Dynamics of Indian Financial System
Markets, Institutions & Services

Dynamics of Indian Financial System
Markets, Institutions & Services

Preeti Singh
Senior Reader,
Jesus & Mary College,
University of Delhi,
New Delhi

GLOBAL
professional
publishing

ISBN: 978-1-906403-50-8

Global Professional Publishing
Random Acres
Slip Mill Lane
Hawkhurst
Cranbrook
Kent TN18 5AD
United Kingdom

Printed in the United Kingdom by Bell & Bain

Preface

It gives me great pleasure to present this book on the Dynamics of the Indian Financial System. This is a book I wanted to write ever since I completed my Ph.D. on Life Insurance Corporation and the Capital Market in India. I did several research studies and a few books in the area of finance and in interdisciplinary areas but despite my best intentions, I did not write this book or publish my thesis. I have to thank my publishers Mr. Sunil Saxena and Mr. J.R. Kapoor of Ane Books India who have brought back my interest in writing on this subject and publishing it for the benefit of students who definitely feel the gap of a simple, comprehensive and clear book. The need of the day being to keep the book brief and yet cover all the important aspects was kept in mind while working on it.

Some of the salient features of the book are as follows:

- It provides an overview of financial system with a historical perspective of the Indian capital market including the current scenario.

- It explains the importance of Reserve Bank of India (RBI) and Securities Exchange Board of India (SEBI), the two controllers in the Indian capital market.

- It presents the internal and external financial instruments useful for raising capital in the market.

- It gives a detailed account of the Primary and Secondary markets, their history, organizational role, market participants and trading methods. It also discusses other important markets like call-money market, treasury bills market and market for commercial papers.

- It gives special coverage to banking and non-bank financial intermediaries. It has a detailed study on commercial banks, small savings, insurance and mutual funds with the latest developments.

- It discusses the financial services necessary for savings volume to increase and be useful for productive investment in India. Some of these financial services are merchant banking, underwriting, leasing and higher purchase, housing and consumer finance, factoring and credit rating.

- It provides the changes and latest developments in the financial environment in India.

The comprehensive package is an attempt to make it a useful book for students and teachers of management, economics, chartered accountants and masters in finance. It would be useful for professionals to understand the financial environment in India for conducting business. The book is written in an easy comprehensible style with many objective type questions. Each chapter begins with a chapter plan to allow the reader to know the focus of the chapter. It provides a summary through points recapitulated at the end of each chapter.

In working on this book, I am inspired by Prof. L.C. Gupta who continues to do research and contribute to the findings of the shortcomings of the capital market and suggestions on improving the mechanisms of trading, supervision, transparency, disclosures and regulation, as well as introducing new instruments to overcome the problems. My thanks are also due to my Ph.D. guide Prof. M.Y. Khan who gave me insights to the subject and with whom I wrote some research papers. I also remember sharing lot of thoughts with Prof. P.K. Jain now in IIT Delhi on the subject as we did our Ph.D. together. Thanks are due to Prof. J.D. Aggarwal, Chairman of Indian Institute of Finance, who has always been supportive on providing library resources for any work done on finance.

I acknowledge with thanks the valuable suggestions and library support provided to me by Prof. Malashri Lal, Joint Director, South Campus while writing this book.

While working on the book my husband, Raminder Singh has been very considerate and supportive. Although I neglected him, he did not complain.

I thank Brajendera Kumar for secretarial assistance in completing the book.

Finally I thank my students as well as my supportive friends teaching in different colleges and universities for their support and would appreciate valuable suggestions for improvement of the book.

—Preeti Singh

Contents

Preface   *v*

Part – One
Financial System—An Overview   **1-42**

---

1. Nature and Role of Financial Systems   **3-14**

- Introduction   3
- Functions of a Financial System   3
- Stages of Financial Development   5
- The Structure of the Financial System   6
- Financial System and its Linkages with Saving and Investment   11
  Summary   12
  Objective Type Questions   12
  Multiple Choice Questions   13
  Short Answer Questions   14
  Long Answer Questions   14

2. An Overview of the Indian Financial System   **15-26**

- Institutional Development (1947-1990)   16
- Institutional Changes Since 1991   17
- Financial Markets   19
- Financial Instruments   21
- Financial Services   23
- Regulators   23
  Summary   24
  Objective Type Questions   25
  Multiple Choice Questions   25
  Short Answer Questions   26
  Long Answer Questions   26

3. Financial Sector Reform in India   **27-42**

- Introduction   27
- Financial Reforms   28
- Objectives of Reforms   28
- Strategies of Reforms   29
- Policy Reforms   30
- New Issue and Stock Market Reforms   31
- Government Securities Market Reforms   32
- Banking Sector Reforms   32
- External Sector Reforms   33
- Vision Document   34
- Impact of Financial Reforms   35
- Flow of Funds   36

  Summary   39
  Objective Type Questions   40
  Multiple Choice Questions   41
  Short Answer Questions   41
  Long Answer Questions   42

Part – Two
Regulatory Authorities   43-84

4. The Reserve Bank of India   **45-60**

- Introduction   45
- Historical Background   46
- Functions of RBI   47
  - Note Issuing Authority   47
  - Bankers' Bank   49
  - Monetary Control   50
- Promotional Role of RBI   52
  - Setting up Specialized Institutions   52
  - Monetary Policy   53
  - Supervision   54
  - Financial Sector   55

  Summary   58
  Objective Type Questions   58
  Multiple Choice Questions   59
  Short Answer Questions   60
  Long Answer Questions   60

5. The Securities Exchange Board of India   **61-84**

- Background   61
- Organization Structure   62
- Objectives of SEBI   63
- Investor Protection   65
- Model Code of Conduct   65
- Investor Grievances   66
- SEBI and Reforms in the Primary Securities Market   66
- SEBI and Reforms in the Secondary Securities Market   68
- SEBI's Failure in Investor Protection   73
- OMBUDSMAN   78
- Investor Education   79
- Fraudulent and Unfair Trade Practices Securities Market Regulation   79
- MAPIN   80
- Investor's Protection Fund   80
  - *Summary*   81
  - *Objective Type Questions*   82
  - *Multiple Choice Questions*   82
  - *Short Answer Questions*   83
  - *Long Answer Questions*   84

Part – Three
Financial Markets   85-164

6. New Issue Market   **87-106**

- Introduction   87
- Role of The New Issue Market   88
- Method of Floating New Issues   90
- Offer to Public Procedure   91
  - Book Building   95
  - Share Application and Allotment Procedure   96
- Intermediaries to The Issue   97
  - Merchant Banker   97
  - Lead Manager   98
  - Portfolio Manager   98
  - Underwriters   99
  - Registrar and Transfer Agents   99
  - Broker   99
- Trends in The New Issue Market   100

- The Relationship of The New Issue Market and Stock Exchange   102
  Summary   104
  Objective Type Questions   104
  Multiple Choice Questions   104
  Short Answer Questions   105
  Long Answer Questions   106

7.   The Secondary Market   **107-134**
- Historical Background   107
- Important Stock Markets in India   108
  - National Stock Exchange (NSE)   109
  - Bombay Stock Exchange (BSE) Mumbai   111
  - Over the Counter Exchange of India (OTCEI)   112
  - Inter-connected Stock Exchange (ISE)   114
- Mechanics of Security Trading In Stock Exchanges   114
- Membership Rules in a Stock Exchange   128
- Listing of Securities   130
- Offer for the Sale of Existing Issued Capital   135
- Legal Control of Stock Exchanges in India   136
- Developments in the Stock Market   140
  - Depository or Paperless Trading   140
  - Insider Trading   143
  - Forward Trading and Badla   144
- Options and Derivatives   144
- Circuit Breakers   146
- Settlement and Clearing   146
  Summary   147
  Objective Type Questions   147
  Multiple Choice Questions   148
  Short Answer Questions   148
  Long Answer Questions   148

8.   Financial Markets for Short Term Funds   **149-164**
- Introduction   149
- Call Money Market   149
- Treasury Bills Market   152
- Commercial Bills Market   154
- Markets for Commercial Paper and Certificate Deposits   156
- The Discount Market   157
- Market for Financial Guarantees   158

- Government (Gift-edged) Securities Market — 160
  Summary — 162
  Objective Type Questions — 163
  Multiple Choice Questions — 163
  Short Answer Questions — 164
  Long Answer Questions — 164

Part – Four
Dimensions of International Financial Markets   165-202

9. Foreign Exchange Market   **167-184**
- Nature of Foreign Exchange Market — 167
- Participants in the Market — 168
- Fixed and Flexible Exchange Rates — 170
- Trends in Foreign Exchange Rates — 173
- Types of Transactions — 175
- Trading Mechanism — 176
- Foreign Exchange Risks — 177
- Developments in the Foreign Exchange Market — 178
  Summary — 181
  Objective Type Questions — 182
  Multiple Choice Questions — 182
  Short Answer Questions — 183
  Long Answer Questions — 183

10. Foreign Capital Flows   **185-202**
- Introduction — 185
- Factors Affecting International Capital Flows — 186
- Importance of Foreign Capital — 187
- Problems in Foreign Capital Flows — 188
- Types of Foreign Capital — 188
- Types of International Financial Instruments — 189
- Global Banking — 192
- Multilateral Financial Agencies — 193
- Developments of Foreign Capital into India — 195
  Summary — 199
  Objective Type Questions — 200
  Multiple Choice Questions — 200
  Short Answer Questions — 201
  Long Answer Questions — 201

Part – Five
Banking Institutions   203-254

11. Commercial Banks   205-236

- Introduction   205
- Types of Banks   205
- Functions of Bank   210
- Distinction Between Bank and Financial Institutions   211
- Phases of Development   211
- Banking Sector Reforms   214
  - Deregulation of Interest Rates   214
  - Reducing Reserve Requirements   214
  - Diversification of Services   215
  - Prudential Norms   216
  - Banking Supervision and Discipline   218
  - Transparency and Disclosure   219
  - Risk Management   219
  - Securitization of Assets   220
  - Non-performing Assets (NPAs)   221
  - Technology   223
  - Customer Services   226
- Regional Rural Banks   229
- Maturity Pattern of Bank Deposits   229
  - Comprehensive Statistics of Commercial Banks   230
  - *Summary*   232
  - *Objective Type Questions*   234
  - *Multiple Choice Questions*   235
  - *Short Answer Questions*   236
  - *Long Answer Questions*   236

12. Co-operative Banks   237-254

- Introduction   237
- Structure of Co-operative Banks   237
- Urban Co-operative Banks   239
- Rural Co-operative Banks   249
  - *Summary*   252
  - *Objective Type Questions*   253
  - *Multiple Choice Questions*   253
  - *Short Answer Questions*   254
  - *Long Answer Questions*   254

Part – Six
Non-banking Financial Intermediaries   255-338

13.   **Non-bank Financial Companies**   **257-268**

- Introduction   257
- Classification of NBFCs   259
- Mutual Benefit Finance Companies (MBFCs)   259
- Fair Practices Code   260
- Corporate Governance   260
- Diversification of Activities   260
- Certificate of Registration   261
- Change of Management   261
- Financial Regulation of Systemically Important NBFCs   261
- Securitization   262
- Prudential Norms of NBFCs   262
- Norms for NBFCs Accepting Public Deposits   263
  - *Summary*   265
  - *Objective Type Questions*   266
  - *Multiple Choice Questions*   266
  - *Short Answer Questions*   267
  - *Long Answer Questions*   267

14.   **Small Savings, Provident Funds & Pension Funds**   **269-278**

- Introduction   269
- Post Office Saving Instruments   269
- Provident Fund   272
- Pension Fund   273
  - *Summary*   276
  - *Objective Type Questions*   276
  - *Multiple Choice Questions*   277
  - *Short Answer Questions*   278
  - *Long Answer Questions*   278

15.   **Insurance Companies**   **279-298**

- Introduction   279
- Life Insurance Corporation (LIC)   280
- Private Insurance Companies   286
- General Insurance Corporation (GIC)   287

- Reforms in Insurance Sector   290
- Control by IRDA   291
  Summary   295
  Objective Type Questions   296
  Multiple Choice Questions   296
  Short Answer Questions   297
  Long Answer Questions   297

16. Unit Trust of India and Mutual Funds   **299-320**
- Introduction   300
- Structure of UTI   300
- Restructure of UTI and Mutual Funds   301
- Methodology of Operations   304
- Objectives of Investing in Mutual Fund   305
- Classification of Mutual Funds   307
- Net Asset Value   310
- Schemes of Unit Trust of India   312
- Significant Mutual Fund Companies in India   315
  Summary   318
  Objective Type Questions   319
  Multiple Choice Questions   319
  Short Answer Questions   320
  Long Answer Questions   320

17. Development Banks   **321-338**
- Introduction   321
- Industrial Development Bank of India (IDBI)   323
- Industrial Finance Corporation (IFC)   326
- Industrial Credit and Investment Corporation of India (ICICI)   329
- Industrial Investment Bank of India Ltd.   333
- State Financial Corporations (SFCS)   334
- Export Import Bank of India (Exim)   335
  Summary   336
  Objective Type Questions   337
  Multiple Choice Questions   338
  Short Answer Questions   338
  Long Answer Questions   338

Part – Seven
Financial Services   **339-380**

18. Financial Services   **341-380**
- Introduction   341
- Types of Financial Services   342
- Financial Services – Players   343
- Merchant Banking   344
- Underwriting   348
- Leasing   350
- Hire Purchase   352
- Consumer Finance   353
- Housing Finance   355
- Venture Capital Finance   358
- Factoring & Forfaiting   366
- Securitization   370
- Credit Rating   372

Summary   375
Objective Type Questions   377
Multiple Choice Questions   378
Short Answer Questions   378
Long Answer Questions   379

Glassary   **381**
Index   **387**

Part – One
Financial System—An Overview

1. Nature and Role of Financial Systems
2. An Overview of the Indian Financial System
3. Financial Sector Reform in India

Chapter 1

Nature and Role of Financial Systems

Chapter Plan

- Functions of a Financial System
- Stages of Financial Development
- The Structure of the Financial System
- Financial System and its Linkages with Saving and Investment
- Financial System and its Linkages with Saving and Investment

INTRODUCTION

The Financial system of a country consists of a network of an interconnected system of markets, institutions and services. This system contributes to the economic development of a country. It connects the savingssurplus and savingsdeficit institutions and establishes a regular flow of funds in the capital market of a country. The role of the financial system is to make an efficient allocation of the savings and investments through the transfer process. The main functions of the financial system can be categorized as the following:

- *Savings: The main function of financial system is to mobilize savings in a country for the development process to take place. Low level of savings hinders development as funds are important for making development successful.*

- *Transfer process: The efficiency in which finance is converted is through a transfer process into investments which will begin an earning for the economy.*

- *Investments: These are resources used for production to take place. All types of securities and bonds which earn interest or dividends and help in the activity of development are called investments.*

The functions of the financial system can be elaborated with a detailed description of the three main functions of savings, transfer process and investments:

FUNCTIONS OF A FINANCIAL SYSTEM

The financial system performs the following functions.

Efficient Transformation of Funds

One of the most important functions of the financial system is to make the transformation of savings into investments in an efficient manner. There are five important parameters of achieving efficiency which the financial sector must achieve. These are: (i) Funds can be allocated efficiently or inefficiently. When investments are made in productive assets and their marginal efficiency is high after adjusting the risk difference, then funds have been allocated efficiently in the economy. The financial sector aims to make the process of transformation of funds in the most productive and profitable manner. (ii) The market is efficient when information is wide-spread. Perfect capital markets are those where equal information is provided to all the investors and there are less chances of making a high gain by an individual because the prices of securities reflect all known information. (iii) The market must be efficient in valuing its securities. This possibility arises when the intrinsic value of an asset is the present value of the future stream of its cash flows in competitive markets. (iv) Market is efficient when risk is reduced to a minimum. This can be ensured through hedging against future contingencies. (v) Funds should be chanellized by minimum expenditure in administrative costs and maximum returns for providing efficiency. Hence it is the function of the financial sector to bring about maximum efficiency through financial market, attractive instruments and good services to provide efficiency in mobilizing savings and making productive investments.

Creating Innovative Schemes for savings and investment

The financial sector has the role of creating innovative schemes and features to make financial instruments attractive to investors. They should also take steps to create savings in tax, reduce costs of transaction, costs of intermediaries and agency costs. Innovations should help in streamlining administrative procedures and bringing about technological changes and suggestions to help the economy to grow.

Globalization

The financial sector has the function of extending its services not only in its own country but also in international arenas. Extending beyond the home countries boundaries integrates business in different markets. This has the advantage of convergence of interest rates in different markets. Financial instruments become varied and greater choices can be offered to investors. New foreign financial instruments can be used in the domestic front and the country can also float its securities outside its own country. The advantage of certain foreign bonds and global depository receipts can be utilized. Different currencies can be interlinked with each other. Hence the financial sector should perform the role of internationalizing itself.

Diversification

The financial sector has the important function of diversifying the savings of the people by purchasing different kinds of securities to provide the maximum benefit to an investor. This will achieve the purpose of minimizing risk in the portfolio of an investor and he will benefit in his return from the investments.

Financial Engineering

Financial innovation can be performed only if the financial sector develops it by creating value to the instruments. By engineering the instruments it can skillfully make changes and develop new techniques for hedging, speculation and arbitrage.

Reforms

The financial sector has the function of making reforms to add value to savings and investments. New regulations and guidelines and discipline is important to function. The financial sector has to constantly make reforms like regulating certain sectors or by liberalizing them. It has to make reforms for streamlining and bringing about good administrative and operational practices.

Thus the functions of the financial system can be summarized as:

- *Creating Efficiency in transformation of funds from savings into investments by information efficiency, allocation efficiency, valuation of securities, and operational efficiency.*
- *Planning Innovative Schemes for savings and investment for creating an environment of sound and speedy transactions.*
- *Globalizing for making gains by integrating with markets, institutions, instruments and services of other countries.*
- *Diversifying the funds into different investment outlets for maximum returns and minimum risk*
- *To engineer new and innovative instruments to add value to them for providing choices to the savers and investors.*
- *To make reforms for providing value to financial instruments for creating confidence amongst the investors in the working of the financial system.*

In order to get the maximum benefit a financial system has to depend on direct and indirect finance. A rudimentary economy will have equal savings and investments. All that is earned is consumed but as a country develops the possibility of both direct and indirect finance begins with business organizations beginning to flourish. These are linked to stages of financial development.

STAGES OF FINANCIAL DEVELOPMENT

An economy moves through different stages of development. In the rudimentary stage it is a traditional and underdeveloped economy marked with the absence of financial instruments, financial institutions and financial services.[1] Since financial facilitating agencies do not exist there is a hindrance to the development of an economy.[2]

The development phase begins with ***direct finance.*** The primary securities are issued directly by investors to savers. There is no intermediary link through financial institutions or instruments. This means that a savings surplus unit will directly identify a surplus deficit unit and thus the funds will flow

---

1. Read Bennet R.L. *Financial Sector and Economic Development*, Baltimore, John Hopkins Press, 1965 p. 22.
2. For a greater understanding read Gurley and Shaw, *Money in a theory of finance*, New York, Columbia, 1960 p. 12.

from one to another. The process of development will be slow as the amount of capital mobilized will be in a low volume because the efficiency of the transfer process will be slow as there are few financial instruments to convert the available surplus into productive channels in a country. Thus transfer of funds is important to build an efficient financial system. When direct finance is available then it is restricted to financial assets, brokers and investment bankers and stock exchanges.

The modernization phase in the economy creates ***indirect finance*** where there is the existence of savings surplus, savings deficit and savings neutral units. The intermediation process takes place through financial markets, institutions, instruments and savings. It is in fact the flow of funds through financial institutions, which are intermediaries in the process of saving and investments between ultimate borrowers and lenders. In the process of intermediation, the transmutation effect[3] takes place. This refers to different kind of contracts that are made by the financial institutions with the borrowers and the lenders. When a savings surplus unit provides finance, the financial institutions make a contract with some important features. The contract signed with the savings deficit unit is quite different. These features are then converted by taking into consideration the preferences of both types of units. The transfer process is carried out by financial institutions with different set of choices between the savers and the lenders. Indirect finance thus refers to the following:

- *Purchase of primary securities by financial intermediaries at low cost from non-financial economic units.*

- *Transfer direct claims into indirect financial instruments through the collection of funds from a large number of small funds.*

- *Providing benefits through indirect securities to both savings surplus and savings deficit units by matching their expectations through attractive features like income, liquidity, economies of scale, diversification, options regarding maturity period, risk and professional management of securities to get a maximum expected return.*

- *Mobilizing savings through skill and expertise which is necessary for development of an economy.*

THE STRUCTURE OF THE FINANCIAL SYSTEM

The financial system consists of financial markets, financial institutions, financial assets and financial services. The above discussion has explained the functions of these facilitating agencies. It is clear that mobilization of savings and transfer process provides development in the economy. Let us understand the working of each of these important and integral parts of the process through which the financial system functions in an economy.

Financial Markets

The financial markets support the transfer process in a country through the sale and purchase of securities. There are many financial markets in a country depending upon the functions that they perform. The transactions can be for investment of long term or short term period. They can also refer to industrial

---

3. Smith, P.F., *Economics of Financial Institutions and Markets*, Richard D. Irwin, Illinois, 1971, p. 65.

securities or Government securities. Due to globalization and reforms taking place inter-linkages are developed in different markets extending beyond the boundaries of the home country. Information should be efficient to make perfect markets and to reduce undue benefits to a single individual. In fact, though perfect markets are desired, imperfections do arise and the market becomes imperfect. Markets should also create the confidence of the people. They should be assured that their transactions are safe and there are no fraudulent dealings. This helps in the movement of capital from buyers to sellers and like wise from the sellers to the buyers.

The purchase and sale of financial assets can be direct through the primary market or indirect through the secondary market. The primary market is known as the new issue market and only those securities are dealt with in these markets which are offered for the first time to the public. Thereafter all the securities must be purchased and sold through the secondary market better known as the stock market. The primary and the secondary market are complementary in nature and co-exist to make the financial system efficient in its functions. The financial markets can be *organized* as well as *unorganized*. They can also be *formal and informal*. A financial market within the country would be called a *domestic market* and a market in another country would be termed a *foreign market*. There are many types of markets. They are *long term capital markets, short-term money markets, Government gilt edged securities markets, market for financial guarantees*. They are named according to the specialization provided by them in financial products. They help individuals to get the benefits of time preference, liquidity preference and portfolio management. This is discussed in detail in chapters 6 to 10.

Table 1.1: Financial Markets

Organized	Unorganized
• It is a market which is governed by rules and regulations.	• The procedures are not standardized. Interest rates and transactions are variable.
• It is controlled by a market regulator like SEBI.	• Rates of interest are exorbitant. There is no Investor protection regulator.
• The market is recognized and formal for example new issue market, stock exchange.	• The market is informal with the presence of chit funds and lotteries.
• There are many financial intermediaries which mobilize savings and make investments.	• There is no intermediation of funds as it is operated by people for their own private advantage.

Money Markets	Capital Markets
• It is a market for financial assets of maturity of less than one year.	• It is a market for long term funds.
• In this market assets are at short notice converted into cash. Transaction cost is low. Assets are treasury bonds, commercial papers, bills, inter-corporate deposits.	• It dealers in shares debentures, mutual funds investments. The dealings are usually for a period of more than one year.
• The participants are large institutional investors. Short term transactions are conducted.	• The primary or new issue Market deals with the first time issue of securities. Stock market or secondary market deals with trading of second hand securities. Individuals and institutions are participants.

Primary Market	Secondary Market
• The market mobilizes savings of individuals. The participants are merchant banker, underwriter stock broker, portfolio manager. • This market helps in raising funds for industry or corporate organizations. • This market is termed the new issue market. The IPO's are offered through it.	• The market for second hand securities. Only listed securities can be traded. • It is complementary to the primary market. It helps in the distributive mechanism of securities. • It is popularly called the stock market. Individuals, brokers, corporate organizations, are the main participants.
Domestic Market	**International Market**
• A domestic market deals in all the transactions that take place within the home country.	• An international market is known for its home transactions as well as those taking place in trading with other countries. Ex, Bonds issued outside the country, listing securities in NYSE or London stock exchange.

Financial Institutions

Mobilization of savings and transformation of direct claims into indirect are the focus of these institutions. They can be distinguished from other institutions through the way they conduct their business. Business organizations perform their business activities through physical assets such as machinery, goods, equipment, or real estate. Banks perform their work through deposits made by the public. Their main function is to create credit and expand it through the deposits made by the account holders. Financial institutions lend out of the savings mobilized by them. They create a reservoir of funds through a large number of small savers and offer financial assets with attractive features and transform the funds from savings surplus to savings deficit units through various instruments issued by them[4]. The financial institutions engage in different kinds of transformation of funds. These may be referred to as liability transformation, size transformation, risk transformation, maturity transformation. *Liability transformation* is the method of converting deposits or liabilities with the bank into assets through grant of loans. Banks are a good example of such a transformation. *Size transformation* is the service provided by financial institutions relating to increase in the volume of finance by creating small deposits through units of capital like in a mutual fund and then investing the funds and increasing the volume of funds. *Risk transformation* by the financial institutions is the act of distributing risk by diversification of funds into different kinds of risks and returns. Financial institutions also bring about liquidity preference by providing *Maturity transformation* or different dates of maturity depending on the preference of the savers.

The financial intermediaries thus provide various services to individuals and try to mobilize the savings of individuals. They help the small savers to reduce their risk by diversification into different kinds of securities. They lend their expert services through specialized knowledge in making investments. They are able to create economies of scale by collecting small funds but investing large amounts in a particular sector. Finally they are able to boost savings by offering convenience to the small saver by

4. Goldsmith, R.W., *Financial Institutions*, Randon, New York 1969, p. 22.

managing their funds with knowledge and skill bringing about diversification, high profitability and reducing risk to the minimum.

Financial institutions which bridge the savers and the investors together are called *'intermediaries'*. In a financial system there exist non-intermediaries as well. The difference between the two is due to the business that they perform. Intermediaries link savers and investors, performing the function of mobilization of savings and their investment thereof. Non-intermediary financial institutions are engaged in lending business but their resources are not collected from the savers. In India there are both intermediaries and non-intermediary finance institutions. The life insurance, general insurance and mutual fund institutions are intermediaries. Banks act as intermediaries taking deposits from individuals and then lending those funds. Examples of non-intermediary finance institutions in India are the Industrial Finance Corporation of India (IFCI), National Bank for Agricultural Development (NABARD). The Industrial Credit and Investment Corporation of India (ICICI) and The Industrial Development Bank of India (IDBI) began as solely non-intermediary financial institutions in India but later started intermediary business by opening commercial banks and are no longer pure lending institutions.

Table 1.2: Functions of Financial Intermediaries

- Liabilities Transformation
- Size Transformation
- Risk Transformation
- Maturity Transformation

Financial Assets

Transformation from savings to investments can be done efficiently if there are a variety of financial assets available to the savers. Financial instruments also called financial assets can be simple instruments with one feature or those offering many features. The saving surplus units will be attracted to purchase these instruments if they have attractive options of high return coupled with other benefits like tax, liquidity and marketability. To make the assets acceptable to people financial engineering is done. Financial assets may be industrial securities issued by Public Ltd. companies or securities issued by financial institutions and banks. Banks issue fixed deposits. Mutual funds issue units and are convenient for the small savers. Post offices have special saving certificates. Insurance companies primarily issue security to life or physical assets and at the same time provide savings plans because they give a return on the deposits. Bonds of various kinds may also be issued.

Financial instruments represent claims to future interest or dividend payments which may be periodic or regular in nature. They can be in the form of *primary securities* which are issued directly by investors to savers in the *new issue market* and indirectly through the *secondary market*. Since many kinds of financial instruments are available, they are distinguished through the various benefits they offer through specific features relating to liquidity, marketability, maturity period, interest, tax and dividends. These features are important as liquidity decides the conversion of instruments into cash; marketability reflects the ease in trading of an instrument. Similarly maturity gives the date when the instrument will become liquid and interest dividends and taxes show how much an investor will earn.

Table 1.3: Functions of Financial Instruments

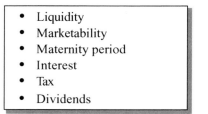

- Liquidity
- Marketability
- Maternity period
- Interest
- Tax
- Dividends

Financial Services

Services facilitate mobilizing of savings and their transformation into investments. When an economy is in the rudimentary stage there is the absence of financial assets and services. This is the reason for the slow movement of funds in the economy. When a large number of new financial instruments are introduced in the economy the services should be simultaneously developed because this provides a quicker movement of funds. Specialized financial services help in different kinds of schemes. The various kinds of services include merchant banking, underwriting, leasing, higher-purchase, consumer and housing finance, venture capital finance, factoring services, bank guarantees and letter of credit, credit rating and financial counseling.

The functions of financial services are to provide help in raising funds from surplus units like individuals, institutions and corporate organizations. They participate in making effective movement of funds by offering innovative equity instruments, debt instruments, and hybrid instruments. The constituents of the financial services market consist of market players like banks, financial institutions, mutual funds, merchant bankers, stockbrokers, consultants, underwriters and market makers. The services are provides by specialized institutions like acceptance houses, discount houses, depositories, venture capitalists and credit agencies The participants are regulated by agencies like the Reserve Bank of India, Securities exchange board of India, Department of Banking and Insurance.

Table 1.4: Financial Services

- Acceptance house
- Mutual fund
- Merchant banking
- Underwriting
- Discount houses
- Depositories
- Venture capital
- Credit agencies
- Stock broking
- Consultants

Thus the structure of a financial system is inter-related. Financial markets, institutions, assets and services are connected and each plays an important part in transformation of savings into investments. Figure 1.1 depicts it.

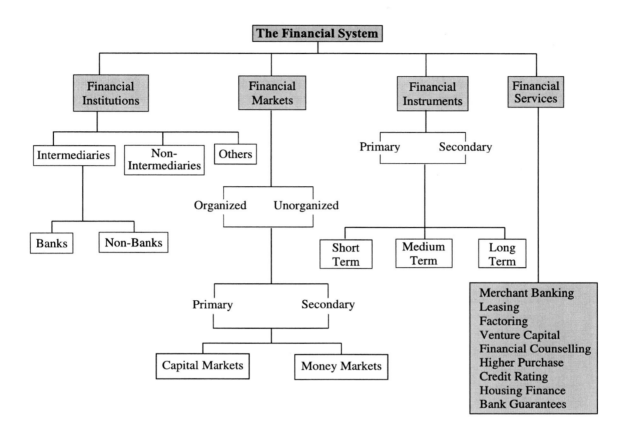

Fig. 1.1: The Financial System

FINANCIAL SYSTEM AND ITS LINKAGES WITH SAVING AND INVESTMENT

A question that is often asked is whether the financial system has any relationship with saving and investment leading to development in an economy. There are many views. One of the linkages with saving and investment is that it assists the economy in transforming surplus wealth into productive outlets. By offering a variety of financial assets it attracts savers to move from gold and other precious metals into assets like shares, bonds and units. It inculcates the habit of savings through the returns provided by banks and makes it convenient for people to use banking facilities thus increasing the volume of savings in the economy. Financial intermediaries can enhance growth because they transform savings to finance productive activities.

Summary

⇒ The main functions of the financial system are to encourage savings and to transfer them efficiently into investments.

⇒ The functions can be elaborated into efficient transformation of funds, creating Innovative Schemes for savings and investment, globalization, diversification and financial engineering.

⇒ The transforming of funds in an economy can be direct or indirect depending on the type of an economy in terms of development.

⇒ A rudimentary economy transfers savings into investments directly whereas a developed economy has indirect channelization of funds as financial institutions are instrumental in the process of intermediation by offering their own securities.

⇒ The financial system consists of financial markets, financial institutions, financial assets and financial services.

⇒ Financial markets consist of primary or new issue market and secondary market or stock exchange. The primary market is for new issues and the stock market is for second hand sale of securities.

⇒ Markets can be long term capital markets or short term money markets. They can also be organized or unorganized, national or international. They can also be Government Gilt Edged Securities, Market for Financial Guarantees.

⇒ Financial institutions are engaged in liability transformation, size transformation, maturity transformation and risk transformation.

⇒ Financial assets can be shares of Public Ltd. companies, units of mutual funds, bank deposits, post office schemes, insurance schemes and new innovative instruments to encourage people to save.

⇒ Efficient financial services hasten the movement of funds in the capital markets. They are merchant banking activities, discount houses, underwriters, credit rating, financial counseling and many other services.

⇒ Financial system links the savers with the investors.

Objective Type Questions, Answer True (T) or False (F)

(a) A financial system comprises of financial institutions, markets, assets and services.

(b) Financial institutions are mainly banking institutions.

(c) Financial instruments provide different kinds of services to an individual.

(d) Financial markets can be classified into primary or indirect markets and secondary or direct markets.

(e) In a developed economy there is usually direct supply of capital.

(f) Financial markets are classified as organized and unorganized, formal and informal, domestic and foreign markets.

(g) Financial institutions offer services for transformation of savings into investments.

(h) Financial markets help in increasing the volume of purchase and sale of securities.

(i) A developed financial system induces growth through its investments, services, institutions and markets.

(j) The functions of the financial system are to allocate efficiently, bring about efficiency, reduce risk, innovate and diversify funds in the economy.

Answer: (a) T, (b) F, (c) F, (d) F, (e) F, (f) T, (g) T, (h) T, (i) T, (j) T.

Multiple Choice Questions (Tick mark (✓) the right answer)

1. Financial markets can be classified as:
   (a) Markets with financial institutions
   (b) As markets for sale and purchase of goods
   (c) As brokers transaction place
   (d) As a place for sale and purchase of securities

2. Financial intermediaries have the function of:
   (a) Risk Transformation through diversification
   (b) Tax exemption for share holders
   (c) A banking institution
   (d) Bringing about discipline in markets

3. Financial instruments are useful for:
   (a) Creating benefits for Government
   (b) Providing credit creation for Banks
   (c) Mobilization of savings
   (d) For creating direct securities

4. Financial engineering:
   (a) Is to create financial instruments through different features
   (b) Bringing about reforms
   (c) To globalize production.
   (d) To bring about operational efficiency at low cost

5. Financial system comprises of:
   (a) Share holders in the economy
   (b) Funds and financial institutions
   (c) Surplus and deficit funds
   (d) Financial institutions, financial markets and financial assets

Answers: 1 (d), 2 (a), 3 (c), 4 (a), 5 (d).

Short Answer Questions

1. A financial system consists of savers and investors. Discuss this statement.

2. Distinguish between the savings and investment process in a rudimentary and developed economy.

3. Financial markets consist of primary and secondary market. Discuss.

4. Name some important financial services in the capital market.

Long Answer Questions

1. Discuss the composition of the financial system. What are its main objectives?

2. What are the functions of the financial system? In what way is it possible to bring about a perfect capital market?

3. How do financial services create value in a financial system?

4. A financial system has many intermediaries and services comment on this statement.

Chapter 2

An Overview of the Indian Financial System

Chapter Plan

- Institutional Development
- Institutional Changes Since 1991
- Financial Markets

- Financial Instruments
- Financial Services
- Regulators

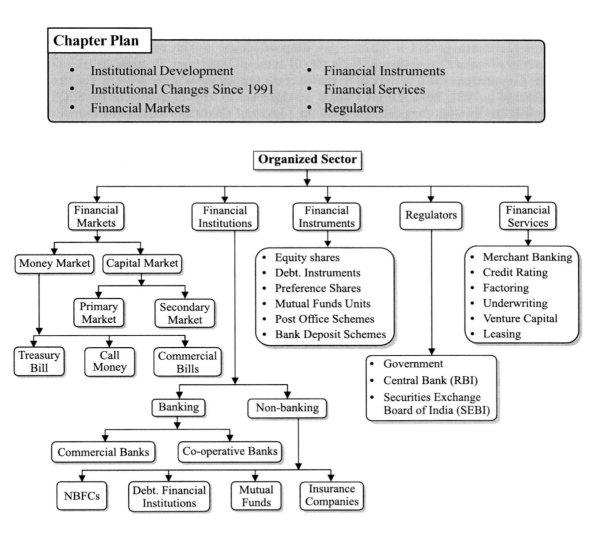

Fig. 2.1: The Indian Financial System

The last chapter discussed the nature and role of financial systems. This chapter is focused on the Indian financial system. It is an overview of India's financial institutions, markets, instruments and services. It traces the development of the institutions and the changes after 1991. The institutional setup was restrictive and there was the absence of institutions and instruments before the year 1951. L.C. Gupta described the Indian finance system as 'a semi organized and narrow industrial securities market, devoid of issuing institutions and the virtual absence of participation by intermediary financial institutions in the long term financing of industry'.[1] In these circumstances, government decided to set up new development banks and financial institutions and to reorganize existing organizations to fit with its development policy.

INSTITUTIONAL DEVELOPMENT (1947-1990)

The Indian Financial system was planned according to the socio-economic and political objectives of the country. The most significant development was the setting up of *Reserve Bank of India (RBI)* in 1948 under government control. In the same year the development banking era also began by setting up the *Industrial Finance Corporation of India (IFCI)* at the all India level. To assist the IFCI the *State Financial Corporations (SFC's)* were to be started at the various states in the country. The first SFC's was established in 1951. While the IFCI would provide loans to large organizations the SFC's would finance small and medium companies. In 1955 the *Industrial Credit and investment Corporation of India (ICICI)* was setup with a modern approach to assist in financing of the private corporate sector. In the mean while government decided to nationalize the *Life Insurance Corporation of India (LIC)* in 1956 by amalgamating 245 life insurance companies. In 1958 the *Refinance Corporation of India (RCI)* to provide refinance to banks against term loans granted by them to medium and small enterprises. In 1964 the *Unit Trust of India (UTI)* was setup for mobilizing the savings of the people of the country. It was to provide units to small investors and issue different types of securities to issue the requirement of different classes of investors. In 1964 the *Industrial Development Bank of India (IDBI)* was established as a subsidiary of the RBI and RCI was merged with IDBI. In 1969, 14 existing *Commercial Banks* were nationalized to give loans to the priority sector. In 1971 the *Industrial Reconstruction Corporation of India (IRCI)* was setup jointly by LIC and IDBI to rehabilitate sick mills. In 1972 the *General Insurance Corporation (GIC)* was nationalized by merging different general insurance companies. In 1976 IDBI was de-linked from the RBI and elevated to the position of an apex bank to oversee the activities of the different development banks. At the state level the *State Industrial Development Corporations (SIDC's) / State Industrial Investment Corporations (SIIC's)* was setup to meet financial requirements and to promote balanced regional development. By the end of 1980 a large number of institutions were developed and existing ones were either reorganized or nationalized.

The new economic policy in 1991 brought about a complete change from the previous controlled policy and mixed economy consisting of public and private ownership. Due to the process of globalization and liberalization, India began to deregulate its industries to shift to free flow of capital through demand and supply mechanics. This brought about a complete shift in institutional reorganization. The development banks which were formed under government control now had to plan to become independent entities.

Let us briefly describe the changes in the development banks and financial institutions since 1991.

---

1. Gupta L.C., *Changing Structure of Industrial Financing in India*, Oxford Printing Press, New Delhi, P. 9.

INSTITUTIONAL CHANGES SINCE 1991

Development Banks

In India there is a distinct difference between ***Development Banks and Financial Institutions***. The development banks are those institutions which were introduced in India with the specific purpose of 'development' of industries in the Centre and the State level. They had a promotional role to play. Their main activity was to develop industries by providing finance and guidance to them. They were to act as *'gap fillers'* to industries and to finance those industries which could not get loans from any other sources. The development banks were IDBI, IFCI, ICICI and SFC's. The financial institutions were LIC, UTI and GIC. There main function was to mobilize the savings of the people by issuing claims against themselves and to use the reservoir of funds so collected to invest in the capital market. Development banks were significant as their role was both quantitative and qualitative. The first development bank to be setup was the IFCI. It was started to work on traditional lines of financial development of industries. Since 1991 the IFCI shifted into investor services. It setup the IFCI financial services limited, IFCI investor services limited and IFCI custodial services limited. It also made a public issue of shares. The IDBI shifted to promoting institutional infrastructure development in the capital market. It also converted into a commercial bank. The ICICI converted into a commercial bank and was so successful that the parent company merged with it and it became a reverse merger. The ICICI has a good reputation in the capital market and its shares are being sold at a premium. Its public issue was very successful. The ICICI has now formed the ICICI securities and finance limited in (I-SEC). The development banks have jointly sponsored credit rating agencies such as ***Credit Rating Information Services of India Limited (CRISIL), Investment Information and Credit Rating Agency Limited (ICRA)*** and ***Credit Analysis and Research Limited (CARE)***. Other infrastructural development made jointly by the development banks are establishment of stock exchanges like ***Over the Counter Stock Exchange of India Ltd. (OTCEI)*** and the ***National Stock Exchange Ltd. (NSE). Stock Holding Corporation of India Ltd. (SHCI***) and ***Investor Service of India (ISI)*** were specifically sponsored for the needs of the investor.

The development banks became financial super markets and engaged in traditional and modern services. Their new role was underwriting, lease financing, merchant banking, portfolio management, new issue management, mergers and acquisition counseling, corporate advisory services and credit syndication. The development banks have also began to sponsor new areas like industrial services and financial services. Thus there is a complete transformation of development banks and now they have entered new areas of financial in the capital market.

Financial Institutions

The financial institutions link the savers to the investors through conversion of instruments issued by them into indirect securities. The Life Insurance Corporation of India (LIC), The Unit Trust of India (UTI) and GIC were the well known financial institutions of the country. LIC was a monolithic institution. Its main aim was to mobilize the savings of the house hold and to protect the investor by offering protection against death and sickness. The LIC was a very powerful share holder in the capital market. It was a underwriter of the capital issues and it preferred to underwrite large and established companies.

It was amongst the top ten share holders in out of three companies registered in the stock exchange until 1978. With the emergence of UTI the LIC was relegated to the second position as it began to take greater interest in capital market affair. The LIC moved on to socially oriented projects and development work such as sewerage, road and transport and electricity generation. LIC's new role began since 1991 when reorganization began and insurance companies were allowed to the setup as private companies co-existing with the LIC. There large number of life insurance companies now present in the Indian capital market. The ***Insurance Regulatory and Development Authority (IRDA)*** Act was passed in 1999 to regulate a promote insurance activities. The General Insurance Company (GIC) also underwrote capital issues and invested in the capital market but its investments were less than the LIC and UTI. Since 1999 changes have been brought about by IRDA by allowing private insurance companies to operate in the insurance sector. Both LIC and GIC have sufficient competition from the private sector.

The Unit Trust of India was formed with its flagships unit scheme of 1964. This scheme was open ended and it was able to collect the savings of the small investors. It started many different types of scheme to provide a choice to the individuals. Its schemes covered children, retired people, women, education, insurance, stock exchange, monthly income plans, charitable trust and institutions. In India it was the sole mutual fund in 1987. UTI emerged as a dominative underwriter of capital issues. It promoted financial institutions like CRISIL, SHCI, Housing Promotion and Finance Companies, Tourism Finance Corporation of India (TFCI) and UTI institute of capital market. It started the UTI commercial bank in 1994 which is now AXIS bank. In 2001 the UTI could not fulfill its promises to the investors. Its 1964 scheme crashed. In 2002 government restructured the UTI.

Mutual Funds

Since 1991 among the financial intermediaries mutual funds have been incorporated. Mutual funds emerged with the existence of the master share of the UTI. In 1991 Guidelines were formed for the introduction of mutual funds in India. 5 mutual funds were setup in 1993. They were subsidiaries of public sector banks. They were SBI mutual funds, CAN bank mutual fund, PNB mutual fund, BOI mutual fund and IND bank mutual fund. The financial intermediaries like the LIC and GIC also floated mutual fund after 1992. The mutual funds were opened to the private corporate sector sum of these were Sriram mutual fund, Birla global finance, Tata mutual fund and Morgan Stanley mutual fund. Mutual funds in India have both open-end and closed and schemes. They provide regular income, capital appreciation and tax saving schemes.

Commercial Banks

Commercial banks have changed from traditional lending to dynamic and vibrant lending to industry. The focus was to lend to priority industries but due to large non-profitable assets (NPA's) there was a change in the lending pattern. After the reforms of Narsimham committee, banking system made many changes to become commercially viable. Banks closed their non-profitable branches. Many banks merged for example, the New Bank of India merged with Punjab national bank. Banks became more professional and worked for solutions in their internal management and upgraded the services. They improved their internal asset management and credit risk management. Banks have now started many new functions in lending. They have entered into new services like merchant banking, leasing, portfolio management, credit cards, car financing, personal loans and insurance. Commercial banks have now become super markets or financial conglomerates and are called universal banks because they have a large number of financial services under one roof.

Non-Bank Financial Companies (NBFC's)

The Indian financial system has new types of financial companies dealing in financial services. These new types of companies are called non-bank financial companies. They are fund based and fees based. They are engaged in fund based activities like hire purchase finance, lease financing, venture capital and housing finance and factoring. Their advisory services are fees based. They are corporate counseling, portfolio management, lease syndication, merger and acquisition. The RBI has setup a Department of Non-Banking Supervision to have a control on such service based companies.

To summarize, the following important aspects may be reviewed:

- The institutions before 1991 followed the policy of mixed economy whereas after the reforms the institutions were reorganized and the bias was towards privatization.
- The Indian economy was controlled. There was no free play of demand and supply but after 1991 the economy was liberalized and deregulated towards globalization.
- The development banks were formed to be the backbone of Indian industry because government was keen to develop industries in India both at the central and state level.
- The institutional setup in India was marked by priority area development but this brought about imbalance and non-profitability in the institutions. The reforms were specifically made to make the institutions more diversified in their approach towards lending and becoming competitive and profitable.
- The institutional structure was heavily dependent on special institutions and it could not link it self to the ultimate source of savings.[2] Reforms became necessary for linking the expanding corporate sector of the private industry with the financing method.
- Since 1991 changes have come about in development banks. Many of them have become commercial banks.
- Commercial banks have enlarged their activities and they have become financial super markets called universal banks.
- Life insurance and general insurance have been encouraged in the private sector.
- Mutual funds have been introduced and non-bank financial companies have also been setup.

FINANCIAL MARKETS

The financial system of any country has financial institutions and financial markets. A well organized structure of the markets encourages public and institutional support. As discussed about the financial institutions have grown and reorganized during the planning period. The financial markets which exist in

---

2. For a detailed account refer Gupta L.C., *Changing Structure of Industrial Finance in India*, Oxford University Press London, 1969, P. 70.

India are ***Industrial Securities Market, Call Money Market, Commercial Bills Market, Market for Financial Guarantees, Government Gilt as Securities and Treasury Bills Market.***

The industrial securities market is the long term capital market. It consists of the primary market and secondary market. These are complementary to each other in their functions. They are called the new issue market and the stock market. The call money market is for short term maturity. Let us take a brief look at the changes in the industrial securities market and the call money market.

New Issue Market

This is the primary market. Shares are issued for the first time to the public. Before 1990 the new issue market was not well organized but many changes have been brought about since the setting up of ***Securities Exchange Board of India (SEBI)*** in 1986. The participants in this market are merchant bankers, lead managers and underwriters, bankers to the issue, portfolio managers and brokers. The new issue market works in conformity with the regulations of SEBI. The procedures regarding issue of shares have been streamlined and after 1991, it has become developed and is geared towards investor protection measures. Complaints from investors regarding late refunds and allotment longer than the usual time have been attended to by companies due to SEBI's strict procedures.

Stock Market

The stock market provides liquidity and ready marketability to shares through trading carried out in the market. In India the stock market was dominated by speculators. It was controlled by controller of capital issues but since 1992 SEBI has developed the market and regulated the transactions in the stock market. '***Badla***' trade or the Indian name for forward trading was being carried out but it was abolished and derivatives came into the Indian market in 2002. This brought safe trade and limited losses for individuals. The ***National Stock Exchange (NSE)*** was established and the ***Over The Counter Exchange of India (OTCEI)*** was setup to develop a strong and matured securities market. Another land mark towards a sound securities market was the setting up of the ***National Securities Depositary Ltd. (NSDL)***. Through these institutions, dematerialized and paperless trading in India was started. SEBI made many notable changes for developing the stock market. It made rules and regulations for brokers and dealers which they had to strictly adhere to in trading of securities. Changes also came about in capital adequacy norms for intermediaries. Trading and settlement practices were simplified but more rigorous for the protection of investors. Another important move that is planned is towards demutualization of stock exchanges which will separate trading from ownership and management of securities.

Call Money Market

The call money market in India deals with inter-bank uses, bill market, stock exchanges, bullion markets and individuals. It is highly liquid and deals with short term funds which are required to fulfill the needs of the investors for a temporary period. The call money market in India is controlled to the reserve bank of India. When RBI follows a restrictive policy the money market becomes active but when it follows a liberal policy the banks stop borrowing from the call market. In this way the call money market has dull and active borrowing period. The call money market was liberalized by allowing the private sector companies to issue commercial papers for a period of 3 to 6 months if they were able to get credit rating. After 1990 the market has been strengthened by appointing Primary Dealers to deal with the inter-connected treasury and commercial bills market and foreign exchange markets.

To summarized, financial markets before 1991 was controlled and had many restrictions on flow funds and did not have any liquidity. The transaction costs were high. After 1991 there has been a transformation and the markets have been integrated. They have also become stable and efficient.

FINANCIAL INSTRUMENTS

Financial instruments help in the process of intermediation. A choice of financial instruments to cater to the needs of the different types of investors will provide dynamism in trade of the securities in the financial markets. An array of securities creates development in the financial system. As discussed in chapter 1 an economy devoid of financial instruments is financially backward.

The following instruments are traded in the Indian capital market. Financial instrument consists of ownership securities, debt securities, mutual funds units and financial engineering securities.

Equity Shares

The shares are ownership securities. Investors find equity shares the best type of investment as the shares can be traded. The investor participates in the earnings of the company and receives dividends. The equity share value increases and during inflation it acts as a hedge, increasing the importance of such shares. The equity shares also have capital appreciation. They are however very risky shares as the prices can also fall and there can be losses.

Preference Shares

Preference shares are fixed dividend bearing instruments. They are called hybrid instruments because they have the features of both the equity shares and bonds. They have certain important features like cumulative dividends and are redeemable after some years.

Debentures/Bonds

There are many kinds of debentures/bonds in the Indian capital market. These are redeemable, perpetual, convertible, registered and bearer issues. They have a fixed interest called '*coupon*' rate. These are debt securities and the holders do not have any right to attend the annual general meeting of the company. They are also not allowed to vote in any issues.

Financial Engineering Securities

These are new type of securities which combine different features in one security. They are called innovative instruments. Many companies have tried to innovate to give a choice to the investors. The financial institutions and development banks in India have also issued such securities. The following are some financial engineering securities issued in India.

Participating Debentures have been issued by companies. The investors are given a part of the excess profits that it has earned after giving a dividend to equity share holders.

Convertible Debentures Redeemable at Premium: These securities are issued by a company at the par value but the holders have a '*put option*'. This enables the holders to sell the security at of premium. *Zero Interest Fully Convertible Debentures (FCD's):* These debentures do not carry any interest but on the specified date they are converted to in to shares.

Floating Rate Bonds (FRB's): These bonds are issued by financial institutions by linking the interest on the bond to a benchmark interest rate. The benchmark may be the interest rate on treasury bills, prime lending rate or interest rate of term deposits. The floating rate may be either above or below the benchmark rate.

Zero Interest Coupons Bonds: Such bonds do not pay interest but are offered at a low price. The investors get returns from the difference he receives between the acquisition and redemption amount.

Deep Discount Bonds: Such bonds have a long term maturity period between 20 to 25 years. They carry the feature of '*call*' which means that the company can call back the bond after 5or 10 years. It is sold at a discount but has no interest for example, a 25 year bond is issued at rupees 10,000 but is redeemed at rupees 1, 00,000. The discount makes up for not receiving any interest during the waiting period.

Regular Income Bonds: These bonds have '*call*' and '*put*' options. They are for a fix period of kind and they pay interest after every 6 months. The period can also be monthly and the bond can be called monthly income bonds. It also carries a front end discount.

Retirement Bonds: These bonds are useful for investors who are in the retirement stage. They are issued at a discount with the option of monthly income and for a specified fix term period. On the exit time of the bond the investor gets a lump-sum amount.

Mutual Fund Securities

Mutual fund securities are called unit. Investors prefer mutual funds because they offer low risk and stable income. Small severs find the mutual fund schemes beneficial because they offer advantage of diversification and professional management. Mutual fund offer growth, income and index funds. They can be open ended or closed ended schemes.

Post Office Securities

Post offices offer certificates like Indra Vikas Patra, Kisan Vikas Patra and National Savings Certificates. They also provide monthly income schemes and schemes for retired investors. They have the scheme of public provident funds. The investor has certain advantages like tax benefits, higher rates of interest for special schemes and liquidity in investment. The Indian investor can choose from the various securities of the post offices.

Thus there are many instruments from which an investor can select the security of his choice. From the above the following important aspects should be remembered. These are given below:

- Equity shares have quick conversion into cash but are highly risky. However, an investor has both dividends and capital appreciation to look forward to in his investments.
- Debt securities which offer fixed rate of interest for a fixed term and with a definite maturity period. The investor will benefit with continuous return in the form of coupon rate.

- Financial engineering securities which have many options like liquidity, marketability, convertibility, flexibility, and maturity period and tax benefits. These are innovative securities and combine the advantages of different types of securities.
- Mutual funds securities that offer units. They offer freedom from management and diversification coupled with a good and stable return.
- Post office securities offer different types of schemes like fixed period with interest and monthly income schemes.

The investor should select securities after carefully analyzing the features of liquidity, collateral value, marketability, transferability, maturity period, and risk and tax factor. In the Indian financial system the number of instruments has increased since 1991 and this facilitates the linkage between depositors and investors. It is also able to encourage savings and distribute it in the right director through proper investment. The financial instruments may be ownership securities or debt securities but the choice available to the investors will help in developing the capital market.

FINANCIAL SERVICES

Financial services are provided to raise funds from individuals, investors, institutions and corporate organization. Financial services ensure effective mobilization of savings into productive units. There are many financial services like credit rating, venture capital, lease financing, factoring, mutual funds, merchant banking, stock lending, depository, credit cards, housing finance, book building and banking and insurance services.

Financial services have to be innovative and creative to mobilize savings. They also have to be dynamic and must respond to the socio-economic changes in a country. In India financial services were extremely limited. Up to 1980 merchant banking was the main function but it was limited. It helped in identifying projects and preparing feasibility reports and developing projects. Their services have since 1991 now grown into technical services, syndication facility, technical advise, legal advice, assistance in designing the capital structure of a company, underwriting and arranging working capital loans.

In India many new financial services have increased. The depository system was a landmark to bring about dematerialization of shares and bonds and creating paperless trading. Book building was introduced as a new concept of bidding for the purchase price of a share. The online trading system in Bombay stock exchange and national stock exchange also helped in developing the financial services in India.

The Indian financial system has now provided regulatory authorities to bring about discipline in financial services. The SEBI, RBI and the Department of Banking and Insurance of the government of India regulate the functioning of financial services.

REGULATORS

The regulators in the Indian financial system are government, RBI and SEBI. Government is an important regulator because it prepares the policies and within the frame work, the financial system has to work. RBI prepares the economic policies of the country and has a monetary control over the flow of funds.

RBI has strengthened the technological and procedural system for payment and supplement in the capital market. It has planned safety, security and efficiency in the capital market. SEBI has been formed with the view that the mechanics of buying and selling shares, nominations and transfers required simplification. Further, new companies required to be disciplined as they were no standardized procedures of allotment of shares. Investor protection was necessary for developing the financial system.

The regulators have helped in reorganizing and making the financial system liberalized. The introduction of new financial institutions, financial engineering and innovative instruments, and financial intermediation has brought about improvement in the system. It has given confidence in the minds of the investor with many investor protection measures brought about in the system. There is a closer link between different financial institutions and the capital market in India. To some extent the deficiencies in the capital market as pointed of L.C. Gupta have been removed. This has improved the financial system of India. The intermediation of saving through direct and indirect securities has brought about a growth in equity culture. The proportion of savings has increased since 2000-2001. Finally, it can be stated that the Indian financial system is more sophisticated, innovative and creative, with a large number of instruments, institutions and investor protection measures. The financial system can be called a dynamic and well diversified system.

Summary

➡ The development of the Indian financial systems can be marked by two important periods of time. Development from 1947 to 1990 and 1991 onwards.

➡ The Indian financial system was developed first as a controlled financial system with no free flow of demand and supply of funds. At that time most of the institutions were created in the Public Sector.

➡ After 1991 there has been a policy change. Privatization of development, financial institutions and banks is being encouraged.

➡ Development banks were formed to finance and develop industries. They did not have any link with the source of savings but they were to finance industries.

➡ Financial institutions were intermediaries linking the savings sources with the investment outlets.

➡ Development banks created a deficiency in the Indian capital market because industries became dependent on them. However, this has now being changed with the new policy in 1991.

➡ Many development banks like ICICI, IDBI and IFCI entered in to business of commercial banking and became very successful.

➡ There has been the introduction of a large number of new instruments in the economy. Besides, equity and debt instruments, there are financial engineering and innovative instruments.

➡ New financial services have been introduced for making the financial system more efficient. These services include venture capital, credit rating, factoring, leasing, book building, and merchant banking and depository functions.

➡ SEBI, RBI and Government have tried to bring about discipline in the capital market. Their focus has been on investor protection measures.

Objective Type Questions, Answer True (T) or False (F)

(a) The ICICI was setup in 1955 as pioneer financial institutions in the public sector.

(b) The IDBI was setup in 1964 as an apex lady to lend finance to small and medium companies.

(c) The financial institutions were formed to lend money directly.

(d) The financial sector in India before 1991 was controlled by government.

(e) The LIC was established a monolithic institution by merging 245 insurance companies in 1956.

(f) The concept of mutual funds was first started by the UTI in India.

(g) Since 1992 the development banks have been liberalized. They have entered into the field of commercial banking.

Answer: (a) F, (b) F, (c) F, (d) T, (e) T, (f) T, (g) T.

Multiple Choice Questions (Tick mark (✓) the right answer)

1. Which of the following started functioning as the first development bank in India?

   (a) The UTI started as the first development bank

   (b) The IFCI was developed by government as the first development bank in India

   (c) The ICICI was considered to be the first development bank even though it was not instituted first

   (d) The State Bank of India was given the responsibility of being the first development bank of India

2. Financial engineering means:

   (a) A package with new financial instruments

   (b) Innovative instruments with a variety of between to provide a choice to the investors

   (c) The interconnections between different financial instructions to make financial instruments

   (d) A direction from the RBI relating to the formation of different financial instruments

3. Mutual funds were imitated:

   (a) To being discipline in the financial

   (b) To provide high returns to markets investors

   (c) To being a stable returns to investors

   (d) To create awareness of unit schemes

4. A secondary is useful and known for its many functions:

   (a) The functions of issuing Initial Public Offerings (IPO's) to investors

   (b) It helps in mobilizing the savings of the people

   (c) It has the function of lending liquidity and marketability to a security

   (d) It helps in raising funds for industry

5. The objective of a commercial bank is:

    (a) To provide loans to industry

    (b) To provide merchant banking activities

    (c) To create deposits for different financing

    (d) To provide travellers cheques and cash credit to investors

    Answers: 1 (b), 2 (b), 3 (c), 4 (c), 5 (c).

Short Answer Questions

1. Give a brief description of the different financial instruments in India.

2. What is the role of SEBI in the Indian capital market?

3. What is the difference in the pattern of financing before and after 1990 in the development banks?

4. What is the changing role of commercial banks in India?

Long Answer Questions

1. Discuss the structure of the Indian financial system.

2. What are changes in the Indian financial system being about development is India?

3. Discuss the differences in the role of development banks and financial which one of there has played institutions in India more dominating role in the Indian financial system?

Chapter 3

Financial Sector Reforms in India

Chapter Plan	
• Financial Reforms	• Banking Sector Reforms
• Objectives of Reforms	• External Sector Reforms
• Strategies for Reforms	• Vision Document
• Policy Reforms	• Impact of Financial Reforms
• New Issue and stock Market Reforms	• Flow of Fund
• Government Securities Market Reforms	

INTRODUCTION

The last chapter discussed the financial system in India before and after 1991. This chapter discusses the reforms made to strengthen the financial system. The financial sector comprises of financial institutions, markets, instruments and services. The developments in the financial sector have been impressive but distortions have arisen. The industries had become heavily dependant on the development banks and relied totally for their financial requirements. Government intervention was to some extent necessary to bring about the possibility of financial development though imbalances arose due to too much interference and control.

The background to financial reforms is that the controlled economy had created the problem of low business, reduced number of transactions, high cost, low productivity and bureaucratic interference. Since the institutions did not give attention to internal management practices there was the prevalence of high risk and low returns in investments. There were mounting non-performing assets (NPA's) with financial institutions and commercial banks. Many institutions had become sick and required to be revived. Since technology was not developed most of the work carried out was done manually. Financial markets were not well organized and the participants in the capital market were not disciplined. There were restrictive practices and interest rates were high on loans but deposit gave a low rate of return.

To bring about a vibrant financial system it was necessary to create financial health through a flexible, de-regulated and liberalized system. It was important to bring about quality in services to allocate the savings of the people efficiently. It was necessary to update technology especially in transmitting information quickly to different sections of the constituents of the financial system. Disclosure practices had to be improved. Profitability and efficiency had to be brought about to make the financial system in a developed state.

The basic objective of creating reforms would be to improve operational matters with respect to the financial markets, institutions and banking systems. This should be possible through a new policy which would create facilities for competitive ability. The controls in the economy would have to be removed and a new policy would have to be prepared to globalize the Indian capital markets. The most important aspect required for modernizing, deregulating and globalizing of the financial system was to create a confidence amongst the investors. Several reforms were required for investor protection.

The reforms were made in the following areas.

- Reforms in the policies of the financial sector.
- Reforms in the new issue market and stock markets.
- Reforms in the government securities markets.
- Reforms relating to modernization in banks.
- Reforms for globalization of financial markets.

FINANCIAL REFORMS

The financial reforms in 1991 were focused on bringing about efficiency in the financial sector. Efficiency would be related to the transformation of the financial sector. It would bring about a free system with adequate protection in a deregulated environment. One of the major activities would be to have good procedures in trading, settlement, clearing of securities and investor protection in transactions.

OBJECTIVES OF REFORMS

The objectives of the reforms introduced in the financial sector in 1992 can be discussed entry categories. These are enabling measures, institutional measures and strengthening measures. ***The objectives of the financial sector reforms were the following:***

- ***Developing financial sector infrastructure***: It was necessary to upgrade the existing framework, facilities, services and technology for modernizing the financial sector.
- ***Financial supervision***: Although the financial sector was to be deregulated, supervision and inspection was important so that the flow of funds moves in the right direction and there is maximum benefit, achieved due to reforms. It would also provide investor protection and make the capital market vibrant and dynamic.
- ***Liberalization***: Openness and an environment of deregulation to bring about ease in transactions were desired. The absence of bureaucratic control and movement of funds from a controlled economy to a market economy would make it efficient.

- *Quality of Services*: Improvement in services and introduction of new services would help in high returns and low risk to home to the investors. It would bring about confidence in the minds of the saving population, thus encouraging savings in the economy.

STRATEGY OF REFORMS

The reforms in the Indian financial sector had to be made according to some strategies to achieve the above objectives.

Developing Financial Infrastructure (Enabling)

The most important aspect of reforms in the financial sector was the up-gradation of the basic infrastructure. Technology was lacking in this area. The stock market required computerization for trading. It also required re-organization of the stock markets and opening of new stock markets. Credits rating institutions had to be developed. Competition for making it a market economy had to be introduced for making the financial sector from a controlled to an open one. The basic strategy of government was to first develop all these infrastructural requirements.

Development in the financial sector was possible by developing and strengthening financial institutions and financial markets. In this directions government planned to allow foreign banks to begin business in India. New private banks were allowed to enter in the banking business. This was required to bring about competitiveness and openness in the economy. It allowed banks to raise funds through the capital market in India and internationally. It also introduced the concept of privatization by allowing entry of private life insurance companies and general insurance companies. Another infrastructural development was to allow the mutual funds to setup business in the private sector.

Computerization and depository system were the landmark infrastructural up-gradation in technology in the financial system. The acceptance of government towards a competitive economy and steps taken by it to develop and modernize the financial sector was the first step for development and change.

Legal Supervision

In order to bring about protection measures for investors, the strategy towards regulation was important to create an organized system. Government took a very important step by appointing the *Board for Financial Supervision (BFS)* in 1994. The board was to be engaged in inspection and supervision of financial institutions, banks and non-banking financial companies.

The BFS would monitor and supervise the credit planning and allocation of banks and financial institutions. Banks had high non-performing assets. The BFS had to control the practices of the banks and financial institutions on income recognition, asset classification at the time of providing credit.

Legal supervision was not only necessary within India but also for a monitoring cross border flows, international banking and international exchange transactions. The Securities Exchange Board of India was given statutory recognition in 1992 to regulate the capital market. SEBI had to create an environment which would facilitate mobilization of resources and its efficient allocation in the securities market. It also had to promote investor education and training of intermediaries in the stock market. Under its purview was the regulation of the working of stock brokers and stock markets. The Reserve

Bank of India was to create legislative supervisions of government securities and foreign exchange markets and Insurance Regulatory and Development Authority was created to regulate the insurance sector. **Clearing Corporation of India Ltd. (CCIL)** was established as a central counter party for payments and settlement system regarding fixed income and money market securities. **Credit Information Bureau India Ltd. (CIBIL)** was setup in 2000 to provide credit information on borrowers of credit institutions.

Easing of Restrictions (Openness)

In making reforms effective, de-regulation and liberalization was another steps in globalizing India. The strategy towards *openness and easing of restrictions* was taken up. Banks were given freedom to operate in financial markets internationally. The foreign institutional investors were encouraged to make investments in India. International standards were adopted and liberalization measures were taken to make them effective. The financial environment was made investor friendly. Information and awareness was provided to investors. Controls over pricing of financial assets and restrictions on transactions were reduced.

Let us now discuss the different reforms specifically made in the financial sector such as *policy reforms, new issue market and stock market reforms, government securities reforms, banking sector reforms and external sector reforms.*

POLICY REFORMS

The following policies were made to make the financial sector effective in India.

Abolition of bureaucratic control: The controller of capital issues was removed following the abolishment of capital issues Act.

Deregulation: The interest rates were deregulated by removing administered interest rates. The structure of interest rates was simplified and government securities were made market oriented.

Capital adequacy norms: The Basle committee prepared the capital adequacy norms. These adopted by banks financial institutions and other intermediaries.

Financial Supervision: The board of financial supervision was established as an independent department of RBI. Its function was to supervise banks, financial institutions and non-banking companies. It would also keep under control earnings, liquidity, capital adequacy, asset quality and management of financial institutions and banks.

Recovery of Debts: Special Recovery Tribunals were setup through the Recovery of Debts Due to Banks and Financial Institutions Act which was past in 1993. Its aim was to recover loan arrears.

Ceiling on ad-hoc issue of Treasury Bills (TB's): In 1994 (September) government and RBI jointly made an agreement to phase out ad-hoc treasury bills and in 1997 (April) it was decided to abolish them.

Statutory body initiated: SEBI was made a statutory body in 1992. It had powers and authority for regulations and reforms of the capital market.

Registration with RBI: All non-bank finance companies which owned a net (minimum) of Rs. 25 lakhs had to register themselves with RBI. This was in accordance with the RBI (amendment) Act of 1997.

Establishing stock exchanges: The National Stock Exchange (NSE) and the Over The Counter Exchange of India (OTCEI) were established with facilities such as trading through electronic display and clearing and settlement.

Floating interest rate: The all India development banks were allowed to have a floating interest rate on financial assistance which was linked to treasury bills of 364 days interest.

Conversion into public limited companies: SBI, IFCI and IDBI became public limited companies. IDBI raised capital from the public up to 49% of its paid of capital. The board of directors could be elected from the private sector.

Setting up institutions in the private sector: Government allowed the setting up of banks mutual funds and insurance companies in the private sector. Banks were also allowed to diversify their ownership by having 51% as a government quota.

Reducing cash reserve ratio: The cash reserve ratio which the banks had to keep as a statutory requirement was to be reduced from 15% to 10%. This reform would help the banks to have a higher cash balance for making investments.

Statutory liquidity ratio decreased: This ratio was to be reduced from 38% to 25% to bring about liquidity in the market.

NEW ISSUES AND STOCK MARKET REFORMS

The primary market for new issues and the stock market for sale and purchase of secondary securities a complementary to each other. There were many problems faced by shareholders and public at large. Reforms were necessary relating to issue of securities, listing, stockbrokers, promoters and merchant bankers. Many changes were brought about in these issues for a efficiency in the financial markets.

Book building process: The price of securities would be arrived at through the demand and supply interaction. The method of bidding for the security would be used.

Ownership record: The Depository Act was passed in 1996. The details of ownership would be recorded in a book entry form. It would help in dematerialization of securities.

Listing agreement: Modifications were brought about for listing of securities. This move would enable the investors to receive interest from companies from the 30th day of closing of a public issue.

Modernization of stock exchanges: The electronic trading system was to be introduced. The Bombay stock exchange started its online trading system called BOLT. Stock exchanges which were screen based were allowed to expand their trading terminals to those places which did not have any stock exchanges.

Ceiling on forward transaction: A ceiling on stock market members was made of business up to Rs. 10 crores for carry forward transactions.

Disclosure of transactions: Stock markets had to disclose the carry forward position of securities by classifying the broker carry on transactions. This disclosure was to be made in the beginning of every carry forward transaction. Further short and long sales were to be disclosed everyday.

Listing of Debt securities: Companies were allowed to list their debt securities on stock exchanges even though their equity was not listed.

Collection of daily margins: In the reform process restrictions were placed on gross traded value of a broker. Stock exchanges had to collect 100% of daily margins on the notional loss of a broker for every security that he traded. The gross traded value of a broker was to be a maximum of 33.33% of his basic capital.

Many changes were made by SEBI after 1992 to bring about uniformity and control in the financial markets. This was the beginning of the change and thus provided a back drop for discipline and investor protection. The primary and secondary markets are discussed in detail in chapters?

GOVERNMENT SECURITIES MARKET REFORMS

Reforms were made in the government securities market relating to introduction of new instruments, changes in features of treasury bills and introduction of new facilities. These are discussed briefly:

Maturity period: Central government securities had a maturity period of 20 years. This was reduced to 10 years. Similarly, State Government securities matured in 15 years but with the reforms it was reduced to 10 years maturity.

New instruments: Many new instruments were introduced. Some of them are floating rate bonds (1995), capital indexed bonds (1997), zero coupon bonds (1994), partly paid government stock (1994).

Treasury bills auctions: Provident funds and State Governments were allowed to participate in treasury bills of 91 days from 1994. The RBI could also option government securities as open market operations from its own portfolio (1995).

Establishment of dealers: Primary dealers were established for making deals in government securities. Guidelines were issued in 1995.

Replacement of treasury bills: The treasury bills of 182 days were replaced by 364 days treasury bills in 1992.

Introduction of new Treasury bills: 91 days treasury bills were introduced in 1993.

Reverse repo facility: The RBI extended its reverse repo facility to Discount and Finance House of India (DFHI) and Securities Trading Corporation of India (STCI).

BANKING SECTOR REFORMS

Banks were facing many problems. They had mounting non performing assets. They were controlled and had to fulfill many norms of lending. Their interest rates were regulated. Efficiency was lacking and human resource development was important. Modernization and deregulation of interest rates was necessary to make improvements in the system. A few reforms which were made after 1991 are given below:

Transparency: In accordance with The International Accounts Standards Committees banks had to bring about transparency in their accounting system. Their balance sheet was to make disclosure of all the material facts regarding their funds.

Liberalization: Banks were given the right to open new branches to bring about more business. They were given greater freedom to diversify into related areas like merchant banking and leasing equipment.

Introduction of Prudential norms: Banks have to adopt a uniform system in accounting and valuation of their investments. Prudential norms have been identified for income recognition, classification of assets and provision for bad debts.

Relaxation of banking issues: Banks were given relaxation on consortium lending, project finance, prior credit authorization and inventory and receivable norms.

Customers' grievances: Customer service helps the bank to growth. The banking Ombudsman schemes were introduced in 1995. RBI would appoint 15 Ombudsmen. They would solve customer grievances quickly.

Performance parameters: Banks would have to follow performs parameters relating to generation of income and profits, increased low cost deposits, lending for exports, reducing expenditures, improving quality and creating better standards of productivity.

Issue of capital: The nationalized banks and SBI would be allowed to issue equity and debt capital to public.

Fixing interest rate: Banks were given the freedom to fix their on interest on post shipment export credit for over 90 days.

Fixing foreign exchange position: Banks were allowed to fix their own foreign exchange open position. However, they have to take the approval of the RBI.

Components of finance: Banks were required to furnished details about bank credit. Bank finance was to be divided into two components. These components consist of short term working capital loan and cash credit.

Budgetary support: Those public sector banks which were financially weak would be given support depending upon banks budget.

EXTERNAL SECTOR REFORMS

The financial sector in India was controlled. The external financial markets required openness and introduction of a flexible system to bring about foreign investment in the country. There was a virtual stoppage of financial transactions between India and other countries. To revive these transactions, reforms were made. Some of the changes are discussed below:

Flexible exchange rate: Exchange controls were abolished and in its place the flexible exchange rate system was introduced.

Permission towards international access: The Indian companies were allowed to introduce new instruments and to register their instruments in the foreign markets to have an access in the international capital markets. They were allowed to issue euro-equities.

Rupee convertibility: The Indian currency (rupees) was made convertible on current account to be subsequently followed by capital account convertibility.

Receipts of proposal: The single window for accepting receipts and for disposing of the proposals was made functional through the RBI for foreign proposals by Indian companies.

Promoting investment in India: It was important to have an inflow of foreign direct investment in India. To promote foreign investment in India, the **Foreign Investment Promotion Council (FIPC)** was established.

Legal framework: There was a proposal to replace The *Foreign Exchange Regulation Act (FERA)* by *Foreign Exchange Management Act (FEMA)* in 1997. The reason for this change was to increase the foreign flow of capital.

Investments of Non-Resident Indians (NRI's): The NRI's were encouraged to bring their inflow of funds into the Indian economy. To promote their savings into the financial markets in India the rate on long term capital gains tax on their investment was reduced to 10%. They were earlier paying a tax of 20%. With this reduction the tax was at par with the *Foreign Institutional Investors (FII's)*. NRI's were also permitted to invest in Indian companies up to a maximum of 24% in equity shares with the exception of agriculture and plantation.

Foreign Institutional Investors (FII's): Permission was granted to FII's to enter the Indian capital market. FII's had to register themselves with SEBI and were allowed to invest in the equity shares of a company. They could invest in listed and unlisted companies. They could also establish 100% pure debt funds; make an investment in government securities, charitable trust, societies, university, foundations and foreign endowment funds. They could invest up to 24% in equities of Indian companies except for those engaged in agriculture and plantations.

These financial reforms were made to have a safe and sound financial sector, for sustained growth in India. Deregulation and liberalization was brought about to globalize the Indian financial markets with other countries. Reforms were made in the internal and external environment of the financial market to integrate the various constituents of the financial system. The banking sector was made competitive and according to the expectations of international standards.

The regulatory mechanism is expected to provide a cover for future risks in business. The Liberalization in the financial system will bring about a high volume of funds. There will also be competition with foreign markets. India has to bring about technological advancement to take the advantage of business opportunities. It also has to be ready to deal with high volatility in funds. The reforms were the first step towards financial integration. They have made changes with view of transforming the economy from a closed economy to a vibrant, dynamic and confident one. The climate has been setup. The financial sector reforms were reviewed and the RBI was faced with new challenges in the form of standardization and technology up-gradation. It developed vision documents to take up those areas which required attention for development and growth.

VISION DOCUMENT

A Vision document 2005-2008 was prepared by RBI to take a feedback from stakeholders like banks, experts, technology solution providers and members of the public. The document focuses is on safety, security, soundness and efficiency. It is called triple S and E. This document stressed on risk reduction measures. It also aimed at providing confidence in the payment systems. Efficiency would be enhanced through cost effective technological solutions. The RBI released a financial sector technology vision document (draft) in 2005. This focused on information technology for regulation, supervision in the financial sector and in government related functions. This document also has a plan for *Institute for Development and Research in Banking Technology (IDRBT).* For research and development to link the business processes with e-governances to achieve goals. The RBI also proposes the need for making reforms in foreign banks operating in India. It released a road map which was divided in two phases. The first phase would cover March 2005 to 2009. This document had number of proposals for banks already operating in India and foreign banks which wanted to establish themselves for the first time in India. Foreign banks already operating in India would be allowed to setup or convert themselves into a *Wholly Owned Subsidiary (WOS).* However, such banks would have to follow the financial soundness, supervisory rating, ownership pattern and international ranking. A WOS would have to keep a minimum capital of 300 crores and keep in line with sound corporate governance. RBI was also keen to go beyond the *World Trade Organization's (WTO)* commitment for opening new branches and expanding their branches. The second phase would be from April 2009 after making a review and in consultation with the stakeholders in the banking sector. In this phase 3 important issues would be considered. The first issue consists of opening up the obstructions and treating WOS at par with Indian banks. The second issue is related to WOS of foreign banks which may be allowed to dilute their stake after completing a minimum period of operation. This dilution should be according to the guidelines in 2004 issued to a minimum of 26% of paid up capital of the subsidiary to Indians. The dilution can be either issued to public or it may be an offer for sale. A third issue is to allow the foreign banks into merger and acquisition agreements with any private sector bank in India with a total investment level of 74%.

IMPACT OF FINANCIAL REFORMS

The financial reforms brought about changes in the financial sector. Most of the institutions were keen to bring about technology changes as well as quality in services. Banks tried to reduce their NPA's and improve their profitability. They had to follow capital adequacy and other prudential norms. The period from 1992 to 2002 clearly shows that the non performing assets as a percentage of total assets reduced but the volume of NPA's continued to be high. Banks had another problem. The interest rates due to reforms had been decreased. This reduced the household sectors investments in bank deposits. Since bank deposits gave low rates of interest and interest on such deposits was taxable, the preference of the household sector shifted to other saving avenues.[1]

The reforms increased competition amongst banks. However, it created an imbalance in the financial system because the distinction between commercial banks, development banks and investment banks narrowed down. Banks entered into many new functions to become supermarkets and financial conglomerates and were termed universal banks. Thus they took over most of the functions of the financial institutions and development banks. The functions of life insurance as well as opening of mutual funds in the banks increased their operations and services. The development banks looked for reverse mergers- the ICICI being the first to apply for it. The imbalance created high NPA's in development banks.

---

1. See N.A. Majumdar, *Financial Sector Reforms* (Vol. 1) Academic Foundation, India 2002, p. 40.

The financial markets had a number of reforms but remained depressed. The primary market did not grow immediately and issue of new capital also did not rise. In 2006 the markets had a change and witnessed a continuous rise in sensex. SEBI as a market regulator was not strong. It issued a multiplicity of laws and guidelines but was unable to enforce them. The stock market became highly speculative until the derivatives trade was started and *badla* was abolished.

The market based rates certainly helped the Indian economy to open up and become global. However, there was external pressure and exchange rates were quite volatile. The Americans criticized the Indian reforms to be ideological and fashionable rather than operational. Some experts called the Indian reforms as '*Americanization of finance*'.

The financial sector in India has witnessed many structural changes even though it has been criticized. It can be said that there has been a transformation in the financial system. Due to liberalization rigidity in the system has been removed. The country has high exchange reserves and deserves credit for with standing many crisis situations in volatility in external transactions.

Let us study the role of savings and investments to find out the progress that has been made after the reforms. We now take a look at the flow of funds in the Indian economy.

FLOW OF FUNDS

The flow of funds in an economy helps to understand the financial structure and its inter-relationships. The flow of funds account consists of each sector as well as aggregate sources and uses of funds in an economy. The fund flow matrix depends on the various financial claims and complex nature of the sectors and securities of a country in India. The economy is divided into 6 sectors. These are private corporate business, financial institutions, banking, government, household and external financing. The inter-relationships of the flows are analyzed through savings/investments, sources/uses, and assets/liabilities and borrowing/lending.

The flow and funds-matrix can be prepared by making a review of the balance sheets of different sectors both in the beginning as well as at the end of the time period. *When net assets increase they are treated as uses of funds and when liabilities increase it becomes a source of funds.* Certain items are negative sources of funds, for example debt repayment. Similarly real assets disinvestments/sale or securities are negative uses. Sectoral flows should also be analyzed on a net basis. Flows between different sectors are recorded but within the same sector it is not recorded. For example, public to private sector flows would be recorded but a transfer from one unit in the private sector to another unit in the same sector will not be recorded. Although sources and uses should balance, they normally do not balance because of discrepancies.

Savings and Investments

The following Table 3.1 indicates the flow of funds in savings and investments sector wise. The gross household savings has been 22.04% from 1999 to 2005-2006 out of these financial assets has been 10.73%. Physical assets comprise of 11.31% thus household sector contributes the highest savings amongst all the sectors. The savings minus investment balance indicates that it is positive between the years 2001-2004. This shows that investment was less than domestic savings. This means that savings have not been effectively used in those years. However, the provisional figures of 2004 to 2006 show that utilization of savings is taking place.

In India the household savings have played an important part. A study was made by Newlyn in 1977. He made a comparison of 32 countries in which he found that the corporate sector participated in greater savings than the household sector. In India household savings has always made a greater impact than the corporate sector, in accumulation of savings.[2] In a country it is important to note that collection of savings must be used in a useful manner. Savings should be productive. They can be useful and productive if savings is in the form of financial assets (excluding currency). To accelerate development savings should be higher in financial assets then in other assets like gold or non-agricultural land. In India traditions and cultural bonds create the demand for non-productive assets. It is difficult to explain to the various households that financial assets will also give them a good return. The attachment to land and gold continues. A survey of household investor was conducted by society for capital market research and development shows that households of every class an income have a high preference for fixed deposits in banks.[3]

Table 3.1: Rates of Gross Domestic Saving and Investment

(Per cent of GDP at Current Market Prices)

Item	1999-00	2000-01	2001-02	2002-03	2003-04	2004-05 (PE)	2005-06 (QE)
1	2	3	4	5	6	7	8
1. Household Saving	21.1	21.0	21.8	22.7	23.8	21.6	22.3
(a) Financial assets	10.6	10.2	10.8	10.3	11.3	10.2	11.7
(b) Physical assets	10.5	10.8	10.9	12.4	12.4	11.4	10.7
2. Private Corporate Saving	4.5	4.3	3.7	4.2	4.7	7.1	8.1
3. Public Sector Saving	− 0.8	− 1.7	− 2.0	− 0.6	1.2	2.4	2.0
4. Gross Domestic Saving	24.8	23.7	23.5	26.4	29.7	31.1	32.4
5. Gross Domestic Capital Formation	25.9	24.3	22.9	25.2	28.0	31.5	33.8
6. Gross Capital Formation	26.1	24.1	23.8	25.0	26.6	29.7	32.2
(a) Public sector	7.4	6.9	6.9	6.1	6.3	7.1	7.4
(b) Private corporate sector	7.4	5.7	5.4	5.9	6.9	9.9	12.9
(c) Household sector	10.5	10.8	10.9	12.4	12.4	11.4	10.7
7. Saving-Investment Balance (4-5)	− 1.1	− 0.6	0.6	1.2	1.6	− 0.4	− 1.3
(a) Public Sector Balance	− 8.2	− 8.5	− 8.9	− 6.6	− 5.2	− 4.7	− 5.4
(b) Private Corporate Sector	− 2.9	− 1.4	− 1.7	− 1.7	− 2.2	− 2.8	− 4.8
(c) Household Sector	10.6	10.2	10.8	10.3	11.3	10.2	11.7

PE : Provisional Estimates.

QE : Quick Estimates.

Notes : 1. Figures may not add up to the roles due to rounding off.

2. Sectoral saving-investment balances are calculated as the difference between saving and gross Capital formation at sectoral level.

Source : RBI Bulletin government of India, July 2007.

---

2. W.T. Newlyn, *The Financing of Economic Development*, Clarendon Press Oxford, 1977 p.12.

3. L.C. Gupta, *Indian Household Investors Survey*, Society for Capital Market Research and Development, New Delhi, 2005, p. 129 to 136.

There is however a change and investors have ranked the equity shares higher than the bank deposits in preference for saving. It can be stated that about 50% of the total funds invested by the household sector is in equity shares and bank deposits.[4] The study also states that when the income level is high the importance of bank deposits reduces Table 3.2 shows household savings in financial assets for the years 2003-2006. The figures show that bank deposits, non-bank deposits and trade debts are the highest in household savings.[5] The investment in shares and debentures including units of UTI and mutual funds form 0.1% of the financial assets in which the savings was made by household.

Savings of the household sector in currency reduced from 11.2% in 2003-2004 to 8.5% in 2004-2005 and was 8.8% in 2005-2006 but the preference although reduced is still high in holding currency.

Table 3.2: Household Saving in Financial Assets

(Amount in Rupees crore)

Item	2003-04P	2004-05P	2005-06#
1	2	3	4
A. Financial Assets (Gross)	3,80,090	4,35,706	5,88,656
	(13.8)	(14.0)	(16.7)
1. Currency	42,675	36,997	51,954
	(1.5)	(1.2)	(1.5)
	[11.2]	[8.5]	[8.8]
2. Deposits@	1,45,657	1,61,416	2,78,985
	(5.3)	(5.2)	(7.9)
	[38.3]	[37.0]	[47.4]
3. Claims on Government	87,372	1,06,420	86,755
	(3.2)	(3.4)	(2.5)
	[23.0]	[24.4]	[14.7]
4. Investment in Shares and Debentures +	492	4,967	29,008
	(0.0)	(0.2)	(0.8)
	[0.1]	[1.1]	[4.9]
5. Contractual Saving**	1,03,895	1,25,926	1,41,954
	(3.8)	(4.0)	(4.0)
	[27.3]	[28.9]	[24.1]
B. Financial Liabilities	70,732	1,21,187	1,82,539
	(2.6)	(3.9)	(5.2)
C. Saving in Financial Assets (Net) (A-B)	3,09,358	3,14,519	4,06,117
	(11.2)	(10.1)	(11.5)

P : Provisional.   # : Preliminary Estimates.
@ : Comprise bank deposits, non-bank deposits and trade debt (net).
+ : Including units of Unit Trust of India and other mutual funds.
** : Comprise life insurance, provident and pension funds.
Notes:1. Components may not add up to the total due to rounding off.
     2. Figures in ( ) indicate per cent of GDP at current market prices and [ ] indicate per cent of financial assets (gross).
Source: Reserve Bank of India, Annual report 2005-2006.

4. ibid p. 73, table 5.4.
5. Reserve Bank of India: Annual Report, Government of India, 2006, p. 31.

Household Sector Liabilities

The above table 3.2 indicates that the household sector as the savings minus investments is higher than its financial liabilities. Therefore, it is a net surplus sector. In the above table the financial liabilities are much lower than the financial assets in the years 2004, 2005 and 2006. While financial liabilities were 5.2% of Gross Domestic Product (GDP) in 2006, the financial assets in the same year were 16.7%. This table also shows that savings and financial assets were as high as 11.5%. However, financial liabilities increased sharply into 2005 and 2006 due to high loans and advances for purchasing consumer durables and housing loans. Despite this change the net financial savings of the household sector was 10.7% of GDP at current market prices.[6]

To sum up the total household savings in India has increased from 25% to 47% approximately in 2004-2005 but the rate of financial saving increased less than 2% between 1950 and 2004-2005. In 2000-2001 households preferred physical assets especially housing. In financial assets the preference of the households is shifting to contractual savings life insurance, provident and pension funds. Claims on government have decreased. Financial liabilities have increased. Since the GDP was reflecting a growth of 8% in 2005-2006. It can be said that there is positive development in the Indian economy.

Thus the above discussion has been like an opening towards the various financial markets and institutions to be studied in the next few chapters. It will be useful to find out how these reforms have had an impact and what the new developments are in the financial sector.

Summary

➥ The financial sector reform process was started on the recommendation of the committee on the financial system in 1991. The chairman of this committee was M. Narsimham.

➥ The focus of these reforms was to have a sound financial sector which would be competitive in a global situation.

➥ The reforms were made with the aim of globalization, deregulation and liberalization of the financial sector to revive dynamism and competition in the financial sector.

➥ The reforms were meant to create a transparent system for creating confidence in the minds of the investors for encouraging savings and investment.

➥ Technology up-gradation was important to create an environment for bringing about significant changes in the financial sector.

➥ The objectives of reforms were developing financial sector infrastructure, financial supervision, liberalization and quality in services.

Contd.....

---

6. According to RBI annual report 2005-2006 (supplement) it stated that household sector was the pre dominant source of domestic savings since 1950s and in 2004-2005 it has contributed 76% of total domestic savings 2004-2005. See op. cit. p. 30.

➡ The strategies to make the reforms successful were followed. They were enabling and strengthening measures, supervision and legal framework, and openness and easing of restrictions.

➡ The reforms were made in general policy matters, new issue market and stock exchange market, commercial banks, government securities markets and external sector.

➡ The reforms were a background to further reforms after feedback and review.

➡ RBI made new reforms in technology up-gradation and in the efficiency of the payment and settlement systems by creating vision document 2005-2008.

➡ Reforms also made through a roadmap for foreign banks in India. This was to be done in phases. The first phase was to be the implementation and the second phase was to start in 2009 after reviewing the first phase and looking into its positive and negative aspects.

➡ The reforms have brought about imbalances in the financial sector and differences between banks and development banks have narrowed down.

➡ The NPA's of banks have reduced but the volume is till high.

➡ Although there are limitations yet there has been a transformation in the financial sector.

➡ After the reforms a review of the flow of funds through the saving and investment channels has been made. Savings from the household sector is highest.

➡ The household sector preferred physical assets but in the financial assets contractual savings was becoming popular.

➡ The GDP of the country is showing a growth of 8% in 2005-2006. This is positive.

Objective Type Questions, Answer True (T) or False (F)

(a) The financial reforms were made in India due to inflation and closure of industries.

(b) The focus of the reforms was to being about transparency, competition and deregulation for development.

(c) The banking reforms were made to private banks.

(d) The depository system existed before the reforms but technology was updated after the reforms to make it to denationalize shows.

(e) The financial institutions are merged into banks.

(f) Banks provide many devices like merchant banking, underwriting, leasing and venture capital in the post reforms period.

(g) Mutual funds are in the private and public sector.

(h) The ICICI went into a reverse merger with the ICICI bank.

(i) In India development banks are the same as financial institutions.

(j) Banks have the same functions as development banks.

Answers: (a) F, (b) T, (c) F, (d) F, (e) F, (f) T, (g) T, (h) T, (i) F, (j) F.

Multiple Choice Questions (Tick mark (✓) the right answer)

1. The financial reforms in India were necessary:
   (a) To revitalize the economy
   (b) To encourage mobilization of savings and their allocation into investments
   (c) To control the economy
   (d) To create responsibility in the different sectors of the economy

2. The reforms in the public sector banks were made:
   (a) To privatize the banks for encouraging savings and investments
   (b) To being about capital adequacy and lending norms, transparency and competition
   (c) To create infrastructural development in industries
   (d) To make an efficient and controlled system of banking

3. Reforms were made in the government securities market:
   (a) To bring about new features in securities
   (b) To establish links with other sectors in the economy
   (c) To control money market operations and for reducing black money
   (d) To make changes in the existing pattern of securities, maturity periods and transactions

4. The reforms were initiated through different strategies. These are:
   (a) Legal, control and discipline techniques
   (b) Enabling, strengthening and supervision techniques
   (c) Liberal techniques of credit authorization
   (d) Capital recovery and legal action

5. The Rains in the Indian economy are highest from:
   (a) Government sector
   (b) Banking sector
   (c) Private corporate sector
   (d) Household sector

6. The financial reforms in India were through the financial recommendation in 1991 of the:
   (a) Tandon committee report
   (b) Narsimham committee report
   (c) Vision document
   (d) Dutt enquiry committee

   Answer: 1 (b), 2 (b), 3 (d), 4 (b), 5 (d), 6 (b).

Short Answer Questions

1. What are the different sectors in which financial reforms were made? Discuss the focus of these informs.

2. Why do you think that it was necessary to have reforms in the banking sector?

3. What is the reason for reverse mergers post financial sector reforms?

4. Discuss the strategies for bringing about financial reforms.

5. Write notes on:

    (a) Vision Document,

    (b) Reforms in the new issue and stock market.

Long Answer Questions

1. Discuss the reforms made in the primary and secondary markets in India.

2. What is 'vision document'? Why was it initiated? In which sectors is it directed?

3. Discuss the flow of funds in the different sectors in the economy. What is the significance of the household sector in the savings of the economy?

4. Evaluate the financial sector reforms in India.

Part – Two

Regulatory Authorities

4.   The Reserve Bank of India

5.   The Securities Exchange Board of India

Chapter 4

The Reserve Bank of India

Chapter Plan

- Historical Background
- Function of RBI
  Note Issuing Authority
  Bankers' Bank
  Monetary Control
- Promotional Role of RBI
  Setting up specialized institutions
  Monetary policy
  Supervision
  Financial sector

INTRODUCTION

The Reserve Bank of India was the established on April 1st 1935 as the Central Bank of the country. It was nationalized on 1st January, 1949. It is a regulatory authority at the head of the monetary system in the country. It also regulates monitors and controls the financial system in India. Since the financial sector reforms in 1992 it has played and important role in supervising the financial system. The traditional function of RBI was issue of currency, being banker to government and banker to other banks. This has now been extended to the development of the financial sector.

The RBI regulates the issue of currency and keeps currency reserves for bringing about monetary stability in the country. It has promoted savings and investment through development banks and financial institutions. It has also regulated the investment and business activity of the country. It has played and important role in economic development by adhering with the priorities of India's planning program.

The RBI tried to bring about technological, institutional and legal changes for the initiation of reforms in the financial sector. It worked on integration of domestic financial sector with the global system.

In 1992 the first phase of reforms was started for improving efficiency and creating operational flexibility in the financial sector. In the second phase it proposed to bring about structural improvements in developing the system. Therefore, the role and responsibilities of the RBI was enlarged after the new economic reforms were started in India.

RBI's responsibilities covered not only the Indian domestic market but also the external sector. It played a traditional role in maintenance of foreign exchange reserves for the country. After the reforms it had to cope with exchange control and manage the reserves by investing and utilizing them for the benefit of the country. It acts as stabilizer of the foreign exchange market and manages India's reserves in gold accounts and transactions in international shares and securities.

HISTORICAL BACKGROUND

The Reserve Bank of India was started as a private bank by a statute on March 6, 1934. During this period it was under the colonial government and its main function was to be the banker to the government and to be the note issuing authority. During the World War its main function was to look after the finances of the war. In the post war years it conducted all the traditional functions plus the administration of exchange control and the repatriation of sterling debt. In 1934 it took over the function of controller of currency. It issued notes of rupees 5 and rupees 10 in 1938. Then in 1937 RBI looked after the monetary problems which were due to the separation of Burma. From 1937 to 1942 RBI was a banker to the Burmese Government. From 1947 to 1948 the RBI provided its services to Pakistan as well as India. In 1948 it severed its connections with Pakistan and it was nationalized in 1949 to become the apex bank of the country. It became State-owned. Its head office is in Mumbai and its executive head is the governor of the bank. Nationalization of the bank was by transferring the share capital to the Central Government. An Act was past in 1948 for the transfer and the act empowered the Central Government to issue directions which were considered important in the interest of the public.

Organizational Structure

The organization structure of the bank was to be governor at the head and four deputy governors which were to be appointed by the Central Government. RBI was to be managed by a central board of 15 directors, local board of directors and a committee of the central board of directors. The governor and 2 deputy governors are appointed by the central government. 4 directors are nominated by the Central Government, 1 from each of the 4 local boards. 10 directors are to be nominated by the Central Government. 1 government official is to be nominated by the Central Government. The local board of directors was to advise the central board on important matters which were referred to them. They would also be accepted to participate in the duties given to them. The central board comprising of governor, deputy governors and directors were to be nominated by central government. The committee of the central board consisted of governor, deputy governors and directors. The governor and deputy governor would the appointed for 5 years and were eligible for reappointment. 10 directors appointed by the government had a term period of 4 years. The directors would represent different sections of the society like charter accountants, traders, industrialist, and exporters and so on. As functions of the RBI began to increase, the number of departments also increased. These have been updated and changed according to the requirements of the banks.

RBI as the head of the monetary system is also a central force in the Indian financial system. Its main function has been to monitor, guide, promote, regulate and control the Indian economy in monetary and financial matters. After the new economic reforms it had helped in nation building process and

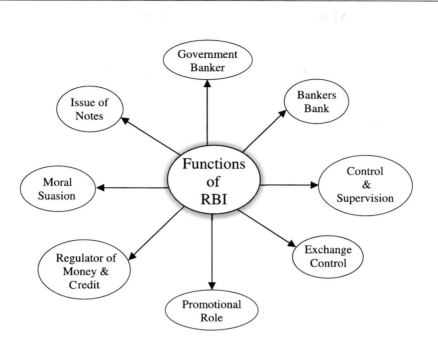

Fig 4.1: Functions of RBI

development of the financial sector. The bank is the central bank of India. It issues currency. It is a banker to the Indian government and it is also a banker to other banks. Truly, it has played a promotional role in India.

FUNCTIONS OF RBI

The RBI is the central bank of India and has many functions. The Preamble of the Reserve Bank of India describes the basic functions of the Reserve Bank as: "...to regulate the issue of Bank Notes and keeping of reserves with a view to securing monetary stability in India and generally to operate the currency and credit system of the country to its advantage."

The traditional functions are note issue authority, banker to the government, bankers bank and control of money and credit. Its modern functions include promotional role in institutional building and developing the financial sector.

Note Issuing Authority

As a note issuing authority it issues currency notes and coins with the exception of rupees one which is issued by the central government. Under this function the RBI conducts printing of currency notes, clean notes policy, has security features of notes, computerizes currency operations and issues coins of lower denomination notes.

Printing of currency notes: The Bhartiya Reserve Bank Note Mudran Private Limited (BRBNMPL) which is a wholly own subsidiary of the RBI at Mysore in Karnataka and Salboni in West Bengal has been setup and made operational in 1999 and 2000 respectively. It prints all the notes in a secure environment with modern facilities of printing, checking and process control. These two printing presses were in three sifts everyday and have a combined capacity of 19.8 billion notes per year.

Clean note policy: This policy was created to remove the non-usable notes from the market and to print new notes and put them in circulation. The RBI installed high speed automatic machines for processing 50,000 to 60,000 soiled notes per hours. The machine sorted out the good and bad notes. The notes which can be reused are put in fresh packets. The bad notes are sent to an online shredding unit and torn into small pieces. They are then put into a briquetting unit and disposed of according to environment friendly regulations.

Security features of notes: The RBI reviews the security features and tries to improve the design of the notes whenever it takes out a new series of notes. The security features consist of an image like for example Mahatma Gandhi. A water mark a security thread, a latent image and intaglio features. RBI had also brought a new feature in 2005 in which security features are machine readable. It takes proper caution with notes of high denomination like rupees 100, 500 and 1000. The security features are constantly updated with the latest technology. They are also changed so that they can be copied.

Computerizing currency operations: The RBI has tried to modernize the currency system through an Integrated Computerized Currency Operations and Management Systems (ICCOMS). The objective of computerization is to provide with care efficient services to the customers. The system would bring about uniformity in processing, accounting and management of currency transactions. This would also provide security of the currency in the currency chests.

Issue of lower Denomination points: In 2005 the volume of notes in circulation was high. RBI decided to limit this volume to a manageable amount by issuing coins instead of notes. Rupees 5, 2 and 1 were made into coins and high denomination currency was issued into notes. To sum up:

> RBI issues all the notes in the country. It takes care in printing of notes through two specialized printing presses. It removes from circulation all the soiled notes by completely destroying them through automatic machines. It has special security features on the notes consisting of water mark, thread, image and machine readable quality. Its currency operations are computerized and it issues notes of high denomination and coins of small denomination currency.

Banker to the Government

The RBI provides the government with a wide range of services.

Payments and collections: It makes payments and collects them for government. It accepts deposits, withdrawal of funds by cheques and any transfers of funds on behalf of government. The RBI has agreements with the central and state governments and according to those agreements it provides service to them. It offers all the services to government that are provided by a commercial bank to its customers.

Minimum balance: The central and state governments have a current account with the RBI in which they keep their cash balances. The governments as per agreements have to keep minimum cash balance with the RBI.

Government Borrowing from RBI: Government tries to keep minimum cash balance as required by the RBI but it usually has a deficit cash balance in the beginning of the financial year. It takes measures for replenishing the funds but when its expenditures exceed its receipts it borrows funds from the RBI. As a short term measures the central government borrows through the sale of ad-hoc treasury bills. State governments take short term loans for a maximum term of three months through '*Ways and Means Advances*'. This advance is classified into *normal or clean advances,* in which money is borrowed without providing a collateral security. *Secure advances* in which the pledge of government securities is taken as a security. *Special advances* which are given by the RBI at its discretion. RBI has prescribed limits for borrowing by state governments.

Loans for agricultural development: RBI provides loans to state government for agricultural development. This borrowing is in addition to the short term advances made to state government.

Overdrafts: RBI has given the facility of overdrafts or drawing in excess of their credit limits to state governments. RBI charges a minimum bank rate for 7 days of providing on overdraft. From the 8th days it charges 3% above the bank rate.

Administration of public debt: RBI as the government banker manages its public debt. It administers and services out-standings in public debts. It provides management services for all the new issues of government loans. It charges a commission for its services to government.

Advisor to government: The RBI functions as an advisor to government on matters regarding banking legislation, international finance and issues relating to mobilization of resources for 5 years plans of India.

Bankers' Bank

The RBI has the power to supervise, regulate and control commercial and cooperative banks.

Reserves with RBI: It controls the reserves of the commercial banks. Every bank has to keep a reserve with the RBI. It is a statutory requirement that every bank has to compulsorily deposit between 3% and 15% of their total liabilities.

Licensing banks: The RBI has the power of licensing banks. It can give permission to banks to expand their branches. It may allow banks to amalgamate or merge. It has the powers for issuing licenses for establishing new banks.

Controlling authority: The RBI has the right to control the commercial banks. It can prescribe minimum requirements of a bank for reserves, paid up capital and transfers to reserve fund. It can inspect the operational aspects of banks relating to any complaints or irregularities. It can appoint or terminate the chairman as well as the chief executive officers. It also has the right to investigate into the working of a bank in their activities relating to deposits, investment, advances, portfolio management and profit planning.

Banker of last resort: When commercial banks require funds temporarily and they are unable to get funds from alternate sources they borrow from the RBI. Therefore the RBI is known as the *banker of last resort.*

Monetary Control

The RBI has the main function of preparing monetary policy and using different techniques to control credit and money supply in India. The monetary policy is prepared in India to accelerate its economic development and ensure price stability through controlled bank credit and money supply. Monetary policy has the function of conserving the country resources and take decisions to ensure equitable and balanced growth. The monetary policy should also achieve growth without deflation. The credit expansion and inflation should be controlled to achieve growth in output. Similarly they would be a likelihood of increase in prices with growth but the increase should be within limits. The monetary policy would also have to emphasize the promotion of exports to earn a foreign exchange with external transactions. The goal of the monetary policy would be to bring about an increase in productivity through channeling investments in the right directions.

Since, the new economic reforms, the monetary policy of India, directed through the RBI, has been focused, to bring about competition, deregulation, flexibility and discipline in the financial system of the country.

RBI has different instruments to control the monetary policy. These are quantitative and qualitative instruments. The quantitative measures used are bank rate; cash reserve ratio (CRR), statutory liquidity ratio (SLR), open market operations and moral suasions. The qualitative credit controls are selective controls.

Bank rate: The RBI lends to other banks at an interest rates which is called the bank rate. The RBI provides credit to banks by rediscounting their eligible government securities. When the RBI increases the bank rate it reduces the willingness of the commercial banks to borrow at a higher rate. At the same time the commercial banks would increase their rate of interest and the general public would be dissuaded to borrow from commercial banks. This policy has to be carefully applied as there are certain seasonal requirements which are higher then in other season.

Cash reserve ratio (CRR): In India all scheduled banks are under statute, required to have cash reserves with the RBI. The commercial banks have to maintain a percentage of their demand and time liabilities. The maximum CRR is 15%. Co-operative banks and Rural Regional Banks have to maintain only 3% as CRR. If banks fall below their CRR they have to pay an interest of 3% above the bank rate for the first week in which they are defaulting and after than 5% above bank rate until the balance required is maintained. RBI can withdraw re-financing facility if banks default in their CRR.

The RBI since 1973 pays an interest on the cash reserves maintained by banks. The interest is paid between the averages plus marginal prescribed CRR and the minimum CRR of 3%. The interest is paid only to those banks that do not make a default. Interest is paid on the prescribed CRR and not on any extra reserve beyond the stipulated amount.

The RBI uses this control to increase or decrease the supply of money in the country. It increases the CRR to reduce the money supply and it decreases the CRR when the country requires a smooth flow of funds. This policy was not used between 1950 and 1972 but between 1973 and 1989 RBI used it to control the flow of credit in the economy. In 1993 it reduced the maximum cash reserve to 10% from the earlier required reserve of 15%. From 1998 the CRR was reduced from 10% to 4.5%. Since 1997 the

RBI has changed the interest rates that it would pay on the cash balance maintained with it. Until 2001 it paid 4% and for a short while it paid 6% and in the end of 2001 it changed and made the rate of interest to be given to banks equal to the bank rate.

Statutory liquidity ratio (SLR): The RBI uses the CRR technique of control with the SLR. The commercial banks, financial institutions like LIC, GIC and provident funds have to invest a minimum of their prescribed assets and liabilities in government securities and approved securities. The reason for this is that a certain reserve is kept in government securities. This becomes a supplementary reserve while the primary reserve is the CRR.

The SLR can be used as a control measure to expand or restrict bank credit. When SLR is increased the banks expansion of credit gets restricted and when it is reduced then the credit can be expanded. The SLR does not affect the total expenditure of the economy but it restricts the private sector expenditure. Therefore, SLR helps to distribute bank resources to give important to government securities.

The SLR has been declining since 1991 it was 38.25% in 1992. It reduced to 38% and then 37.25% in 1997 the credit policy further rationalized the credit policy uniform rate of 25% was imposed on the banks. This rate is unchanged.

Open market operations: RBI has used the open market operations by buying and selling government securities in the money market. When it buys the securities then there is increase in the money supply but when it sells it the money reduces. The effect of this money control is useful because this control is flexible and does not have any problems in trade. The effect of making this announcement is not drastic like in the case of the bank rate changes. In India it has not worked effectively because the treasury bill market is limited by the RBI and the commercial banks which already have to under statute have a minimum reserve in government securities.

Moral suasion: This control is based on advice, suggestions as well as discussions to influence credit policies of commercial banks. The RBI can request or advise certain changes in allocation of credit but cannot enforce any of the suggestions because they are not enactments or legally binding. They are moral controls and do not have any quantitative implications.

RBI has used moral suasion to convince commercial banks in matters which are important for the economy. Since the RBI uses this technique for attaining national objectives, the banks usually adhere to the measures suggested by RBI.

Selective credit control (SCC): This control mechanism was introduced to India in 1956 for regulating credit for certain specific requirements. It has been used by RBI for fixing the maximum limit of advances to be given to an individual borrower on the minimum stocks of certain specific commodities. It has been used to control speculative holdings of commodities such as price beet oil and vanaspati. SCC's have been used to reduce supply of credit or to encourage it in certain directions. It has also been used when the composition of credit has required a change. Since 2000 selective credit controls have been abolished except in sugar.

Management of foreign exchange: Foreign exchange must used in an optimum manner. RBI controls and manages foreign exchange functions of the rupee. It makes transactions at the official rate of exchange. It has introduced new products in the foreign exchange market. These are hedging

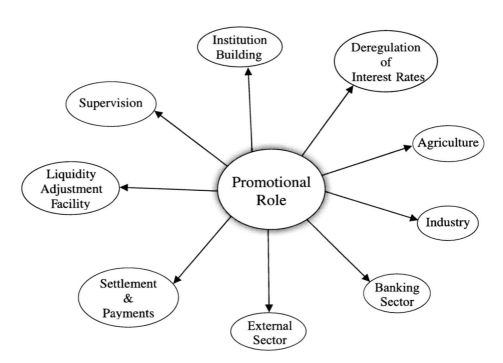

Fig. 4.2: Promotional Role of RBI

instruments, cross currency options, interest rates and currency swaps, caps, collars and forward rate agreements in the international foreign exchange markets. With current account convertibility foreign investments in foreign equity, loans to foreigners and purchase of property of foreign lands have been permitted in India. It has a given a boost to direct investment, portfolio equity investment and transfer of technology. The RBI also controls the foreign exchange exposure limits.

PROMOTIONAL ROLE OF RBI

The RBI as an apex bank is an institution which has a wide range of powers. It uses these powers for strengthening and consolidating the financial structure in India. Its policies have been directed in accordance with the 5 years plans of India. It has tried to play a useful role in allocating credit to priority sector. It has extended the banking services in urban and rural areas.

Setting up Specialized Institutions

RBI was instrumental in setting up special financial institutions both at the national level and the state level to provide financial services in the country. It promoted *the Industrial Development Bank of India (IDBI) and Unit Trust of India (UTI).*

Its started the Deposit Insurance Corporation (DIC) as its subsidiary in 1962 to provide insurance to deposits with co-operative banks. This increased bank deposits. It introduced the system of credit guarantee schemes by promoting Credit Guarantee Corporation (CGC) in 1971. The corporation was the support the commercial banks to meet credit requirements of neglected sectors such as the weaker sections of the society and those engaged in non-industrial activities. In 1978 both these were merged to form the *Deposit Insurance and Credit Guarantee Corporation of India (DICGC)* with the objectives of protecting small banks depositors and giving them a guarantee cover to credit facilities.

The RBI was also keen to develop the agricultural sector in the economy. It setup the *Agricultural Refinance Corporation (ARC)* in 1963 for providing medium and long term finance to agriculture. In 1982 it established the *National Bank for Agriculture and Rural Development Bank (NABARD)*. Its focus was on rural credit, dissemination of information and awareness of agricultural techniques and equipment.

Export-Import Bank of India (EXIM) was setup by RBI in 1982 as part of the export functions of the IDBI. It was committed by the RBI to make use of loan and advances from national industrial credit fund (long term). EXIM was given the charge of providing assistance to exporters and importers to encourage foreign trade.

Commercial Banks in India existed. The RBI played a promotional role in 1969 by nationalizing 14 major Indian banks which had deposits of 50 crores and above. The focus of these banks after nationalization was to provide credit to priority areas, agriculture, rural areas and weaker sections of the society. When the banks were nationalized RBI looked after their operational aspects and the central government had the ownership of the bank. The nationalized banks mobilized the savings of the people into the credit requirements of the priority sector. In 1980 RBI began the initiative of nationalizing more banks as small private banks had also become big and were required to direct the flow of funds into productive credit requirements.

The RBI took some steps in consolidation of the nationalized commercial banks and diversifying them especially to rural areas, to mobilize savings of the people in the rural areas.

The RBI promoted the *Discount and Finance House of India (DFHI)* in 1988 to promote the secondary market with money market instruments.

Thus the RBI played an important role in setting up institutions, developing and consolidating them to direct and diversify their activities for working according to the Five Years Plans of the country.

Monetary Policy

RBI played an important role in directing the monetary policy of the country. The suggestions of the Sukhamoy Chakravarty Committee in 1980 were taken up by the RBI for monetary targeting in a formal and secured manner. The RBI provided credit to government and commercial sector in a consistent manner and kept a check on the money supply and the credit budget.

The RBI also supported the committees decisions and paid special attention to seasonal demand of credit and supported refinancing of short fall of such credit. It created a formal framework for the monetary policy. It directed its policy for the whole money supply but in particular M3.

It introduced many new money market instruments. These are 182 days treasury bills, Inter Bank Participation Certificates (IBPC's), Certificates of Deposits (CD's), commercial papers.

Supervision

The board of financial supervision was constituted by the RBI. The governor of RBI was the chairman of the board with the deputy governor as the vice chairman and 6 members were appointed. This board was setup to implement the regulations of income recognition, capital adequacy, credit management, asset classification and treasury operation of commercial banks. The RBI monitors and inspects the working of the private banks, public sector banks, foreign banks all India financial institutions and non-bank financial companies. It adopts the CAMEL rating system which was recommended by the Padmanabhan Working Committee. According to the CAMEL system there are 6 rating factors for Indian banks and 4 foreign banks.[1]

In 1995 the Khanna Committee advised the RBI on financial supervision. There after the RBI had a stratified approach to supervision of non-bank financial companies depending upon the size of the operations and assets. The RBI made on-site inspections and did off-site monitoring and introduced the supervisory rating system for the companies. In this way it tries to direct the commercial banks and financial institutions into priority areas of finance. Since 1995 the commercial banks have to submit information on profile of ownership and control and management. The RBI has also introduced a new prudential supervisory reporting through which quarterly reports have to be furnished to it giving details of volume of NPA's, assets and liabilities in balance sheets, risk exposures, capital base and information on single borrowers.

The three important functions of the board has been debt recovery, Lok Adalats (People Courts) and asset reconstructions.

In this manner the RBI has played a promotional role by disciplining the commercial banks and financial institutions to give credit for the development of the country in accordance with the financial planning period of India. Although discipline may appear rigorous and restrictive it is necessary to control the functions of difference banks and institutions to make it harmonious with the development of the system. Financial supervision has been a measure to strengthen the financial institutions, banking and non-banking financial companies through prudential norms, improvement in payments and in debt recovery.

Prudential norms were introduced for meeting the international standards of requirement. RBI has been active in improving the capital adequacy ratio, taking care of market risks and assigning risk weights to government approved securities. It has also introduced norms for income recognition. Thus financial supervision has been promotional.

Financial Sector

The RBI contributed to the development of the financial markets by trying to remove the problems face by them. It tried to integrate the internal financial markets with the external world markets to improve the process of financial intermediation. Since 1992 the following reforms have been made to upgrade the financial sector.

---

1. CAMEL is a bank rating first introduced in the United State of America as an alternative to bank supervision. It refers to 5 areas. These are capital adequacy (C), asset quality (A), management (M), earnings (E) and liquidity (L). The bank financial health is a valuated in which 1 is the highest rating and 5 is lowest. Banks with 1 and 2 rating are sound. Ratings with 4 or 5 are problem banks in which restrictions were necessary.

Deregulation of interest rates: To have the full advantage of the reforms RBI deregulated and simplified interest rates structure. In 1994 the interest rates of the bank was deregulated and they were given the flexibility to take decisions on their deposits and lending rates. The RBI provided guidelines on Non-Resident Indians (NRI's) deposits and saving banks deposits. The lending rates on export credit and small loans up to Rs 2 lakhs are still regulated. All other interest rates are deregulated.

Opening up of the capital market: The RBI permitted the Indian corporate sector to register with the international markets and become global through new instruments like American Depository Receipts (ADR's), Global Depository Receipts (GDR's), Foreign Currency Convertible Bonds (FCCB's) and External Commercial Borrowings (ECB's). In India the Foreign Institutional Investors (FII's) were permitted to operate since 1992. NRI's were invited to invest in Indian companies. FII's were allowed full capital convertibility. They have been permitted to participate in government securities. Mutual funds can begin the operations through off shore funds for investing in equity investments in foreign countries. Thus the RBI brought about openness and freedom to operate in the capital market. It moved from control to liberalization.

Consortium of banks and financial institutions: RBI promoted a participatory approach between banks, co-operative banks and financial institutions. It encouraged consortium lending amongst the different institutions. This brought about efficiency in providing credit and giving good service to the industries.

Control of refinance: The RBI rediscount bills of exchange and promissory notes and loans and advances to commercial and co-operative banks and financial institutions like State Financial Corporations, Industrial Development Bank of India, Industrial Finance Corporation of India, Export and Import Bank of India for providing financial accommodation. The rate of discount or refinance was the bank rate but now RBI provides refinance facilities according to different rates depending upon the sector specific facilities for refinance.

Credit allocation: RBI has been keen to extend credit to create an assured balance in the urban and rural areas. It asked the banks to give information on the credit deposit ratios of the urban and rural areas separately.

Liquidity adjustment facility: This facility was started in 2000. It has brought about innovation in monetary control measures. Through this method the RBI does discretionary market operations instead of standing facilities. This helps to bring about market liquidity. Discretionary liquidity is applied out of the funds which arise from money market operations. It is the change which is produced when discretionary policy is directed upon. It helps in movement of interest rates in the inter bank call money market. This is done through the liquidity adjustment facility and through the repo and the reverse repo rates. These funds are operated through the sale of government securities from the RBI portfolio. It is also called a repo auction. The repo is purchase everyday to get call money rate and short term interest rates. The funds are used by the banks daily to balance the liquidity. The repos maximum maturity is 14 days. The minimum repo size is 5 crores and it continues in lots 5 crores. The usefulness of this facility is its effect on short term rates. The RBI sets its repos and reverse repos everyday at given rates of interest. The RBI also provides liquidity through refinancing at the bank rate. In the call money market the rates a call rate, a ceiling rate, a bank rate and the floor rate. The call rate is normally higher than the repo rate. The bank rate and the repo rate determine the movement of interest rates in the money market. This technique is useful for short periods of time. The RBI uses this facility for liquidity to adjust and manage the money market. This facility can be used with other monetary controls of the RBI.

Banking sector: The RBI made several reforms in the banking sector. The reforms were taken up in stages. It first deregulated the banking sector by allowing the private sector banks to begin their operations. Foreign banks were also permitted to establish themselves in India. It tried to strengthen the institutional structure of the banks. RBI has issued guidelines to banks to improve their position and bring about transparency by disclosures of their financial position. The RBI took the initiative to give licenses to new banks and to open more branches of the existing bank. It also permitted the banks to diversify into new products.

In the second stage it brought about prudential reforms which were required for stability and international standardization. It strengthened the banks by insisting on capital adequacy ratio, income recognition and risk weights to assess market risks. The RBI has initiated that there would be a review and Basel II would be applied for international standardization for minimum credit risk.

Non-bank financial intermediaries: The RBI took steps to reform both the banking sector and non-banking financial intermediaries. It regulated them through the financial supervision board. It took care to make the system uniform for all the institutions through prudential regulation. To develop this system the RBI brought about reforms which covered development financial institutions, non-banking financial companies, term lending institutions and urban co-operative banks.

Government securities: Interest rates on government papers were made market related. The ad-hoc treasury bills were discontinued from April 1st, 1997. The maturity period of government securities was changed to make it according to the market preference. The government borrowing and its open market operations was based on price discovery in the market.

Payments and settlements: The payment and settlements system in a country should be safe and efficient. The RBI focused its attention on technology for reducing risks and making international payments and their settlements efficient. It has introduced the Real Time Gross Settlement (RTGS) system. According to this system the inter bank transactions would take place quickly. The RTGS system is an electronic mode through which transactions take place with reduced risks. It has started the system of MICR based cheque processing centers. It allows the clearing system to be managed by banks and clearing houses but it performs the settlement systems.

A vision document was prepared by RBI for payments system it had action points framed for different years. It stresses on information technology for payments.

Agricultural sector: The RBI played an important role in increasing the supply of agricultural credit. It strengthened to co-operative banks by providing short term finance at low rates for seasonal demands of agriculture especially in the sowing of seeds and harvesting season. It offered the co-operative banks through the state co-operative banks short term finances for temporary requirements. It also provided finance for marketing of crops. It operated the national agricultural credit fund for long term requirements. It also established (NABARD) for providing medium and long term finance for agriculture. It was instrumental in promoting the agricultural finance corporation.

Industrial finance: The RBI setup a large number of special financial institutions. Its objective was that these institutions would provide finance to industries. These financial institutions were instituted both in the centre and at the state level to provide long term funds to large industries. At the state level funds were to be given to both small industries and medium industries engaged in developing the resources of the state. It has helped sick units to revive and it has provided guarantees to small industries.

External sector: The RBI made notable changes in the external sector after the new economic reforms were initiated. On the recommendation of the Ranga Rajan Committee in 1993 the RBI made important changes like introducing market determined exchange rates and current account convertibility through liberalization. It regulated external commercial borrowings and moved from debt to non-debt capital flows. It regulated short term debt and non-resident Indians flow of funds. It instituted the Liberalized Exchange Rate Management System (LERMS) in 1992 with dual exchange rates. In 1993 it was further improved to be market determined exchange rate. In 1994 the current account convertibility was achieved.

The RBI then tried to develop the forex market on the recommendation of Sodhani Committee. It introduced new products, tried to reduce risk and increase efficiency. The RBI further tried to create reserves in foreign currency. The foreign exchange reserves with low interest rates have helped the government to repay foreign currency loans of approximately 5 billions in 2003. RBI has also relaxed capital controls. Indian residents are permitted to invest in mutual funds abroad.

Dissemination of information: The RBI creates awareness about the economy and its financial sector through different journals and magazines that it provides through its in house printing. The RBI regularly publishers a monthly journal called the Reserve Bank of India bulletin. It prepares annually information on different financial aspects of India through its report on currency and finance. The third journal is on the statistic of the Indian economy. The RBI has an in house research department through which the research activity and the planning of the journals takes place. This is an important service as it creates awareness in the minds of the people about the country statistics.

Thus the Reserve Bank of India has played a prominent role in promoting the financial sector. As a promotional effort it has made reforms and changes in difference sectors of the financial system. It has setup many institutions for developing the financial structure. It has made reforms in interest structure by deregulating it. It has tried to bring in liquidity in the money market through the repo and reverse repos. It has brought about changes in the banking sector, government securities sector, payment and settlement, credit allocation, agriculture and industrial finance. Through its supervision it has tried to bring about stability and international standards. It has brought about modernization through computerization in banks.

The next chapter discusses securities exchange board of India which has been formed to be the market regulator for purchase and sale of securities.

Summary

➠ The RBI is the apex bank of the country. It started its operations on April 1st, 1935.

➠ The RBI was nationalized in 1949.

➠ The composition of the bank consists of the governor, deputy governor, and 15 directors.

➠ The functions of the RBI are to print issue and manage currency, to be a banker to the government, to be a bankers bank, to supervise and control commercial banks co-operative banks and non-bank financial intermediaries, to promote and develop financial markets and institutions, to administrator foreign exchange reserves and manage rupee exchange rate and to control money and credit in India.

➠ The RBI has used both traditional and innovative techniques to manage and control money in the country.

➠ The RBI uses the Cash Reserve Ratio, Statutory Liquidity Ratio and Open Market Operations to control money.

➠ It has also used moral suasion and selective credit controls wherever the need has arisen.

➠ Since 1991 it has actively played a promotional role in the Indian financial system.

➠ RBI's monetary policy has been directed towards price stability, discipline control and promotion of the financial system.

➠ It has deregulated interest rates, made reforms in the money market, capital market, government sector, banking sector, payments and settlements, supervision, external sector, and industrial finance.

➠ It has introduced Real Time Gross Settlement.

➠ It has brought about liquidity adjustment facility which is an innovative aspect in the in bringing about liquidity in the money market through repos and reverse repos.

Objective Type Questions, Answer True (T) or False (F)

(a) The Reserve Bank of India was nationalized in 1947.

(b) The Reserve Bank of India began its operations on April 1, 1935.

(c) The Reserve Bank of India issues the entire currency except Rs. 5 coins.

(d) The clean note policy is used to institute security features in notes.

(e) The integrated computerized currency operations and management system is a technological innovating for operations efficiency and good customer services.

(f) The central government is empowered to make short terms borrowings from the RBI though the 'Ways and Means' advances.

(g) RBI manages all new issues of government loans.

(h) The commercial banks have to compulsorily keep a balance with RBI based on a specified ration of their total deposits.

(i) The RBI has introduced the real time settlement system for reducing risks in inter bank transactions.

(j) RBI is applying Basel I on all the banks for efficiency.

Answers: (a) F, (b) T, (c) F, (d) F, (e) T, (f) F, (g) T, (h) T, (i) T, (j) F.

Multiple Choice Questions (Tick mark (✓) the right answer)

1. As a bankers' bank the RBI has the authority of allow the banks:
   - (a) To issue currency notes
   - (b) To control the volume of reserves of banks
   - (c) To allow every bank to frame its own policies for classification of their assets
   - (d) To make policies for banks of make capital gains

2. As a banker to the government RBI provides to the government:
   - (a) Ways and means advances
   - (b) Bills of exchange
   - (c) Clean notes
   - (d) Supervision on investments

3. As a supervising authority the RBI has the following powers:
   - (a) Issue licenses for establishing new banks
   - (b) Give overdrafts to exporters and control them
   - (c) Issue notes in its printing press
   - (d) Provide startup facilities to NRI's

4. The cash reserve ratio refers to:
   - (a) Statutory liquidity ratio
   - (b) Selective credit controls
   - (c) Cash maintained with RBI as percentage of their demand and time liabilities
   - (d) Process of credit control

5. The RBI points notes according to:
   - (a) Maximum value of gold and silver
   - (b) Value of foreign securities
   - (c) Value of bills of exchange and promissory notes
   - (d) Minimum value of gold coins, bullion and foreign securities

6. They ways and means advances RBI are:
   - (a) Long term advance by RBI
   - (b) Short term advances
   - (c) Medium term advances
   - (d) Advances to small business owners

Answers: 1 (b), 2 (a), 3 (a), 4 (c), 5 (d), 6 (b).

Short Answer Questions

1. What is financial supervision? Is it a promotional or restrictive role of RBI?

2. What is Cash Reserve Ratio? Why do banks have to keep this reserve?

3. Discuss the reforms made by RBI for fulfilling international standards of efficiency.

4. Give the importance of Real Time Gross Settlement System (RTGS).

5. What is moral suasion technique? Has the RBI used it as a control means?

6. Write notes on: (a) RBI as a note issuing authority, (b) Ways and means advances, (c) Financial supervision, (d) Techniques of monetary control.

Long Answer Questions

1. Discuss the promotional role of RBI.

2. What is the payment and settlement system? What reform was made to bring in efficiency?

3. Why is the RBI called the lender of the last resort?

4. What is the Role of RBI as a banker to the government?

Chapter 5

The Securities Exchange Board of India

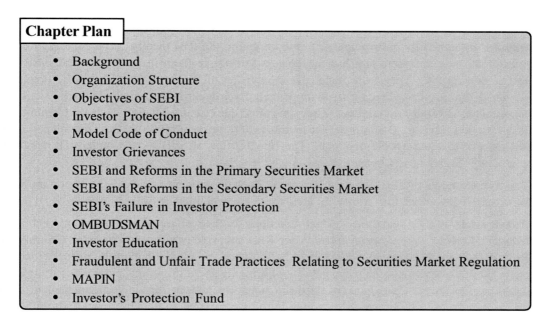

Chapter Plan

- Background
- Organization Structure
- Objectives of SEBI
- Investor Protection
- Model Code of Conduct
- Investor Grievances
- SEBI and Reforms in the Primary Securities Market
- SEBI and Reforms in the Secondary Securities Market
- SEBI's Failure in Investor Protection
- OMBUDSMAN
- Investor Education
- Fraudulent and Unfair Trade Practices Relating to Securities Market Regulation
- MAPIN
- Investor's Protection Fund

BACKGROUND

The Securities and Exchange Board of India (SEBI) was established by an Act of Parliament in 1992 as a regulatory authority, for the investment market in India. It has been established under Section 3 of SEBI Act 1992. The purpose of this board is to maintain stable and efficient markets by creating and enforcing regulations in the market place. The Securities and Exchange Board of India is similar to the U.S. Securities Exchange Commission (SEC). It was formed following the dissolution of the Controller of Capital Issues (CCI), which derived and exercised its powers in terms of Capital Issue (Control) Act 1947. The Controller of Capital Issue regulated the private sector companies in their activities relating to, securities to be issued in the primary market, timing of new issues, composition of securities to be issued, interest and dividend rates to be offered on debentures and preference shares, issues relating to price of right issues and premium on securities. The Controller of Capital Issues was considered to be an ineffective and dormant institution and not responsive to changes in the stock market and issues relevant to the dynamic developing economy. SEBI was set up to take up these new challenges through promotional but regulatory measures. SEBI was given regulatory powers over intermediaries like Underwriters, Registrars to Issue, Bankers entrusted with Issue Work, Share Transfer Agents and Debenture Trustees. The objective of the board was two-fold-protecting investor's interest and developing the securities market. The preamble of the SEBI Act 1992 describes the objectives of the board in the following word:

"To protect the interests of investors in securities and to promote the development of and to regulate the securities market and for matters connected therewith or incidental thereto".

ORGANIZATION STRUCTURE

SEBI was formed with a Chairman in the top most position, two members of Government of India, Ministry of Law and Finance, one member from the RBI and two other professional members. The members are appointed by government with the exception the RBI member. The central government approves of all new members and has the powers to remove them in public interest. SEBI has 5 operational departments. They work under the supervision of the executive director. He prepares the policies which the executive director has to implement. Each department is divided into divisions. It has two non-statutory advisory committees. They are called the Primary Market Advisory Committee and Secondary Market Advisory Committee. The members of these committees are from market participants, investor associations and people of repute. The Head Office of SEBI is at Bombay.[1] It has regional offices at Delhi, Kolkata and Chennai.

The 5 departments of SEBI are very important. Each department carries out an important function and the scope of their work is in a specific area, these are explained below.

Primary market: The department which functions for the welfare of the primary market is called the ***Primary Market Policy, Intermediaries, Self Regulatory Organizations, Investor Grievance and Guidance Department.*** Under this department, all policies and regulations of the primary market are prepared. This department has the responsibility of bringing about discipline and correct attitude of the intermediaries like the merchant bankers, portfolio managers, underwriters, investment bankers and self regulatory organizations. Their purpose would be to give services to the customers and not have any intentions of cheating and defrauding investors. This department has to prepare awareness programs for educating the investor and guiding him to make his investments properly. It also has to try and solve the problems and grievances of the investors.

Issue management: The department which has to vet prospectus of companies and their letters of offer to public is called the ***Issue Management and Intermediaries Department.*** Besides new issues it

---

1. Two other important acts which are constituent to the Indian financial system are Companies Act 1956 and Securities Contract Regulation Act ICRA, 1956. The Companies Act covers financial and Non-financial aspects of corporate affairs and helps in integrated relationship between promoters, investors and management. The SCRA regulates Stock Exchanges to prevent undesirable transactions and speculations and stipulates laws for strong investment markets. The companies act is under Ministry of Law Department of Company Affairs and the SCRA is under the Ministry of Finance Department of Economic affairs, Government of India certain powers of Companies Act and SCRA have been delegated to SEBI.

also monitors, regulates and registers the intermediaries. It co-ordinates and works according to the primary market policies.

Secondary market: There are two specific departments for the secondary market. Other departments are also responsible for problems of the secondary market. *The Secondary Market Policy, Operations and Exchange Administration, New Investment Product and Insider Trading Department* prepares policies and regulations. It is the department for registration and monitoring of stock exchange members. It administers large stock markets, monitors price movement. Market surveillance and new products are under this department. It is responsible for curbing insider trading and it prepares a data base for SEBI.

The secondary market has another department also. This is called *The Secondary Market Exchange Administration, Inspection and Non-Member Intermediaries Department.* This department has the function of inspecting stock exchanges. Another function of this department is to monitor, regulate and register non member intermediaries. An example of non-member is the sub-broker. This department has be responsibility of administering small stock exchanges. For example, Hyderabad, Ludhiana, Cochin, Kanpur, Indore and Bhuvaneshwar.

Institutional investment and publication: The Institutional Investment, Mergers and Acquisitions, Research and Publications and International Relations and International Organization of Security Commissions Department is responsible for preparing policies, registrations and regulations. It monitors foreign institutions investors', mutual funds and merger and acquisitions of companies. Its functions are comprehensive. It has to maintain international relations, it is engaged in research and publications were of the annual reports of SEBI.

In addition to the above 5 departments SEBI has a legal and an investigations department. The legal department carries out the function of legal matters. It is supervised by the general counsel. The investigation department has the work of inspecting and investigating matters under the supervision of the chief of investigation.

OBJECTIVES OF SEBI

There are 5 major areas of reforms, which SEBI took up. These are Primary Market, Secondary Stock Market, Investors Protection, Mutual Funds and Foreign Institutional Agencies.

The main objective of SEBI in the *Primary Securities Market* was to improve the transparency and standards of disclosure in public issues.

In the *Secondary Stock Market*, SEBI was to help in the transformation process of Stock Exchanges through modernization, raising accounting standards of firms and intermediaries and professionalizing Stock Broking System and having uniform By-laws for stock exchanges.

Amongst the *promotional steps*, SEBI was to promote investors education and training of intermediaries in the Securities Market, conduct research and regulate substantial acquisition of shares and takeover of companies and thereby curb unfair and fraudulent practices relating to securities market especially relating with insider trading practices.

SEBI was to take an interest in mutual funds. All *mutual funds* were to be registered with SEBI and were to provide portfolio disclosure and standardization of accounting policies. SEBI would provide guidelines for valuation norms and pricing of issues.

SEBI had a role with *Foreign Institutional Investors (FIIs).* It was to issue guidelines to FIIs and, business could be conducted by them after registering themselves with SEBI.

> *The most important function of SEBI was to protect investors by acting as a regulatory mechanism enlightening and guiding them on various issues related to the securities market and providing an insight to them of their rights and limitations and remedies to the situation by handling investors' complaints through an efficient system. Investor's complaints relating to delay in receiving shares or refund orders and to ensure that no malpractice take place in allotment of shares.*

Its main objective is to protect the interests of the investors in the *new issue market* and *stock exchange* and to regulate, develop and improve the quality, of the securities market in India. **SEBI** has been actively interested in protecting the investor: the following aspects have been dealt with by SEBI to achieve its objectives:

- SEBI has issued guidelines for investor protections in four areas, these are
  - Guidelines to companies issuing public offers.
  - Guidelines to the intermediaries who are functioning between the investor and companies in the new issue market.
  - Issue of directions to these intermediaries in the stock market.
  - Guidelines for investor's rights and liabilities.
- SEBI has a grievance cell for protection of investors who face problems while making investments. Some of these problems are delays in refunds, delays in transfer of securities and misleading statements in advertisements.
- The third area refers is investor education. SEBI is engaged in investor information and workshops for them to know their rights as shareholders and investors.
- SEBI has issued a prohibition of fraudulent and unfair trade practices regulation in 2003. These regulations relate to securities markets for protection of investors.
- SEBI has issued a model code of conduct for listed companies.
- SEBI has issued regulation of 1992 for investigation of insider trading and also prohibition of insider trade practices.
- To have a transparent system of redressal of grievances. SEBI has passed a regulation called Ombudsman Regulations of 2003.
- It has also provided a facility at National Stock Exchange for arbitration of investor grievances.

Let us find out the performance of SEBI in its role as a regulatory mechanism. Has SEBI been able to exercise control in capital market? Has it fulfilled the objective of investor protection for which it was conceived? Is the role of SEBI promotional or merely one with a plethora of legislations and no follow up programs are some questions it seeks answers to. The role of SEBI has been analyzed on different aspects. In this chapter we discuss the developments in the Primary Market and seek to find out the major reforms in the stock market and how SEBI protects investors' interest.

The functions of SEBI and its investor protection measures are now discussed in detail:

INVESTOR PROTECTION

The first area, which is important for the protection of the investor's, is to keep a discipline of the companies, which issue securities. SEBI has issued guidelines, rules and regulations (2000) to protect the investor by making it compulsory for companies to provide information through documents so that the investors can take decisions in purchasing securities in a fair manner. Some of the important aspects are:

- A company has to prepare its offer document giving information of general and financial nature according to SEBI's guidelines.
- A company has to file a draft prospectus with SEBI before making a public offer.
- A Company cannot issue securities until it applies for listing of its shares at a stock exchange.
- A company can make a rights issue or public issue only when the existing shares of a company are fully paid up.
- SEBI restricts companies to make a debt issue without obtaining a credit rating and an investment grade.
- SEBI restricts unlisted companies from issuing their shares. It makes an exception in some cases. An unlisted company can issue shares if its promoters contribute at least 20% of post issue capital. The company should have a track record of distributing profits, having a net worth of Rs.1 crore and tangible assets of Rs.3 Crores in previous 3 out of 5 years.
- SEBI also monitors companies. It may carry out inspection of the books of accounts and other records of a listed company in respect of matters covered by its guidelines.

A company usually advertises a public issue. Such advertisements should contain statements, which are fair, clear and truthful giving the risk factor to enable an investor to make his judgment and not be misled by any wrong statements.

SEBI has issued a model code of conduct for listed companies this is discussed below:

MODEL CODE OF CONDUCT

The SEBI regulations of 1992 also provided a model code of conduct for listed companies. Companies listed on the stock exchange have to frame a code of Internal Procedures and Conduct of Corporate Disclosure Practices. Some of the provisions are given below:

- The code of conduct has to be strictly observed and those employees, officers, or directors of the company who violate the code of conduct will be subject to disciplinary action by SEBI or by the company.
- Every listed company is required to employ a compliance officer who has to report to the Managing director or to the Chief Executive Officer of the company.
- Confidential files should be protected and kept secure. These pertain to all files but especially computer files and passwords, which are likely to have sensitive price information.
- Every company should have a closed trading window period when no trade takes place .It should be a closed period when the Annual Profit and Loss and Balance Sheet have to be

declared, when dividends have to be declared and when amalgamations and mergers take place.

- SEBI has also provided that these trading windows would open only after 24 hours of making sensitive prices available to the public.
- To avoid insider trading practices each listed company has to provide price sensitive information on a continuous basis to the stock exchange.

SEBI also deals with problems faced by investors. These are dealt with the investor grievance cell. The process of grievances and their settlement are now discussed.

INVESTOR GRIEVANCES

Investor grievances are usually due to delays in dispatch of allotment letters, refund orders, misleading statements in advertisements or in the prospectus, delay in transfer of securities, non-payment of interest or dividend. Theses grievances are dealt with either SEBI or department of company affairs. Stock exchanges have information centers where investors can put in their complaints about problems relating to shares and complaints of traders.

SEBI deals with complaints, which are regarding:

- Securities traded or listed with the exchanges.
- The trades effected by listed company or by the members of the stock exchange.

The Department of Company Affairs and Registrar of Companies (ROC) deal with the following complaints:

- Complaints against unlisted companies.
- Complaints regarding non-receipt of annual report, notice of Annual General Meeting.
- Complaints regarding Fixed deposit in manufacturing companies.
- Complaints regarding Forfeiture of Shares.

The Reserve Bank of India looks into problems of investors relating to fixed deposits in Banks and Non-Bank Financial Institutions.

SEBI AND REFORMS IN THE PRIMARY SECURITIES MARKET

The developments in the Primary Securities Market were as a result of the recommendations of the Malegam Committee Report which was implemented by SEBI in 1995.

Eligibility for Public Issue

One of the most important issues in the primary securities Market was to protect the investors from fraudulent dealings. Hence SEBI made certain important reforms. SEBI made eligibility criteria for New Issues. A company could issue shares in the New Issue Market only if it had paid a dividend for at least three years prior to the public issue. If a company did not have a record of payment of dividends in the previous three years it should get its project appraised by banks or financial institutions which have a 10% stake in equity participation of the issuing company. A third criteria is that the securities of the company should be listed with OTCEI (over the counter exchange of India). It has also been stated by M.T. Raju that for transparency SEBI also asked such companies to make draft prospectus of company available to public and to give financial projections in their offer documents.[2]

Allotment of Shares

Reforms relating to allotment of shares to investors were also made by SEBI. In case preferential allotment was to be applied by a company 50% of the public offer was to be reserved for individual investors applying for less than 1000 securities and 50% to be allotted to these who apply for more than 1000 shares. Also shareholders allotted shares were to receive their allotment within 30 days of closure of the issue after which the company would have to pay 15% rate of interest. Merchant Bankers of SEBI imposed Mandatory restrictions on costs of public issue on underwriting commission, brokerage, fee of managers of issue, fee to registrars to the issue, listing fees and advertisement cost and compulsory registration of Merchant Bankers and Bankers to the Issue. Only corporate bodies would be allowed to function as Merchant Bankers, Restriction was imposed upon them for carrying out funds based activities exclusively in the capital markets. They were prohibited from accepting deposits and leasing and Bill discounting.

Book Building

Book building facility was developed in the initial Public Offer to bring about the flexibility of price and quantity which would be decided on the basis of demand.[3] In India book building was developed for issues above 100 crores and consists of that portion which is reserved for institutional and corporate investors. It is a flexible pricing method based on feedback from investors and in the US it is called *soft underwriting*.

It has become an extremely popular method for pricing of new issues in India. All new issues are made through book building. Price bands are given and the investor is allowed to make a bid within that band.

Free Pricing of Issue

Keeping in view the changes in the capital market emanating from *free pricing of shares* and free access to market for funds by the issuers, the SEBI with the objective of broadening the investors' base, dispensed with the requirement of standard denomination of Rs.10 and Rs.100, gave freedom to companies with dematerialized shares, to issue shares at any denomination. The existing companies, with shares at Rs.10 and Rs.100, also can avail of this facility by consolidating or splitting their existing shares.

In order to enable the investors to take informed investment decisions, the stock exchanges were directed to indicate the denomination value of shares as fixed by the company along with the market quotation. However, the companies availing of this facility are required to strictly adhere to disclosures

---

2. M.T. Raju Prospects of Indian Capital Markets, in depth information and reforms UTI Institute of Capital Markets & Birla Institute of Management and Technology. All India Management Convention 1997 papers, page 1.2. Convention held by BIMTECH and UTI Capital Markets PHD House, Delhi 1997.

3. For more information on Book Building read H.R Machiraju, 1998 Indian Financial System, Vikas Publishing House, New Delhi, , pp. 12.16-12.19.

and accounting norms. SEBI also decided that there would be only one set of disclosures and entry norms for all the issues irrespective of the issue price. Thus, the different requirements for making issues at par and premium were merged to create a common set of requirements.

In India free pricing of shares has become common as companies have priced their shares at Re. 1 and Rs. 2. Such pricing is expected to have a positive effect on the volume of trade and transactions of securities in the securities market.

SEBI AND REFORMS IN THE SECONDARY SECURITIES MARKET

There are twenty three recognized stock exchanges in India.[4] The major reform made by SEBI has been to encourage modernization and develop the Stock Exchanges. Most of the Stock Exchanges have computerized or screen based trading. Over The Trade Counter Exchange of India (OTCEI) was the first automated Exchange in India in 1992. Trading was done electronically on similar lines on the Stock Exchanges. The G.S. Patel Committee, Dave Committee, recommendations have been accepted for improvement in the Stock market.

The following departments take care of the activities in the secondary market. They provide support for registration of companies, their supervision, monitoring their work and brining about transparency in their books of account. Although there are five main departments of SEBI, 2 of which are specifically for the secondary market, they have further subdivisions to look after the activities. The following 3 departments of the secondary market have been allotted certain specific duties. They are described in table 5.1. Since derivatives are new, they have to be developed. A department takes care of derivatives and all new products in the market.

Table 5.1: Departments and their activities in regulating the secondary market

Department	Activities
Market Intermediaries Registration and Supervision department (MIRSD)	Registration, supervision, compliance monitoring and inspections of all market intermediaries in respect of all segments of the markets viz. equity, equity derivatives, debt and debt related derivatives.
Market Regulation Department (MRD)	Formulating new policies and supervising the functioning and operations excluding derivatives of securities exchanges, their subsidiaries, and market institutions such as Clearing and settlement organizations and Depositories (These are collectively called 'Market SROs').
Derivatives and New Products Departments (DNPD)	Supervising trading at derivatives segments of stock exchanges, introducing new products to be traded, and consequent policy changes.

The important reforms by SEBI in the secondary market are discussed below:

---

4. A detailed study of secondary securities market is provided in M.Y. Khan, 1996, Indian Financial System, Tata McGraw Hill, New Delhi, pp. 10.2-10.41.

Screen Based Trading

In 1993, SEBI made the policy of bringing about screen based trading. In March 1995, BSE online trading (BOLT) was started. It brought about the facility of trading with order book functioning as an *ancillary jobber*. The order book allows retention and matching of orders and improves the price competitive character. It provides investors to place orders at prices better than the quotes presently available. Jobbers quote would be given priority as incoming orders would first be matched against jobber quote. On the remaining quantity if the best price in the market is through order book then incoming order would be matched against the order book. This is called *Price Jobber Time Priority Matching*.

BOLT brought about improvement in trading of volumes of transactions. Trade takes place through electronically transmitted terminals. The brokers trade for the clients through the terminals. Individuals can directly also trade in the stock market through the terminals. The signal is sent through the terminal to find out if there is a buyer/seller of a security as soon as the order is given by the client. When the price of the seller matches the buyer the transaction is made. The depository agent then sends to the depository for clearing. Within 48 hours the buyer pays his cheque and ready delivery contracts are cleared within a week.

Settlements and Clearing

Settlements in Indian Stock Exchanges have an account period of settlement. It involves netting of trades and drawing up of statements by members, amount of securities due, scrip wise and member wise. In a physical trade environment trades were stuck on the floor statements had to be generated and confirmed by the members but in the computerized environment information the exchange can download the information to the member at the end of the day. There is a risk involved in the absence of a clearinghouse. In 1996 after the M.S. Shoes scam (1995) involving 18 crores of Rupees, a National Securities Clearing Corporation was started to guarantee all trades in NSE. Regional clearing facilities have also been provided.

Depository or Paperless Trading

The Depository Act was passed in 1996 allowing dematerializing of securities and transfer of security through electronic book entry to help in reducing settlement risks and infrastructure bottlenecks. The dematerialized securities will not have any identification numbers or distinctive numbers. *The National Securities Depository Ltd. (NSDL)*, was set up in Nov 1996. Trading of new Initial public offers were to be in dematerialized form upon listing. An exclusive feature of the Indian Capital Market is that multiple depository system has been encouraged. Hence there are two Depository Services. The other depository system is also registered. It is called *Central Depository Service Ltd. (CDSL)*. Debt instruments however, are not transferable by endorsement delivery.

Dematerialization of securities is one of the major steps for improving and modernizing market and enhancing the level of investor protection through elimination of bad deliveries and forgery of shares and expediting the transfer of shares. Long-term benefits were expected to accrue to the market through the removal of physical securities.

Surveillance on Price Manipulation

SEBI introduced surveillance and enforcement measures against intermediaries for violation of laws especially in price manipulations. All exchanges have surveillance departments which co-ordinate with SEBI. SEBI has enforced information to be submitted by exchanges on daily settlement and monitoring reports. SEBI has also created a database for trading on National and Bombay Stock Exchanges. If price manipulation is detected auction proceeds may be impounded or frozen so that the manipulation cannot use it.

SEBI has introduced *'Stock Watch'* an advances software for surveillance of market activities programmed *to show movements from historical patterns* through follow ups by analyst and trained investigators to act as a deterrent to trading and price rigging.

Insider Trading

Insider Trading Regulations in 1992 notified by SEBI, prohibited Insider trading, as it is unfair upon investors. Persons who posses price sensitive information because they have connections with a company take advantage of the situation to *'peg up'* or *'down'* prices of securities to their advantage. The TISCOs case is an example, whereby there was intense activity in trading volume of shares between October 22, 1992, and October 29, 1992, as there was insider information on poor performance of the companies working. Profits of the company had declined. After having brought trading under their control the prices of shares brought about a sharp fall in the prices from October 29 to Nov 6, 1992. Insiders had manipulated the market. When a probe took place the presence of insider information was considered to be the main problem area. As a result of this case, Insider Regulation took place in November 1992, to prohibit insider trading practices and avoid creation of problems for small investors.

Insider trading is not allowed by SEBI. The reason for this prohibition is that it gives an individual, a group of people or a company an edge over others trading in the market. Such people have the advantage of knowing important information, which may benefit those who have information. However, it is not fair to those who do not have this information. SEBI issued regulations in 1992 for prohibition of Insider Trading. SEBI has defined an insider in the following way.

An insider is a person who is internally connected to a company. He may be an employee, a director, promoter, a relative or a friend or an ex-employee who in someway has an access to price sensitive information. In a formal way an insider may be defined as the following:

- Any company in the same management or group of companies.
- Any intermediary, asset management company, clearing corporation, an official of a stock exchange, a director or an employee who has access to information.
- A merchant banker, registrars to an issue, underwriters, portfolio managers, bankers to an issue, members of board of directors or their relatives.

According to these regulations, insiders having an access to unpublished price sensitive information will not use it or communicate to other persons to use it for trading purposes. The price sensitive information has been defined as information, which is unpublished and available to a few people. Such information is usually concerned with changes in policy matters of a company, dividend declaration, merger or amalgamation plans of a company, issue buy-back, delisting of companies and to financial reports of a company.

SEBI can investigate into complaints from investors or intermediaries and also take action against the individual or companies, which use price sensitive information for making gains.

Regulation of Stock Brokers

Stock Broker and sub Brokers Regulation Act, was passed in 1992. Brokers had to have a dual registration both with SEBI and with Stock Exchange. Penal action would be taken against any broker for violation of laws. Capital adequacy norms were introduced and they were 3% for individual brokers and 6% for corporate brokers. For investor protection measures brokers have been disciplined by introducing the system of maintaining accounts for clients and brokers own account and disclosure of transaction price and brokerage separately in contract note. Audit has been made compulsory of the brokers' books and filing of auditor's report with the SEBI has been made mandatory.[5] SEBI has also extended regulations to sub-brokers. Sub brokers have to be registered by entering into an agreement with the stock brokers from whom he seeks affiliation. Sub brokers can transact business only through stock broker with whom he is registered. If he wants to do business through more than one stock broker he has to be registered separately with each one of them.

Forward Trading and Badla

Forward trading had been in practice in India as it was the main speculative activity in stock exchange. *Futures* and *Options* were absent in the Indian Market and *Forward Trading* was called *Contracts for Clearing*. This system enables a trader to play with price expectations, transfer outstanding buy or sell positions and delivery of securities. In 1969, *Contract trading* was banned in India. However, a new system called *Badla* was developed which was used in Carry forward of trades to the settlement period.[6] This system was regulated in 1983 by permitting trade through specified securities[7] and carry forward facility up to 90 days.

Controls were also set on margins and limits were placed on positions. In December 1993, Badla was banned. In 1995, it was reviewed by Patel Committee and SEBI reintroduced carry forward system with restrictions. 90-day limit was fixed for carry forward, trade settlements could be made in 75 days with delivery. For investor protection exchanges had to adopt a twin track trading system where

---

5. See information on SEBI in L.M. Bhole1999, *Financial Institutions and Markets*, Tata McGraw Hills Publishing Co. Ltd., New Delhi, pp. 116-125.

6. In this Badla system – off-setting transaction on the last day of settlement with the intent of reversing the positions in the following accounting period was undertaken. The make up price was called Havala and was fixed by the Stock Exchange, while interest on transaction was determined by borrowers and lenders.

7. There are 3 groups of shares A or specified group "B1" and "B2" shares, on Bombay Stock Exchange. A group is with weekly settlement on which forward trading is allowed. B1 is with weekly settlement without facility of carry forward and B2 with fortnightly settlement. In September 1996, all settlement duration were reduced to one week. Distinctions between B1 & B2 have therefore no meaning. F group includes debt securities.

transactions for delivery were separated from those that were carried forwards. Limits were also imposed on carry forwards positions and on scrip wise limits on brokers. Badla was again reviewed in 1997 by Varma Committee. SEBI increased carry forward limits of brokers to 20 crores and reduced margins from 15% to 10% and after the *Ketan Parekh* scam Badla was again banned from July 1, 2001. Trading in 246 scrips including all stocks that make of group A of Bombay Stock Exchange became *cash down* and *day trade*.

Options and Derivatives

Options can be classified as *call option* or *put options*. The National Stock Exchange (NSE) and the Bombay Stock Exchange (BSE) have launched *derivatives.* They will offer derivatives for three tenures one in the first instance each for subsequent 3 months. So in July Nifty call and put options can be purchased for July end, August end and September end. The last day of the contract would be the expiration date.[8] In an options contract a premium has to be paid to enter a contract. Buyer's losses are limited to the extent of premium paid but his gains are unlimited. Seller's profits are limited to premiums received but losses are unlimited. These derivatives have been started by SEBI to bring about investor confidence to establish the market and to reduce risk. Initially options trading were allowed only in 14 stocks. Option will not allow a person to defer settlement of sale/purchase but they will enable placing of bets on Stock Markets.

Regulation of Mutual Funds

SEBI regulates the Mutual Funds to provide portfolio disclosure and standardization of accounting procedures. It is a requirement of SEBI that Mutual Funds should have a trustee company which is separate from the asset Management company and the securities of the various schemes should be kept with a custodian independent of the Mutual Fund. All Mutual Funds should be regulated with the SEBI. All schemes of UTI after 1994 have also been brought under the control of SEBI. SEBI created certain procedures of valuation norms and asset value and pricing for the Mutual Funds. The primary interest of SEBI to control Mutual Fund schemes was to protect investors from fraudulent deals.

Regulation of Foreign Institutional Investors (FIIs)

FII's had a large volume of funds. By the nature of their trading volumes FII's can retain control over a stock market. SEBI had to keep these FII's under its control for protecting the investors. Hence, all FII's had to be registered with the SEBI. FII's having a capital of 100 crores could register themselves as depositories and their procedures were to be evaluated by an independent agency. FIIs are also allowed to invest in debt securities but investment in equity and debt securities should be in the ratio of

---

8. Expiration date is the last date of the contract. There are European options in which the Buyer can exercise option on expiration. There are American options also in which a buyer can exercise his options any day before or on the day of the expiration. The difference between index options and stock options is the mode of settlement. Index options are settled in cash, while Stock Options result in delivery. Indian Options are based on European style if they are indexed options and American style if they are Stock Options. They will be settled in cash for the first 6 months.

70:30. The FII's under SEBI include Pension Funds, Mutual Funds, Asset Management Companies, Investment Trust and Charitable Institutions.

SEBI'S FAILURE IN INVESTOR PROTECTION

SEBI had been formed in India as a regulatory mechanism. It was to bring reforms in the Indian capital market with the main aim that protective measures are taken towards the investors. While speculation is encouraged and the standard of transparency are maintained through the disclosures and audited financial statements of companies, underwriters, promoters and brokers in the market. It is time to make an appraisal of SEBI's contribution towards investor's protection.

Legislations

SEBI has a plethora of legislations. There have been many committees on reforms of Primary New Issue Market and Stock Market in India. The number of Legislations that have taken place are shown in table I. These legislations basically aim at *investor protection*. However, the number of committees and sub-committees and laws are often very confusing. L.C. Gupta has pointed out that there are many clarification and additions to legislations and guidelines, which often makes them incomprehensible. According to him some of the rules are so 'difficult to comprehend that different interpretations of the rules are made and too often these rules are changed. SEBI is not fulfilling purpose of *self regulation* which is its objective. It may wield undue power with interpretation of its own rules and regulations.[9] Hence laws and rules must be initiated but if these laws are actually a deterrent towards investor protection as confusions can bring out many loops holes which will not be beneficial for the protection of the investor as it can be interpreted differently by different people. It is important to bring about clarity for the understanding of the common investor. As the situation prevails, brokers have often taken advantages of the system. The example of the *Ketan Parekh* case shows loopholes in the inherent system of laws. SEBI has not been able to regulate the capital market agencies despite rules and regulations and committees for regulating the market mechanism. Companies, brokers, underwriters, promoters and investors have been able to take advantage due to the inherent weakness of the system. SEBI was formed after the Harshad Mehta scam in 1992 ands in less than a decade a scam of a greater magnitude than the 1992 scam took place in India which shook the securities market and many investors lost their total personal belongings leading to many suicide cases. This shows that SEBI has failed as a regulatory mechanism. The Ketan Parekh scam has been as a result of broker-bank-corporate nexus, and it is the small investor which has had a magnitude of losses and the SEBI cannot be said to have fulfilled its role as a *Watch Dog* or as a surveillance institution which was one of the major reforms it was to undertake in the capital market.

---

9. Gupta L.C., *"Challenges before Securities and Exchange Board of India"* Economic and Political Weekly, March 23, 1996, and Keynote Address in All India Management Convention 1997 on Indian Capital Market: Opportunities and Challenges UTI Institute of Capital markets and Birla Institute of Management Technology, Nov 15, 1997.

Table 5.2: Legislations in primary and secondary market

Primary Market	Secondary Market
• Merchant Banker, 1992.	• Stock Brokers & Sub-Brokers Regulations, 1992.
• Debenture Trustee, 1993	• Insider Trading, 1992.
• Portfolio Managers, 1993.	• Unfair Trade Practices, 1995.
• Registrar to Issue, 1993.	• Depositories Act, 1996.
• Underwriters Regulations, 1993.	• D&P Regulations, 1996.
• Bankers to an Issue, 1994.	• Credit Rating Agencies Regulations, 1999.
• Buy back of Securities Regulations, 1998.	• Procedure for Board Meetings 2001.
• Foreign Venture Capital Investors, Regulation 2000.	• Prohibition of Unfair Trade Practices 2003.
• Sweat Equity Regulations 2002.	• Database of Market Precipitant Regulation 2003.
• Listing Regulations 2002.	• Holding Enquiry and Imposing Penalty Regulation 2004, 2005.
• Self-regulations 2004.	• Guidelines for Disclosure and Investor Protection 2000 Updated in 2005.
• Criteria for Fit and Proper Person Regulations 2004.	
• Interest Liabilities Regulation Scheme.	

Source: SEBI.

Discipline for Investor Protection

The small investors have several problems. They purchase securities for long term investments but according to them they have many complaints related with receipts of allotment/refund letters, share transfers and brokers services. A large number of shareholders have common complaints of delays with brokers. Brokers have not been able to perform their role well especially in view of occurrence of delay and the extent thereof in receipts of payments for the sale of scrips in the market. Companies delay share transfers beyond 30 days which is the stipulated time. On allotment of new issues share certificates are sent beyond 60 days. Such delays create problems for small investors. This is due to the fact that SEBI has investor guidelines but not enforcements.

There are several letters in newspapers and magazine which substantiate the fact that delays are common with company issues and brokers dealing with small investors are also not satisfactory. These problems of the small investors in relation to company matters or brokers dealings have been overlooked by SEBI despite legislations in this regard. There is a Brokers Act as well as Companies Act which is binding on these agencies and SEBI's objective of protecting the investor is a mere eyewash if these problems however small they appear are continuous. It clearly means that SEBI has not been able to use its control mechanism to the advantage of the investors in disciplining the brokers, companies, banks and other agencies. Such failings on the part of these agencies have not been given due consideration by SEBI.

SEBI has not been able to discipline UTI, which had a large number of shares of Ketan Parekh companies on its portfolios. SEBI's regulating mechanism through surveillance and watch dog operations should have seen unusual stock movements while UTI was purchasing shares of Ketan Parekh companies in large volumes. It is at that time it should have investigated into such purchases as the dividend of UTI 1964 Plan would be affected. Such shares are now worthless and affect the small share-holders as they will not be able to avail of dividends expected by them from UTI, which was supposed to be a stable mutual fund.

These problems have arisen because SEBI has a programme for investor awareness and education and guidelines for protection but no enforcement of guidelines are made.

Transparency in Transactions

The random walk hypothesis states that in perfect competitive market conditions there should be equal information for all operators and there should be transparency in dealings and transactions. Hence there should not be any insider trading or rigging in the stock market. SEBI as a regulator has prohibited insider trading as per the Act. Insider trading takes place in other economies as well but it is illegal and the regulator has to be careful that insider trading does not take place. In the USA it is severely punished. One of the well known cases being SEC vs. Texas, Gulf Sulphur and in Shapiro vs. Merrillynch, both the *tipper* and the *tipee* were prosecuted but in India Harshad Mehta who was responsible for a scam in 1992 was again in the price rigging scam through insider trading in 1998 in BPL, Sterlite and Videocon shares. There are further instances of Anand Rathi the Ex-president of Bombay Stock Exchange who gained insider information and used his official position for getting information into share prices and then was able to bring down the market through *'bear'* operations. Finally Ketan Parekh manipulated the market through 10 software companies Table 5.3. He purchased stocks of new software companies and in 6 months their prices reached at a very high level in 2000. In this way he *cornered* the market. The price of these shares fell and this is shown in Table 5.3.

Table 5.3: KP – 10 Stocks

	High Price of 2000 *(Rs.)*	Price on 11.4.01 *(Rs.)*
Himachal Futuristic	2,553	83
Global Tele System	3,550	116
Zee	1,630	100
Aftek Infosys	5,000	98
Silverline	1,361	62
Pentamedia	2,272	60
DSQ	2,372	67
Ranbaxy	1,240	468
SSI	6,640	490
Satyam Computers	1,430	230

Source: Stock Exchange & SEBI.

The question to be asked here is how did SEBI allow price rigging and not regulate the market at any time. How was Harshad Mehta allowed to operate again in the market after the scam of 1992? Why was his entry to the stock market not banned? 67 companies are now under inspection and surveillance Table 5.4. Why was timely action not taken against them? The Videocon International was initiated only in the 3rd Week of June in 1998. In a stock market, which is highly volatile action should be taken at a fast pace.

Table 5.4: Inspection and surveillance under DCA*

K P Group	**35.** Krishna Securities Ltd.
1. N. H. Securities Ltd.	36. Avenue Stock Brokers Pvt. Ltd.
2. Triumph Investment Finance Ltd.	**Ajay Keyan Group**
3. Classic Share & Stock Broking Services Ltd.	37. Makertich Ltd.
4. K.N.P. Securities Pvt. Ltd.	38. SMIFS Securities Ltd.
5. V.N. Parekh Securities Ltd.	39. Stewart Securities Ltd.
6. Panther Fincap Management Services Ltd.	40. Maya Trade Link Ltd.
7. Panther Investrade Ltd.	41. Powerflow Holdings Ltd.
8. Classic Credit Ltd.	42. Makertich Consultancy Services Ltd.
9. Saimangal Investrade Ltd.	43. PNR Securities Ltd.
10. Classic Infin Ltd.	**Consortium Group**
11. Panther Industrial Products Ltd.	44. Consortium Securities Ltd.
12. Goldfish Computer Pvt. Ltd.	45. CSL Securities Ltd.
13. Nakshatra Software Pvt. Ltd.	46. CSL Stock Broking Pvt. Ltd.
14. Chitrakoot Computyard Ltd.	**BLB Group**
15. Luminant Investment Pvt. Ltd.	47. BLB Ltd.
16. Triumph Securities Pvt. Ltd.	**Rathi Group**
Nirmal Bang Group	48. Rathi Global Finance Ltd.
17. Bama Securities Ltd.	**Zee Tele Group**
18. Nirmal Bang Securities Ltd.	49. Zee Telefilms Ltd.
19. Bang Equity Broking Ltd.	50. Zee Gold Refinery Ltd.
20. Bang Securities Pvt. Ltd.	51. Siticable Network Pvt. Ltd.
21. Suresh Rathi Securities Ltd.	**Others**
22. Nadi Finance & Investment Pvt. Ltd.	52. Palombe Securities and Finance Ltd.
Shankar Sharma & Devina Mehra Group	53. Global Tele Systems Ltd.
23. First Global Finance Pvt. Ltd.	54. HFCL
24. First Global Stock Broking Pvt. Ltd.	55. Digital Superhighway.
25. Vruddhi Confinvest India Pvt. Ltd.	56. Bulington Finance Ltd.
Shailesh Shah Group	57. Briggs Trading Co.
26. Dolat Capital Market Ltd.	58. Prajamata Trading Co.
27. Nirpan Securities Ltd.	59. Gajan Trading Co.
28. Shailesh Shah Securities Ltd.	60. Churu Trading Co.
Radha Krishnan Damani Group	61. Nirma Ltd.
29. Damani Share & Stock Brokers Pvt. Ltd.	62. Ranbaxy Lab Ltd.
30. Maheshwari Equity Brokers Pvt. Ltd.	63. Kopran Ltd.
31. Pratik Stockvision Pvt. Ltd.	64. Adani Export Ltd.
32. Pruthi Share and Broking Ltd.	65. Lupin Laboratories.
33. Damani Estate and Finance Ltd.	66. Padmini Polymers.
34. Brightstar Investment Ltd.	67. Shonkh Technologies Ltd.

*Directorate of Company Affairs.
Source: Economic Times, 23rd June, 2001.

There were 18 brokers who were part of the scam Table 5.5 and as SEBI has established that they had close links with Harshad Mehta and Strelite Industries showed abnormal movements in April-May 1998 but investigation by SEBI. How could a regulatory mechanism not adopt systems and steps before such a scam could take place? Lakshman Singhvi, Executive Director, SEBI pointed out that there should be integrity in the market and not artificial price rigging. In this market SEBI should take up the matter seriously.

Table 5.5: Videocon Sterlite BPL Scam

Name of Broker
1. GNH Global Securities Ltd. – BSE Broker
2. Satyanarayan Nangalia – BSE Broker
3. R.R. Mehta – BSE Broker
4. M/s. Sharukh N. Tara & Co. – BSE Broker.
5. P.R. Shah Share & Stock Brokers Pvt. Ltd. – BSE Broker.
6. M/s. Ramrakh R. Bohra – BSE Broker.
7. Mahico Pvt. Ltd. – BSE Broker.
8. M/s. Mefcon Securities Ltd. Broker BSE and Broker NSE.
9. Lalkar Securities Pvt. Ltd. – BSE Broker.
10. Harvest Deal securities Pvt. Ltd. – BSE Broker.
11. Bharat J. Patel – BSE Broker.
12. Sony Securities Ltd. – NSE Broker.
13. Digital Leasing & Finance Ltd. – NSE Broker.
14. Valfin Financial Services Pvt. Ltd. – NSE Broker.
15. Stenly Credit Capital Ltd. – NSE Broker.
16. Asian Securities & stocks Ltd. – NSE Broker.
17. Star Share & stock Brokers Ltd. – NSE Broker.
18. Malar Share Shopper Ltd. – NSE Broker.

* **Source:** SEBI (18 Brokers)

Badla Trade

The Badla or carry forward system is said to have encouraged malpractice in the stock market in India. According to Bhole "the regulatory ineffectiveness of SEBI in certain cases has been due to its concentration on symptoms rather than root causes. The present delivery system is highly conducive for manipulative operations and unhealthy speculation. SEBI has kept on tinkering with trading laws instead of doing away with such an outdated delivery system".[10] According to him SEBI has been corporate friendly rather than investor friendly. L.C. Gupta[11] has also stated that "the defect in the Indian Stock Exchange is the mixing of cash market with futures. From July 2, 2001, Badla has been banned and the introduction of derivatives like *call* and *put* options has been introduced with daily settlements. Rolling settlement has been extended to all the scrips with effect from December 2001 and rolling settlement cycle has been made T+3 from 1st April, 2002.

---

10. Bhole, 1999, *Financial Institutions and Markets*, Tata McGraw Hills Publishing Co. Ltd., New Delhi, , p. 125.

11. L.C. Gupta, is Director Society for Capital Market Research and former member of SEBI.

"Preventive measures should be taken by SEBI rather than corrective actions after the event and scams are over". L.C. Gupta has time and again warned SEBI not to take ad-hoc decisions in *Badla* trade and to evolve a long term policy through the use of derivatives.

Hence in the interest of the shareholders SEBI should regulate the market in such a way that scams are avoided and the Primary New Issue Market and Securities Market is controlled and small investors are protected from the fraudulent games played by brokers, bankers and corporate organizations. This requires a continuous watch over the market with inspection and effective policies, which are *investor friendly*.

SEBI's experience in the protection of investors was considered faulty as explained above. SEBI had to make changes in regulating and improving the situation in the capital market. As a follow up measure it introduced new techniques for a transparent system. It introduced new regulations and guidelines for investor protection. It brought about the OMBUDSMAN regulations in 2003 to bring about transparency in the system. It strengthened be investor protection measures by focusing on the problems of the investors. SEBI has given a lot of attention to investor awareness and education. To protect investors it has taken certain steps like MAPIN and arbitration facilities. It has setup investor protection fund and a regulation has been made against fraudulent practices. These are discussed in the following paragraphs.

OMBUDSMAN

SEBI issued **OMBUDSMAN** regulations in 2003 following scams and problems in investor protection. This regulation was made to provide fair and transparent systems of redressal of grievances. These regulations empower an investor to get redressal against both listed companies and intermediaries. According to Act an investor can make a complaint for any of the following problems that it faces. This act will help in solving disputes between parties.

The complaints dealt with by the OMBUDSMAN act are in respect of:

(i) Delays in receiving refund orders, allotment letters, dividend or interest.

(ii) Non-receipt of dividends, certificates, bonus shares, annual reports, refunds in allotments or redemption of mutual fund unit.

(iii) Non-receipt of letters of offer in respect of Buy Back of Shares or in the case of delisting.

(iv) Complaints regarding grievances against intermediaries or listed companies.

The OMBUDSMAN is empowered to receive complaints of listed companies and intermediaries and to deal with them in a way to make a settlement between the investor and the companies as early as possible.

National Stock Exchange and Arbitration Facilities: The complaints of investors are also dealt with at the National Stock Exchange. This stock exchange provides for arbitration facilities for investors problems. This is a mechanism, which resolve disputes between trading members and clients in those trades, which takes place on this exchange. Arbitration is much faster in this stock exchange. The arbitrators selected by the National Stock Exchange are list of persons approved by SEBI and have an expertise in banking, finance and capital market activities. The stock exchange accepts application for arbitration in a prescribed format within six months from the date of the dispute. The members can apply to any of the four regional centres, which have been opened in metropolitan cities. The stock exchange enters into arbitration facilities for the following members:

- Investors dealing on the exchange having a valid contract note issued to them by the trading member of the exchange.

- Investors who deal through registered brokers and registered sub- brokers of the trading members of National Stock Exchange.

- Any trading member who has a dispute, difference of opinion or claim against another member of the exchange.

INVESTOR'S EDUCATION

To bring about transparency in the primary and secondary markets to protect the investor's, education of investors has become necessary in matter relating to companies, the security markets and intermediaries. SEBI has education programmes, workshops and published material to inform the investor on issues relating to the market. The investors have the responsibilities of exercising their rights by being informed, vigilant and participating in annual general meetings. SEBI has also established an education and protection fund for protection of the investors' education and awareness.

SEBI makes investors aware of the procedure relating to trading and transfer of securities and also the risk that they are surrounded with in the market. The investor is also given information on his rights and responsibilities and the kind of problems that may be encountered. The investors have the following rights:

- To participate and vote in annual general meetings and the right to receive a notice for them or their proxy to attend the meeting.

- To receive dividends, rights shares, bonus offers from the company after approval of the board.

- To receive and inspect minutes of the general meeting.

- To receive balance sheet, profit and loss account, auditors report and directors reports.

- To receive allotment letters and share certificates.

- To requisition an extra ordinary general meeting.

- To apply for winding up of the company.

- To proceed in civil or criminal proceedings against the company.

FRAUDULENT AND UNFAIR TRADE PRACTICES RELATING TO SECURITIES MARKET REGULATION

Another Act to protect the investor was made in 2003 and it was called the Prohibition of *Fraudulent and Unfair Trade Practices Relating to Securities Market Regulation*. This regulation was made to prohibit any false or misleading advertisements as well as activities intended to defraud an investor. This regulation was also intended to debar any intermediary from entering into transactions to increase his commission or brokerage. The regulation was also in favour of investors and it was meant to protect them from any false or misleading statements, which would induce them to sell or purchase their securities. This Act had its main focus on the following issues:

- Prohibition of misleading statements.

- Prohibition of manipulation of price of securities by traders and intermediaries

- Prohibition of entering into a transaction without the intention of ownership of a security.

- Prohibition of intermediaries promising clients falsely not wanting to actually completing the contract.

To regulate the market participants SEBI introduced a system of their identification through MAPIN.

MAPIN

SEBI introduced MAPIN which is the Market Participants and Investors Integrated Database in 2003. According to this regulation all the participants, registered intermediaries, listed companies, and investors would get registered and obtain a unique identification number. (The major objective was to create a comprehensive database of market participants to establish identity of those people who are doing trading in large volume to enable SEBI to take preventive or remedial measures to identify defaulters and manipulators. SEBI has suspended fresh registrations for applications of unique identification number from July 1st 2005.

INVESTOR'S PROTECTION FUND

An investor's protection fund has been set up. The trustees appointed by the stock exchange manage it. An Investor who has been defrauded can be compensated to the extent of Rs.10 lakhs or the amount under default whichever is lower. The arbitration awards obtained by investors against defaulters are scrutinized by the Defaulters Committee, a Standing Committee constituted by the Exchange, to ascertain their genuineness, of the claim. It makes a recommendation if it is satisfied about the claim to the trustees of the fund for release of the award amount. The Investors protection fund consists of contributions from some of the following sources:

- Members of stock exchange provide Rs 0.15 per Rs. 1 lakh of their gross turnover. This is debited to their general charges account.

- On a quarterly basis stock exchange contributes 2.5% on a quarterly basis out of the listing fees collected by it.

- Interest earned by stock exchange on security deposits of companies making public issues.

- SEBI added another directive. According to this directive auctions proceeds of cases where price manipulations and rigging had taken place were also to be transferred to this fund.

SEBI as a regulatory department brought about several developments in the stock market. A transparent system for protection of investors was developed through the following changes.

- Depository or paperless trading.
- Dematerialization through depositories
- Surveillance on price manipulation
- Regulation of stock brokers
- Regulation of merchant bakers
- Prohibition of insider trading
- Regulation of mutual funds
- Regulation of foreign institutional investors
- Screen based trading
- Circuit breakers
- Settlement and clearing
- Credit rating of debt securities
- Introduction of financial derivatives

All these changes have been discussed in chapters 6 and 7 of the book. SEBI is still developing rules and regulation to bring about discipline in the capital market in India. These changes usually take place to rectify problems after they have occurred. SEBI has many guidelines for protection of investors. Although there is an improvement over the previous years, SEBI has to make many more changes for developing the market and protecting the interest of the investors. This chapter provides some of the measures of investor protection by SEBI. SEBI is a market regulator and it was formed in 1992 for the introduction of reforms in the capital market to ensure fair dealings for investors and for development of he market. Investor protection measures consist of regulations and guidelines. SEBI has prepared a model code of conduct for listed companies. It has also brought about a regulation to prohibit unfair trade practices. It has prohibited insider trading, and it has played an active part with the stock exchanges, in the creation of an investor protection fund. This fund is to compensate those investors who have been fraudulently manipulated in buying and selling of securities through unfair practices.

The next chapter discusses the new issue market, its operations, functions and developments.

Summary

➡ There are a large number of reforms in the primary and secondary markets with a plethora of legislations, which are confusing and there are loopholes through which it is possible to perpetuate frauds in the Stock Market.

➡ The reforms made by SEBI are useful but timely action and prosecution is not taken. It is more favourable towards the *corporate sector* than towards the *investors*.

➡ SEBI as a regulatory mechanism failed to initiate discipline amongst the different stock market, agencies like Brokers, Corporate Entities, Mutual Funds and Banks.

➡ SEBI is known to review situations rather than take preventive measures in regulating the market. Badla should have been discontinued as long back as in 1994.

Contd.....

➡ SEBI has failed in protecting the small investor because it is not an effective controlling agency. The presence of RBI, Company Law Board, and Government of India weaken its position and bring about duplication of laws. SEBI should be made an autonomous institution for better control.

➡ SEBI protects investors against fraud, manipulation and unfair trade practices.

➡ SEBI has issued a model code of conduct for listed companies.

➡ SEBI has issued guidelines (2000) for redressal of investor grievances.

➡ OMBUDSMAN (2003) had been passed for a transparent system of receiving complaints and amiable settlement of disputes.

➡ Investor awareness through education of investor's rights and liabilities has become a very important part of SEBI's activities.

➡ Insider trading has been prohibited by SEBI, as some people would have unfair advantage over others in trading securities.

➡ An investor protection fund has been established to provide relief to those who have been defrauded.

Objective Type Questions, Answer True (T) or False (F)

(a) The Securities Exchange Board of India was established in 1996.

(b) SEBI is a subsidiary of the U.S. Securities Exchange Commission.

(c) It provides guidance for the protection of mutual funds.

(d) It helps the intermediaries in protecting the investors.

(e) SEBI has brought about a model code of conduct for unlisted companies.

(f) OMBUDSMAN regulations were issued in 2003 for providing a system for receiving investor companies.

(g) The most important function of SEBI is to protect investors and bring discipline in the capital market.

(h) The depository Act was passed in 1996 for trading of new issues.

(i) SEBI allowed the forcing institutional investors to invest in debt securities.

(j) SEBI regulates mutual funds through standardizing of accounting procedures and transparency in disclosures.

Answer: (a) F, (b) F, (c) F, (d) F, (e) F, (g) T, (h) F, (i) T, (j) T.

Multiple Choice Questions (Tick mark (✓) the right answer)

1. Model code of conduct:
   (a) is a prohibitory order by SEBI
   (b) A code of internal procedures and disclosure practices

(c)   An order for conducting trade on stock exchange

(d)   A code for external procedures and practices of companies

2.   SEBI deals with investor grievance relating to the following:

(a)   Securities listed or traded with stock exchanges

(b)   Complaints against unlisted companies

(c)   Fixed deposits with non bank financial institutions

(d)   Complaints relating to for feature of shares

3.   The fraudulent and unfair trade practices relating to securities market regulation in 2003 was passed to prohibit.

(a)   Insides trading practices

(b)   Brokers from illegal trading

(c)   Foreign institutional investors in the market

(d)   Manipulation of prices and misleading statements

4.   OMBUDSMAN regulations were issued in 2003 for dealing with

(a)   Delay in refunds and allotment of shares

(b)   Arbitration of disputes between trading members and clients

(c)   Annual general meeting and inspection of minutes of the general meeting

(d)   Market participants and investors integrated database

5.   Insider trading means:

(a)   Purchase of securities by owners of the company

(b)   Taking advantage of internal price sensitive informational for trading

(c)   Trade for purchase of shares only by employees

(d)   Investors sell their financial paper to relatives of the firms

Answer: 1 (b), 2 (a), 3 (d), 4 (a) and 5 (b).

Short Answer Questions

1.   What are some of the common grievances of an investor? Give the process of redressal system to the investors.

2.   What is insider trading? Who is an insider? How does SEBI deal with such practices?

3.   What is a trading window? In what circumstances is it closed?

4.   Discuss the provisions of model code of conduct for companies.

5.   Write notes on:

(i)   OMBUDSMAN

(ii)   Investor protection fund

(iii) Investor education

(iv) Insider trading

Long Answer Questions

1. The twin objective of SEBI was two to protect the investors and develop the securities market. In the light of this observation discuss whether SEBI has fulfilled its objectives in the capital market in India.

2. Discuss the reforms made by SEBI in the primary securities market.

3. SEBI created many changes in the working of the secondary market. Discuss some of the important reforms.

4. SEBI has failed in investor protection measures despite a plethora of legislations. Comment and explain this statement.

5. What are the steps taken by SEBI in investor grievance and education?

Part – Three
Financial Markets

6. New Issue Market

7. The Secondary Market

8. Financial Markets for Short Term Funds
   - Call Money Market
   - Treasury Bills Market
   - Commercial Bills Market
   - Markets for Commercial Paper and Certificate of Deposits
   - The Discount Market
   - Market for Financial Guarantees
   - Government (Gift-edged) Securities Market

Chapter **6**

New Issue Market

Chapter Plan

- Introduction
- Role of the New Issue Market
- Method of New Issue Market
- Offer to Public Procedure
    Book building,
    Application and allotment
- Intermediaries to the Issue
    Merchant banker

Lead manager
Portfolio manager
Underwriter
Registrar and transfer agent
Broker
- Trends in the New Issue Market
- The Relationship of the New Issue
  Market and Stock Exchange

INTRODUCTION

This chapter discusses the operations in the New Issue Market (NIM). The New Issue Market and Stock Exchanges are the constituents of the industrial securities market in India. The New Issue Market (NIM) deals with those securities which have been made available to the public for the first time. The mechanism of floatation of new issues, share application and allotment and the intermediaries which help in the process of the issue are presented in this chapter.

The broad features of the Indian financial system were discussed in chapter 2. It gave an account of the structure of the securities market in India. A critique of the Indian capital market pointed out certain weaknesses of the capital market structure. One of the needs of the day is to form an organic link between the saving populace and avoidance of duplication of activities among the various financial institutions. Whilst the Indian capital market consists of a variegated number of financial institutions who have been giving financial help to the industrial sector, few have participated in the management of these firms. A study in the *Economic Times* indicated that more than 75% of the total resources financed to industry was through the financial institutions but it was the non-resident individual and especially Swaraj Paul in 1985 who woke up the financial institutions and showed them their responsibilities toward the corporate sector where they hold a major share but their nominee directors are in a sleeping position, the stock exchanges in India serve not only the private sector, but also the joint and public sectors, by providing a forum for free transferability of shares held by the public. The stock exchanges work in conjunction with the new issue market. The shares issued in the new issue market are listed on stock exchanges and then offered for sale. The shares issued, not only affect purchases and sales of securities but also make a continuous valuation of securities traded in the market. The New Issue Market (NIM) has emerged as an important source of corporate financing in India after 1992. The New Issue Market was being regulated by Controller of Capital Issues. In 1992, it was abolished and the Securities and Exchange Board of India (SEBI) was established for providing protection to investors and toning up the operations of the NIM. It was also given the responsibility of development and regulation of the NIM. The SEBI was to cover all the activities of the NIM beginning with the planning of the capital issues and completing the formalities until the post issue activities. Let us now discuss the procedure of making a new issue and allotting shares to investors while discussing the procedures the role of intermediaries and the methodology of allotting shares will be explained.

ROLE OF THE NEW ISSUE MARKET

The NIM has three functions to perform. These may be put together to be called the 'performing' role of the NIM. These functions as described by Briston are: (a) Origination, (b) Underwriting, and (c) Distribution. The interplay of these functions helps to transfer resources from the sources of surplus funds to those who require these funds, *i.e.,* the ultimate users of these funds.

Origination

Origination is the work, which begins before an issue is actually floated in the market. It is the stage where initial 'spade work' is conducted to find out the investment climate and to be sure that if the issue is floated it will be subscribed to by the public. The factors, which have to be carefully analyzed, are regarding the soundness of the project. Soundness of the project refers to its technical feasibility backed by its economic and financial viability. It is also concerned with background factors, which facilitate the success of an issue. The underlying conditions are:

The Time of Floating of an Issue: This determines the mood of the investment market. Timing is crucial because it has a reflection on the subscription of an issue. Periods of buoyancy will clearly show over-subscription to even ordinary quality issues and are marked by the general lack of public support during depression.

Type of Issue: This refers to the kind of securities to be issued whether equity, preference, debentures or convertible securities. These have significance with the trends in the investment market. Sometimes there is a sudden spurt of new issue of shares marked with government support and tax incentives. Investors are keen buyers of such an issue. The success of one encourages issues of these kinds to be floated. In times when the market is depressed it will have little support from even sound and good issues of other types of securities. The kind of marketability of the issue is an important analysis at the time of origination.

Price: The encouragement of public to a particular issue will largely depend on the price of an issue. Well-established firms of some group connections may be able to sell their shares at a premium at the times of a new issue but relatively unknown firms will have to be cautious of the price. Price of shares of these firms should be fixed at par. There is a danger of fixing prices at a discount as these may undervalue the firm and bring down their reputation.

In India shares are now priced through book building. Free pricing of shares is also allowed. Most of the new issues in 2006-2007 have been priced at a premium. An equity share of ICICI bank with the face value of Rs. 10 was fixed through book building at Rs. 900 per share. It was over subscribed. Thus shares with a reputation can be priced at very high price.

The functions of the NIM at the time of origination are, based on preliminary investigation and are mainly advisory in nature. This function was performed by banks which created merchant banking divisions. Since 1992 merchant banking institutions and other intermediaries have been created to do the work of origination. SEBI is empowered to regulate them. The functions of the merchant bankers' are to draft the prospectus prepare application forms and deal with legal procedures.

Underwriting

Underwriting is a kind of guarantee undertaken by an institution or a firm of brokers ensuring the marketability of an issue. It is a method whereby the guarantor makes a promise to see the stock issuing company that he would purchase a certain specified number of shares in the event of their not being invested by the public. Subscription is thus guaranteed even if the public does not purchase the shares for a commission from the issuing company. These are: Life Insurance Corporation of India (LIC), Unit Trust of India (UTI), Development Banks like Industrial Development Bank of India, Industrial Finance Corporation of India, Industrial Credit and Investment Corporation of India (ICICI), General Insurance Companies, Commercial Banks, and Brokers. The methods adopted by these groups and their pattern of underwriting show a definite type of institutional role.

The Commercial Banks, to a great extent, have remained away from the underwriting sphere. They are better known for their function as agents engaged in the distribution of shares for a commission. Even if they have underwritten issues it has been on an ad-hoc basis. They have not believed in underwriting firm. They may keep the shares in their own portfolio or off-load them in the stock market for a price. They, therefore, do not have a particular direction in underwriting. They are also known to underwrite small amounts only.

The brokers do not underwrite 'firm'. They guarantee shares only with the view of earning commission from the company floating its shares. They are known to off-load their shares later again to make a profit. The broker's policy can thus be identified with 'profit motive' in underwriting industrial securities.

In case the issue is not subscribed the underwriter makes a commitment to lend support to the issue. Financial institutions and development banks used to underwrite firm and it was mandatory to subscribe the issues by underwriters. Since 1995 it is not legally required to have an issue underwritten but it is a good support for any new issue which is being marketed.

Distribution

The New Issue Market has a third function besides the function of origination and underwriting. The third function is that of distribution of shares. Distribution means the function of sale of shares and debentures to the investors. This is performed by brokers and agents. They maintain regular lists of clients and directly contact them for purchase and sale of securities. The companies can appoint brokers for sale of securities but brokers have to be registered with stock markets.

METHOD OF FLOATING NEW ISSUES

The objective of the New Issue Market is to centre its activities towards floatation of New Issues. The methods by which the new issues are placed in the market are: public issue, offer for sale, placement, and right issues.

Public Issue

The most popular methods for floating shares in the new issue market is through a legal document called the 'Prospectus'. The issuing company makes an offer to the public directly of a fixed number of shares at a specific price. The company has to incur expenses on administration, advertisement, printing, prospectus, paper announcements, bank's commission, underwriting commission, agents' fees, legal charges, stamp duty, document fees, listing fees and registration charges.

Offer for Sale

Offer for sale is a method of floatation of shares through an 'intermediary' and 'indirectly' through an 'issuing house'. It involves sale of securities through two distinct steps. The first step is a direct sale by the issuing company to issuing houses and brokers. The second step is also a second sale of these securities involving the issue house and the public. The price of the shares is obviously at a higher rate to the public that for which the 'issuing house' (or intermediary) purchases from the 'issuing company'. The profit charged by the issuing house is called a 'turn'. Offer for sale method is not used in India. It is widely used for floatation as described in the public offer method. In India, offer for sale method is sometimes used when a foreign company floats its shares. Offer for sale as used in Indian terminology has a different meaning. It is used not for selling securities to the public but to comply with certain stock exchange regulations at the time of listing of shares. In India, the existing shareholders make an offer to the public for subscription so that the securities become widely distributed to the public. This offer would grant a stock exchange quotation. Offer for sale even in this sense is not used often in India as a method of floatation of securities.

Placement

This is another method of floatation not used normally in the Indian capital market. In the London Stock Exchange this is operative and is used for an issuing house to sell shares to its own clients. 'The Issuing House' or 'Intermediaries' purchase shares from companies issuing their shares. Subsequently, the issuing house sells these shares for a profit. The issuing houses maintain their own list of clients and through customer contacts sell shares.

The main disadvantage of this method is that the issues remain relatively unknown. A small number of investors buy a large number of shares and are in this way able to corner shares of firms.

This method is useful when small companies are issuing their shares. They can avoid the expenses of issue and also have their shares placed. Timing is crucial from the point of view of floatation of shares. In a depressed market condition when these issues are not likely to get proper public response through prospectus placement method, this is an excellent process for floatation of shares.

Right Issues

Shares floated through 'right issues' are a measure for distribution of shares normally used for established companies, which are already listed in the stock exchange. Sometimes, this method of floatation is used by new companies also.

Right issues are an inexpensive mode of floatation of shares. This is an offer made to existing shareholders through a formal letter of information. In India, according to Section 81 of the Companies Act, 1956: (a) one year after the company's first issue, (b) or two years after its existence, right shares must be issued first to existing shareholders. The shares can also be offered to the public after the rights of the existing shareholders have been satisfied. These shares are issued in proportion to the shares held by the existing shareholders. This right can be taken away by the company by passing a special resolution to this effect.

The four methods of floatation discussed above are: (a) Offer to public, (b) Offer for sale, (c) Private Placement, and (d) Right issues. In India, offer to public through prospectus and right issues to existing shareholders is popular for floatation of shares. Let us discuss the procedure for allotment of shares to public through offer to public method.

OFFER TO PUBLIC PROCEDURE

The SEBI has also made certain procedural changes in the mode of issue of capital for removing deficiencies in the issue procedure. Those companies, which intend to issue capital, have been classified into existing listed companies, existing unlisted companies and new companies. These are divided into 8 categories. These are:

Category A : This category consists of new companies with less than 12 months in operation. At least 25% and 20% of total issued capital of Rs. 100 crores and above Rs. 100 crores respectively should be through promoters like friends, relatives and associates. The first public issue must be made at par.

Category B : In this category are those companies, which have a good record of making profits for the last five years, and are making their first public issue. They are free to price their issue at par or premium.

Category C : Consists of private, closely held and unlisted companies, which are making their first public issue. Such companies have a good past record of profits in at least three out of five years. It can issue shares at premium but it must provide a justification to the SEBI.

Category D :   Is of private, closely held and unlisted companies without a consistent record of past profitability.

Category E :   Consists of the same group of companies without a consistent past record of profitability but supported by existing companies with a consistent record of profitability in the last five years.

Category F :   Is of existing listed companies that are making a public issue.

Category G :   Existing companies—private, closely held and unlisted companies of past profitability by offering to public without issuing fresh capital and seeking dis-investment. The promoters' share should be at least 25% and they can offer their shares at premium.

Category H :   Existed companies—private, closely held and unlisted without a record of profitability by offering securities to the public without issue of fresh capital. They can make their issue only at par.

Promoters

The contribution of the promoters in the public issue has to compulsorily be made before the opening of the public issue. In a public issue by a listed company promoters have to contribute at list 20% of the purposed issue and it should be help as his post issue capital. The full amount of contribution with premium should be deposited at least one day before issue opening day. The Promoters contribution is not required in a public issue of securities which have been listed in stock market for at least 3 years and it has a good record of paying dividend for at least 3 preceding years. It is also not required when rights issues are made. However, where companies are issuing shares of above Rs. 100 crores, 50% of their contribution is to be made before the opening of the issue and the balance is to be collected before the calls are made. After receiving the contribution of the promoters the company has to file a copy of the amount received from the promoters with the SEBI. The promoters' contribution has a lock in period of 3 years. When promoters' contribution is an excess of required minimum contribution, the excess is lock for period of 1 year. The locked in securities of the promoters can be used as a pledge with banks and financial institutions as collateral securities for loans which have been granted by those banks or financial institutions, during which they are not transferable. These shares can be used as security with banks on loans granted by them.

Eligibility for Public Issue

One of the most important issues in the primary securities market was to protect the investors from fraudulent dealings. Hence SEBI made certain important reforms. SEBI made eligibility criteria for New Issues. A company could issue shares in the New Issue Market only if it had paid a dividend for at least three years prior to the public issue. If a company did not have a record of payment of dividends in the previous three years it should get its project appraised by banks or financial institutions which have a 10% stake in equity participation of the issuing company. A third criteria is that the securities of the company should be listed with OTCEI (over the counter exchange of India). It has also been stated by M.T. Raju that for transparency SEBI also asked such companies to make draft prospectus of company available to public and to give financial projections in their offer documents.

Offer to the public is made by a company by issuing a notice of its offer document. The most important offer document that is prepared in this connection is the ***prospectus*** of the company. When there is flexible pricing of securities and the price has to be decided through bids a ***red herring prospectus*** has to be issued. There are many formalities in issuing shares to the public. To make a proposal the company must project itself by providing its identity and the productive activities it conducts. The offer document should give adequate information about the company to allow the investor to take an informed decision. The document should be true and correct. It should be signed by the directors and the managing director of company, the chief executive officer and the chief financial officer of the company. All material facts should be disclosed. The offer document should be filed with the registrar of companies and SEBI. The names of the stock exchanges where listing is applied for should also be given. The contents of the prospectus are the following:

Prospectus

The prospectus is part of the offer document. It is important that all information in this document is disclosed correctly. Some of the important aspects of the prospectus are given below:

- Name of the company.
- Address of the Registered Office of the company.
- Activities of the company. Existing business functions and its proposal for the future.
- Location of the industry.
- Names of the Directors of the firm.
- Minimum subscription.
- Dates when subscription is opened and date of closing offer.
- Institutions underwriting the issue, their names, address and amounts underwritten.
- A statement made by the company that it will apply to the stock exchange for quotation of its shares.
- Rating of debentures/preference shares through credit rating agencies.

The prospectus has to be registered at least 21 days before the issue with the registrar of companies. If a debt instrument is issued it is mandatory to have a credit rating.

Red Herring Prospectus

This is a prospectus which is introduced with the concept of book building. It does not give any details of number of shares offered or price of shares that are offered or the amount of the issue.

Green Shoe Option (GSO)

The GSO (Green Shoe Option) is a stabilizing mechanism in the form of an option available to a company to allocate shares at a price, which is higher, then that of the public issue. It operates a post-listing price through stabilizing agent. This provision has been allowed by SEBI from August 2003 to those companies, which issue shares through book building mechanism for stabilizing the post-listing price of the shares.

Employees Stock Option

This is a right given to the employees, officers as well as directors of a company to purchase shares at a future date but at a pre-determined price. This option is only for the employee and is not transferable to other people.

Sweat Equity

The company act of 1956 and the rules as per SEBI Sweat Equity Regulation 2003 allows a company to issue its shares to its employees or directors at a discount or free for consideration other than cash for providing services or knowledge based activities to the company. Sweat Equity can be sold even below the par value. It is a method of recognizing the employees' contribution to intellectual property rights to the company, which may be in a form of contribution towards research, strategy, or additions to the companies profitability. SEBI allows such an issue to a company if: (i) such shares have already been issued, (ii) commercial activity has taken placed for at least one year, (iii) the issue has been authorized by special a resolution.

Free Pricing of Issue

Keeping in view the changes in the capital market emanating from *free pricing of shares* and free access to market for funds by the issuers, the SEBI with the objective of broadening the investors' base, dispensed with the requirement of standard denomination of Rs. 10 and Rs. 100, gave freedom to companies with dematerialized shares, to issue shares at any denomination. The existing companies, with shares at Rs. 10 and Rs. 100, also can avail of this facility by consolidating or splitting their existing shares. In order to enable the investors to take informed investment decisions, the stock exchanges were directed to indicate the denomination value of shares as fixed by the company along with the market quotation. However, the companies availing of this facility are required to strictly adhere to disclosures and accounting norms. SEBI also decided that there would be only one set of disclosures and entry norms for all the issues irrespective of the issue price. Thus, the different requirements for making issues at par and premium were merged to create a common set of requirement.

Issue Advertisement

A new issue is required to be advertised in the news papers and through brochures, pamphlets and circulars. It can be advertised through radio and television and through hoardings at prominent places. The advertisement should be true and correct and full facts should be disclosed. It should not be misleading. It should not be a promise or a guarantee of any fact which is not present in the offer document. Models and celebrities cannot be part of the advertisement displays. The advertisement should be released with risk factors. The announcement for closure of the issues should be made after the lead banker has given his consent. This announcement can be made only if 90% of the issue has been subscribed and a certificate has been issued by the registrar. Before the public issue is made it is mandatory that a prospectus is filled by the lead managers to the SEBI. Although it is not compulsory to make an appraisal of a project it is quite useful to do so for purposes of term loans and underwriting of capital issues. In their own interest whether SEBI makes it mandatory or not a company can have its project appraised. However, SEBI has issued guidelines regarding code of 'advertisement' for issue of shares. The statements in these advertisements should be clear and fair and not misleading and false. Since shares are usually given the option of book building, companies in India go through the process of bidding for their issue. The following is the book building process.

Book Building

Book building is a process of offering securities in which bids at different prices are made by investors. The demand for the security is assessed based on these bids and the price is discovered. In a new issue price is given by the company in advance when it is a fixed price issue. In that situation the investor knows the price when he applies for the share, but in book building process the price is based on demand and bids. It is known only when the issue is closed. In a book building process the floor price is indicated but there is no ceiling price and bids have to be open for 5 days. The retail bidder has the option to bid at cut off price, they are allowed to revise their bids and the bidding demand is displayed at the closing time each day. The syndicate members can bid at any price. Allotment of shares is done within 15 days of closing the issue. If a certain category is under subscribed, the unsubscribed portion can be allotted to bidders in other categories. The book building portion has to be underwritten by book runners or syndicate members. Book building facility was developed in the initial public offer to bring about the flexibility of price and quantity, which would be decided on the basis of demand. In India book building was first developed for issues above 100 crores and consisted of that portion which is reserved for institutional and corporate investors. It is a flexible pricing method based on feedback from investors and in the US it is called *soft underwriting*.

In November 2001, the book building guidelines brought about 100% book building for companies which wanted to bring out a public issue. The issuer company was allowed to issue securities to public through a prospectus either through 100% of the net offer to the public through book building process or 75% of the net offer to the public through book building process and 25% of the price determined through book building. The Red Herring Prospectus would disclose the floor price of the securities and not the maximum price. The lead manager would make the bids on a real time basis. The bidding centres for 100% book building of the net offer to the public would be made through all recognized stock exchanges. When the offer is made in accordance with 75% of the net offer to the public then the process would be according to the collection from the number of mandatory collection centres.

When a company issues 100% of the net offer to the public through book building, the new issue would have to be offered in the following way:

- Retail bidders would be allotted not less than 25% of the net offer to public. The investors eligible under this category were those who applied up to 1000 shares.
- 15% of the net offer to public would be allotted to investors which apply for more than 1000 securities.
- 60% of the net offer would be offer to qualified institutional buyers.

When a company issues 75% of the net offer to public and 25% is determined through book building:

- 15% of the net offer to public would be allotted to non-institutional investors.
- 60% of the offer would be allotted to qualified institutional buyers.
- 25% of the balance through book building would be provided for individual investors. Who have not participated or received any allocation of the book build portion.

Share Application Procedure

The application for shares is also made in accordance with SEBI guidelines. The minimum application money paid is 25% of the issue price. If the face value is Rs. 10, a minimum of Rs. 2.50 should be paid at the time of application of shares. There should be a minimum of 30 collection centres at which money can be collected. The collection agents are authorized to collect application money by cheques or drafts but not in cash. The application money so collected should be deposited in the share application account with the authorized banker. If money received is 90% of the amount issued within 120 days of opening of the issue it will be a valid issue and within 45 days of the closing of the issue a report signed by the chartered accountant must be sent to the SEBI.

Allotment Procedure

Allotment to investors is made according to the legal formalities as described by SEBI. When an issue is oversubscribed, proportionate allotment is to be made to all the investors. The allotment is made according to the number of shares which has been applied for and according to the category of investor. The investor may be a retail bidder or an individual investor. He can be an institutional investor as well. The number of share allotted to each category is according to the number of applicants in each category multiplied by the number of share applied for. The company will then have to find out the number of times in each category that the share has been oversubscribed. For example,

- Total number of applicants 2000.
- Total number of shares applied for in this category Rs. 2,00,00,000.
- Number of times oversubscribed 5.
- Proportionate allotment 2,00,00,000/5 = 40,00,000.

The investors who have been allotted shares would now be allotted the shares proportionately. For example,

- Number of shares applied by each applicant 500.
- Number of times oversubscribed 5.
- Proportionate allotment to each applicant 500/5 = 100.

Therefore, the individual will be allotted only 100 shares although he has applied for 500 shares. Sometimes shares are allotted by rounding off. When the proportionate allotment works out to 110 shares, only 100 shares will be allotted after rounding off.

When shares are allotted in any category and there is a balance which is left over due to rounding off, the available shares would be adjusted in the categories where the applicants are high but shares are less. Sometimes due to rounding off the allotment may be higher than the number of shares offered. An adjustment up to 10% can be made in this case. If the minimum subscription amount of 90% of the issue amount is not received by the company within 120 days of the opening of the issue, the subscription money must be returned to the investor.

Shareholders allotted shares were to receive their allotment within 30 days of closure of the issue after which the company would have to pay 15% rate of interest. Merchant Bankers of SEBI imposed Mandatory restrictions on costs of public issue on underwriting commission, brokerage, fee of managers of issue, fee to registrars to the issue, listing fees and advertisement cost and compulsory registration of Merchant Bankers and Bankers to the Issue. Only corporate bodies would be allowed to function as Merchant Bankers, Restriction was imposed upon them for carrying out funds based activities exclusively in the capital markets. They were prohibited from accepting deposits and leasing and Bill discounting.

SEBI has also issued guidelines for Bonus issues and right issues and debentures. A new development in the NIM relates to 'Bought Out Deals' in sale of securities. Bought out deals involve the promotion, sponsors and investors. It is an outright sale of a larger amount of equity to one single sponsor by an unlisted company. The price settled for purchase of those shares depends on negotiations and project evaluation and the price is competitive. The shares can be treated at the OTCEI or any recognized stock exchange to help the company to get listed. This is a specific activity of a merchant banker. The main difference between bought out deals and private placements is that bought out deals are usually in unlisted companies and private placements are dealings of listed companies.

INTERMEDIARIES TO THE ISSUE

The changes in the NIM especially those relating to market intermediaries, issue procedures and disclosures have helped in removing inadequacies and deficiencies in the New Issue Market and in bringing about significant improvement in compliance with the New Economic Policy of the economy which came into force in 1991. One of the developments in the NIM was the role of intermediaries in selling 'new issues'. The most important being the merchant banker.

Merchant Banker

The company has to appoint a merchant banker. They advise the firm in drawing up the capital structure of the company. It has now become mandatory for all companies who are bringing out new issues to appoint merchant bankers.

The role of the Merchant bankers was considered complementary to the NIM as they carry out all the activities relating to issue of shares. They draft prospectus, appoint registrars for share application and transfers, provide arrangements for underwriting, select brokers, bankers to the issue and handle past issue problems. SEBI has made it mandatory for all firms issuing shares to appoint merchant bankers. Merchant bankers must be regulated with the SEBI and is granted recognition on the basis of its capital adequacy norms in terms of its net worth. A merchant banker has to pay a registration fee annually. There are 4 categories of merchant bankers:

Category I to carry out activities relating to issue management have to pay fees of Rs. 2.5 lakhs for the first two years and 1.50 for the third year. Category II merchant bankers were to pay Rs. 1,50,000 for the first two years and 50,000 for the 3rd year. Merchant bankers in this category were to act as advisor, consultant, portfolio manager, underwriter or manager. Those in Category III were to act as advisor, underwriter and consultant. Category IV acts only as advisors or consultants to the issue. Therefore, merchant bankers in category I are the lead managers to an issue.

A merchant banker has to abide by the code of conduct laid down by SEBI. They have to submit documents and records and other legal papers under the guidelines of the SEBI. A lead manager has to prepare prospectus and submit it to the SEBI at least two weeks before the issue. The numbers of lead managers are related to the size of the issue. Two lead managers are appointed for an issue of less than Rs. 50 crores. Rs. 50-100 crores issue requires 3 lead managers and for Rs. 100-200 crores 4 lead managers may be appointed.

Lead Manager

The commercial or investment bank which has primary responsibility for organizing a given Initial Public Offering (IPO) or bond issues is called a lead manager. The lead merchant banker plays a very important role in all the pre-issue procedures of the company. This bank will find other lending organizations or underwriters to create the syndicate, negotiate terms with the issuer, and assess market conditions. He is also called syndicate manager, managing underwriter or lead underwriter. Every company which issues securities has to make a Memorandum Of Understanding (MOU) with the lead banker. The MOU specifies their mutual rights, liabilities and obligations to the issue. SEBI merchant banking regulation 1992 states that all issues of a company should be managed by at least one merchant banker functioning as a lead merchant banker known as a lead manager. In a rights issues up to Rs.50 lakhs it is not necessary to have a lead manager. A lead manager is supposed to make an underwriting commitment which is 5% of total underwriting commitment or Rs. 25 lakhs whichever is lower. If there are two lead managers they should have separate responsibility areas. Their main interest is to protect the investors. They have to ensure that all the procedures of the issue are complete and the disclosures in the offer document are complete. They have to send particulars of an issue to SEBI.

Portfolio Manager

The Portfolio Manager tracks and monitors investments, cash flow and assets, through price updates. Investments like equity, mutual funds, assets, cash flows, and borrowing funds is the work of the portfolio manager it is the most up-to-date and precise indicator of net worth and investments at each stage. It can be used as a record of holdings to base any future investments decisions.

The Portfolio Manager has useful tools to gain an insight of volatile markets this help to track the trends of current investments and stocks. Under the SEBI portfolio manager regulation of 1993 any person can work as a portfolio manager but he should be registered with SEBI. He should have adequate infrastructure, professional qualifications and capital adequacy of Rs.50 lakhs. A portfolio manager advices, directs, and under takes on behalf of the client. He is under a contract with a client and he is entitled to a fees.

Underwriters

Since 1995, another change in the NIM is with respect to intermediaries in the role of underwriters. Underwriting is no longer mandatory. Underwriters should have a certificate of registration with the SEBI and are governed by the rules and regulations of the SEBI. He has to abide by a code of conduct. The third intermediary is the banker to the issue. He has also to be registered with the SEBI and has to pay fees of 2.5 lakhs for the first 2 years and Rs. 1 lakh for the third year. He has also to abide by the code of conduct laid down by the SEBI. Another intermediary, *i.e.,* Brokers to the issue is extremely important in the stock market but it is not compulsory in the NIM. An important activity in NIM which has been carried on after 1985 is to appoint Registrars and share transfer agents to an issue.

Registrars and Transfer Agents

An important activity in NIM, which has been carried on after 1985, is to appoint registrars and share transfer agents to an issue. The role of the registrars is extremely useful. They keep a record of the investor and assist companies for allotment of securities. They despatch allotment letters, refund orders, certificates and other documents relating to the issue of capital. The transfer agents maintain records of holders of security and deal with transfers and redemptions of securities.

In Category I are placed those who are both Registrars and transfer agents and in Category II is those who are either transfer agents or registrars. They must be compulsory registered with the SEBI and the capital adequacy requirement in Rs. 6 lakhs for Category I and 3 lakhs for Category II. They also have to maintain a code of conduct and act within the legal jurisdiction of the SEBI. A debenture trustee is also a necessary intermediary in the NIM. The debenture trustee has to be registered with SEBI. Only scheduled commercial banks, public financial institutions, insurance companies and companies are entitled to act as debenture trustees. The registration fee for a debenture trustee is Rs. 2 lakhs for the first two years and 1 lakh for the third year. The role of debenture trustee is to look after the trust property and carry out all the activities for the protection of the debenture holders. Since the work requires integrity and fairness in discharging their duties. SEBI has a code of conduct for debenture trustees within which they have to carry out their duties.

The intermediaries have thus to follow a code of conduct, should fulfill capital adequacy norms and be disciplined in their dealing in the NIM. In case they do not follow the SEBI guidelines their registration can be cancelled and they may be penalized by a penalty also.

Broker

A broker is an agent which buys and sells securities for a commission. Brokers to the issue are extremely important in the stock market but it is not compulsory in the NIM. The role of the broker in the new issue market is to distribute forms of the public issues that are made by the company to investors. In a stock exchange a broker has to be registered before he can trade in securities. His role will be discussed in detail in the next chapter on stock market.

TRENDS IN THE NEW ISSUE MARKET

The New Issue Market (NIM) has emerged as an important source of corporate financing in India after 1985. The New Issue Market was being regulated by Controller of Capital Issues in 1992. It was abolished and the *Securities and Exchange Board of India (SEBI)* was established for providing protection to investors and toning up the operations of the NIM. It was also given the responsibility of development and regulation of the NIM. The SEBI was to cover all the activities of the NIM beginning with the planning of the capital issues and completing the formalities until the post issue activities.

The NIM continued to make changes for improvements and toning up the quality of work in the market. SEBI appointed the Malegam Committee in 1995 to offer guidance in respect of disclosures made by companies to the SEBI in respect of documents such as prospectus, financial information through the annual balance sheet and accounts and information to be given to SEBI on different issues from time to time. The Malegam Committee has suggested requirements on disclosures in documents of a company. This has come into effect since October 1, 1995. They cover all aspects such as prospectus, advertisements, new issues and right issues, pricing of shares, issue of shares at a premium, pure rigging and mergers.

The performance of the securities market improved with transparency as the confidence of the investor increased. The economics survey 2005-2006 stated that there was a lot of activity in the new issue market since 2002. There were 55 IPO's in the year 2005 but difficulty was faced in collecting funds from debt securities. Table 6.1 depicts IPO's of both equity and debt in the years 2002-2005. The amount of equity during 2005 was Rs. 30,325 crores and debt Rs. 66 crores.

The new issue market is connected with the stock market. The Initial Public Offerings are listed on stock exchanges and obtain the permission of SEBI to trade on stock markets. The trends of new issues can also be depicted through data on size of issues. Table 6.2 presents data on new issues according to the size of the issue.

Table 6.1: Primary market

(Rs. Crore)

	Calendar year			
	2002	**2003**	**2004**	**2005**
Debt	4,549	5,284	2,383	66
Equity	2,420	2,891	33,475	30,325
Of which, IPOs	1,981	1,708	12,402	9,918
Number of IPOs	6	12	26	55
Mean IPO size	330	142	477	180
Total	6,970	8,175	35,859	30,391
Number	28	43	65	109

Source: SEBI

Table 6.2: Size-wise classification of capital raised (1993-94 to 2005-06)

Year	Total		< 5 cr.		≥ 5 cr. – < 10 cr.		≥ 10 cr. – < 50cr.		≥ 50 cr. – < 100 cr.		≥ 100 cr.	
	No.	Amount	No.	Amount	No.	Amount	No.	Amount	No.	Amount	No.	Amount
1	2	3	4	5	6	7	8	9	10	11	12	13
1993-94	1,143	24,372	–	–	–	–	–	–	–	–	–	–
1994-95	1,692	27,633	853	2,569	442	3,033	305	6,356	51	3,584	41	12,090
1995-96	1,725	20,804	1066	3,183	418	2,833	175	3,344	43	2,934	23	8,511
1996-97	882	14,276	547	1,760	215	1,473	87	1,621	14	908	19	8,465
1997-98	111	4,570	52	122	26	177	15	368	6	420	12	3,484
1998-99	58	5,587	15	35	9	63	14	297	9	581	11	4,611
1999-00	93	7,817	19	53	15	105	26	629	14	997	19	6,034
2000-01	151	6,108	66	186	25	165	34	764	8	507	18	4,486
2001-02	35	7,543	3	7	3	20	8	199	3	177	18	7,140
2002-03	26	40,703	2	6	1	8	10	255	0	0	13	3,801
2003-04	57	27,272	6	16	5	36	16	330	5	351	25	22,539
2004-05	60	28,256	2	3	5	44	17	461	11	723	25	27,025
2005-06	139	27,382	6	20	4	32	47	1,325	33	2,189	49	23,815

Source: SEBI – Handbook of Statistics on the Indian Securities Market January 2006.

The data source that their have been 139 issues in the year 2005-06 of which 49 are above 100 crores and there are 6 small issues. The amount collected by large issues above 10 crores was Rs. 27,329 crores. However, small issues (up to 10,000 crores) could collect only 56 crores. From 2003 the new issue market has increased its volume of amount issued. In 2002-03 the total amount issued was Rs. 4070 crores and in 2003-04 it became 27,272 and it has been growing steadily. In 2004-2005 the amount collected in the new issue market was Rs, 28,256 crores. This was as a result of very large issues made in the new issue market. In contrast 2004-05 the years 2005-06 had more issues in different categories starting from 10 crores. Table 6.3 depicts the number of issues which were made at par and those which were issued at a premium. It shows that from 2003-04 to 2006 there are an increasing number of equity shares being issued at a premium. The equity issues at par were very high from 1993-96 and the number of issues from 1997-98 to 2000 the trend remained the same but number of issues was very low. From 2001 the trend changed and the number of equity issues made at a premium has been increasing steadily. Trading in bonds has been not as high as in equity issues. The table shows that in 2005-06 the amount collected from bonds was nil. The Indian capital market is known for the equity issues rather than bonds. This is truly reflected from the data in Table 6.3.

Table 6.3: New issues – instrument-wise (1993-94 to 2005-06)

Year	Instrument-wise									
	Equities				CCPS		Bonds		Others	
	At par		At Premium							
	No.	Amount	No.	Amount	No.	Amount	No.	Amount	No.	Amount
1	2	3	4	5	6	7	8	9	10	11
1993-94	608	3,808	383	9,220	1	2	9	1,991	142	9,351
1994-95	942	5,529	651	12,441	7	124	0	0	135	9,538
1995-96	1,181	4,958	480	9,727	8	145	6	2,086	63	3,888
1996-97	697	3,433	148	4,412	5	75	10	5,400	29	957
1997-98	64	271	33	1,610	3	10	4	1,550	10	1,128
1998-99	20	197	20	660	3	78	10	4,450	6	202
1999-00	30	786	52	3,780	0	0	10	3,200	2	51
2000-01	84	818	54	2,408	2	142	10	2,704	1	36
2001-02	7	151	8	1,121	0	0	16	5,601	4	670
2002-03	6	143	11	1,314	0	0	8	2,600	2	13
2003-04	14	360	37	18,589	0	0	6	4,324	0	0
2004-05	6	420	49	23,968	0	0	5	3,867	0	0
2005-06	10	372	128	27,000	0	0	0	0	1	10

The relationship of the new issue market and stock market are discussed below and the next chapter gives a detailed description of the stock market.

THE RELATIONSHIP OF THE NEW ISSUE MARKET AND STOCK EXCHANGE

The New Issue Market and Stock Exchange are inter-linked and work in conjunction with each other. They cannot be described as two separate markets because of the kind of functions they perform.

Although they differ from each other in the sense that the New Issue Market deals with 'new securities' issued for the first time to the public and the stock exchange deals with those securities, which have already been issued once to the public, they are complementary in nature because of this particular function. The 'new issues' first placed with the NIM have a regular and continuous purchase and sale in the stock exchange when secondary purchases have to be made by the investor. The NIM, therefore, functions as a 'direct' link between the companies, which require a provision for funds, and the investing public. The Stock Exchange provides capital to firms 'indirectly'. The transactions relating to purchase and sale of securities provide both liquidity and marketability and do not involve firms in the transfer of stocks from one person to another. The stock exchange is, thus an important medium of transfer of resources for those shares, which have already been issued. It also plays a role in the transfer of securities with the companies whose shares are being dealt with, as the process of registration of shares must be conducted when they are transferred.

The second factor which makes the role of the NIM and Stock Exchange complementary to each other is the infrastructural facilities provided for 'sale and purchase' of securities. The NIM does not have a physical existence but the service as provided in India is taken up entirely by the brokers and commercial banks. The new issues, in the private corporate sector are subscribed and go through the application forms supplied by the brokers before the date of commencement of the issue. On the opening day of the issue these forms can also be collected from the authorized banks. The authorized bankers also undertake the function of collection of forms and receiving the amount on application. The NIM thus does not have a physical form or existence but there are agencies, which provide the facilities, which are conducive to the sale of the new issues. The stock exchange unlike the NIM provides all the facilities in the form of a market. It is a well-established organization with professional brokers, financial literature, information about companies and the daily stock exchange lists are supplied for information to investors. This is also a place where dealers of security meet regularly at an appointed time announced by the market. The Bombay Stock Exchange is well organized with proper electronic gadgets to receive information about stock prices from other parts of the country. It also gives the daily changes in prices of stocks.

Another related factor between the NIM and Stock Exchange is the relative strength and public confidence in their joint participation in the sale, purchase and transfer of securities. In India, the NIM and stock exchanges are connected to each other even at the time of the 'new issue'. The usual practice by the firms issuing securities is to register themselves on a stock exchange by applying for *listing of shares*. Listing of shares provides the firm with an added prestige and the investing public is encouraged with this service. The advantage of listing on a recognized stock exchange is that it widens the market for the investor. It provides the investor with the facility of sale of his shares thus offering him a 'market' for immediate liquidity of funds. Secondly, the working of the stock exchange and NIM provides a greater protection for the investing public as the companies applying for stock exchange registration are bound by the statutory rules and regulations of the market.

Further, the securities markets are closely connected to each other because of the sensitive nature of the movements of stock prices. Stock prices are to a great extent affected by environmental conditions such as political stability, economic and social conditions, industrial pattern, monetary and fiscal policies of the government. The long-term and short-term changes in these factors have an effect on the day-to-day changes in prices of stocks. The NIM depends on the stock exchange to find out these price movements and the general economic outlook to forecast the climate for investing and the success of new issues floated in the NIM.[1] Thus, the prices of shares in the NIM are sensitive to changes in the stock market and act and react accordingly and in the same direction and the general outlook in the market will show a "downswing" in trading activity of securities.

The next chapter discusses the operations and mechanics of trading in the stock market.

---

1. For a detailed description of similarities of NIM and Stock Exchange read Chapter-XVII, Khan, M.Y., *Indian Financial System: Theory and Practice,* Vikas Publishing House, New Delhi, 1980.

Summary

➡ The new issue market deals with new securities which have been issued for the first time. There are also called Initial Public Offerings (IPOs).

➡ The new issue market is called the Primary Market and the Stock Market which is complementary to it is called the Secondary Market.

➡ The new issue market has 3 functions. These are origination, underwriting and distribution.

➡ The new issue consists of flotation of shares through offer of sale, placement and right issues.

➡ The most important document for the new offer is the prospectus. If book building is desired a red herring prospectus should be issued.

➡ The prospectus should contain all material facts and complete disclosure for transparency.

➡ The role of the intermediaries has become very important in the new issue market. Some of the intermediaries are merchant bankers, lead manager and portfolio manager.

➡ Since 1992 many reforms were made in the new issue market. Transparency and disclosure norms have given confidence to the investor. The number of new issue has been increasing since 2002.

➡ The new issues are listed on the stock market and then traded in the secondary market.

Objective Type Questions, Answer True (T) or False (F)

(a) The new issue market is a place for purchase and sale of securities after they are issued.

(b) The most important intermediary in the new issue market is the broker.

(c) The green shoe option is for post issue stabilization of share.

(d) Sweat equity is offered free for services rendered by directors.

(e) Book building helps to establish the price of shares through the bidding process.

(f) The share application procedure differs from one company to another.

(g) Shares are allotted to all the applicants by bidding.

(h) Free pricing of shares is allowed to companies subject to the permission of SEBI.

(i) The minimum offer made to public should the 25% of each type of securities offered.

Answer: (a) F, (b) F, (c) T, (d) T, (e) T, (f) F, (g) F, (h) T, (i) T.

Multiple Choice Questions: (Tick mark (✓) the right answer)

1. Book building is for:
   (a) Fixation of price of share
   (b) Preparing a price index
   (c) Writing a book for a publisher
   (d) An auction for sale of a book

2. A merchant banker:
   (a) Buys and sells securities for a commission
   (b) Is a divisional head in a bank
   (c) Is a share holder of a company
   (d) Manages the issue of a company

3. Underwriting helps in:
   (a) Lending strength to the new issue by
   (b) Fixing a proportion of capital for firm subscription
   (c) Book building
   (d) Private placement

4. The are issues market and stock market:
   (a) Are complementary to each other
   (b) Independent of each other
   (c) Are amalgamated into one another
   (d) Trade in shares and debentures

5. In a 'category A' company there are:
   (a) New companies with less than 12 months in operation
   (b) Companies having a good track record of profits
   (c) Privately hold companies
   (d) Unlisted companies

6. A portfolio manager is:
   (a) A banker to the issue
   (b) A merchant banker
   (c) An advisor to the company on investment months
   (d) A share transfer agent

7. A registrar of a company:
   (a) Records accounting items of a company
   (b) Transfers shares from one company to another
   (c) Establishes the registered office of a company
   (d) Keeps records of investor and helps in allotment, transfer and redemption of securities

   Answer: 1 (a), 2 (d), 3 (b), 4 (a), 5 (a), 6 (c), 7 (d).

Short Answer Questions

1. Give the importance of the following terms: (i) red herring prospectus, (ii) green shoe option, (iii) prospectus.

2. How is the new issue market complimentary to the stock market?

3. Discuss the role of the promoters in issuing new capital.

4. Explain the requirement of a lead manager in new issues.

5. Discuss the role of merchant bankers in issuing capital.

6. What is the importance and procedure of 'book building'?

Long Answer Questions

1. Discuss the share application and allotment procedure in the new issue market.

2. What are the rules prescribed for a 'public offer'? When is book building necessary? What is its procedure?

3. Discuss the mechanics of floating share in the new issues market.

4. Explain the importance and role of intermediaries in the new issue market.

5. Discuss the relationship between the new issue market and the stock market.

Chapter 7

The Secondary Market

Chapter Plan

- Historical Background
- Important Stock Markets in India
    National Stock Exchange
    Bombay Stock Exchange
    OTCEI
    Inter Connected Stock Exchange
    NCDEX
- Mechanics of Security Trading in Stock Exchanges

- Membership Rules in a Stock Exchange
- Listing of Securities
- Legal Control of Stock Exchanges in India
- Developments in the Stock Market
- Depository or Paperless Trading
- Insider Trading
- Forward Trading and Badla
- Options and Derivatives, Regulation of Mutual Funds, Settlement and Clearing, Circuit Breakers

This chapter discusses the working of the stock markets which help in the secondary sale of securities. As we have seen in the last chapter that the primary market is concerned with new issues and complementary to its role is the secondary market where the industrial securities are listed and traded. In India the equity market is known for trading and not for development of business and industry. The financing of real investment and transformation of saving into investment has been in India through the commercial banks and financial institutions and development banks. The main function of the stock market in India has been to create liquidity and promote growth through trading of securities. Thus secondary market deals with financial assets.

HISTORICAL BACKGROUND

The stock market originated in the 19th century. In 1860-61, stock markets were introduced. Table 7.1 depicts the largest exchange in the world by the number of transaction that has taken place. The National Stock Exchange (NSE) and the Bombay stock exchange (BSE) are two Indian Stock Markets which occupy or dominating position in the world NSE remains at a steady position of number 3 amongst the 10 largest in the world. The BSE is 5th in world ranking. It is thus necessary that the trading is done in an orderly manner in these exchanges. In India in 1875 the Native Share and stock brokers association was formed in Bombay. This was followed by establishing Bombay Stock Exchange. Ahemdabad was formed in 1894, Calcutta exchange was formed in 1908 and Madras in 1937. The stock exchanges established in some towns before and during the First and Second World Wars did not have any technical background. The trade was mainly speculative. The Securities and Contract Regulation Act of 1956 brought about powers for the central government to regulate the stock exchanges. With this legislation every stock market was required to apply for recognition to government. There are 23 recognized stock markets in India. The most well known stock markets are the National Stock Exchange (NSE) and the Bombay Stock Exchange (BSE) the other recognized stock markets are in Ahemdabad, Bangalore, Baroda, Bhubaneshwar, Kolkata, Chennai, Cochin, Coimbatore, Delhi, Guwahati, Hyderabad, Indore, Jaipur, Kanpur, Ludhiana, Mangalore, Mumbai (Bombay Stock Exchange and National Stock Exchange and Over The Counter Exchange of India exchange of India), Patna, Pune and Rajkot.

Table 7.1: Biggest exchanges by number of transactions in 2005

Rank by number of Transactions				
	2002	2003	2004	2005
NASDAQ	1	1	1	2
NYSE	2	3	2	1
NSE	3	3	3	3
Shanghai	5	4	4	6
BSE	7	5	5	5
Korea	4	7	6	4
Taiwan	6	6	7	8
Shenzhen	8	8	8	7
Deutsche Borse	9	9	9	9
London/Euronet	12	11	10	10

Source: Economic survey, government of India publication, 2005-2006.

The Bombay Stock Exchange was the most important exchange of India. The National Stock Exchange was established in 1994 and it became the top most stock exchange of India. The regional stock markets found it difficult to survive with the entry of NSE. Most of them have become the institutional members of the NSE and BSE by setting up subsidiaries of their own. Members of such stock markets can do business both in NSE and BSE as well as their regional stock market. Some of the large stock markets in India are discussed below:

IMPORTANT STOCK MARKETS IN INDIA

In India some of the well known stock markets are the National Stock Exchange, Bombay Stock Exchange, Inter Connected Stock Exchange of India and Over the Counter Exchange of India.

National Stock Exchange (NSE)

The National Stock Exchange was incorporated in 1992 and was given recognition as a stock exchange in April 1993 and started its operations in June 1994. The objectives of the NSE was

- To establish a nation wide trading facility for all types of securities:
- To have an equal access of information for all the investor in the country through an appropriate communication network.
- To provide an efficient and transparent securities market which is fair and equal all the investors.
- To use the electronic trading system and meet international standards and benchmarks.
- To have book entry settlements as well as enable shorter settlement cycles.

The NSE operates in 3 markets segments. These are:

- Whole sale debt market segment which was begun in June 1994.
- The capital market segment which started in November 1994 and.
- Futures and options segment which started in June 2003.

Ownership and Management: NSE is owned by leading financial institutions, banks, insurance companies, and financial intermediaries. It is managed by professionals who do not trade in the stock exchange. Its Board consists of professional senior executives. The board prepares the policy of the stock market. It has executive committees which were formed under the Articles of Association and rules of NSE for different market segment to manage the working and administration of the exchange. The executive committees have members some of which may also be traders in the market. There are several committees. For example committee on trade related issues, settlement issues, and regulatory issues. The managing director and CEO is the head of the professional staff.

NSE was set up to bring about a nation wide facility of equity debentures and hybrid securities. It is a fully automated screen based trading system having a wholesale debt market and capital market segment and future option segment. The equity and derivative segment account for the maximum trading volume. The system provides full transparency of trading operations.

Wholesale Debt Market Segment: The wholesale debt market segment in NSE offers financial services of high value transactions. It facilitated transactions for institutions and banks in instruments of public sector bonds, treasury bills, government securities, units of unit trust of India, certificate of deposits, and floating yield bonds. The trading members of Wholesale Debt Market (WDM) consist of institutional members, subsidiaries of banks and body co-operates. These members should have a minimum net worth of Rs. 2 crores and an annual fees of Rs. 30 lakhs with a minimum period of membership for 5 years. The securities traded in this segment are listed at the NSE. In the wholesale debt market sector, NSE introduced trading in Rupees in Government securities and Treasury Bills, Repo is restricted from 2 to 14 days. A Repo is essentially the sale of a security but with the agreement that it will be repurchased at a later date.

Capital Market Segment: The trading members of the capital market may be either individuals, registered firms or institutional members having a minimum net worth of Rs. 75 lakhs but corporate bodies should have a minimum of Rs. 100 lakhs. The members in whole sale debt segment and capital market segment should be actively engaged in purchase and sale of securities. They should also have a background and experience of securities. Only securities listed and NSE can be traded. Trading on equity segment takes place on all days of the week accept Saturday, Sunday and holidays declared by NSE. The market timing of NSE is 9:55 AM to 15:30 hours.

Futures and Options Trading: The NSE deals in many products. It is active in the derivatives market. It trades in NIFTY Futures, NIFTY Options, individual stock options and individual stock futures. The NSE has a settlement guarantee system which is like the Chicago Futures Exchange.

Criteria for Listing of Shares: The NSE is very particular that trade is carried out in securities only after the companies are listed with it. There are strict rules for listing of shares. A new company can list its shares if it has an equity capital of more than 10 crores and its market capitalization is not less than 25 crores. The application for listing should be from a company which has at least a 3 years good past record. For existing companies entry to NSE can be gained if such a company was listed on any other recognized stock exchange for a minimum of 3 years or it should have a net worth of 50 crores. It should have paid a dividend in 2 out of last 3 financial years. The NSE started equity trading functions since November 1994. It provides listing to only those companies which have a minimum paid up capital of Rs. 10 crores.

Settlement of Securities: The NSE clears and settles its securities according to a periodic settlement cycle. The trading period begins on Wednesday and ends on Tuesday, in the following week settlement is made. For all outstations the NSE is the only stock exchange for inter bank securities. It also enters into government securities, treasury bills, public sector bonds and units. The settlement on the Retail Debt Market is on T+2 rolling basis. That is on a second working day for arriving at the settlement day all holidays are excluded. If trade takes place on Monday, it is settled by Wednesday. Clearing and settlement is based on netting of the trades in a day. In NSE trade in rolling settlement are settled on a T+2 bases. The National Securities Clearing Corporation Ltd. (NSCCL) is the clearing and settlement agencies for all deals made at the NSE.

Nation Wide Trading: The National Stock Exchange provides the service of trading securities at the same price at any stock exchange in the country. The NSE brokers can link themselves to the automated quotation system and allow brokers to buy and sell electronically. NSE Operates on National Exchange for Automated Trading (NEAT) system. Equipped with the date of the National Stock Exchange the price data will be broadcasted by Press Trust of India. The National Clearing House will be able to give information about the owner of the scrips and the number of scrips owned by a specific person.

NSE provides many services and index related services and products. Its main index is the 50 shares S&P CNX NIFTY. The index consists of 50 companies representing 25 sectors of the economy. It represents 47% of the traded value of all stocks on the National Stock Exchange in India. It is calculated as a weighted average, so the changes in the share prices of large companies have an effect. The base is defined as one thousand at the price level of November 3rd, 1995 when the market capitalization total was 20,60,000 million.

Developments in NSE: NSE has launched internet trading services since 2000. In the same year it started index futures derivatives trading. In 2001 it began trading in Index Options, and Options and

Futures on individual securities. In 2002 it launched the exchange traded funds and NSE government securities index. It also won the Wharton-Infosys Business Transformation Award in organization wide transformation category. In 2003 it's started trading in Retail Debt Market. It also started trading in Interest Rate Futures and in 2004 it began the electronic interface for listed companies. In 2005 it instituted the Futures and Options Bank NIFTY Index. In this way the NSE has continuously tried to develop new activities and it ranks amongst the largest stock markets in the world.

Bombay Stock Exchange (BSE) Mumbai

The Bombay Stock Exchange was established in 1875. It is situated in Dalal Street Mumbai. It is the oldest stock exchange in Asia.

Origin: It was started with stock brokers trading under the banyan tree opposite the town hall of Bombay. This group of stock brokers formed an association called The Native Share and Stock Brokers Association and 1875 it became of a formal stock market. In 1928 BSE was shifted to Dalal Street. It is the first stock market in India which got permanent recognition from government of India under the Securities Contract Regulation Act 1956. In 1955 BSE became screen based trading system.

Index: The BSE Sensex is the most popular value weighted index. It is composed of 30 companies with April 1979 = 100 as its base. The companies in the sensex are about one fifth of the market capitalization of BSE. BSE uses other stock indices besides the popular sensex. These indices are BSE-100 and BSE-500. Sensex was introduced in 1986 which has become the barometer of the movements of the share prices in the stock market. It is a market capitalization weighted index. It reflects the total market value of all 30 stocks from different industries. The total market value is determined by multiplying the price of the stock with the number of shares outstanding. The daily calculation of sensex is done by dividing the aggregate market value of the 30 companies in the index by a number called the index divisor. The divisor is dealing with the original base period of sensex.

Importance: BSE has been a pioneer in many areas. It was the first stock market to introduce Equity Derivatives. It introduced Free Float Index. It enabled the internet trading platform. It was the first to obtain the ISO certification for Surveillance, Clearing and Settlement. It had the facility for financial training and it was the first stock market to become electronic. It also launched the nation wide investor awareness campaign and dissemination of information through print and electronic media.

BOLT: The BSE Online Trading System (BOLT) started in March 1995 to bring about transparency and liquidity and to increase market depth. It was started to eliminate mismatches and settlement risks. It brings about dissemination of information and volumes in trade.

Investor Protection Fund: BSE has setup an investor protection fund since 1987 to help the investors against defaulting members. The fund is managed by the trustees appointed by the stock exchange. The members contribute to it. The stock market contributes 2.5% of the listing fees collected by it. The stock market also credits the interest on securities deposit kept by it with companies making a public issue. The exchange also released 5% of its surplus to this fund. The maximum amount payable to an investor from this fund in the case of default by a member is Rs. 10 lakhs. There is a defaulter committee which finds out the genuineness of the claim. It is then released by the trustees of the fund.

Investor Education and Training: BSE has been giving a lot of attention to investor education and training. It provides safety and security in the capital market mechanism to ensure investor protection. It provides financial assistance up to Rs. 1 crore to recognized investor associations for their development expenditure towards investor protection measures. It has setup an Investor Assistance centre in many cities. These centres provide redressal of investor grievances and information and other facilities to investors. BSE has trend more than 20,000 investors on the capital market mechanisms in the BSE Training Institute. It brings out many publications providing information to the investor. It has arranged seminars and lecturers for creating awareness among investors. It is associated with professional bodies. It has initiated many research projects in collaboration with the management institutes. Its websites bseindia.com provides information on capital markets. It uses audio-visual media and internet for education and training of investors.

BSE has collaborated with ZEE Interactive Learning Systems to provide knowledge, information and awareness through structured training on various aspects of the capital market to investors. The collaboration would have a pilot series of 26 episodes and it will be aired 3 times in a week. The television series would be called the BSE investor awareness program.

Corporatization and Demutualization: The Securities and Exchange Board of India (SEBI) has approved the Scheme for corporatization and demutualization of the stock exchange. The stock market would become a company limited by shares. The ownership and management of BSE Ltd. would be separate from the trading rights of the members. The initial membership will be from cardholders of BSE who will become its share holder and can also become their trading members. A trading member of BSE will also become a trading member of BSE Ltd. After the organization they will be only one class of trading members with similarity in rights. There will be uniforms standards in capital adequacy, deposits and fees. The governing board would be constituted in a manner that the trading members do not exceed one fourth of the total strength of the government board. The existing assets and reserves would be transferred from BSE to BSE Ltd. There would be at least 51% of equity shares held by public other than the share holders which have trading rights.

Over the Counter Exchange of India (OTCEI)

Formation: OTCEI is a unique experience in India. It was established in October 1990 under section 25 of the companies Act 1956. The objective of setting up the OTCEI was to have a recognized stock exchange under the securities contract regulation Act of 1956. It was to be the first screen based and automated exchange and to replace the ring system with the ring-less trading system. Its focus was to have transparency in transactions and to help new projects or existing companies to expend their activities by raising capital in a cost effective manner. It was formed through a consortium of financial institutions like UTI, ICICI Bank, IDBI, IFCI, LIC, GIC, SBI and Can Bank Financial Service Ltd.

Listing: OTCEI was setup for small and medium size companies. Companies applying to OTCEI for listing should be 'public limited' having a minimum equity capital of 30 lakhs and maximum of 25 crores. Companies with an issued capital of more than 3 crores must be listed with OTCEI. The minimum offer made to public should be 25% of the issued capital or equity shares of the face value of Rs. 20 lakhs whichever being highest. The OTCEI has trading of listed securities, permitted securities and initiated securities. Instead of brokers it has 'members' and 'dealers'. Only members can be 'sponsors' and can help in getting the shares of a company appraised by him. He performs pre issue and post issue functions and does voluntary market making. OTCEI network is nationwide. Sometimes listing can be done through 'bought out deals'. In this case a member/sponsor/merchant banker agrees to buy the entire equity from the company. He then sells the shares of the company later through offer for sale method. Through this method, listing can be done immediately without any past records of profitability. The sponsor can sell the shares at par or at a premium. He can hold the shares for a long time as there are no restrictions. He can sell them whenever he finds the market and price appropriate for the sale.

Participants: Members and dealers can both engage in voluntary market making (VMM) and additional market making but dealers cannot act as sponsors. A member of the OTCEI should have a good organizational set up. The members may be merchant banks approved by SEBI, mutual funds banking and financial institutions. A dealer should be an individual, a firm or a corporate body with a net worth of 5 lakhs and sound capital packing. Members have to pay non-refundable fees of Rs. 20 lakhs and annual subscription of Rs. 1 lakh. Dealers have to pay Rs. 6 lakhs on admission and Rs. 5000 yearly.

Market maker: A market maker provides liquidity by buying and selling securities. He analyses companies and provides information to investors. There are 3 kinds of market makers. These are compulsory market maker, additional market maker and voluntary market maker. The market makers generate investor's interest by quoting the buying and selling rates and creating a competitive environment.

Trading mechanism: The trading mechanism on OTCEI is quite different to other stock exchanges. It is based on a created tradable document called counter receipt (CR). Share certificates have to be converted to CR to begin trading. A Sale Confirmation Slip (SCS) is given to an investor when he sells the CR and the transaction is completed.

A listed company may either make a direct sale to the public or offer for sale and bought out offer. In a direct public issue a sponsor does not have to take any shares. If the sponsor takes up shares he can offer these later to the public and the price can be in accordance with the OTCEI.

If an investor purchases a security at a public offer he is issued a counter receipt which gives information about the investor as well as the company, share price, date of transaction, brokerage and total value of transactions. When an investor wishes to sell the security he has to produce the counter receipt (CR).

Transfer process: The transfer procedure is little different to other stock exchanges. The transfer and the transferee signs separate transfer deeds. The registrars of the company match the two transfer documents and execute the deal. The OTCEI has a 5 day trading cycle. As the exchange does not allow short selling or forward buying the deals are concluded at the time of confirmation.

The advantage of OTCEI is that the small and medium companies are encouraged. It is cost effective and it has nationwide trading by listing only one stock exchange. The transactions are fast and investor friendly with single window request. It is computerized and it is traded through permanent counter receipt. It has an OTC Index based at 100 since 23rd July, 1993. Only listed equities are included in the OTCEI compose it index.

One of the' over the counter exchanges' operating in U.S.A. is called National Association for Securities Dealers Automated Quotation.(NASDAQ).The majority of the shares traded in it are those of software companies.

Inter-connected Stock Exchange (ISE)

The Inter-Connected Stock Exchange of India Ltd is a National level Stock Exchange and is promoted by 15 Stock Exchanges in India. It was setup as a trading facility at regional stock market inter connected with the national market. ISE provides protection and support required for trading, clearance, settlement and risk management.

Inter-Connectivity: Inter-Connectivity of Stock Exchanges is a mechanism to enable a trader member broker of any Participating Exchange or a Dealer Trading member who is directly enrolled by ISE to deal with another Trader or Dealer through his own Local Trader Work Station. All trading members have to satisfy the capital adequacy requirements of ICSE separate from the requirements of their regional stock exchange.

Clearing: ISE has appointed ABN-Amro Bank and Vysya Bank as the Central Clearing Bank to ensure that all collection and movement of funds is centralized. The margin in the inter-connected market would be collected by directly debiting the accounts of the Traders or Dealers in the Central Clearing bank. This account at the Central Clearing Bank acts as a control account for monitoring margin collection and risk management. The funds collected during the settlement are adjusted during pay-in and pay-out of that settlement.

Listing: Only listed security can be traded on the stock exchange. The listing agreement between a company and SEBI has to be filled by providing disclosure of information and payment of listing fees. The security can be traded at all the stock markets which are inter-connected ones it is listed on a regional stock market.

National Commodity and Derivatives Exchange Limited (NCDEX)

In 2003 the NCDEX was formed as an online multi commodity exchange. It is recognized by government of India as a national level exchange in commodities. It has eight shareholders. These are Canara Bank, CRISIL, ICICI Bank Ltd., Indian Farmers Fertilizers Co-operative Ltd., and Life Insurance Corporation of India, NABARD, National Stock Exchange and Punjab National Bank. NCDEX trades in 45 different commodities it covers agricultural commodities, bullion, energy and metals. The forward market commission is the regulator for commodities exchanges in India. It provides sport prices of commodities traded on the exchange. It has participated in many pilot projects for encouraging farmers to hedge their price risk. It works in an electronic mode. It has dematerialized system for settlement of trades through National Securities Depository Ltd. and Central Depository Services Ltd.

MECHANICS OF SECURITY TRADING IN STOCK EXCHANGES

The stock market is complementary to the new issue market. However, the operations of stock market are different to that of the new issue market. While the new issue market operates through the sale of issues for the first time, trading continues everyday except on holidays and Sundays. Shares can be bought and sold bringing about liquidity in the market.

An investor must have some knowledge of how the securities markets operate. The marketing of old or new securities of the stock markets can be done only through members of the Stock Exchange.

These members are either individuals or partnership firms. An individual must use the facilities of these members for trading in securities unless he himself is a registered dealer or member of an organized stock exchange. Trading among the members of a recognised stock exchange is to be done under the statutory regulations of the stock exchange. The members carrying on business are known as *'brokers'* and can trade only on *listed securities*. These members execute customer's orders to buy and sell on the exchange and their firms receive negotiated commissions on those transactions. About one-fourth of all members of the exchange are 'specialists', so called because they specialize in 'making a market' for one or more particular kind of stock. In the process of trading in stock exchanges there is the basic need for a 'transaction' between an individual and broker. A transaction to buy and sell securities is also called 'trades'. This is to be done through selection of a broker.

Types of Securities

It is useful to know that three kinds of securities can be traded upon in the Mumbai Stock Exchange— *specified, non-specified and odd lot.* In the specified category of equity shares the criteria are that the share should be listed on the stock exchange for at least 3 years and the issued capital should not be less than Rs. 75 crores. It should have a market capitalization of two or three times. At least 20,000 shareholders should be on the dividend receiving list. It should be a growth company with shares of Rs. 4.5 crores face value and its shares should be actively traded on the Bombay Stock Exchange. The companies which do not have specified securities are in the **non-specified securities** list. The odd lot includes odd lots of shares and debentures. In India specified securities are fewer in number compared to other securities but they influence the stock market. To stabilize the market, limits have been imposed. When the stock market is on the rise being bullish or when it is bearish, limits on brokers and jobbers help in keeping the market firm and stabilized. In normal periods of time, the total outstanding purchases and sales which can be made at one point of time is Rs. 5 crores. If these have to be carried forward the limit is Rs. 3 crores. A broker's carry forward business should not exceed one-fourth of this daily transaction. 75% of his daily transaction should be in cash. This system is called the "thin track" system whereby SEBI keeps a strict vigil on brokers dealings in the stock market. A capital adequacy norm has also been suggested for individual brokers. These reforms have been brought about after recommendations were made by G.S. Patel Committee in 1995. SEBI was set up to regulate the organization and working of the stock exchanges and members operating within it. SEBI has brought about uniformity in the different stock exchanges. Nine stock exchanges were given permanent recognition. Every stock exchange is to be managed by a committee called a governing board consisting of brokers, directors, government, SEBI and public representatives.

Selection of a Broker

The selection of broker depends largely on the kind of service rendered by a particular broker as well as upon the kind of transaction that a person wishes to undertake. An individual usually prefers to select a broker who can render the following services:

Provide Information: A broker to be selected should be able to give information about the available investments. These may be in the form of capital structure of companies earnings, dividend policies, and prospects. These could also take the form of advice about taxes, portfolio planning and investment management.

Availability of Investment Literature: Secondly, a broker should be able to supply financial periodicals, prospectuses and reports. He should also prepare and analyze valuable advisory literature to educate the investor.

Appoint Competent Representatives: Brokers should have registered competent representatives who can assist customers with most of their problems. In other words, to personalize brokerage business so that the customers need not have to look after for their broker, the broker should be able to give the services at the residence or office of the investor.

The investor who is satisfied with the qualities of the broker will have to look next for a specialized broker. The second process is to find a good, reputed and established broker in the kind of deal that the investor is interested. In India, the stock exchange rules, by-laws and regulations do not prescribe any functional distinction between the members. However, brokers do establish themselves and are known for their specialization. In India, the following specialists can be contacted for trading the 'Securities' market.

Types of Brokers

Commission Broker: All brokers buy and sell securities for earning a commission. From the investor's point of view he is the most important member of the exchange because his main function and responsibility is to buy and sell stock for his customers. He acts as an agent for his customer and earns a commission for the service performed. He is an independent dealer in securities. He purchases and sells securities in his own name. He is not allowed to deal with non-members. He can either deal with a broker or another jobber.

Jobber: A jobber is a professional speculator. He works for a profit called 'turn'.

Floor broker: The floor broker buys and sells shares for other brokers on the floor of the exchange. He is an individual member, owns his own seat and receives commissions on the orders he executes. He helps other brokers when they are busy and as compensation receives a portion of the brokerage charged by the commission agent to his customer.

Taraniwalla: The Taraniwalla is also called a jobber. He makes an orderly and continuous auction in the market in the stock in which he specialises. He is a localised dealer and often handles transactions on a commission basis for other brokers who are acting for their customers. He trades in the market even for small differences in prices and help to maintain liquidity in the stock exchange.

Odd Lot Dealer: The standard trading unit for listed stocks is designated as a round lot which is usually a hundred shares. Anything less that the round lot is an odd lot is traded on the floor of the exchange because odd lots appear in odd quantities – 8 shares, 10 shares or 15, 20, 25, 27, 33 and it is impossible to match buying and selling orders in them. The specialists handle odd lots. They buy odd lots which other members wish to sell for their customers and sell odd lots which others wish to buy. If dealers buy more than they sell or sell more than they buy they can clear their position by engaging in round lot transactions. The price of the odd lot is determined by the round lot transactions. The odd lot dealer earns his profit on the difference between the price at which he buys and sells the securities. He does not rely on commission.

Budliwalla: The financier in the stock exchange is also called the Budliwalla. For giving credit facilities to the market, the budliwalla charges a fee called 'contango' or 'backwardation' charge. The budliwalla gives a fully secured loan for a short period of two to three weeks. This loan is governed according to prevailing rate of interest in the market. The Budliwalla's technique of lending is to take up delivery on the due date at the end of the clearing to those who wish to carry over their sales. These transactions help him to make a profit on the prevailing rates of interest, subject to regulations of the stock exchange.

Arbitrageur: An arbitrageur is specialist in dealing with securities in different stock exchange centres at the same time. He makes a profit by the difference in the prices prevailing in different centres of market activity. His profit depends on the ability to get the prices from different centres before other trading in the stock exchange.

Security Dealers: The purchase and sale of government securities is carried on the stock exchange by Security Dealers. Each transaction of purchase or sale has to be separately negotiated. The dealer takes risk in ready purchase and sale of securities for current requirements. The dealer has information about several kinds of government securities as well as statutory public bodies, but the presence of large investors like the LIC and commercial banks makes his role rather restricted.

Opening an Account with Broker

After a broker has been selected the investor has to place an 'order' on the broker. The broker will open an account in the name of the investor in his books. He will also ask the investor for a small sum of money called margin money as advance. In case, the investor wishes to sell his securities he will have to give his dematerialized (DEMAT) account number and trading account number.

Opening an account with the broker can also be optional on the part of the broker. Usually the broker also satisfies himself that the prospective investor has a good credit rating, that he will actually pay for the stock that he orders for purchase and that he is in a financial position to invest in securities. The broker may ask for bank reference and two or three credit references from the investor. He may also enquire from his customer, whether he is interested in stability of principal, liberal dividend income, growth issues or speculative issues. Knowledge of type of securities the customer is seeking and the degree of market risk he is willing to assume will help the broker in knowing the customer's requirements in the stock market. When the broker is satisfied about the customer's intention to trade in the market, the broker and the investor have come to an agreement. The broker then writes the name of the customers in his books and opens an account. The next step for the investor is to place an order on the broker.

Order

Brokers receive a number of different types of buying and selling orders from their customers. Brokerage varies as to the price at which the order may be filled, the time for which the order is valid, and contingencies which affect the order. The customer's specifications are strictly followed. The broker is responsible for getting the best price for his customer at the time the order is placed. The price is established independently by brokers on an auction basis through internet. The following transactions take place on orders in the stock exchange.

Types of Transactions

Long, Short, Spot Delivery, Hand Delivery, Special Delivery: When an investor buys securities, he is said to be 'long' in the issue, if he sells securities, he eliminates his long position, and when he strongly believes that an issue is overpriced and will in most likelihood fall short within the foreseeable future he may his brother to sell 'short'. A short sale involves selling an issue that one does not own and must borrow to settle the account, or does possess but does not wish to deliver. Financial institutions are not allowed to sell short. In short sales the broker buys securities for his customer to make delivery but expects the seller to buy back at a later date in order to repay the borrowed share certificate. Short selling is legal and the most obvious reasons for buying short is to cover stock in declining pricing.

Spot Delivery: Spot delivery means delivery and payment on the same day as the date of the contract or on the next day.

Hand Delivery: Hand delivery is the transaction involving delivery and payment within the time of the contract or on the date stipulated when entering into the bargain which time or date is usually not more than 14 days following the date of the contract.

Special Delivery: Special delivery is the delivery and payment exceeding 14 days following the date of the contract as specified when entering into a bargain, with a specific permission of the President or Governing Board. These transactions are conducted at the time of executing an order. The types of orders that can be made by the broker for his customer are described below:

Types of Orders

Market Orders: Market orders are instructions to a broker to buy or sell at the best price immediately available. Market orders are commonly used when trading in active stocks or when a desire to buy or sell is urgent. With this order a broker is to obtain the best price he can for his customer – that is the lowest price if it is an order to buy and highest price if it is one to sell at the time when the order is executed. This is a firm order.

Limit Orders: Limit orders instruct a broker to buy or sell as a stated price 'or better'. When a buyer or seller of stock feels that he can purchase or sell a stock at a slight advantage to himself within the next two or three days, he may place a limited order to sell at a specified price. A limit order protects the customer against paying more or selling for less than intended. A limit, therefore, specifies the maximum or minimum price the investor is willing to accept for his trade. The only risk attached to a limit order is that the investor might lose the desired purchase or sale altogether for a trifle margin. For example, if an investor instructs his broker to buy 10 shares of company, at limit price of Rs. 20/-, the market price at the time of this limit order is placed at 21. The order will 'go on' the broker's records at 20 and 'stay in' for however long the investor specifies. It cannot be executed except at 20. Indeed it may never be executed at all. On the other hand, if he wishes to sell stock which is selling at 21 in the market and he enters a limit order of 23, he runs the risk that the stock may never go up to 23 and he may not be able to sell, on the contrary the price may go down.

Stop Order: Another type of order that may be used to limit the amount of losses or to protect the amount of capital gains is called the stop order. This order is sometimes also called the "stop loss order". Stop orders are useful to both speculators and investors. Stop orders to sell can be used to sell out holdings automatically in case a major decline in the market occurs. Stop orders to buy can be used to limit possible losses on a short position. It may also be used to buy if a market price seems to indicate a major upswing in the market. Stop orders are most frequently used as a basis for selling a stock once its price reaches a certain point. Suppose that an investor owns securities in a company X whose current market price is Rs. 44/-. After an analysis he finds that the market conditions are uncertain and the price can move either way. To minimize the potential loss he stops order at Rs. 42/-. If the market price goes down his shares will sell at 42. If the market price rises, he has nothing to lose. On the contrary, if the market price rises to 50, to ensure some gain on this price rise the investor might raise the stop loss order at 48. The investor may gain if all his securities are sold at 48. Most likely he will not be able to off-load all at the price but he will ensure that no loss arises out of this transaction. He might even be expecting some profit.

The market order, limit order and the stop order are three main kinds of order. There are various other discretionary orders also in the securities market. Some examples are the Best Rate Order, Net Rate Order. These orders are executed through various trading techniques.

Kinds of Trading Activity

Firm contract: The firm contract is done through market order. It is sold and bought at the price of the day and the time at which the order is given. The price is settled immediately. Such contracts are settled through rolling settlement of T + 2. The payment and delivery is completed in 2 or 3 days. The contract note is given by the broker and the settlement is made through cheque. Since there is no involvement of paper work, it is electronically executed immediately and the shares are transferred.

Options: An 'Option' is a contract which involves the right to buy or sell securities (usually 100 shares) at specified prices within a stated time. There are various types of such contract, of which 'puts' and 'calls' are most important. A 'put' is a negotiable contract which gives the holder the right to sell a certain number of shares at a specified price within a limited time. A 'call' is the right to buy under a negotiable contract.

Example: Mr. X is an investor holding 100 shares of a certain stock selling at Rs. 60/- per share. He wishes to hold the stock but fears a decline in the price. He may purchase a 'put' which gives him the right to sell stock at Rs. 45 a share to the seller of the option. Similarly, another investor may purchase a 'call' if he wishes to buy 100 shares at the market price of Rs. 60/-. He may buy if he gets the right to buy the stock of Rs. 55 a share from the seller of the option. That investor may purchase this call who knows that the time is not opportune/appropriate but fears that the price may rise suddenly when he is waiting. The purchase of an option runs the risk of losing his entire investment in a short period of time. If the market price of the security fails to rise above the required price, the option will become worthless on its expiry. Sometimes these option transactions are combined. These are called options and are exercised through the following strategies:

- *Establishing a Spread:* A spread involves the simultaneous purchase and sale of different options of the same security. A vertical spread is the purchase of two options with the same expiry date but different striking prices. In a horizontal spread, the striking price is the same but the expiry date differs.
- *Buying a Call:* Buyers of Call look for option profits from some probable advance in the price

of specified stock with a relatively small investment compared with buying the stock outright. The maximum that can be lost is the cost of the option itself.

- *Writing Options:* A written option may be 'covered' or 'uncovered'. A covered option is written against an owned stock position. An uncovered or 'naked' option is written without owning the security. A covered option is very conservative. The income derived from the sale of a covered option offsets the decline in the value of the specified security.

- *Wash Sales:* A wash sale is a fictitious transaction in which the speculators sells the security and then buys it a higher price through another broker. This gives a misleading and incorrect position about the value of the security in the market. The price of the security in the market rises in such a misleading situation and the broker makes a profit by 'selling' or 'unloading' his security to the public. This kind of trading is considered undesirable by the stock exchange regulations and a penalty is charged for such sales.

- *Rigging the Market:* This is a technique through which the market value of securities is artificially forced up in the stock exchange. The demands of the buyers force up the price. The brokers holding large chunks of securities buy and sell to be able to widen and improve the market and gradually unload their securities. This activity interferes with the normal interplay of demand and supply functions in the stock market.

- *Cornering:* Sometimes brokers create a condition where the entire supply of particular securities is purchased by a small group of individuals. In this situation those who have dealt with 'short sales' will be 'squeezed' and will not be able to make their deliveries in time. The buyers, therefore, assume superior position and dictate terms to short sellers. This is also an unhealthy technique of trading in stock exchange.

- *Blank Transfers:* A blank transfer is one which the transferor signs the form but does not fill in the name of the transferee while transferring shares. Such a transfer facilitates speculation in securities. It involves temporary purchases and sales of securities without regulation.

Blank transfers encourage: (i) Non-payment of transfer fees of shares, (ii) Evasion of tax, and (iii) Unhealthy trading.

Non-registration of transfer of shares gives rise to non-disclosure of the name of the transferee in the books of the company. The shareholders of the company thus do not get a true picture of the members. Moreover, the 'transferor' or the 'seller' of the shares remains liable for the un-called part of a partly paid share if the name is not transferred in due course according to the procedure of the company. The stamp duty on transfer of shares also remains unpaid unless proper transfer is executed.

Due to problems associated with blank transfers, the Companies Act of 1966 has made certain changes and regulated blank transfers. Since 1st April, 1966, shares which have to be transferred must be on a prescribed form and presented to the Registrar of Companies, i.e., the prescribed authority before it is signed by the transferor for endorsement thereon of the date of presentation. It must, therefore, be delivered to the company for registration of the transfer, in case of listed securities before the first closure of Register of Members after the date of presentation and in the case of non-listed securities within two months of presentation. These measures have been taken for discouraging blank transfers. Since the depository system has been introduced in 1996 there cannot he any blank transfers. Trade has become transparent and systematized.

- *Arbitrage:* Arbitrage is a technique of making profit on stock exchange trading through difference in prices of two different markets. If advantages of price are taken between two markets in the same country it is called 'domestic arbitrage'. Sometimes arbitrage my also be between one country and another. It is called 'foreign arbitrage'. Such an advantage in prices between two countries can be taken when the currencies of both the countries can be easily converted.

Arbitrage usually equalises the price of security in different places. When the security is sold at a high price in a market, more of the supply of the security will tend to bring a fall in the price, thus neutralising the price and making it equal to the price in the cheaper market.

On placing an order, the brokers get busy through different kinds of trading activities, which may also include options and other speculations such as wash sales, rigging, cornering, blank transfers or arbitrage. The speculators in the stock market are generally represented by 'bull', 'bear', 'stag', and 'lame duck'.

Types of Speculators

Bull: A bull is a person on the stock exchange who expects a rise in the price of a certain security. A bull is also called a *'tejiwala'* because of his expectation of price rise. The usual technique followed by a bull is to *buy security without taking actual delivery* to sell it in further when the price rises. The bull raises the price in the stock market of those securities in which he deals. He is said to be on the 'long side of the market'.

If the price falls (since there is no actual delivery) the bull pays the difference at a loss. The 'bull' may thus close his deals if the price continues to fall or *carry forward* the deal to the next settlement day by paying an amount called *'contango'* charge. The bull may carry forward his deal if he expects a price rise in the future which will cover the contango charge and also bring him profit.

Thus active bulls in a stock exchange put pressure in a stock market and raise the price of the security. The increase in prices is generated through bulk purchasing of securities.

Example of Bull Transaction: A person asks his broker to buy for him 500 shares at Rs. 10 each for which there is no immediate payment. Before he pays for the shares on the date of settlement, the price of shares rises by Rs. 5 per share. He would instruct his broker to sell the shares on his behalf. The transaction may not be real. Only the difference may be paid for on the date of settlement. The Bull's profit is calculated below:

Solution:

Profit of Bull

	Rs.
500 shares sold @ Rs. 15 each	7,500
500 shares bought @ Rs. 10 each	5,000
Profit	2,500

Bear: A bear is the opposite of a bull. He expects a fall in prices always. He is popularly known as *'Mandiwalla'*. He agrees to sell for delivery, securities on a fixed date. He may of may not be in actual possession of these securities. On the due date he purchases securities at a lower price and fulfils his promise at a higher price. In this way he makes a profit on a transaction which may be 'real' or 'notional' with settlement of difference only.

The bear makes a loss if the price rises on the date of delivery. In such a situation he will have to buy at a higher price and sell at a lower rate in fulfillment of his agreement.

The share market usually shows a decline in price when 'bears' operate and sell securities not in their possession. On the date of settlement the bear has an option either to close the deal or carry it forward by an amount called the 'backwardation' charges. If the bear is able to make a profit on the settlement date it is called 'cover' because the bear buys the requisite number of shares and sells them at a specified price on the delivery date.

Example: A person expects a fall in the price of shares of a company. He may agree to sell 500 shares at Rs. 12/- each on a specified date. If before the fixed date the price of the shares has fallen to Rs. 10/- he makes a profit of Rs. 2/- per share

Solution:

Total Profit on 500 shares

	Rs.
500 shares sold @ Rs. 12 each	6,000
500 shares bought @ Rs. 10 each	5,000
Profit	1,000

Bullish and Bearish: When the price is rising and the 'bulls' are active in the market, there is buoyancy and optimism in the share market. The market in this situation is reigning 'bullish'. Where there is decline in prices, the market is said to go 'bearish'. This is followed by pessimism and decline in share market activity.

Bull Campaign and Bear Raid: The bulls begin to spread rumours in the market about rise in prices where there is an over-bought condition in the market, *i.e.,* the purchases made by the speculators exceed sales made by them. This called a *'bull campaign'*. Similarly, a *'bear raid'* is a condition when speculative made by bear speculators exceed the purchases made by them and they spread rumours to bring the price down.

Lame Duck: A bear cannot always keep his commitments because the price does not move the way he wants the shares to move. He is, therefore, said to be struggling like a *'lame duck'*.

Example: A bear may agree to sell 500 shares for Rs. 12/- each on a specified date. On the due date, he may not be able to settle his agreement for scarcity or non-availability of security in the market. When the other party insists on delivery on that date itself, the bear is said to be a *'lame duce'*.

Stag: A stag is a cautious speculator. He does not buy or sell securities but applies for shares in the new issue market just like a genuine investor on the expectation that the price of the share will soon rise and be sold for a premium. The stag shares the same approach as a bull, always expecting a rise in price. As soon as the stag receives an allotment of his shares, he sells them. He is, therefore, taking advantage in the rise in price of shares and is called *'premium hunter'*.

The stag does not always make a profit. Sometimes public response is not extraordinarily good and he may have to acquire all the shares allotted to him and he may have to sell at a lower price than he purchased it for when the stag sells at a discount he makes a loss. The market also suffers a decline. The stag is not looked upon with favour.

Hedging: Hedging is a technique applied by a person to protect himself against losses. A 'bull' agreeing to purchase a security for someone may *'hedge'* or protect himself by buying a 'put option' so that any loss that he may suffer in his transaction may be offset. Similarly, a seller can hedge against loss through 'call'.

After the order has been placed on the broker and the various instructions have been given to him so that he can execute the order in the market the broker asks his customer for a 'margin'.

Giving Margin Money to Broker

Margin: Margin is the amount of money provided by customers to the brokers who have agreed to trade their securities. It may also be called a provision to absorb any probable loss. When a customer buys on margin the customer pays only part of the margin, the broker lends the remainder. For example, if a customer purchases Rs. 10,000 market value of stocks and bonds, the customer might provide 60% margin or Rs. 6,000 and the broker would lend the margin, the securities bought become collateral for the loan and have to be left with the broker. The collateral in banks is carried in the broker's name but is the purchaser's property. He is entitled to receive dividends and to vote in the shareholders' meeting. Therefore, margin may be expressed in the following manner:

$$\text{Margin} = \frac{\text{Value of Collateral} - \text{Debit Balance}}{\text{Value of Collateral}}$$

$$\text{or} \quad \text{Margin} = \frac{\text{Equity}}{\text{Value of Collateral}}$$

Example: If X purchases 100 shares @ Rs. 100 per share or a total of Rs. 10,000 worth of stock at a margin of 70% (Rs. 7,000) and he borrows Rs. 3,000 from the broker. Assuming no commission is paid. (i) Calculate X's Margin (ii) If value of stock falls to 75 calculate X's margin (iii) If value of stock falls to Rs. 50 Calculate X's margin.

Solution:

(a) X's margin   = 7,000 (70%)

     Debit balance   = 3,000

     Equity   = Current market value (Rs. 10,000)

                          = Current debit balance (Rs. 3,000)

                          = Rs. 7,000/-

     Margin $= \dfrac{7,000}{10,000} \times 100 = 70\%$

(b) If value of stock falls to Rs. 75

     Calculate X's margin

     Debit balance   = 3,000

     Equity (7,500 – 3,000) = 4,500

$$\text{Margin} = \frac{4,500}{7,000} \times 100 = 60\%$$

(c)   If value of stock fall to Rs. 50

Calculate X's margin

Equity (5,000 – 3,000)   =   2,000

$$\text{Margin} = \frac{2,000}{5,000} \times 100 = 40\%$$

Margin System: 'Margin trading' must be distinguished from 'margin system'. Margin system is the deposit which the members have to maintain with the clearing house of the stock exchange. The deposit is a certain percentage of the value of the security which is being traded by members. In India, the margin system is applied in Mumbai, Kolkata, Ahmedabad and Delhi Stock Exchanges. In these exchanges if a member buys of sells securities marked for margin above the free limit, a specified amount per share has to be deposited with the clearing house.

Procedure of Trade in Stock Market

Trade in the stock market can be conducted by first selecting a broker, then making a deal, a contract note settlement and transfer of shares through the depository. Settlement can be for ready delivery contract, forward contracts and rolling settlement. Transfer of shares is done through clearing by the clearing house.

- ***Selection of Broker:*** The right agent or broker has to be found and the market deal best suited to the investor has to be made by the broker.

- ***Making a Deal:*** When the broker receives the margin money and is clear about the order received by him he puts the details in the 'order book'. The broker in the beginning of his career makes the deals himself. Once his business grows he employs clerks to transact his orders.

- ***Contract Note:*** The clerk takes the details of the day's transaction to the broker at the end of the working day. The broker scrutinizes all transactions of the day and prepares a *contract note* and signs it on a prescribed form. The contract note gives the details of the contract for the purchase or sale of securities. It records the number of shares, rate and date of purchase or sale. It also gives the 'brokerage' entitlement to the broker.

- ***Settlement:*** The last step is the settlement of the contract by the broker for his client. The procedure for settlement is to be made for ready delivery contracts, for forward delivery contracts and Rolling settlements.

  - ***Ready Delivery Contracts:*** A ready delivery contract is to be settled within 3 days in Kolkata Stock Exchange and 7 days at the Mumbai and Chennai Stock Exchange. A ready delivery contract is also called a 'spot' contract. The settlement under this contract can be made on the same day or during the maximum period of 7 days and there can be no *extension, or postponement* of the time of settlement. Ready delivery contracts can be settled in two ways.

- **By Actual Delivery:** The securities may be purchased or sold and the price is paid or received in full.

- **By Paying the Difference:** The securities are not actually delivered but on the settlement day the transaction is squared by paying the difference. For example, a broker may contract to sell 500 shares at Rs. 110. On the settlement day if the price falls to Rs. 105 in the stock market, he receives Rs. 5 on each share for his client, thus receiving a difference only without actual delivery. The total gain is Rs. 2,500.

- **Rolling Settlement:** Rolling Settlements are based on the total net of the issue traded during the day. The NSE (National Stock Exchange) System of settlement on T + 2 basis. T stands for the trading day. E.g., if a trade has been executed on Wednesday then it should settled after two working days i.e., Friday. An investor has to give the securities immediately when he gets the contract note. If he is buying securities then he has to pay within two days. The trading member has to pay within 48 hours.

- **Transfer of Shares:** The depository participant 'DP' has to take instruction from the investor to give delivery by transferring the shares from his beneficiary account to the pool account of the trading member to whom the shares have to be transferred. If shares are sold it is called Delivery Out and when the shares are purchased it is called Delivery In. Instruction has to be given regarding the number of shares, which are to be transferred with details of scrip and quantity to be delivered. If an investor is buying shares then the trading member has to directly credit the beneficiary account as soon as he receives a receipt from the clearing house.

Clearing House

Ready delivery contracts may be either for *cleared securities* or *non-cleared securities*. The procedure or settlement of securities will depend on the group to which the securities belong. Cleared securities must be delivered and paid for through a clearing house. In India, these clearing houses exist in five stock exchanges—Mumbai, Chennai, Kolkata, Ahmedabad and Delhi. A clearing house is used for settling contracts between buyers and sellers. The clearing house makes and receives total amounts on transactions. The buyers and sellers have only to give or receive the dues. Those securities which are active in the stock exchange are cleared through the clearing houses. Transfer deeds are delivered to the clearing house on the date of clearing. The clearing house maintains an account of the securities purchased and sold by each transaction party. The broker as a rule has to send a cheque for any balance due by him on Wednesday preceding the clearing day.

The *'non-cleared securities'* are settled by hand delivery. On the date of settlement, the selling broker delivers the contract, signed by the transferor to the purchasing broker's office. The actual settlement is done in the presence of an official of the exchange on the 'Monday' following the date of the contract. Thus the non-cleared securities are not delivered or paid for through a clearing house.

Forward Delivery Contracts: Forward dealings can be made in stock exchanges only in those securities which are placed on the forward list by an exchange. Forward delivery contracts are done with the object of making profit. The intention of the parties involved is not to take delivery or make payment on buying and selling securities. These forward delivery contracts are settled on a fixed settlement day occurring at fortnightly intervals. These contracts can be settled on agreement between the parties involved in the next settlement period. Thus date of transaction can be 'postponed' or 'carried over' or 'budla'.

On the date of settlement of forward delivery contract one of the following situations may arise: delivery of securities is actually made, transaction is reversed through a neutralizing purchase or sale, and transaction is 'carried over' to the next settlement day.

Generally the first situation rarely arises.

Time of Settlement

Forward contracts are settled over a period of six days.

- *First Day:* The memorandum slips are compared by the buying and selling brokers.
- *Second Day:* The clearance lists are submitted by the brokers to the clearing house. The members' lists indicated the balance of securities to be taken or to be delivered and the net amount due in the clearing lists. This is called the Ticked Day or Clearance Day.
- *Third Day:* The day of actual delivery of shares to clearing houses.
- *Fourth Day:* The fourth day like the third day is also for the purpose of actual delivery of shares to clearing houses.
- *Fifth Day:* The members submit their statements. Balance in statements is debited or credited to the account of the person. This is also called the 'Pay Day' or 'Account Day'. A member unable to pay his balance before noon the next day after the Pay Day is declared a 'defaulter'. If the account of the member is squared up, it is scored out.
- *Sixth Day:* Sixth day is also known as 'Settlement Day' when members receive payments from the clearing house.

'Carry Over' or 'Budla'

'Carry Over or 'Budla' is the facility of postponing a transaction till the next settlement day. This facility is available only in forward delivery contracts. Postponement of a transaction is effected by payment of an amount called 'Budla Charge'. Budla is transacted in the following manner:

First cancel existing contract by squaring it up. Cancellation is to be made at the price determined by Stock Exchange authorities.

Second prepare a new transaction through the original transaction for settlement on the next settlement day.

Third make the payment of a 'budla' charge. When a bull speculator wishes to defer his transaction, he pays a 'contango charge' to the bear speculator for carrying over of his purchase agreement to the next settlement.

When the sellers or the *bears* deals with the bull buyers they have to pay the charge called 'backwardation'.

Budla charges are a higher rate of interest.

Example of Carry Over or Budla

A. (Bull) or (Buyer) 1st January, 1990	Purchases 500 shares at Rs. 20/-	Rs. 10,000

For carry over on settlement
On 31st January, 1990

I. To sell 500 shares at Rs. 22/-
(making up price) — Rs. 11,000

Balance to be received — Rs. 1,000

II. To re-purchase 500 shares at Rs. 20/-
on next settlement in February 1990 — Rs. 10,000

Payment of contango charges 1%
per month. — Rs. 100

B. (Bear) or (Seller)
1st January, 1990 — Sells 500 shares @ Rs. 20/- — Rs. 10,000

For carry over on settlement
14 days later in February

I. To purchase 500 shares @ Rs. 22/-
Making up price — Rs. 11,000

Balance to be paid — Rs. 1,000

II. To resell 500 shares @ Rs. 20/- on the
Next settlement in the end of
February 1990 — Rs. 10,000

Payment to purchaser for carry over
Backwardation rate at 90 paise per
Month. — Rs. 90

'Budla' or 'Carry Over' transaction can be effected several times and it is important to sustain speculation. As Budla system brings about speculation, the SEBI has banned it since 1993. The Patel Committee recommended a revised carry forward system instead of Budla. In July 1995 the revised carry forward system was brought about. Permission has to be taken for carrying on Budla. These were again revised on April 1, 1996. A capital adequacy norm of 3% for individual brokers and 6% for corporate or institutional investors was imposed. The carry forward deals limiting it to 25% would also be revised if capital adequacy norms are fulfilled. Forward trading would only be allowed on stock exchanges which have screen based trading and an effective reporting and monitoring system. The SEBI would review the Budla system after every 3 months. Both SEBI and Patel Committee suggested that there should be a margin on securities kept by a broker for forward trading but SEBI suggested a gross margin whereas Patel Committee had decided a uniform 15% on the net margin and this was imposed in 1995. This margin would be recovered from the market on a weekly basis. Brokers would also be allowed to give self certification instead of monthly audits. Publishing of carry forward position of each broker for forward trading has also been revised as it gives a negative feeling to brokers' dealings. These changes have been brought about to create liquidity in the stock market as well as to bring in regulation to the trading system. Shares in the share market can be bought both *Cum-Dividend* and *Ex-Dividend*.

Cum-Dividend: Cum-Dividend is also written as *cum-div* in the stock exchange lists. It is the right acquired by the buyer of shares to receive dividend declared by the buyer on shares but not paid by the company up to the time of purchase of shares. The purchase price of cum-dividend shares usually includes the value of the dividend and, therefore, the price of such shares is higher than shares without this right. Under the Companies Act of 1956 only registered shareholders have the right to receive dividend even if the dividend declared relates to a period before acquiring shares. Therefore, the purchase price of shares is treated in the investment account and the price paid for the dividend is considered as a revenue expense.

Ex-Dividend: When shares are bought *Ex-div* or Ex-Dividend the purchase price paid for the shares does not include any dividend in it. Usually the person purchasing shares buys them ex-dividend when the company closes its share register and the buyer cannot get his name registered in time for claiming the dividend. The buyer does not acquire any right to claims on dividend on shares which he acquires Ex-Dividend.

Option dealings and forward trading are both banned in India. Option dealings are illegal and are prohibited under the Securities Contracts (Regulation) Act, 1956. Forward trading is banned under an order of the government in the Indian Stock Exchanges. To sum up, trading on Stock Exchange as described in the various steps involves the following order:

- Selection of broker.
- Opening an account with a broker.
- Placing an order with a broker.
- Preparing the contract note in the Stock Exchange.
- Settlement of contracts.
- Transfer of shares.

MEMBERSHIP RULES IN A STOCK EXCHANGE

In a Stock Exchange as we have seen earlier the contract can be made only by brokers or other registered members of the stock exchange. To be a member a person has to conform to certain rules and regulations specified under the Securities Exchange Board of India.

Eligibility of Members

The membership rules provide that the following cannot be members:

- No person shall be eligible to be elected as a member if he is less than 21 years of age.
- A person cannot be a member if he is not an Indian citizen.
- Adjudged bankrupt or proved to be insolvent or has compounded with his creditors.
- Convicted of an offence involving fraud or dishonesty.

- Engaged as principal or employee in any business other than that of securities.
- Member of any other association in India where dealings in securities are carried on.
- Director or employee of company whose principal business is that of dealing in securities.
- Lastly, firms and companies are not eligible for membership of a recognised stock exchange and individuals are ordinarily not deemed to be qualified unless they have at least two years' market experience as an apprentice or as a partner or authorized assistant or authorized clerk or their remisiers.

Rights of Members

- Members of the Exchange are entitled to work either as individual entities, or in partnership, or as representative members transacting business on the floor of the market not in their own name but in the name of the appointing members who assume the market responsibility for the business so transacted. The formation of partnerships and appointment of representative members is subject to the approval of the Governing Body.
- Members are entitled to appoint attorneys to supervise their stock exchange business. Such persons must satisfy in all respects the conditions of eligibility prescribed for membership of the Exchange and their appointment must be approved by the Governing Body.
- Active members are also entitled to appoint authorized assistants or clerks to enter into bargains in the market on their behalf and to introduce clientele business. Remisiers to bring in customers' business may also be appointed.
- Registered members are given entry to the floor of the exchange and remunerated with a share of brokerage but they are not permitted to transact any business except through the appointed members or their authorized assistants or clerks. But their appointments as well as of authorized assistants and clerks are subject to the approval of the Governing Body.

The Governing Body of a recognised Stock Exchange has wide government and administrative powers. It has the power, subject to government approval, to make, amend and suspend the operation of the rule, by-laws and regulations of the Exchange. It also has complete jurisdiction over all members and in practice, its power of management and control are almost absolute.

Rules for Members

A member of the stock exchange must have the necessary infrastructure, manpower and experience to conduct the business of purchasing and selling securities. He has to work under the rules, regulations and bye-laws of the different stock exchanges. SEBI exerts control over the members through the various rules and regulations and inspection of records and premises.

Registration of brokers: Every broker has to be registered by paying a fees and forwarding an application to the SEBI through the stock exchange where he wants to become a member. He has to maintain a high standard of integrity and protect the interest of the investor by making prompt deliveries and payments.

Maintenance of records: He has to maintain a record of his dealings through books of accounts such as Journal, ledger, cash book, bank pass book, contract notes to clients and details of contracts. These books should be maintained and a record of 5 years should be preserved.

Penalty: If a member fails to comply with the conditions of registration his membership can be cancelled or he may be penalized by the SEBI. SEBI is also empowered to inspect the books of members and in the interest of investors attend to any complaints made by them about a stock broker through investigations and audit of documents and organizational activities.

Capital adequacy norms: SEBI has also brought about control over members by insisting on capital adequacy norms. A member is required to have a lease capital and an additional capital which is related to the value of business. The base or minimum capital required by Mumbai and Kolkata Stock Exchanges is Rs. 5 lakhs. Ahmedabad and Delhi Stock Exchanges require a minimum of Rs. 3.5 lakhs from members. Other stock exchanges require Rs. 2 lakhs as a minimum deposit. One-fourth of the minimum requirements is to be maintained by the brokers in cash with the stock exchange. 25% is to be maintained as a long-term fixed deposit with a bank with a lien of the stock exchange. The rest of the 50% is to be maintained in the form of securities with a margin of at least 30%. The gross outstanding business should not be more than 12.5 times of the combined base and additional capital. For any additional business there should be additional capital. As a rule this should not be less than 8% of the gross outstanding business of the broker. The member's capital is calculated by taking into account all his assets minus non-allowable assets. A member or broker must maintain separate accounts for himself and his client but the broker can claim his charges from his client.

Code of conduct: SEBI insists that stock brokers (members) of a stock exchange should maintain a code of conduct in their dealings with other brokers of the same stock exchange. In the interest of the investors he should be disciplined and should not make false statements to fellow brokers as it is likely to jeopardise the interest of the investors.

Sub-broker: A stock broker may allow a sub-broker to act on his behalf for helping the investor in purchase or sale of securities but sub-brokers are not members of the stock exchange. A sub-broker has to pay a fee, get a recommendation letter from a broker on whose behalf he wants to act in the stock exchange. He has to pay a fee of one thousand Rupees a year for 5 years to continue his registration. After 5 years his fees will be five hundred every year. The rules applying to a stock broker also apply to a sub-broker. A sub-broker should protect the interest of the investor and maintain books of account and carry out all the legal requirement of the stock exchange. He should extent co-operation to the broker and also see that the necessary facilities and rights of investors are duly protected relating to issues of rights shares, bonus issues and dividends. To maintain a relationship with the broker he should draw out an agreement with him specifying his rights and liabilities and also that of the main broker on whose behalf he is carrying on the transactions.

LISTING OF SECURITIES

Members deal both in listed and non-listed securities. Listed securities, however, have certain advantages. When listing is granted to a company, it means that the securities are included in the official list of the stock exchange for the purpose of trading. Security listing ensures that, a company is solvent and its existence is legal. Government security is not required to be listed. Listing provides the following advantages:

Advantages of Listing on Stock Exchange

- Detailed information about the company is available.
- Information increases the activity of purchase and sale of the security of that organization.
- Continuous trade of the securities creates confidence in the value of the security.
- Convenience of sale of security leads to liquidity to the shares.
- It ensures creditworthiness and safety to the investor.
- The investor. Has a favorable impression of the company whose share is being purchased or sold.
- Listing gives collateral value in making loans and advances from banks who prefers quoted securities.

Thus, listing benefits both the investor as well as the company. Listing on stock exchange is done only when the company follows the statutory rules laid down under the Securities Exchange Board of India (SEBI).

Rules for Listing of Securities

The following statutory rules have been laid down for the listing of securities under the SEBI. A company requiring a quotation for its shares (i.e., desiring its securities to be listed) must apply in the prescribed form supported by the documentary evidence given below:

Documents to be Attached

- Copies of Memorandum and Articles of Association, Prospectus or Statement in lieu of Prospectus, Directors' Reports, Balance Sheets, and Agreement with Underwriters etc.
- Specimen copies of Share and Debenture Certificates, Letter of Allotment, Acceptance, Renunciation etc.
- Particulars regarding its capital structure.
- A statement showing the distribution of shares.
- Particulars of dividends and cash bonuses during the last ten years.
- Particulars of shares or debentures for which permission to deal is applied for.
- A brief history of the company's activities since its incorporation.

Criteria for Listing

The Stock Exchange has to direct special attention to the following particulars while scrutinizing the application:

Articles

- Whether the articles contain the following provisions:
    - A common form of transfer shall be used.
    - Fully paid shares will be free from lien.
    - Calls paid in advance may carry interest, but shall not confer a right to dividend.
    - Unclaimed dividends shall not be forfeited before the claim becomes time barred.
    - Option to call on shares shall be given only after sanction by the general meeting.
- Whether at least 49% of each class of securities issued was offered to the public for subscription through newspapers for not less than three days.
- Whether the company is of a fair size, has a broad based capital structure and there is sufficient public interest in its securities.

Listing of Agreement

After scrutiny of the application, the stock exchange authorities may, if they are satisfied, call upon the company to execute a listing agreement which contains the obligations and restrictions which listing will entail. This agreement contains 39 clauses with a number of sub-clauses. These cover various aspects of the issue of letters of allotment, share certificates, transfer of shares, information to be given to the stock exchanges regarding closure of register of members for the purpose of payment of dividend, issue of bonus and right shares and convertible debentures, holding of meetings of the board of directors for recommendation or declaration of dividend or issue of rights or bonus shares or convertible debentures, submission of copies of directors' report, annual accounts and other notices, and resolutions.

The basic purpose behind making these provisions in the listing agreement is to keep the shareholders and investors informed about the various activities which are likely to affect the share prices of such companies so that equal opportunity is provided to all concerned for buying or selling of the securities. On the basis of these details, investors are able to make investment decisions based on correct information.

The stock exchange enlisting the securities of a company for the purpose of trading insists that all applicants for shares will be treated with equal fairness in the matter of allotment. In fact, in the event of over-subscription, the stock exchange will advise the company regarding the basis for allotment of shares. It will try to ensure that applicants for large blocks of shares are not given undue preference over others.

A company whose securities are listed with a stock exchange must keep the stock exchange fully informed about the following matters which affect the company:

- to notify the stock exchange promptly of the date of the Board Meeting at which dividend will be declared;
- to forward immediately to the stock exchange copies of its annual audited accounts after they are issued;
- to notify the stock exchange of any material change in the general nature or character of the company's business.

- to notify the stock exchange of any change in the company's capital; and
- to notify the stock exchange (even before shareholders) of the issue of any new shares (right shares or otherwise) as the issue of any privileges or bonus to members.

The company must also undertake:

- not to commit a breach of any condition on the basis of which listing has been obtained;
- to notify the exchange of any occasion which will result in the redemption, cancellation or retirement of any listed securities;
- avoid as far as possible the establishment of a false market for the company's shares;
- to intimate the stock exchange of any other information necessary to enable the shareholders to appraise the company's position.

According to Section 73 of the Companies Act, 1976, if a company indicate in its prospectus that an application has been made or will be made to a recognised stock exchange for admitting the company's shares or debentures to dealings therein, such permission must be applied for within a stipulated period to time.

The Securities contracts (Regulation) Act, 1956, gives the Central Government power to compel an incorporated company to get its securities with a recognised stock exchange in accordance with the rules and regulations prescribed for the purpose. If a recognised exchange refuses to list the securities of a company, the company can file an appeal against such a decision with the government. The Act empowers the government to set aside or change the decision after giving proper opportunity to both the parties to explain their position in this regard.

Guidelines for Listing Securities

To ensure the effective working of the recognised stock exchange in the public interest, Government framed Securities Contracts (Regulation) Rules, 1957. Form time to time these Rules have been revised whenever it has been necessary to do so depending on the environmental requirements through guidelines issued by the government in this regard. In November, 1982, certain administrative guidelines governing the listing of securities on recognised stock exchanges, in relaxation of Rule-19 (2) (b) if these Rules were issued. These guidelines broadly cover the following:

Established Non-FERA Companies

According to the Act, 'Non-FERA Companies' mean (1) those companies which are incorporated in India at least ten years prior to the date of applying for the listing regulation; or companies which have a profit earning record for a continuos period of at least five years prior to the date of the listing application; and (2) in which foreign equity does not exceed 40 per cent.

The rule provides that in relation to these non-FERA companies, public offer should ordinarily be at least 49% of the issued capital of the company. But in certain cases, where there is already a considerable public shareholding in the company, a further reduction in the public offer may also be considered if the following conditions are satisfied:

- The shares are held by persons not connected with the management, their associates and associate companies.
- The shares have remained widely distributed, without undue concentration of large holdings in the hands of the shareholders on record (or their predecessors in title) for a period of at least 3 years prior to the date of the listing application.
- The number of such shareholders is at least 20 for every Rs. 1 lakh of capital held by them.

Other Established or New Non-FERA Companies

In respect of:

- Other established Non-FERA companies, that is, companies incorporated in India within ten years of the date of the listing application and in which foreign equity does not exceed 40 per cent.
- New companies without any foreign equity participation, the provisions of Rule 19 (2) (b) of the Securities Contracts (Regulation) Rules will apply. In other words, the public offer should be at least 60 per cent of the issued capital of the company in such cases.
- Notice that subscriptions by the Central Government, State Government and their agencies and public financial institutions will be counted as a part of the public offer up to a maximum extent of 11 per cent of the issued capital of the company.

Existing FERA Companies

In respect of existing companies having more than 40 per cent foreign equity and undergoing the process of becoming an Indian company under the Foreign Exchange (Regulation) Act, 1973, the public offer should be balance of the issued capital after deduction of the permissible level of foreign equity and the holding of existing Indian shareholders. However, in no case should the public offer be less than 20 per cent of the issued capital of the company.

New Companies with Foreign Equity Participation

In respect of new companies with approved foreign equity participation, the public offer should be the balance of the issued capital after deduction of the capital subscribed by the foreign participants and the Indian promoters. The following conditions should, however, be fulfilled:

- The public offer should in no case be less than $33\frac{1}{3}$ per cent of the issued capital of the company.
- The share of the Indian promoters should not be more than 40 per cent of the issued capital of the company.

New Companies with Non-Resident Indian Equity Participation

Where non-residents of Indian nationally or origin of overseas companies, partnership firms, trusts, societies and other corporate bodies, owned predominant ownership is that at least 60 per cent of the ownership of these entitles should be with non-residents of Indian nationality or origin (the criterion for determining such predominant ownership is that at least 60 per cent of the ownership of these entities should be with non-residents of Indian nationality or origin) are themselves the promoters of the company after deduction of the capital subscribed by them. However, public offer in such a case should not be less than 26% of the issued capital of the company.

If the non-resident Indian equity is 74 per cent, the public offer should be 26 per cent of the issued capital of the company.

If the non-resident Indian equity is 40 per cent, the public offer should be 60 per cent of the issued capital of the company. [There is no relaxation of Rule 19(2) (b) in this case].

If the non-resident Indian equity is 30 per cent, the public offer need not exceed 60 per cent, and the balance of 10 per cent can be allotted to friends, relatives and associates of the promoters. [Here again, there is no relaxation of Rule 19(2) (b)].

Joint Sector Companies

In a Joint sector company, the principal promoter will be a State Government and/or its agencies and the co-promoter will be a private party. The shareholding of the State Government and/or its agencies will not ordinarily be less than that of the co-promoter. In such cases, the public offer should be the balance of the issued capital of the company after deduction of the capital subscribed by the promoters and the co-promoters subject to the condition that the public offer should not normally be less than $33\frac{1}{3}$ per cent of the issued capital of the company. To illustrate, if the State Government and/or its agencies take up 26 per cent and the co-promoter takes up 25 per cent of the issued capital of the company, the balance of 49 per cent should be offered to the public.

OFFER FOR THE SALE OF EXISTING ISSUED CAPITAL

Companies can have their shares listed on recognised Stock Exchange by arranging for an offer for sale of their existing issued capital. Such an offer for sale can be combined with a fresh issue of capital also. The extent of public offer in these cases should be in conformity with the provisions detailed above.

In addition, the following conditions should also be fulfilled:

- The net worth (i.e., existing paid up equity capital plus free reserves, excluding reserves created out of revaluation of fixed assets) of the company should not be less than its existing paid up capital and the company should not have incurred a loss in each of the three years preceding the listing application.
- The offer should result in a wide distribution of shares among the general public without undue concentration of large holdings, and the number of public shareholders should be at least 20 for every Rs. 1 lakh of the public offer.
- If the share is offered at a price above its par value, the price should have been approved by the Central Government.
- The offer should set out all material particulars relating to the company and the shares offered to the public. It must be in a form approved by the Stock Exchange concerned and must comply with all conditions pertaining to public advertisement, opening and closing of subscription lists, payment of application money, disposal of applications, basis

of allotment, etc., as are applicable to a company offering fresh shares for public subscription in accordance with the listing regulations and instructions and instructions issued by the government from time to time.

LEGAL CONTROL OF STOCK EXCHANGES IN INDIA

Control is an important factor for a stock exchange where speculation takes place. The salient points of the Act are discussed below:

The Stock Exchanges in India are regulated by the Securities Contracts (Regulation) Act of February 20, 1957. It has the following features:

- Functioning of recognised stock exchanges.
- Control over the stock exchanges by Central Government.
- Regulatory measures in the working of stock exchange.
- Curbs on speculation.
- Setting up Directorate of Stock Exchanges for administration and control of stock exchanges.

Recognized Stock Exchanges: Under the Act every stock exchange must apply for recognition to the Central Government. A recognised Stock Exchange has to ensure:

- That it will follow the rules and bye-laws of Statute.
- That it will act in accordance with the conditions laid down by the Central Government failing which the Central Government may withdraw recognition.

Control by Central Government: Under the Act the Central Government has the right to control the stock exchange in the following ways:

- By requiring stock exchanges to furnish periodical returns about their affairs.
- By requiring stock exchanges to provide any explanations and information.
- By requiring the submission of the annual report.
- By exerting its right the Central Government may take an enquiry into the working of any recognised stock exchange.
- The Central Government may also order suspension of business and supersede Governing Boards of Stock Exchanges if business is conducted in violation of rules.
- The Central Government may appoint its own nominees on any stock exchange subject to a maximum limit of three.
- It may also compel companies to get themselves listed and also to comply with listing arrangements.

Regulatory Measures: Central Government regulates the working of a stock exchange in the following manner:

- It frames bye-laws regarding time of trade and hours of work in stock exchange.
- Regulation or abolition of speculative trades like options, budla and blank transfers.

- Maintenance of clearing houses.
- Frames arbitration rules to be followed during disputes.
- Fixation of brokerage fees and license.

Curbs on Speculation: The Act has made various curbs on speculation. These are:

- Making option dealings illegal.
- Making option dealings before the Act void.
- Discouraging blank transfers.

Directorate of Stock Exchanges: A Directorate of Stock Exchanges was set up in 1959. It administers and implements the bye-laws contained in the Securities Regulation Act. It is both in an advisory position as well as in a position of implementing laws. It controls the activities of the stock exchange and maintains a close watch over operations and other illegal dealings. It also gives licenses to dealers on unrecognized stock exchanges. It maintains a liaison between Government and the Stock Markets in India.

Securities Exchange Board: In 1987 as a measure of legislative reform as well as to bring in confidence among the investors, a Securities Exchange Board was set up. Every company issuing capital was to register itself with the board and abide by its rules and regulations. The securities exchange board would held in streamlining procedures regarding issue and transfer of shares. It would bring discipline among existing companies and provide information to the investors about the working of these companies.

OTC Market: As an extension to the stock market activity on 'over the trading counter' has been formed. The primary objective of an 'OTC' market is to help small or medium companies with viable projects but high risks. The capital base of the companies which would be benefited would be between 50 lakhs and 3 crores. The OTC market would extent their services to semi urban and rural areas. They would be decentralized and extend their operations beyond the frontiers of the Stock Exchange.

Capital Issues Control

Capital Issues Control Act was passed in 1947 with the objective of: (a) giving some direction to new issues so that they are in consonance with the planned period, (b) to ensure protection to investor through legal rules, regulations and controls, (c) to widen the distribution of shares to public so that there is greater participation of the investing public, (d) to incorporate within its control: (i) all companies which have made a floatation of capital in India, whether incorporated in India or abroad, and (ii) all companies registered in India whether floating capital in India or abroad. This Act has been withdrawn since 1992 and SEBI has taken over the issues.

Principal Criteria of Control

The capital issues are controlled according to the directions notified in the Act and changes made from time to time. The emphasis is on the soundness of company's capital structure, adequacy of capital and timing of issues.

Sound Capital Structure: The capital issues control maintains that every company should have a proper balance between its debt obligations and equity and preference capital. The following aspects should be considered:

- *Debt Equity Ratio:* The company should have a proper debt equity ratio and in no condition should this exceed a ratio of 2:1, Debt 100: Equity 50. While capital intensive industries may have a higher debt equity ratio, a conservative investor should not prefer a highly levered firm. Shipping companies are permitted to have a ratio of 4:1 because of their narrow capital base. A public sector company should have debt equity parity.

  Equity for calculation of debt equity ration includes irredeemable and preference shares, redeemable preference shares above 12 years redeemability share premium, reserves, free reserves and development rebate reserve.

  Debt includes redeemable preference shares below 12 years, secured and unsecured loans except short-term working capital loans such as loans against hypothecation from banks (stocks, stores, tools, raw materials) and deferred payments.

- *Bonus Issues:* Bonus issues are to be made out of free reserves, development relate reserve account and premiums collected in cash. The maximum amount of bonus issue that can be declared is to the proportion of 1:1. The pre tax profits of the company should give a return of a minimum of 10% on the increase in the capital of the company. A bonus issue can be declared only after the gap of 12 months of a previous Bonus issue. Before raising a fresh bonus issue, a residual reserve of 40% must be with the company.

- *Debenture Issue:* The debt equity ratio after the issue should be 2. The rate of interest on debentures would be according to the market forces and conditions. The debentures should not exceed 20% of gross current assets. Debentures must be redeemed after 7 years of allotment. Non-convertible debentures may be redeemed at 5% premium.

- *Preference Shares:* The cumulative convertible preference share issue is to be treated like an equity issue. The cumulative convertible (CCP) preference shares can be converted into equity shares. This conversion can take place between 3 to 5 years but they must be approved by Government. Dividend should be at least 10% until it is converted its equity. The CCP's should be converted into equity shares compulsorily. Redeemable preference shares must be redeemed between 9-12 years from the date of issue.

- *Equity Issue:* The new companies have to issue shares at par. Pricing of further issues is according to market forces. Existing unlisted companies are allowed to make a public issue upto 20% of the equity according to the price determined by the market forces. The lead manager can help in fixing the price.

- *Public Sector Bonds:* The rate of interest on tax free bonds should be 9% per annum. The rate of interest on taxable bonds should be 13% per annum. Debt equity ratio should not exceed 4:1. Past dated interest warrants on a half yearly basis are to be issued to the bond holders. Bonds must be redeemed 7 years from the date of allotment.

SEBI-Guidelines for Capital Issues

The SEBI has taken over the functions of the capital issues control. It has brought out guidelines for the issue of securities. These are given as follows:

- Underwriting of Capital Issues is mandatory to ensure success of an issue.
- The debt equity ratio of companies should be 2:1 but it is relaxed in capital intensive projects.

- The equity preference ratio should be 3:1.

- The cast of a public issue has been fixed. It cannot exceed the prescribed limit. Equity and convertible debentures up to 5 crores will consist of mandatory cost + 5%. Issues above 5 crores will be mandatory cost + 2% and non-convertible debenture up to 5 crores is mandatory cost + 2% above 5 crores = mandatory cost + 1%.

- The quota of promoters is fixed up to 25% of the paid up capital of the company.

- There is quota for employees and collaborators.

- The issue price is determined on the company's 3 year track record. The average of the Book value and earnings capitalization model is taken.

- The offer of the issue and prospectus have to be submitted to SEBI with documents, agreements, technical collaborations, full information about the company's capital structure, business activity and the interest of promoters and directors.

- The capital required by a company should be in accordance with the amount that it issues. It should maintain a proper balance and avoid evils of over and under capitalization.

- The issuing company must file the requirement of capital, the reason for the need of the company, projects for the next 5 years, interest charges and working capital charges during early period of formation and construction. The issuing company should also indicate foreign exchange requirements of the company and file its profitability projections of the project also. The issuing company is also supposed to be issuing capital because it should not rely wholly on loans and uncertain sources of capital or on projected future profits. A company issuing capital should be confident that it is raising sufficient capital and does not have to make another public issue before the completion of the project.

- When a company wishes to make an issue at premium after the initial issue, the profit on this premium should be limited. The price of right issues should be such that the profit becomes available to the company for using it productively in its projects.

- The companies can have flexible pricing if red herring prospectus has been issued. Currently most shares are issued at a premium with book building option to the investors. The issue price should, therefore, be dependent on the economic, social and political factors of the economy and the state of the capital market. The profit earning capacity of the firm should be considered. Company analysis should be made regarding its dividend record and reserves position.

- In the case of right issues the existing shareholders should be allowed to take the offer of purchase of additional shares beyond the right of purchase in proportion to their holding offered by the firm. Those shareholders who renounce their rights on right issues will not be given the facility to apply for additional issues. When right shares are not fully subscribed they can be distributed equally to the applicants, small shareholders should be given preference. If balance is still left un-issued the company can sell the shares at the market price.

- The allotment of shares had been very irregular by the issuing companies. Some shareholders allottees received their allotment and refund letters even after six months. Now, according to the regulations placed on companies, allotment of shares or refund of non-allotment of shares should be made within 30 days of receiving applications. If the amount or information is not received by the applicant within the prescribed period the issuing company is liable to pay interest with refunds or allotment letters.

Issues are timed in such a way that both large and small issues are given an equal chance throughout the year open for public subscription. This also has the advantage of spacing issues to get a good public response.

DEVELOPMENTS IN THE STOCK MARKET

The stock markets in India have several reforms with the inception of SEBI. There have been guidelines issued for the protection of the investors. Reforms have been attempted in re-organization and administrative aspects of the stock exchange. Regulations have been made on broker dealings with investors. One major development is the prohibition on insider trading. Other changes are in share transfer procedure, establishment of depositories, Bombay Online Trading System (BOLT). Establishing Over The Counter Exchange of India (OTCEI) and the setting up of National Stock Exchange. These issues are discussed briefly.

The SEBI is empowered to prosecute any company which does not comply with the act and the persons are liable to penalty and fine or imprisonment if they violate the laws. Form time to time SEBI can give directions to the officers of the company, scrutinize records and documents and conduct an investigation of books and accounts on the complaint of an investor.

Depository or Paperless Trading

The Depository Act was passed in 1996 allowing dematerializing of securities and transfer of security through electronic book entry to help in reducing settlement risks and infrastructure bottlenecks. The dematerialized securities will not have any identification numbers or distinctive numbers. The National Securities Depository Ltd., was set up in November 1996. Trading of new Initial (NSDC) public offers were to be in dematerialized form upon listing. An exclusive feature of the Indian Capital Market is that multiple depository system has been encouraged. Hence there are two Depository Services. The other depository system is also registered. It is called Central Depository Service Ltd. (CDSL). Debt instruments however, are not transferable by endorsement delivery.

Dematerialization of securities is one of the major steps for improving and modernizing market and enhancing the level of investor protection through elimination of bad deliveries and forgery of shares and expediting the transfer of shares. Long-term benefits were expected to accrue to the market through the removal of physical securities.

Usefulness of a Depository System

A depository system was required in India to eliminate physical certificates. A depository system has the following advantages:

- It eliminates risks, as this system does not have physical certificates. There are no problems regarding bad deliveries or fake certificates.
- It is an electronic form and provides transfer of securities immediately without any delay;

- A depository provides a demat account with a client identification number and a depository identification number. Therefore, there is a special identity of a member. He also has a trading account, which enables him with identity and immediate transfer.

- There is no stamp duty on transfer of securities because there is no physical transfer. It is transfer through a pass book similar to a bank;

- The DP charges a yearly charge for maintaining the member account, hence there is a reduction of paper work and transaction cost of a frequent transfers of securities.

- Investors had the problem of selling shares in Odd Lots but with the depository system even one share can be sold.

- Since a depository allows a nomination facility, shares can be easily transferred at the time of death of a participant.

- Change in address recorded with DP gets registered with all companies in which investor holds securities electronically eliminating the need to correspond with each of them separately;

- Transmission of securities is done by DP eliminating correspondence with companies;

- There is an automatic credit into demat account of shares, arising out-of bonus, split, consolidation, merger etc.

The Working of a Depository System

A depository consists of the following constituent members:

- **Depository:** This is an institution which is similar to a bank. An investor has the facilities of depositing securities or withdrawing them. He can buy and sell securities through the depository.

- **Depository Participants (DP):** A DP is an agent of a depository. He is the link between the investor and the depository. To avail the services of a depository you require to open an account with any of the depository Participant of any depository. Share brokers, banks, financing institutions and custodians can become a DP after they are registered with the SEBI.

- **Opening of an Account:** An investor has to approach a DP and fill up an account opening form and follow the Account opening procedure. He has to fill a form and give proof of Identity: Signature and photograph of investor must be authenticated by an existing demat account holder or by his banker. He has to submit some proper identification papers. He may submit a copy of a valid passport, voters ID card, driving license or PAN card with photograph. As proof of address he may submit passport, voter ID, PAN card, driving license or bank passbook. Investor should carry original documents for verification by an authorized official of the depository participant, under his signature. Further investor has to sign an agreement with DP in a depository prescribed standard format, which details investor's and DPs rights and duties. DP should provide investor with a copy of the agreement and schedule of charges for his future reference.

- *Identification Number*: The DP will open investors' account in the system and give an account number, which is also called BO ID (Beneficiary owner Identification number). An investor can have multiple accounts in the same name with the same DP and also with different DPs. It is not necessary to have any minimum balance.

- **Broker**: A. Depository/DP can be chosen by an investor to be his broker for sale and purchase of securities as well as his DP. He also has the option of having a trading account with another broker which may not be his DP.

- **Conversion of Shares into Dematerialized Form**: In order to dematerialize physical securities an investor has to fill in a DRF (Demat Request Form) which is available with the DP and submit the same along with physical certificates DRF has to be filled for each ISIN no. The investor has to surrender certificates for dematerialization to the DP (depository participant). Depository participant intimates Depository of the request through the system. He then submits the certificates to the registrar. The Registrar confirms the dematerialization request from depository. After dematerializing certificates, Registrar updates accounts and informs depository of the completion of dematerializations. Depository updates its accounts and informs the depository participant. Depository participant updates the account and informs the investor

- **Re-materialization**: If an investor is interested in getting back his securities in the physical form he has to fill in the RRF (Remat Request Form) and request his DP for re-materialization of the balances in his securities account. He has to make a request for re-materialization. Then the DP intimates the depository of the request through the system. The Depository confirms re-materialization request to the registrar. Registrar updates accounts and prints certificates. Depository updates accounts and downloads details to depository participant. Registrar dispatches certificates to investor.

- **Distinctive Numbers**: Dematerialized shares do not have any distinctive numbers. These shares are fungible, which means that all the holdings of a particular security will be identical and interchangeable.

- **Purchase and Sale of Dematerialized Shares**: The procedure for buying and selling dematerialized shares is similar to the procedure for buying and selling physical shares. The difference lies in the process of delivery (in case of sell) and receipt (in case of Purchase) of securities. If an account holder wants to purchase he will instruct the broker. The broker will receive the securities in his account on the payout day. The broker will give instruction to its DP to debit his account and credit the account of the account holder.

An account holder can give standing instruction for credit into his account so that he will not need to give Receipt Instruction every time. If an account holder once to sell his shares he will give delivery instruction to DP to debit his account and credit the broker's account. Such instruction should reach the DP's office at least 24 hours before the pay-in:

- **Transaction Statement**: The DP gives a Transaction Statement periodically, which details current balances and various transactions made through the depository account. Transaction Statement is received through the DP once in a quarter. If a transaction has been carried out during the quarter, the statement is received within fifteen days of the transaction. In case of any discrepancy in the transaction statement, the account holder must immediately contact the DP.

It can be concluded that the depositories transfer securities like a bank. There is no physical handling of shares and the procedure consists of the following steps:

- **Step 1:** Selecting a Depository.
- **Step 2:** Opening an account with a Depository Participants (DP).
- **Step 3:** Receiving an Identification Number.
- **Step 4:** Selecting a broker. The broker can also be a depository participant.
- **Step 5:** Conversion of Shares into Dematerialized Form.
- **Step 6:** Re-materialization of shares in case it is required.
- **Step 7:** Purchase and Sale of Dematerialized Shares.
- **Step 8:** Receiving a Transaction Statement.

Surveillance on Price Manipulation

SEBI introduced surveillance and enforcement measures against intermediaries' violation of laws especially in price manipulations. All exchanges have surveillance departments which co-ordinate with SEBI. SEBI has enforced information to be submitted by exchanges on daily settlement and monitoring reports. SEBI has also created a database for trading on National and Bombay Stock Exchanges. If price manipulation is detected auction proceeds may be impounded or frozen so that the manipulation cannot use it.

SEBI has introduced '*Stock Watch*' an advances software for surveillance of market activities programmed *to show movements from historical patterns* through follow ups by analyst and trained investigators to act as a deterrent to trading and price rigging.

Insider Trading

Insider trading had become an extremely sensitive and controversial subject in the stock market in India. Any person in power whether an officer or director who had access to information of private matters of the company relating to expansion programmes of the company, changes in policies, amalgamations, joint contracts, collaboration or any information about its financial results was making full use of his position to give an advantage to relatives, friends or known persons by leaking out information leading to frauds and rigging of price relating to securities. SEBI has laid down guidelines by prescribing norms handling information which may be considered sensitive. Price forecasts, changes in investment plans, knowledge of mergers and acquisitions, information about contracts are not to be disclosed. The staff and officers who have such sensitive information are to be identified in each company. Controls are to be made on the handling of sensitive information.

Insider Trading Regulations in 1992 notified by SEBI prohibited Insider trading, as it is unfair upon investors. Persons who posses price sensitive information because they have connections with a company take advantage of the situation to '*peg up*' or '*down*' prices of securities to their advantage. The TISCOs case is an example, whereby there was intense activity in trading volume of shares between October 22, 1992, and October 29, 1992, as there was insider information on poor performance of the companies working. Profits of the company had declined. After having brought trading under their control the prices of shares brought about a sharp fall in the prices from October 29 to Nov 6, 1992. Insiders had manipulated the market. When a probe took place the presence of insider information was considered to be the main problem area. As a result of this case, Insider Regulation took place in November 1992, to avoid creation of problems for small investors.

Regulation of Stock Brokers

Stock Broker and sub Brokers Regulation Act, was passed in 1992. Brokers had to have a dual registration both with SEBI and with Stock Exchange. Penal action would be taken against any broker for violation of laws. Capital adequacy norms were introduced and they were 3% for individual brokers and 6% for corporate brokers. For investor protection measures brokers have been disciplined by introducing the system of maintaining accounts for clients and brokers own account and disclosure of transaction price and brokerage separately in contract note. Audit has been made compulsory of the brokers' books and filing of auditor's report with the SEBI has been made mandatory. SEBI has also extended regulations to sub-brokers. Sub brokers have to be registered by entering into an agreement with the stock brokers from whom he seeks affiliation. Sub brokers can transact business only through stock broker with whom he is registered. If he wants to do business through more than one stock broker he has to be registered separately with each one of them.

Forward Trading and Badla

Forward trading had been in practice in India as it was the main speculative activity in stock exchange. *Futures* and *Options* were absent in the Indian Market and *Forward Trading* was called *Contracts for Clearing*. This system enables a trader to play with price expectations, transfer outstanding buy or sell positions and delivery of securities. In 1969, *Contract trading* was banned in India. However, a new system called *Badla* was developed which was used in Carry forward of trades to the settlement period. This system was regulated in 1983 by permitting trade through specified securities and carry forward facility up to 90 days.

Controls were also set on margins and limits were placed on positions. In December 1993, badla was banned. In 1995, it was reviewed by Patel Committee and SEBI reintroduced carry forward system with restrictions. 90-day limit was fixed for carry forward, trade settlements could be made in 75 days with delivery. For investor protection exchanges had to adopt a twin track trading system where transactions for delivery were separated from those that were carried forwards. Limits were also imposed on carry forwards positions and on scrip wise limits on brokers. Badla was again reviewed in 1997 by Varma Committee. SEBI increased carry forward limits of brokers to 20 crores and reduced margins from 15% to 10% and after the *Ketan Parekh* scam Badla was again banned from July 1, 2001. Trading in 246 scrips including all stocks that make of group A of Bombay Stock Exchange became *cash down* and *day trade*.

Options and Derivatives

Options can be classified as call options or put options. The National Stock Exchange (NSE) and the Bombay Stock Exchange (BSE) have launched *derivatives*. They will offer derivatives for three tenures one in the first instance each for subsequent three months. So in July Nifty call and put options can be purchased for July end, August end and September end. The last day of the contract would be the expiration date. In an options contract a premium has to be paid to enter a contract. Buyer's losses are limited to the extent of premium paid but his gains are unlimited. Seller's profits are limited to premiums received but losses are unlimited. These derivatives have been started by SEBI to bring about investor confidence to establish the market and to reduce risk. Initially options trading will be allowed only in 14 stocks. Option will not allow a person to defer settlement of sale/purchase but they will enable placing of bets on Stock Markets.

Regulation of Mutual Funds

SEBI regulates the Mutual Funds to provide portfolio disclosure and standardization of accounting procedures. It is a requirement of SEBI that Mutual Funds should have a trustee company which is separate from the asset management company and the securities of the various schemes should be kept with a custodian independent of the Mutual Fund. All Mutual Funds should be regulated with the SEBI. All schemes of UTI after 1994 have also been brought under the control of SEBI. SEBI created certain procedures of valuation norms and asset value and pricing for the Mutual Funds. The primary interest of SEBI to control Mutual Fund schemes was to protect investors from fraudulent deals.

To bring transparency in operations, SEBI directed mutual fund investors to mention their permanent account number (PAN) for investments over Rs. 50000. In case where neither the PAN no the GIR number has been allotted, the fact of non-allotment is to be mentioned in the application form. Mutual fund was prohibited from accepting any application without these details.

All mutual funds were also told to obtain a unique client code from the Bombay Stock Exchange or the National Stock Exchange for each of their existing schemes and plans.

Following the collapse of Global Trust Bank (GTB) SEBI asked all mutual funds to provide details of their investments in fixed deposits (FDs) of banks. In particular, SEBI called for specifying FD investments exceeding 25% of the total portfolio of a scheme.

To prevent mutual funds schemes from turning into portfolio management schemes, each has directed mutual funds scheme and individual plan under the schemes should have a minimum of 20 investors and no single investor should account for more than 25% of the corpus of such scheme/plan. In case of non-compliance, the schemes/plans will be wound up and investors' money redeemed at applicable NAV.

SEBI issued a new format for mutual funds to file information details of investment objective of the scheme, asset allocation pattern of the scheme, risk profile of the scheme, plans and options, name of the fund manager, name of the trustee company, performance of the scheme, expenses of the scheme i.e., (i) load structure, and (ii) recurring expenses, tax treatment for the investors (unit holders) and daily net asset value (NAV).

SEBI issued detailed guidelines regarding uniform cut-off time for calculating NAV for the purpose of subscriptions and redemption. In respect of valid applications received up to 3 p.m., the closing NAV of the next business day is be applicable for both purchases and redemption.

In case of liquid schemes, the cut-off timing for applying NAV, in case of purchase, will be closing NAV of the day immediately previous to the day on which funds are available for utilization. In case of redemption, for valid applications received up to 10:00 a.m., the previous day's closing NAV is applicable.

Regulation of Foreign Institutional Investors (FIIs)

FII's had a large volume of funds. By the nature of their trading volumes FII's can retain Control over the stock market. SEBI had to keep these FIIs under its control for protecting the investors. Hence all FIIs had to be registered with SEBI. FIIS having a capital of 100 crores could register themselves as depositories and their procedures were to be evaluated by an independent agency. FIIs are also allowed to invest in debt securities but investment in equity and debt securities should be in the ratio of 70:30. The FIIs under SEBI include Pension Funds, Mutual Funds, Asset Management Companies, Investment Trust and Charitable Institutions.

Screen Based Trading

In 1993, SEBI made the policy of bringing about screen based trading. In March 1995, BSE online trading (BOLT) was started. It brought about the facility of trading with order book functioning as an *ancillary jobber*. The order book allows retention and matching of orders and improves the price competitive character. It provides investors to place orders at prices better than the quotes presently available. Jobbers quote would be given priority as incoming orders would first be matched against jobber quote. On the remaining quantity if the best price in the market is through order book then incoming order would be matched against the order book. This is called *Price Jobber Time Priority Matching*. BOLT brought about improvement in trading of volumes of transactions.

Circuit Breakers

Circuit breakers are a check on excessive fluctuation in stock market prices. It is a control system introduced by SEBI to be effected when there is a great volatility in trading of particular scrip. If the NIFTY or SENSEX shows too much volatility on a particular day and there is a fluctuation of 10% in the index either on NIFTY or SENSEX automatically circuit breakers will apply. Trade would reopen after one hour but if after reopening the prices again fluctuate more than 5% after reopening, the trade will again stop to allow cooling off time. This helps in applying brakes to fluctuations and brings about order in the stock market. In the BSE (Bombay Stock Exchange) circuit breaker was applied on 22nd May, 2006 as trade was volatile and the stocks fell below 10%. Trading was stopped for one hour and then trading was restarted when it was expected that condition would improve.

Settlements and Clearing

Settlements in Indian Stock Exchanges have an account period of settlement. It involves netting of trades and drawing up of statements by members, amount of securities due, scrip-wise and member-wise. In a physical trade environment trades were stuck on the floor statements had to be generated and confirmed by the members but in the computerized environment information the exchange can download the information to the member at the end of the day. There is a risk involved in the absence of a clearinghouse. In 1996 after the M.S. Shoes scam (1995) involving 18 crores of Rupees, a National Securities clearing Corporation was started to guarantee all trades in NSE. Regional clearing facilities have also been provided.

Summary

➡ Stock market trading takes place through stock brokers.

➡ The important stock markets are NSE, BSE, OTCEI, ICE, there are 23 recognized stock markets in India.

➡ The different securities traded in the stock market are specified and non specified securities.

➡ The different types of brokers are commission brokers, jobber, floor brokers, 'taraniwalla', odd lot dealer, 'budliwalla', and arbitrageur.

➡ An order may be a firm order long, short spot delivery hand delivery, special delivery order.

➡ Orders are of different types. They are market orders, limit orders, stop orders.

➡ The different kinds of trading activity are establishing a spread buying a call, writing options, wash sales, market rigging, cornering, blank transfer and arbitrage.

➡ The speculators in the market are bill, bear, stag and lame duck.

➡ A contract note given the details of the transactions. It is a prescribed form giving details of number of shares sold and price of the shares.

➡ In a rolling settlement of NSE, trade is settle in T + 2 days.

➡ Share cannot be traded unless they are listed on a stock exchange.

➡ There are many developments in the stock market. These are prohibition of insider trading, depository or paperless trading, regulation of stock brokers, introduction of options futures and other devolves regulation of mutual funds and foreign in situational investors, reserve based trading, circuits brokers, credit rating and settlement and dealing.

Objective Type Questions, Answer True (T) or False (F)

(a) NSE is the oldest and most organized stock market in India.

(b) Bombay Stock Exchange ranks 5th in the world among the largest stock markets.

(c) A commission brokers buys and sells securities for earning a commission.

(d) A jobber works to make profits.

(e) Spot delivery means shares received at a particular time in a particular stock market.

(f) Arbitrage makes profits by trading in two different markets.

(g) A bull expects to make a profit when prices fall.

(h) A bear is a 'tejiwalla' who expects to buy securities in a rising market.

(i) Securities are listed because it is mandatory for longs companies interested in trading their securities.

(j) A depository systems eliminates physical certificates.

Answer: (a) F, (b) T, (c) T, (d) T, (e) F, (f) T, (g) F, (h) F, (i) T, (j) T.

Multiple Choice Questions (Tick mark (✓) the right answer)

1. The sensex consists of:
   - (a) 30 stocks
   - (b) 25 stocks
   - (c) 50 stocks
   - (d) 100 stocks

2. The base period of NIFTY is:
   - (a) 1992
   - (b) 1978
   - (c) 1987
   - (d) 1995

3. Listing is mandatory for:
   - (a) Trading in stock markets
   - (b) Making a new public issue
   - (c) Trading in international markets
   - (d) Trading in interconnected stock exchange of India

4. A Depository is:
   - (a) An electronic transfer through dematerialization
   - (b) A fixed deposit in a bank
   - (c) A transfer of physical securities
   - (d) Surveillance on price manipulation

5. Stock market index:
   - (a) Shows trends in the market
   - (b) Provides weights to shares
   - (c) Show the volume of stock in the market
   - (d) Depicts transfer of shares

6. A lame duck:
   - (a) Is a bull who does not keep his promise
   - (b) Is a bear who cannot keep his commitments
   - (c) It is a cautious speculator
   - (d) It is a premium hunter

   Answer: 1 (a), 2 (d), 3 (a), 4 (a), 5 (a), 6 (b).

Short Answer Questions

1. Write notes on the following
   (a) bull, (b) bear, (c) stag, (d) margin, (e) wash sales.
2. How should a broker be selected by an investor?
3. How has SEBI regulated, (a) stock brokers, and (b) insider trading in stock markets.
4. Write notes on:
   (a) OTCEI, (b) BOLT, (c) NSE

Long Answer Questions

1. What is a depository? Discuss the procedure for dematerialize action of shares.
2. Discuss the types of brokers in the stock markets.
3. What are the different kinds of orders that an investors can give to his proper?
4. How is security traded on National Stock Exchange?
5. Discuss the developments in the stock markets after the new economic reforms in 1991.
6. Discuss the procedure of buying and selling securities on a stock market.

Chapter 8

Financial Markets for Short Term Funds

Chapter Plan

- Call Money Market
- Treasury Bills Market
- Commercial Bills Market
- Markets for Commercial Papers and Certificate of Deposits

- The Discount Market
- Market for Financial Guarantees
- Government (Gift-edged) Securities Market

INTRODUCTION

The last chapter was a discussion on the industrial securities market where as chapter six gave an insight into the new issue market. This chapter discusses the other important markets like the call money market, treasury bills market, commercial bills market, markets for commercial paper and certificate of deposits, the discount market, market for financial guarantees and government (gift-edged) securities market.

CALL MONEY MARKET

The call money market is for short-term funds which have a maturity period up to 1 year. It brings about liquidity and influences the level of interest rates in the economy. The main instruments in this market are call money, certificate of deposits, repurchase agreements (repos), commercial bills, commercial papers and inter corporate funds. The money market is directory regulated by the RBI. The objectives of money market are the following:

- To provide a mechanism for equilibrium in the demand and supply of funds and to even out any surplus or deficiency in short term funds.
- To be a central point for the Reserve Bank of India to influence liquidity in the economy.
- To provide short term funds at reasonable rates of interest.

The participants in the call money market are:

- Scheduled and non-scheduled Indian commercial banks and foreign banks.
- State, district and urban co-operative banks.
- Discount and Finance House of India.
- Securities Trading Corporation of India (STCI).

The financial institutions like LIC, GIC and UTI also participates in the call money market by offering loans to banks. The development banks like IDBI, ICICI and IFCI indirectly provided facilities in the call money market. It was mainly operated by brokers until 1970, when they were prohibited by the RBI to operate in the call market.

The call money markets are located in India in those towns were there is a high volume of business. Some of these cities are Mumbai, Kolkata, Chennai, Delhi and Ahmedabad. The highest volume of trading takes place in Mumbai and Kolkata. The interest rates in a call money market are very sensitive to the demand on funds. The rates of interest can shift hourly, daily or weekly. The past experience has shown that in India, Mumbai has had the lowest interest rate whereas it has been highest in Kolkata. In USA and UK there are separate call money markets but in India they are associated with the presence of a stock exchange.

Organized and Un-Organized Money Market

The money market was strictly regulated and the number of participants was very small. The total transactions in this market were between 3-4% of bank deposits. The market had very few instruments and most of the transactions were limited to money at short notice of 14 days duration, inter bank loans, reports and bill discounting. The money market was divided into organized and un-organized sector. The un-organized sector had high interest rates which were not market related but the organized sector was based on market rates. The un-organized sector was in the hands of money lenders who charged exorbitant rates of interest and dominated the money market. The unorganized sector provided easy funds but difficult return rates and often cheated their clients. This was due to the fact that the organized money market had several restrictions on borrowing. It was controlled through the RBI. When RBI followed a restrictive monetary policy, the call money market would become active and they would be a heavy demand for funds. When RBI followed a liberal policy the requirement for funds immediately was from banks borrowing from the call money market. The organized call money market loans were limited to the bill market, they were useful for inter bank uses, they were used for dealing in stock exchange in bullion market and individuals used it for trade to save interest on cash credits and overdrafts. Out of these for uses the inter bank loans were most significant in India. They were useful because banks borrowed from one another to meet a spurt of high demand for funds, large payments and to maintain liquidity with the RBI.

In 1985 a committee was formed to review the working of the monetary system in India under the chairman S. Chakravarty. It brought out the need for developing money market instruments in India. In 1987 the Vaghul Committee was formed to review the money market. It recommended changes and improvement for developing the money market. As a result of these two committees the following changes were brought about:

- *Interest rate ceilings withdrawn:* The ceiling on inter bank call money and inter term money was withdrawn. The rediscounting of commercial bills and inter bank participations without risks were also withdrawn in 1989 as interest rate is very high.

- *Changes in money market instruments:* The 182 days Treasury bills were introduced in 1986, certificates of deposits were started in 1989 and commercial papers were begun in 1990 and RBI repos were introduced in 1992.

- *New participants:* The primary and satellite dealers were appointed. The Discount and Finance House of India was setup as an apex body jointly with public sector banks and financial institutions. It was also made a participant in the money market. STCI was also set up as a discount house.

- *Relaxation in restrictions:* There were many relaxations in subscription norms and in money market instruments. The interest rates were to be based on demand and supply mechanism. Therefore it would be market related and there would be a switch from cash credits system to loans based system. There was to be a removal of restrictions in bank guarantees in commercial papers.

- *Inter-linkages:* The call money market would be linked with the foreign exchange market through the market based exchange rate system.

- *Liberalization:* RBI permitted transfer of customer account from one bank to another without any restrictions or objections. It liberalized the credit policy of banks. The credit authorization scheme was renamed and called credit monitoring arrangement. Banks were allowed to sanction working capital requirement up to Rs. 5 crores. Private sector companies were allowed to inter the market to issue commercial papers. If it got a credit rating from Credit Rating and Information Services of India Ltd. (ICRA).

There have been many developments in the money market since 1991. Changes have been brought about in existing money market instruments. New instruments have been adopted and the money market has been developed in many ways to increase liquidity in the market. Primary and satellite dealers have been appointed to improve the lending and borrowing situation in the market. The banks and primary dealers were allowed to lend and borrow in the market whereas other participants could only be lenders in the market. From 2002 primary dealers can lend in the call money market up to 25% of their net owned assets. The primary dealers would have to work within prudential norms.

In 1997 the Narsimham Committee recommended the reforms in the call money market for its development. The call money market became an inter bank market with primary dealers and the repo market was developed. This reform was made in a phased manner between 1999 and 2005. The following developments were brought about in the call money market after this reform was initiated:

- *Introduction of rupee derivatives:* New instruments like interest rate swaps which are forward agreements were introduced in 1999 for providing the participants to hedge their risk.

- *Benchmark rate:* The rupee benchmark was made through the Mumbai inter bank forward offered rate in 2005. This is called MIFOR. It would be reviewed after 6 months to find out its usefulness. However, MIFOR would be used for forex transactions if approved by the RBI.

- *Growth of collateral market:* In 2005 the RBI encouraged a collateral market for bringing out transparency, price discovery and risk management facilities.

- *Liquidity adjustment facility:* In 2000 the liquidity adjustment facility was introduced with the objective of allowing the RBI to adjust market liquidity daily through repos and reverse repo auctions of different frequencies. This helps in stable movement of call money and also brings about order in market commissions.

- *Electronic negotiated quote:* In May 2005 the technical group on money market made a recommendation that all transactions should be on an electronic negotiated quote systems to make the dealing transparence.

- *Inter bank transactions:* The call money market was purposed to be developed into inter bank lending and borrowing market in 2005.

- *Repos:* Repos are money market instruments which help in short term borrowing and lending through sale and purchases in debt instruments. In a repo transaction the holder of securities sells it to the investor with an agreement to repurchase it at a pre determined rate and debt. The 'forward' price is different from the 'spot' price and the difference between the two is adjusted through repo interest and coupon earned on the securities. Due to miss-use by banks the repos were abolished in government dated securities and approved securities in 1992. Repos in Treasury bill were however exempted from prohibition.

These reforms helped in making the money market more organized but it could not reduce the volatility in the market. The changes in the money market have improved market conditions but it requires further development to make it an integrated market for bringing about equilibrium in short term funds.

TREASURY BILLS MARKET

A Treasury bill market deals with short term borrowing instruments of government. It is a promissory note or a finance bill. It is highly liquid and it is guaranteed by government for repayment. It is an instrument of short term borrowing issued by government of India. Up-to 1987 there were only two types of Treasury bills. These were issued for 91 days and 182 days durations. In 1987 the Chakravarty and Vaghul Committees made recommendations for institutional development and introduction of new instruments.

The Treasury bill rate is fixed by RBI and this rate is revised constantly by it according to the requirements of the market. The interest rate at which the RBI sells the bills is very low. They are useful because they do not have any risk of default, they have high liquidity and their transaction cost is low.

In India there were mainly two types of Treasury bills. These are ordinary and ad-hoc bills. The ordinary Treasury bills are issued to public by the RBI to provide the government to need its temporary requirements of finance. The ad-hoc Treasury bills were created in favour of the RBI. Both these bills had a maturity of 91 days. The ad-hoc bills were very useful to government but they started being used by government as a permanent measure for keeping their cash balance positive. In 1994 the ad-hoc were discontinued but in a phase manner.

The participants of the call money market are limited. The RBI, LIC and UTI were participants until 1987 and in 1994 primary dealers were introduced in the primary and secondary segments to play an important role in government securities. The different Treasury bills are given in brief.

91 days Treasury bill: The 91 days Treasury bill was issued in 1965 at a discount rate between 2.5% and 4.6% per year. The yield was low and RBI rediscounted these bills creating disorder in the market by marked fluctuations in the outstanding and trading volume of Treasury bills. In 1986 and early rediscounting fees was imposed if banks rediscounted their Treasury bills as early as 14 days. Through this method fluctuations in trading were reduced in the first week.

182 days Treasury bill: The 182 days Treasury bill was introduced in 1986. Such bills were sold in the market through monthly auctions for short term liquidity. This instrument was specially created for meeting the statutory liquidity requirement. This bill had higher yield than the 91 days bill. The Discount and Finance House of India (DFHI) actively participated in the primary auctions of this bill and traded in it in the secondary market. The RBI provided the DFHI the refinance facility with the limit of 90% of the phase value its holdings in this bill. In the secondary market the DFHI quoted two way prices by giving the daily bid for buying and an offer for sale price. It became an active trading participant through the bid and offer prices quoted and continuous trading in a market. Individual investors approached DFHI and not the RBI for refinance. Banks entered in raising funds from DFHI in tight money situations with buy back arrangements for return to DFHI in easy money conditions. These Treasury bills were transacted through the subsidiary general ledger maintained by RBI for its investors. If they did not have the facility of subsidiary general ledger the Treasury bills would be held by the DFHI on behalf of the investors. On the due date the DFHI paid the investors the amount of the bill. The participants of these bills was limited to RBI, banks, LIC, UTI, GIC, NABARD, IDBI, IFCI and ICICI. This was enlarged to include corporate and other entities. In 1992 the 182 days bills was abolished and this was again reintroduced by RBI in 1998. This bill was again made active and was auctioned after every 14 days and it included the Foreign Institutional Investors (FIIs) to purchase and sell Treasury bills to absorb short term funds. In 1992 the 364 days Treasury bills were introduced.

364 days Treasury bill: The 364 days Treasury bills were issued every forth-night. The bills were attractive and safe as well as liquid offering short term investment opportunities to banks and financial institutions. The RBI auctions these bills in Mumbai and they cannot be rediscounted with it. The yield on 364 days Treasury bill was higher than the 91 days bill and it has been popular with be investors.

14 days Treasury bill: The short term Treasury bills of 14 days duration was introduced in 1997. This bill was to be issued at a discount rate which would be equal to the interest rate on Ways and Means Advances to central government. These bills were to provide liquidity as well as investment of surplus funds of the state government foreign banks and other specified institutions with which the RBI had an arrangement. The bills were non-transferable and the minimum amount of rupees 1 lakh could be issued in a book form. The bills could be purchased in multiples of 1 lakh. The repayment of these bills was 14 days after its issue and could be renewed at the expiry date. It could also be rediscounted at 50 basic points higher than the discount rate. As soon as they are discounted they would be extinguished.

The Treasury bills market is limited in India. The market is not as active as it is in United Kingdom (UK). In UK banks actively engaged in Treasury bills and sell bills to discount housing for settling inter bank transactions and government receipts and payments. Discount houses hold Treasury bills because they can offer security for obtaining loans from banks for short period. They also conduct business dealings in Treasury bills with foreign banks and with clients holding Treasury bills. The banks buy Treasury bills from discount houses when part of the maturity has completed. In India such facility or liquidity is not present the banks have to buy Treasury bills on their account and after their purchase they have to hold it up-to the maturity period. The low rates of return on investment in Treasury bills dissuade banks to operate in them. The market despite development in the post 1991 period is still small. However, due to suggestions of important committees like Chakravarty and Vaghul Committee recommendations there have been changes in the market. Yields have become more attractive and new Treasury bill instruments have been introduced. The ad-hoc Treasury bills have been discontinued and the RBI continues to play an important role in the Treasury bill market. With the introduction of the auction system the interest rates of Treasury bills are determined by the market. With all these limitations the bill market is attractive because of the absence of the risk of default and high liquidity.

COMMERCIAL BILLS MARKET

A bill of exchange is the financial instrument which is traded in the commercial bills market. It is an instrument under the negotiable instruments act of 1981. It is an instrument in writing, with an unconditional order, signed by the writer directing another person to pay a sum of money to the order of a certain person or the bearer of the instrument. Since it is a negotiable instrument it can be transferred from one person to another. It is highly liquid in nature. It is the self liquidating paper and has legal safeguards. The bills of exchange can be classified into demand and usance bills, D/A and D/B bills, inland and foreign bills, accommodation and supply bills. As soon as a sale has been made the funds are made available. When sale has been made the buyer accepts a bill and promises to pay at later date. The seller can ensure payment immediately by discounting the bill. This means that he can release the payment by paying a discount rate to the bank. On the maturity date the banker can claim the amount on the bill from the person who accepts the bill. The bills of exchange are for short term accommodation and the maturity period is usually between 3 to 6 months. The different bills can be described in the following manner:

- *Demand and Usance Bills:* A demand bill is one in which no time of payment is specified. It is payable immediately at sight. Usance is a time bill. In this bill the time period is specified for its release.

- *DA and DP Bills:* A DA bill becomes a clean bill after delivery of the documents. In A DP bill document of title are held by the banker as soon as the bill is accepted by the drawee until the maturity of the bill of exchange.

- *Inland and Foreign Bills:* Bills which are drawn and are payable in India upon a person resident in India are called inland bills. Foreign bills are drawn outside India. They may be payable in or outside India and drawn upon a person resident in India.

- *Accommodation and Supply Bills:* These are also called 'kite' or 'wind mill' because there is no genuine transactions. A person accepts the bill to help another person to meet his financial obligations. Such bills are prepared when a supplier required funds for supplying goods to government. Government does not except the bill which is not a company by documents of title to goods but bank advances can be received through accommodation bills.

- *Hundi:* The Indian trade bill is called is hundi. It has other names such as Shahjog, Namjog, Dekharanjog, Farmainjog, Dhanijog, Jokhani and Darshani.

In India the bill market is small and under developed. In UK there are specialized agencies which are 'acceptance houses'. Banks also accept bills. In USA banks are the acceptance agencies and they keep a record of entrepreneur's credibility. In India there are no specialized agencies for accepting bills. Banks also are not interested in discounting bills. The date on which the payment is due is called the maturity date. Bills do not have any fixed maturity date but they are short term and can be for 30, 60, 90 and 120 days. In India the hundis have 90 days maturity period. This service is required by exporters and importers. While exporters make a 90 days bill, import traders are able to get bills drawn for 60 days from other countries.

In India banks usually accept bills for conversion of cash credit of overdraft of their customers. These bills are strictly not genuine. Banks give loans on the security of bills if the customer is credit worthy. However, there is no rediscounting facility between banks who need funds and those who have excess funds. The RBI in 1974 involved financial institutions like LIC, UTI, GIC and ICICI for rediscounting genuine bills of commercial banks but bill financing is not significant in India.

The bill market rates in India are those which are prevailing in the short term money market but there are two types of rates. One interest rate is to suit the organized sector and the other which is prevalent in the un-organized sector. The un-organized sector was dependant on the Bazar bill rate. The organized sector had the bank rate, SBI hundi rate, commercial bills rate and SBI discount rate. The RBI rediscounted bills at the bank rate. The bill rate also called the bills finance rate was fixed by RBI for the commercial banks to be able to discount bills and the SBI rate is the discounting facility offered by the State bank of India. RBI prescribed ceiling for the rate of discount of bills but this ceiling was withdrawn in 1989.

The RBI tried to develop the bill market by introducing a scheme in 1952 and another scheme in 1970. In 1952 it provided the banks to give the RBI the bills as a security and take a loan on it but there was no rediscounting facility. In 1970 rediscounting scheme was introduced. These schemes were made to cover only genuine bills which could show a trade of exchange of goods for cash. The bill was required to be accepted by the purchaser's bank in a licensed scheduled bank. If it was an un-licensed bank the bill had to be endorsed by a licensed scheduled bank. These bills would have a maturity period of 90 days and in exceptional circumstances 120 days would be allowed. The minimum amount of single bill would be 5,000. Since 1971 these bills were not to be deposited with the RBI. They could be retained by banks themselves. RBI would refinance banks. From May 1990, many new institutions have been permitted to rediscount commercial bills. Changes have taken place since 1991. The number of foreign bills has been higher than inland bills.

In India, besides the short term bill market there is a long term bill market. This was introduced by IDBI in 1965 under the bill rediscounting scheme. The bills have been created through the sale of machinery on deferred payment. This bill was to enable manufacturers of machinery to get the total value of the machine sold by them immediately. Banks and other finance institutions discount these bills or rediscount them from banks and other institutions. The maturity of these bills is for five years extendable to 7 years. The rate of discounting is fixed according to the maturity period of the bill. The long term bill market is more reasonable than the short term bill.

MARKET FOR COMMERCIAL PAPERS AND CERTIFICATE OF DEPOSITS

The market for commercial papers and Certificate of deposits is a new concept in India. They were introduced in 1990.

Commercial Papers (CPs)

The commercial papers are unsecured, short term negotiable instruments with a fixed maturity. Corporate organizations find these papers useful for raising short term debt. With these papers securitization is adopted and the intermediation of banks is removed. At the time of issue of these papers discount is provided on the face value of the paper. The person issuing these papers promises the buyer a fixed amount of money at a future date without pledging any assets. The only guarantee offered by him is his credit worthiness, earnings capacity and his liquidity. It is not necessary to have any trading transaction or sale of goods. A corporate organization can directly issue commercial papers to investors. This direct dealing between a company and an investor is called a *'direct paper'*. The commercial paper can be indirectly issued through a bank or through a dealer. This is called *'dealer paper'*. The dealer buys at a lower price and sells at a higher price and gets a commission.

A commercial paper is very useful because there is no documentation required. The issuer and the investor find it flexible and useful because the maturity period can be designed. It is unsecured and highly liquid. It can be transferred from one person to another as it is negotiable instrument.

The well known participants in this market are banks, mutual funds, UTI, LIC, GIC, DFHI and Corporate organizations. These are useful for dealing by those institutions which have a positive cash flow and require opportunities for short term investment. Commercial papers are also useful for corporate organizations as there able to raise short term funds for their requirements without any difficulties. Through this process the intermediations of banks is not required as securitization can be adopted. In India this is a relatively new instrument it was introduced in 1990 with the objective of providing short term borrowings.

A company is allowed to issue commercial papers. Individuals, non-resident Indians, banks, companies and registered organizations can invest in commercial papers. Non-resident Indians cannot transfer or repatriate the commercial papers issue to them. The commercial papers have which maturity period of 30 days. There are issued at a discount on the face value and their rate is determined through the interplay of market process.

Certificate of Deposits (CDs)

This certificate of deposits is securitized short term deposits issued by banks at high interest rates during period of low liquidity. The liquidity gap is met by banks by issuing CDs for short term periods of time. Since the interest rate is attractive CDs are usually kept till maturity. CDs are becoming popular because since 2004 there has been a reduction on their stamp duty, withdrawal of tax reduction of source, opportunity for trading in the stock market and requirement of closure of deposits only at maturity. In India CDs are being issued by banks either directly or through dealers. A CD is negotiable short term instrument in bearer form. They are a part of bank deposits and are issued for 90 days but the maturity period can vary according to the requirements of corporate organizations. The minimum issue of CDs to single investor is rupees 10 lakhs and can be further issued in multiple of Rs. 5 lakhs. They can issue at a discount on the face value and they are transferable after a lock in period of 30 days from the time of issue. The CDs market is larger than the CPs market. The rate of CDs is determined by the market. They are used for interim requirements and for financing current transactions.

THE DISCOUNT MARKET

The discount market comprises of institutions which provide liquidity in a country. If liquidity is managed efficiently loses in business are reduced to a minimum. The central bank of a country brings about stability by lending to banks and other institutions. In India the RBI provides liquidity through discounting and refinancing of financial papers in emergencies to commercial banks in India and maintains stability. Most countries have specialized institutions such as discount houses to perform the function of discounting and bringing about liquidity. In India the Discount and Finance House of India and Securities Trading Corporation of India were formed to make the money market active by allowing quick liquidity support.

Discount and Finance House of India (DFHI)

To strengthen the infrastructure of fixed income securities market in India, Discount and Finance House of India (DFHI) was incorporated by Reserve Bank of India (RBI) along with other Public Sector Banks (PSBs) and All-India Financial Institutions (FIs) under the Companies Act 1956, on March 8, 1988. The company started its operation with an initial paid up capital of Rs 100 crore (RBI—Rs. 51 crore, PSBs—Rs. 33 crore and FIs—Rs. 16 crore) in April 1998. To broad base the activity of the company, the paid up capital was subsequently increased to Rs. 150 crore in 1989-90 and further to Rs. 200 crore during 1991-92.

DFHI has been actively trading in all the money market instruments (viz. call/notice/term money, commercial bills, treasury bills, certificate of deposit and commercial paper) and its business turnover has grown progressively over the years. From the year 1992-93, DFHI has been authorized to deal in Dated Government Securities. The company was accredited as a Primary Dealer (PD) in February 1996. Its operations have increased significantly especially in Treasury Bills and Dated Government Securities.

In UK discount houses are public limited companies. They are not connected with any financial institutions. Their main objective is to lend and borrow funds as brokers, commission agents or jobbers for earning commissions. They operate in primary and secondary markets as well as in the short term government securities market. In India the DFHI was setup as a follow up to the recommendations of the Chore Committee, Vaghul Committee and Chakravarty Committee. It was to be sponsored by commercial banks, LIC, UTI, GIC and with IDBI, ICICI and SFCs. The RBI would provide clear instructions, but the institutions would be run on commercial lines.

DFHI has provided liquidity both two the primary and secondary markets. It discounts commercial bills and treasury bills. It used to provide two way quotes everyday. It functioned mainly as a broker but after it became a PD it has become a market maker and takes large positions. It has played an important role in money market instruments in the secondary market. It has also provided liquidity to treasury bills in the secondary market. Companies have invested their short term surpluses and have released them for short term liquidity. DFHI has also tried to equalize the short term surpluses and deficiencies of financial institutions, banks and non-bank public and private sector institutions. RBI has extended full support to DFHI by refinancing against the collateral of instruments in which it deals with. The DFHI has been able to make a mark in the money market and its turnover has been steadily increasing in all it's activities in the money market.

Securities Trading Corporation of India (STCI)

The STCI had the objective of bringing about liquidity but its focus was different to that of the DFHI. It was promoted in 1994 with the main objective of providing an environment in the secondary market to support debt instruments. It was started with a paid of capital of rupees 500 crores. The RBI had a share holding of 51% and the other half was contributed by LIC and banks. The STCI was appointed as a primary dealer is government securities its main function was to take up the whole or part of the auctions of government securities. It was to be a market maker at the long end of the market. It was to developed a market for the auctioned government securities and provide them to the investors. The RBI supports the STCI by providing it with refinancing facility.

The main difference between DFHI and STCI may be explained in the following discussion:

- *Focus*: STCI was setup to deal with long dated government securities but DFHI was to play role with Treasury bills.
- *Participation*: STCI was to participate in the long end of the dated government securities. The DFHI was to be at the short end of the dated government securities.
- *Market Operations*: The STCI was to deal with individuals and companies in the retail market where as DFHI was to be a whole sale dealer.
- *Market maker*: The STCI functioned as a market maker but the DFHI was a broker till it became a primary dealer and began to take market positions.
- *Paid up Capital*: The STCI was a larger organization with it paid of capital of Rs. 500 crores where as DFHI was started with Rs. 200 crores.

The main aim of both the organizations was to develop a debt market and to operate independently as well as like ancillary units in each other activities in the money market.

MARKET FOR FINANCIAL GUARANTEES

Guarantee is a contract to discharge the liability of a third party in case of default. Creditors secure their advance against various types of tangible securities. In addition, they also ask guarantees from borrowers. It can be called a security demanded by the creditor. Usually the borrower finds a person himself to guarantee his acts. The purpose of seeking guarantee is to minimize the risk of default. The guarantor should undoubtedly be known to both parties to be a person of repute and a person who has the means to discharge his liability. Guarantee can both written or oral and single or joint. *In India bank guarantees are very common method of giving security in case of default.*

Guarantees may be: (a) 'specific' or 'continuing'. Specific guarantee covers only one particular transaction. Continuing guarantee covers a series of transactions. (b) Guarantees may also be 'unsecured' or 'secured' with tangible asset. (c) Explicit or Implicit. An implicit guarantee arises out of the special nature of the guarantee and explicit guarantees are properly spelled out. (d) Another category of guarantees are 'performance' and 'financial' guarantees. Performance guarantees cover payment of earnest money, retention money, penalty charges, advance payments and non-completion of contracts. Financial guarantees consist of financial contracts only. In India, guarantee contracts consists of: (i) deferred payments for imported and indigenous capital goods, (ii) medium and long-term loans raised abroad, (iii) credit advanced by banks and other institutions. In India, there are generally financial guarantees of varying maturity periods.

The market for financial guarantees is well organized in India. There are various suppliers of guarantee. Personal Guarantee is the oldest form of guarantee service but the institutional market for financial guarantees is also well developed in India. There are specialized guarantee institutions who guarantee payments but the maximum period for guarantee is 15 years. Central and State Government also provide guarantees. Banks also guarantee funds but they are the costliest institutions for guarantee. Insurance Companies and other statutory companies also undertake to make guarantees but there is no specialized private institution providing guarantee service in the credit market in India. A large number of guarantees issued by insurance companies is given to banks or financial institutions like IDBI, ICICI, IFC who in time give guarantees to creditors, suppliers or contractors. The IDBI guarantees deferred payments due from industrial public market or from scheduled banks. The ICICI guarantees loans from other private investment sources. The State Financial Corporations guarantee loans raised by industrial concerns repayable up to 20 years. They issue secured guarantees. State Industrial Corporation extend guarantees for loans and deferred payments for industrial concerns. National Small Industries Corporation guarantees loans from banks to Small Industrial Units. Commercial banks extend guarantees and letters of credit in contracts and large projects.

Government has also set up certain specialized agencies with the central objectives of providing guarantees. These are: (a) *Credit Guarantee Organization (CGO)* which is a part of RBI and guarantees loans from lending institutions to the small-scale industrial units. It guarantees loans to those units which manufacture goods, are engaged in quarrying and mining, servicing and repairing machinery, dealing in medical equipment, processing agricultural products and engaged in research laboratories. The Credit Guarantee Organization had within its purview financial guarantees and not performance guarantees. It also did not duplicate guarantees in areas which were covered by government or by other financial guarantee organizations. The guarantees period was 10 years and it covered credit facilities on working capital advances, term loans, deferred credit and loan guarantees. (b) *The Export Credit Guarantee Corporation (ECGC)* was set up in 1964 to offer financial protection to the exporters, especially in their relationship with bankers. ECGC provides packing credit, post-shipment export credit guarantee, export production and export finance guarantee. ECGC covers up-to 90% of the loans as guarantees. It is popular because its commission is lower than bank and insurance companies. However, its commissions are higher than the credit guarantee organization and the Deposit Insurance and Credit Guarantee Corporation. Its normal charges are 0.9% per annum. It offers concessions to some units if it finds it necessary to do so, in which case it charges up to 0.54% per annum. (c) ***Deposit Insurance and Credit Guarantee Corporation (DICGC)***. This was started in 1971 as a public limited company. It operated three schemes: (i) Small Loans Guarantee Scheme, (ii) Financial Corporation Guarantee Scheme, and (iii) Service Co-operative Societies Guarantee Scheme. In 1981 government integrated Credit Guarantee Organization and Deposit Insurance and Credit Guarantee Corporation under one organization, namely the Deposit Insurance and Credit Guarantee Corporation for greater flexibility. The DICGC provides loans to traders in the retail sector, professionals, farmers, joint hindu families and association of persons. The loans are guaranteed for a maturity period of 15 years. It charges a guarantee fee of 1.5% per annum. Thus, the guarantee market is well organized in India.

GOVERNMENT (GILT-EDGED) SECURITIES MARKET

In India there are many kinds of government securities. These are issued by the Central Government, State Government and Semi-Government authorities including City Corporation Municipalities, Port Trusts, Improvement Trusts, State Electricity Boards, Metropolitan Authorities and Public Sector Corporations. The development banks and agencies are also engaged in the issue of these securities. Included in this category are the IDBI, IFCI, SFCs, SIDCs, ARC, LDBs and Housing Boards.

The Government Securities Market consists of various kinds of participating institutions. Apart from the major contributions of the government agencies who are issuing securities, there are other participants also. They support the issuing institutions. These are the banking sector. They include RBI, SBI, commercial banks and co-operative banks, LIC, Provident Funds, other special financial institutions, joint stock companies, local authorities, trusts, individuals, resident and non-resident.

The most active participation in the government securities market is of the banking and corporate sector. They purchase and sell large quantities of government securities. Apart from these two sectors, government selling is extremely limited. LIC, UTI and other special financial institutions are rarely active in this market. The reason for this is the special kind of policy formation of these organizations. They prefer to hold securities till maturity rather than sell them at an earlier date to make profit. For these reasons, the government securities secondary market is quite dull. Whatever limited dealings are held are confined to Bombay Stock Exchange.

The role of brokers in marketing government securities is also limited. In fact, there is no individual dealer especially for the purpose of government securities. Broker's firms dealing in other securities also include government selling as a part of their function in the stock market. The brokers receive 'over the counter' orders from their customers locally. They have to negotiate each purchase and sale separately. Anyone who purchases government securities from brokers holds it till maturity. The broker thus acts like a mere jobber. He, however, keeps in contact with RBI, LIC and other institutional investors.

Government securities are issued in denominations of Rs. 100. Interest is payable half-yearly. Financial institutions and commercial banks maintain their secondary reserve requirements in the form of these securities. Against collateral of these securities, commercial banks obtain accommodation from the Reserve Bank of India. Since it is the most secure financial instrument guaranteed by government, it is called a 'Gift-Edged Security' or 'near gold', or 'ultimate liquidity'.

The government securities are in many forms. These are: Stock Certificates (SC) or inscribed stock, Promissory notes and Bearer Bonds which are now discounted. Promissory Notes of any loan can be converted into stock certificates of any other loan or vice versa. These are, therefore, most popular. Government issues are sold through the RBI's Public Debt Office (PDO) while Treasury Bills are sold through auctions. The method of selling government securities is through notification before the date of subscription. Subscription is kept open for two or three days. RBI makes an announcement after which it suspends the sale of existing loans till the closure of subscriptions to new loans. Government can retain up to 10% in excess of notified amounts. Applications are received by the RBI and in States by the State Bank Over-subscription to loans of one State are transferable to another State Government whose loan is still open subscription at the option of the subscriber.

Government securities obtained through subscription help the exchequer to obtain inexpensive finance. The RBI (being the Central Bank of the country) is able to fix interest rates on government borrowing and selling and able to influence the behaviour of prices and yields in the gilt-edged market. Thus, RBI can execute its interest rate policy through changes in the bank rate and control the advances policy and liquidity of commercial banks. The government gilt-edged securities market is, therefore, considered important from the point of view of monetary management.

There have been many new developments in the government securities market. These are given below:

- *Fiscal responsibility and budget management Act 2003*: This Act proposes to separate debt management and monetary operations within the RBI. The open market operation of the RBI would become a dominant function and its participation would be withdrawn from the primary issues of the government securities.

- *Technical group on securities market 2005*: There were several recommendations of this group. These were: (a) Primary dealers would be allowed to underwrite hundred percent of each government auction both in the whole sale and retail segment, (b) RBI would be permitted to participate in the secondary market for improving liquidity in government securities, (c) There would be an effective transparency through monitoring and surveillance through the negotiated dealing system.

- *Negotiated dealing system*: This system was an electronic order matching trading module for government securities. All orders will be matched on price and time priority. The Clearing Corporation of India would settle the trades that are executed.

- *Institutional support*: The Securities Trading Corporation of India was setup with all India financial institutions and RBI for developing and supporting the secondary market for government securities. Primary dealers were introduced to provide two way quotes.

- *Structural reforms*: Retail trading of government securities was started in selected stock markets. The participations of non-bank players ware initiated to include private sector mutual funds, finance companies and individuals.

Summary

➡ A synoptic view of all important financial markets besides the new issue market and stock markets are presented in this chapter.

➡ The call money market is very useful for short term funds and caters to requirements between 1 day, 14 days, 1 months and up to 1 year.

➡ Commercial banks and co-operative banks engage in maximize support to this market being lenders and supplies of funds. PD's have been appointed as participants. Institutions like DFHI and STCI have also started participating in the call money market.

➡ The rate of interest is market determined depending on the forces of demand and supply.

➡ The call money market is most active in Mumbai and Kolkata. The rate is highest in Kolkata and lowest in Mumbai. Call rates in this market are highly volatile.

➡ The RBI stabilizes the market through repos, refinancing of government securities foreign exchange purchases and total support to the money market.

➡ Banks generally lend in the money market. PD's are the net borrowers in the market. The inter bank call market is being developed in India.

➡ A Treasury bill market comprises of promissory notes or finance bills issued by government for raising short term funds.

➡ They are 91 days, 182 days, 364 days and 14 days bills. The 91 days ad-hoc bill and 182 days bills have been discontinued in 1997 and 1992 respectively. Wherever 364 days bills were introduced in 1992. The 14 days bill has replaced the 91 days bill.

➡ The auction system has been introduced for treasury bills and the interest rate has become market related.

➡ The commercial bill market deals in short term negotiable instruments called bills. Bills may be demand or usance, inland and foreign, accommodation bills and hundis or the Indian form of bill of exchange.

➡ Bill market in India is small and underdeveloped. It is generally used for accommodation. The bill discount rate dependant on bazaar bill rate, hundi rate, SBI discount rate and commercial banks bill finance rate. There is no ceiling on discount rates since 1989.

➡ Commercial papers and certificate of deposits are two new money market instruments. They are for short term use, highly liquid, unsecured and negotiable in nature.

➡ The maturity period of CPs is between 30 days and 6 months. Their interest rate is market determined.

➡ CD's may be in bearer form or registered. They are deposited in a bank for a specified period at a specified rate of interest. They are transferable, negotiable highly liquid and risk-less money market instruments. They can be issued to individuals, companies, trusts, associations and NRI's.

➡ The discount market consists of two institutions. The discount and finance house of India and the securities trading corporation of India for promoting the flow of funds in the money market.

➡ The DFHI was started to make finds liquid in the money market. The SICI was promoted to trade in secondary markets. This was specifically for debt instruments. Both the institutions are primary dealers in government securities.

➡ RBI has played an active role in setting up to institutions in the market for financial guarantees. Credit guarantees are up to 75% but ECGC sometimes guarantees up-to 90%-100% cover is not extend.

➡ Government securities market plays an important role in asset management of financial instruments. It also stabilizes the monetary and financial system of the country. In India repos have emerged as an important financial instrument.

Objective Type Questions, Answer True (T) or False (F)

(a) Money market is a market for stock market operations.

(b) The most important constituent of the money market in India is the RBI.

(c) Call money market is mainly to bring about liquidity in the market.

(d) Commercial papers were introduced in 1990 to diversify sources for short term borrowings.

(e) Certificates of deposits are short term securitized deposits issued during light liquidity at low rates of interest.

(f) Repos are repurchase agreements of sale and purchase in debt securities.

(g) The electronic negotiated quote driven system has been adopted in the money market.

(h) Primary dealers since 2006 are permitted to underwrite up to 80% of the notified amount of each auction in government securities.

(i) The discount and Finance House of India was to focus on long dated government securities and STCI on short end of dated government securities.

(j) Hundi is the Indian form of bill of exchange.

Answer: (a) F, (b) T, (c) T, (d) T, (e) F, (f) T, (g) T, (h) F, (i) F, (j) T.

Multiple Choice Questions Tick mark (✓) the right answer)

1. The money market is a market for:
   (a) Long term funds
   (b) Negotiable instruments
   (c) Trading in commercial bills
   (d) Short term maturity

2. A certificate of deposits is a:
   (a) Fixed deposit in a bank
   (b) Short term negotiable instruments in bearer form
   (c) A promissory note to pay a sum of money to the issuer
   (d) It is a government treasury bill

3. The Discount and Finance House of India was setup:
   (a) For giving discounts on goods sold in the market
   (b) For discounting bills of exchange
   (c) For inter bank operations
   (d) For promoting the Securities Trading Corporation of India

4. The market for financial guarantees has specialized institutions, these are:
   (a) LIC and UTI
   (b) IDBI, ICICI and IFCI
   (c) RBI and IDBI
   (d) Credit Guarantees Organization and Export Credit and Guarantee Corporation

5. Commercial papers are:
    (a) Papers transacted at business houses
    (b) Papers used for financing
    (c) Unsecured negotiable promissory notes
    (d) Papers for financial guarantees

    Answer: 1 (d), 2 (b), 3 (b), 4 (d), 5 (c).

Short Answer Questions

1. What is the meaning of call money market? Who are its participants?

2. What is a bill of exchange explain the different kinds of bills of exchange in India?

3. Write notes on:
    (a) Commercial papers
    (b) Certificate of deposits
    (c) DFHI
    (c) SICI

4. What are the specialized types of institutions formed for financial guarantees?

5. Discuss the different financial guarantees executed by commercial banks.

6. The price of government securities have remained stable in India explain.

7. Comment of the following statement 'government securities play an important role in the asset management of many financial institutions'.

Long Answer Questions

1. Discuss the developments in the call money market in India.

2. What are measures taken for development of the bill market?

3. Distinguish between commercial papers and certificate of deposits. What is the impact of these instruments in the money market in India?

4. What is the role played by DFHI in increasing liquidity in the economy?

5. How does DFHI differ from STCI? What is the importance of these institutions in the money market?

6. Discuss the developments in the government securities market in the reforms period.

Part – Four
Dimensions of International Financial Markets

9.   Foreign Exchange Market

10.   Foreign Capital Flows

Chapter **9**

Foreign Exchange Market

Chapter Plan

- Nature of Foreign Exchange Market
- Participants in the Market
- Fixed and Flexible Exchange Rates
- Trends in Foreign Exchange Rates
- Types of Transactions
- Trading Mechanism
- Foreign Exchange Risks
- Developments in the Foreign Exchange Market

NATURE OF FOREIGN EXCHANGE MARKET

The foreign exchange market is electronically linked with banks, foreign exchange dealers and brokers. The main objective of this market is to deal in monetary units of different countries. The trading mechanism consists of the linking of the domestic monetary unit with the foreign monetary unit. In India the Foreign Exchange Regulation Act (FERA) of 1973 governed the foreign exchange transactions consisting of foreign currency, deposits, and traveler's cheques, payments in foreign currency and bills of exchange payable in a foreign country. The Act of 1973 regulated the inflow of foreign capital and foreign currency notes and bullion transactions. In 1999 The Foreign Exchange Management Act (FEMA) replaced the 1973 Act. Its objective was to improve, develop and to liberalize the foreign exchange market in India. The aim was to widen and deepen the foreign exchange market. It was also to promote foreign exchange into the country and utilize it in an organized manner.

The foreign exchange market works for 24 hours a day. It is connected by telephones, fax machines and telecommunications. The large foreign exchange markets are in London, New York, Frankfurt, Tokyo, Zurich, Paris and Milan. These markets are internationally linked through computer based communications which is Society for World Wide International Financial Telecommunications popularly called SWIFT. The Foreign Exchange Market is an inter bank market and is in close connectivity with the Euro Dollar market. It brings about parity in prices in different securities markets. The sport and forward exchange rates between two currencies is connected with the interest rate.

Indian banks maintain foreign currencies with banks abroad. Their accounts are called *'Nastro Account'*. This means *'our accounts with you'*. The currencies accumulated in this account are based on the currency where the account is maintained. In a Nastro Account a minimum balance must be maintained. Since 1997-98 the Nastro Accounts of Indian banks have very few restrictions. Similarly foreign banks can also open their accounts with Indian banks. This is called *'Vostro Account'* which means *'your account with us'*. Such accounts are called Non-Residents Account. If this account is debited there is an inflow of foreign exchange in India but when this account is credited it means that there is the movement of foreign exchange from India to other counties. In Nastro Accounts foreign banks have to pay demand drafts which are issued by Indian banks. They also discount bills of exchange. In Vostro Accounts the drafts of the foreign banks are cleared by Indian banks.

PARTICIPANTS IN THE MARKET

The participants in this market are the RBI at the apex, the authorized dealers which are licensed by it, exporters, importers companies and individuals. It is comprised of a wholesale and retail market.

Central Bank: The central bank of a country is the main participant in the foreign exchange market because it has the power of intervention. Currency intervention is different in each country. It is country specific depending on whether it is on the fixed or market determined exchange rate. The central bank uses foreign currencies for maintaining reserves. In India the Reserve Bank of India being the central bank drew a lot of powers as the foreign exchange account was based on fixed rate system. RBI influenced the different countries according to the planned priorities of India. It has also used the foreign exchange market for bringing about stability in foreign currency transactions.

Wholesale market: This market deals with different foreign currencies of large amounts. It has the following activities.

- The market has a credit line with the head office of large banks through which they service their customers.

- The trading is continuous and there is no physical transfer of currencies. Only book entries are made after transactions.

- The wholesale market does not have any central focal location and it works between the major banks of different countries.

- The banks make a profit in this market through a spread between buying and selling rates. They do not charge any commission on transactions.

- Only large commercial banks are entitled to deal as market makers with assets on their own account through their head offices.

Retail Market: The retail market deals with exchange of currencies of small amounts of different countries. It comprises of individuals such as exporters, importers, portfolio managers, investors and tourists.

- It is a market for bank drafts, currencies, bank notes, travelers' cheques.
- The participants in this market tourists and banks.
- Special outlets in the form of firms, hotels and shops deal with currencies and travelers cheques.
- Money changers get special licenses from the RBI for purchase and sale of currencies of different countries.

Authorized Dealers (ADs): The RBI authorizes dealers to participate in foreign exchange transactions. They are called Authorized Dealers (ADs).

- In India, there are 84 banks which are authorized dealers.
- Their main function is to transact foreign exchange dealings.
- The large banks provide two way quotes and perform a large number of transactions.
- Foreign banks also participants which actively operate in the market and give two way quotes.
- The organization of the authorized dealers is called Foreign Exchange Dealers Association of India (FEDAI). It fixes commission on transactions made by the dealers.

Financial Institutions: There are many financial institutions which are participants in this market.

- A license for foreign exchange transactions has been given to IDBI, IFCI and ICICI for transacting business in other currencies.
- The financial institutions conduct their own business of financing and foreign exchange transactions are their incidental business activity.

Inter Bank Participants: The inter bank participants transact foreign exchange business with each other directly and indirectly.

- The inter bank market directly quote the buying and selling prices to each other.
- All participating banks in the foreign exchange market are 'market makers'.
- The direct market is also called 'double auction', 'open bid' and 'continuous' market.
- The indirect market has banks and brokers as participants. Banks usually give others to the brokers. The brokers put them on their books and match the sales and purchases of different currencies. The buyers and sellers are both charged commission on the transactions.
- The indirect market is also called single 'auction', 'quasi centralized', 'continuous' or 'limit book market'.
- The inter bank market both direct and indirect is transacted by specialist brokers. They get a commission for the work of matching the purchases with the sales.

Speculators: Speculators are those participants who make profits by predicting changes in exchange rates.

- Speculators are engaged in buying and selling currencies of different countries for make a profit.
- Speculators do not have any business while making transactions. They deal only in speculation of currency.
- Speculators also deal in short term financial instruments like treasury bills. Their aim is to anticipate prices at a future date and take positions for profit making.

- Banks and investment banks do speculative transactions for making profits.
- Profit is made by the speculators by playing in the market through changes in exchange rates.
- Speculators may also be engaged in arbitrage transactions between different markets to make a profit.

Brokers: Brokers deal in foreign currencies.

- Brokers are specialists in currencies they work in the foreign exchange market to earn a profit.
- Brokers buy and sell the important and popular well known currencies like American Dollar, European Euro, Japanese Yen and British Pound.
- Brokers provide information on the rates of foreign exchange and give tips to speculators dealing in foreign currency.

Thus the participants in the foreign exchange market consist of brokers, authorized dealers, wholesale and retail markets, individuals, brokers, financial institutions, speculators and banks.

FIXED AND FLEXIBLE EXCHANGE RATES

There are different kinds of exchange rates. These may be fixed or flexible exchange rates.

Fixed Exchange Rates

In fixed exchange rates government fixes the exchange rates through its central bank which operates by creating an exchange stabilization fund. The central bank of a country monitors fixed exchange rates by increasing or decreasing the rates through purchases when exchange rate falls and sales when exchange rate rises. The fixed exchange rates have certain advantages. They create confidence and promote long term investments. UK and Denmark prefer fixed exchange rates but other countries do not favour fixed rates. The reason for this is that it is a managed flexible system as rates require to be pegged up and down by the central bank. It also has to keep large foreign exchange reserves. Moreover, it is difficult to attract foreign capital as the demand and supply factors do not operate in fixing exchange rates. Therefore the flexible exchange rates are preferred by the different countries.

The fixed rates systems are of different types. These are: Gold standard, Bretton Woods, Pegged rate and Currency board.

Gold standard: In a gold standard a countries money supply is connected to the gold reserves owned by it central bank. The notes and coins can be changed for gold. This system is good for a country that has a current account deficit as it can adopt self correcting measures. When a country has a higher volume of imports compared to its exports. The currency acquired by it becomes less. The country then reduces its imports by putting high import duties. Thus exports will increase as they would become cheaper and the import will fowl. Thus gold reserves will be stabilized. The central bank will also control the money supply and corrective action can take place.

Bretton Woods: The Bretton Woods was based on both gold as well as foreign currencies. Through this system flexibility was brought about as gold standard was very rigid. This system helped those countries which had a consistent adverse balance of payments to devalue their currencies and bring about order and improvement in their payment system. In 1969, the international monetary fund created it own currencies in the form of Special Drawing Rights (SDRs). This was useful for members to settle inter member debts.

Pegged rate: The pegged rate means that one country holds the value of its currency constant in terms of another currency. Influential currencies like US dollar and British pound dominate in the foreign currency market and are important trading participants for different countries. Therefore, developing countries find it convenient to peg themselves against these currencies.

Currency board: This is type of peg, so that currencies are backed by foreign currency reserve. This keeps the peg rate stabilized in an economy. When domestic currency is sold the reserves are reduced. The money supply within the country also declined. This brings about an increase in the interest rates and reduces economic activity within the country. Currency board and pegged rate are quite similar except that a currency board has to be changed through proper legislations.

Semi Fixed Rate System

Semi fixed rate system is applied through bands, target zones, pegs and baskets and through crawling pegs and floating rate system. They are also called managed floats.

Bands: When bands are applied, the exchange rate moves between the bands. The central bank of a country makes adjustments in interest rates so that the exchange rate floats between the bands.

Target zones: In target zones government decides to trade within a certain range of another currency. This zone can be decided by the government unilaterally or by agreement with other countries multi laterally.

Pegs and Baskets: In this system the exchange rate of a country is pegged against a basket of currencies of different countries instead of only one country. Singapore and Turkey peg their currencies against as basket of other currencies. Sometimes problems arise because of difficulty in fixing the value of the currency against the basket because of variation in rates of currencies.

Crawling pegged: In the crawling peg an adjustment is made by depreciating the currency's exchange rate. This rate is decided by a country's monetary policy and the level at which the economy must operate. Government plays an important role in deciding the rate of depreciation.

Floating rate system: The floating rate is the flexible exchange rate which is derived through demand and supply conditions. It is a market determined rate of interest. There are no restrictions on this rate. It is allowed to move freely in the market. RBI has made the value of the rupee within a band and according to the basket of currencies mechanism. It uses the American dollar as the intervening currency. They RBI buys and sells to Authorized Dealers and from July 5th 1995, it has made many relaxations. It has provided the Authorized Dealers with facilities to carry on international trade without restrictions and tried to make the rupee fully convertible.

Flexible Exchange Rates

Flexible exchange rates are determined by the free play of demand and supply of foreign exchange. The central bank does not peg up or peg down the exchange rates. The market forces help in determining the foreign exchange rate. The flexible exchange rates are known as fluctuating or floating exchange rates. The flexible exchange rates have certain benefits. It has free movement of foreign exchange bringing in free flow of international trade. The exchange rate is continuously adjusted automatically depending on the trade taking place in the international markets. Large foreign exchange reserves do not require to be maintained by central bank of a country. However, flexible exchange rate has certain deficiencies. The exchange rate changes frequently because it is dependent on the market mechanism. If exchange rates are reduced, there is a danger of inflationary forces to operate in an economy. The exchange rate is also influenced by speculative transactions as it affects the normal transactions in the market. The flexible exchange rates also are not able to correct balance of payments position as the market mechanism does not give a correct picture of the payment balance.

In India there was control in the exchange rates. It was governed by the Reserve Bank of India but after the new economic reforms in 1991 government decided to have a more free system of exchange rates. It decided to allow partial convertibility under the liberalized framework.

Liberalized Exchange Rate Management System (LERMS) 1992

In 1991 government made many reforms to globalize India and integrate it with other countries in the world. In 1992 as a measure of these reforms government liberalized its foreign exchange rates. Government of India allowed partial convertibility of its rupee. Under this new scheme there was to be a 40, 60 basis. 60% of the exchange rates would be market determined exchange rate where as 40% was at the official determined exchange rate directed by the RBI. The US dollar replaced the pound sterling as the intervening currency on foreign currency were to be surrendered to the authorized dealers 40% of the total foreign exchange receipts were to be surrendered to the RBI at the official rate and 60% could be sold in the free market. In 1993 government of India introduced a unified exchange rate with current account convertibility.

Unified Exchange Rate 1993

The unified exchange rate and floating rupee rate was started in 1993 to make it market determined exchange rate. Government decided to remove restrictions on foreign capital. As a first step government liberalized its current account and brought about the freedom of convertibility on current account. This reform brought about the sale and purchase of international transactions according to market related measures. All foreign exchange transactions were to be through the Authorized Dealers at market determined exchange rates. The exporters would surrender their export earnings to Authorized Dealers. All payments of foreign exchange were to be made through the Authorized Dealers at the market rate.

Current Account Convertibility

Government of India removed restrictions from convertibility of the rupee on current account. This brought about freedom in buying and selling foreign exchange in international transactions. It covered all payments in connection with foreign trade inclusive of services, short term banking, interest on loans, income from investments and foreign remittances. Government first removed the verification of the exchange rate. It then removed restriction on import by abolishing the foreign exchange budgeting. It then announced relaxations in invisible transactions. In 1994 under article (viii) of International Monetary Fund, government of India accepted full convertibility of the rupee. Since then the authorized dealers have been able to release foreign exchange with out the approval of the RBI. This has helped India to increase its trade because more than hundred countries have full convertibility on current account making it easier for exporters and importers to transact business.

Capital Account Convertibility

Government of India had planned to bring about capital account convertibility. However, there was a problem in Mexico, Brazil and in South East Asia. India decided not to bring about capital account convertibility even though it will remove restrictions on capital payments.

TRENDS IN FOREIGN EXCHANGE RATES

The foreign exchange rate policy in India has been framed to provide a smooth flow of funds, so that volatility in the rates is reduced and adequate reserves of foreign exchange are maintained. The trends in the foreign exchange rates can be depicted through Table 9.1 and 9.2. Table 9.1 presents changes in the rupee exchange rates.

Table 9.1: Exchange rate of the Indian Rupee *v/s-A-vis* the SDR. US Dollar, Pound Sterling, D.M./Euro and Japanese Yen (Calendar Year—Annual Average)

(Rupees per unit of foreign currency)

Year	SDR	US Dollar	Pound Sterling	Deutsche Mark/Euro	Japanese Yen @
1	2	3	4	5	6
1990	23.7922	17.4992	31.2835	10.8694	12.1600
1991	31.0950	22.6890	39.9941	13.6991	16.9200
1992	36.5094	25.9206	45.7104	16.6354	20.4800
1993	42.6318	31.4439	47.2160	19.0264	28.3600
1994	44.9296	31.3742	48.0482	19.4345	30.7370
1995	49.1803	32.4198	51.1662	22.6515	34.6113
1996	51.4350	35.4280	55.3422	23.5694	32.5971
1997	46.9584	36.3195	59.5346	20.9861	30.0495
1998	56.0329	41.2665	68.3525	23.5057	31.6680
1999	58.8799	43.0552	69.6700	45.9561	37.9983
2000	59.2475	44.9401	68.0760	41.4939	41.7258
2001	60.0782	47.1857	67.9826	42.2869	38.8674
2002	62.9532	48.5993	73.0028	45.9261	38.8722
2003	65.2192	46.5818	76.0974	52.6603	40.2047
2004	67.1053	45.3165	82.9983	56.3260	41.8941
2005	65.1404	44.1000	80.2530	54.8993	40.1020
2006	66.7510	45.3325	83.6546	57.0138	39.0195

@ Rupees per 100 Yen.

Notes :1.   Data from 1970 are based on official exchange rates.

2.   Data from 1993 onwards are based on FEDAI (Foreign Exchnage Dealers' Association of India) indicative rates.

3.   The Euro replaced the Deutsche Mark w.e.f January 1, 1999.

Source: RBI Handbook October, 2007 Table 150 (page 261).

The rupee exchange rates have been volatile even after liberalization and convertibility of current account in 1992. From March 1993 to October 1995 the exchange rates were stable. Since them the rates have fluctuated and remained volatile. In the 1990 the external value of the rupee has been declining. The rupee continuously depreciated against the dollar and the pound. In 2003, 2004 it appreciated against the dollar but not against pound sterling. The Deutsche Mark even after conversion into Euro continued to appreciate against the rupee. In 1990 the Deutsche Mark was rupee 10.86 and in 1999 it appreciated to Rs. 45.95 and then it was converted into Euro. In 2000 the rate declined from Rs. 45.95 in 1999 to Rs. 41.49 there after it has continuously increased an appreciated against the rupee. In 2006 it was Rs. 57.01. The pound sterling has fluctuated many times. There was a sharp jump from 1990 when it was Rs. 31.28 continuously until 1999. It declined 2000 and 2001 then there was an increase from the year 2002 to 2004 from Rs. 73 it increased to Rs. 82.99, it decreased in 2005 to Rs. 80.25 and again increased 2006 to Rs. 83.65. At present in October 2007 it is Rs. 80.67. Thus there are wide fluctuations in exchange rates against the pounds sterling. The RBI had to make an intervention in 1996. In 2007 the dollar rate also decreased to Rs. 39.56. Similarly the rupee and Japanese Yen parity also show is a remarkable appreciation in yen. Table 9.2 indicates the Real Effective Exchange Rate (REER) and the Nominal Effective Exchange Rate (NEER).

Nominal, Real and Effective Exchange Rates

The nominal, real and effective rates are depicted of domestic currency as per unit of foreign currency to make an analysis of the effects and changes in the foreign exchange rate.

Table 9.2: Indices of Real Effective Exchange Rate (REER) and Nominal Effective Exchange Rate (NEER) of the Indian Rupee (36-currency bilateral weights) (Financial year—Anual average)

(Base : 1993-94 = 100)

YEAR	Export-based weights		Trade-based weights	
	REER	NEER	REER	NEER
1	2	3	4	5
1993-94	100.00	100.00	100.00	100.00
1994-95	104.88	98.18	104.32	98.91
1995-96	100.10	90.94	98.19	91.54
1996-97	98.95	89.03	96.83	89.27
1997-98	103.07	91.97	100.77	92.04
1998-99	94.34	90.34	93.04	89.05
1999-00	95.28	90.42	95.99	91.02
2000-01	98.67	90.12	100.09	92.12
2001-02	98.59	89.08	100.86	91.58
2002-03	95.99	87.01	98.18	89.12
2003-04	99.07	87.89	99.56	87.14
2004-05	98.30	88.41	100.09	87.31
2005-06	100.54	91.17	102.35	89.85
2006-07P	97.43	87.45	98.50	85.88

P : Provisional.
Notes:1. REER indices are recalculated from 1993-94 onwards using the new Wholesale Price Index (WPI) series (Base : 1993-94 = 100)
      2. The 36-Country REER & NEER are revised as 36-Currency REER & NEER respectively and for "note on Methodology" on the indices, please see December 2005 Issue of RBI Bulletin.
Aslo see Notes on Tables.
Source: RBI Handbook, October 1, 2007 Table 155.

Nominal exchange rate: The nominal exchange rate is the prevailing exchange rate at the time when it is being analyzed. It is the price of one currency in towns of another. For example, if it desired to find out the nominal rate between USA dollar and Indian rupee, it would be Rs. 39.75 to 1 dollar as on October 20th, 2007. This is the nominal rate or the rate at which the official currency can be purchased by an individual. This has no relationship with the kind of purchase value in a country.

Real Exchange rate: The real exchange rate measures the purchasing power of a currency. The real exchange rate can be calculated by adjusting the nominal rate of exchange for relative prices between the countries that are being analyzed. For example, if the real exchange rate of USA is being analyzed with the purchasing power parity of India. It can be calculated through the index of the real exchange rate, the nominal exchange rate index, the domestic price level index and the foreign price level index. The formula will be real exchange rate = (nominal exchange rate X domestic price index)/foreign price level index.

Effective exchange rate: The effective exchange rate measures whether the price of a currency is appreciating or depreciating against the weighted basket of currencies with whom the country desires to trade. The real effective rate changes without any change in exchange rate. This rate can depreciate when duties are imposed because imports will become expensive. Similarly it can appreciate when duties are reduced and imports are easily available. Liberalization and restrictions thus have an effect on the real exchange rate.

The trade based figures in Table 9.2 depict that the real exchange rate of the Indian rupee is quite different to the nominal exchange rate in terms of 36 countries. The fall in the real effective rate is less than the nominal rate from 1993 onwards. The real exchange rate shows that the value of the rupee is not as low as the nominal exchange rate. The real exchange rate also fluctuates as much as the nominal exchange rates from 1993 to 2007. Similarly, the export based weights so that there are wide fluctuations in REER and NEER in 2006-07. It is expected that the NEER and REER rates will both for some trends can be examined in export based weights from 1999 to 2001, so that REER has been continuously increasing. It reduced in 2003, 2003 and continuously fluctuated up to 2007. There have been corrections and rupee appreciates for a short time before it depreciates again. In 2006, 2007 NEER and REER have both declined sharply. These fluctuations are very high since 1992 after liberalization and relaxations in foreign exchange rate have been made by the Indian government and the rupee has become convertible on the current account. Therefore, fluctuating rates are due to flexible rates system adopted in place of restriction.

TYPES OF TRANSACTIONS

In a foreign exchange market there are spot, forward and swap transactions.

Spot Transactions

When business transactions are made between banks and purchases of foreign currency are followed by payment on the next business day, it is called a 'spot transaction'. The date of transaction is called the 'value date' and the rate at which the transaction is made is called the 'spot rate'. The 'CHIP' is the method of settlement based on the New-York methodology of transactions. According to this method the net balance owed by banks is calculated at 6 PM of the day transaction in the Federal Reserve Bank of New-York funds.

Forward Transactions

In a forward transaction a specified amount of currency is exchanged with the specified amount of another currency and the payment is made on a future date. The rate that is quoted is called the 'forward rate'. The delivery and payment is made on a future date which is determined at the time of making the agreement. The rate is also quoted at the time of the agreement. A forward exchange rate can be quoted for value dates of one, two, three, six or twelve months.

Swap Transactions

When foreign currencies are simultaneously purchased and sold for different value dates. It is called a 'swap transaction'. Purchases and sales are made with the same party. Swaps can be of kinds. These are 'spot against forward swap' and 'forward-forward swaps'. When spot again forward swaps are made the currency dealer buys the currency in the spot market and at the same time sells the same amount of currency to the same bank but in the forward market. It is a counter party agreement and the expectation is there that there will be less risk. The forward-forward swap means borrowing of currency through collateral.

TRADING MECHANISM

Trading in the foreign exchange market can take place through spot, forward and swap transactions. The transactions take place through different types of quotations. When the quotations are provided and the agreement is made, the transaction takes place. Therefore, the methods of quotations are most important in the trading mechanism and methodology of profit making.

Inter Bank Quotations

Trading takes place between different banks. One bank expresses the price of foreign currency of one rupee against one unit of US dollar. There are both European terms and American terms which can be used to describe one unit of currency against another country. Most of the inter bank quotations are provided in European terms. The European terms are used for trading widely all over the world. The European terms would be Rs. 39.75/$1. This means Rs. 39.75 Indian Rs. per dollar. The American term is read as $1/Rs. 39.75 = $.025157/rupee 1. The European term is found to be easier to deal with than be American term by different countries.

Direct Quotation

The direct quotation refers to the home country currency price for a unit of foreign currency. The foreign currency unit is kept constant and the change in the exchange rate is expressed as a change in the unit of the home country. For example, the direct quotation of Indian rupee against the US dollar will be Rs. 39.75 / $1. This is a direct quotation in India. The currency of the home unit is depicted first. The value of the home currency fluctuates but the value of foreign currency is constant. In direct quotation the principle that is used is to '***buy high but sell low***'. The region for this is that $1 being the fixed unit of foreign currency would prefer to pay less amount of home currency. For example, Rs. 39 while purchasing as it receipts more units of home currency that is Rs. 39.75 in India. The RBI directives are that direct quotation should be used for sale and purchase of foreign currency notes and coins as well as for traveler's cheques.

Indirect Quotations

As indirect quotation is one where the value of the foreign currency varies but the value of the home currency is constant. In other words the foreign currency price of a home country is an indirect quotation. Changes in the exchange rate are expressed as a change in the unit of foreign currency. In this case the principle will change. It will become '*buy low and sell high*'. The indirect quotation for Indian rupee will be $.025157/rupee 1. This is called an indirect quote for India. The currency unit of foreign country comes first and then the home country. On the basis of this quotation, transactions may be spot, forward or swap.

Bid Quotations

The bid price is the quotation made in one currency at which the dealer will be ready to buy. The '*bid price*' is normally lower than the '*ask price*'. The banks will buy the dollar at the bid price and sell it for ask price. The offer price would be 39.75, there as the bid price would be Rs. 39.

Ask Quotations

The sale price or the quotation in one currency at which the dealer will sale is called the '*ask quotation*' or the '*offer price*'. The ask price of the dealer will be Rs. 39.75 when he has purchased it for Rs. 39. He thus makes a profit of 75 paisa for every dollar.

Cross Rates

Currencies which are not active but require to the determined can be traded through cross rate. An in active currency which requires making a settlement with an active trade participant can easily do so through a third country. For example, if India wants to trade with another country whose rate it does not have it can trade through the US dollar if both active and inactive participants are linked through trade in USA. The dollar can be the common unit between the two countries.

To summarize trading between to countries have to be settled through the currency of the two counties by payment through a pre-determined rate. The Authorized Dealers quote to the buyers and if immediate delivery and payment is made it becomes spot payment through the spot exchange rate. In the forward trade the rate is fixed but actual delivery takes place on a future date. Hedging techniques can help in reducing risks in international trade. Swaps, forward contracts and currency arbitrage methods are used for reducing risks by offsetting commitments.

FOREIGN EXCHANGE RISKS

There are different kinds of foreign exchange risks. These are called transaction exposure, translation exposure and economic exposure.

Transaction Exposure

The transaction exposure is the net amount of existing commitments to make and receive in foreign currency. These are short term commitment and they are known in advance. The forward contracts are used in off setting such commitments through hedging on the basis of overall exposure. Hedging transactions cannot be done through parts. They are usually done on overall exposure.

Translation Exposure

The net book value of assets and liabilities in foreign currency due to changes in exchange rate is called translation exposure. This risk rises when there is a parent company and subsidiary. Changes in the book value of the parent's investments in the subsidiary company, creates a loss in the parent company. Hedging can create reduction in risk.

Economic Exposure

Economic exposure is the risk which is due to the changes in the present value of the firm due to exchange rate changes. Present value depends on the expected commitments. Such changes can occur even though the assets and the liability of the company are not denominated in foreign currency. The economic exposure depends on future commitments, where as translation exposure is based on past events. It is different from transaction exposure because it is a comprehensive risk and transaction exposure is mainly earning short term commitments.

Managing Risks

Risk can be managed to attain a minimum level in transactions. These risks can be hedged through forward contracts in long and short positions. A long position is acquired through sale of forward contracts. Short positions are through the purchase of a forward contract. Futures and currency shops can also be used for hedging. Derivatives can be used for hedging through swaps such as caps, floors, collars and swaption.

- *Caps:* Caps give protection to borrowers in increased interest rates.
- *Floors:* Floors give an assurance that interest rates will not fall below specific level.
- *Collars:* Collars are simultaneous purchases and sales between cap and floor to limit the exposure of interest rate movement.
- *Swaption:* A swaption is an entitlement but not obligation for the buyer to take a swap at a future date on terms specified at the time agreement.

Risks can also be managed through options and through hedging through the money market.

DEVELOPMENT IN THE FOREIGN EXCHANGE MARKET

The foreign exchange market required a wider setup and liberal attitude in trading. This was important to internationalize the transactions. As a consequence three high level committees were made to recommend and make reforms for improvement. The Sadhani Committee report was brought out on foreign exchange markets in India in 1995. In 1997 the Tarapore Committee report was made on 'capital account convertibility' and the Rangarajan Committee report was prepared on 'balance or payments'. The following are some of the reforms and changes which were made in the foreign exchange market to internationalize and liberalize the foreign exchange market. Most of these reforms were made to make trading simple and easy so that the volume of transactions would increase.

Gold Policy

The gold policy brought about liberalization in importing gold. This helped in reducing the difference between the domestic and international prices of gold. The unofficial market in gold became insignificant with this reform as the purchase and sale of gold was allowed freely in the market. This also had an effect on the spot foreign exchange market. Since importing gold became easy for the traders it had an impact on the emotions and sentiments of the market.

Banking Sector

The banking operations were given freedom for managing, arbitraging and hedging their own positions between difference currencies. Banks are allowed to buy and sell foreign currency at market related interest rates. Inter bank transactions were given freedom. The RBI permitted the banks to make transaction abroad. According to the new positions the RBI became the apex organization. The other participants were Authorized Dealers, money changes and importer and exporters. The FEDAI has issued guidelines for the Authorized dealers and money changes are not allowed to deal in foreign exchange on their own account. The Authorized Dealers can however make transactions between themselves, importers, exporters and other customers.

Foreign Exchange Reserves

Liberalization in foreign exchange dealings has brought about high reserves of foreign exchange in the country. One point of view is that reserves in foreign exchange indicate positive health conditions of an economy. It provides help for growth in developing countries. Some economies are of the view that high reserves in India show that India's reforms have been successful. India will be able to have greater liquidity and use the funds wherever development is required. Other economists feel that high reserves are expensive because the cost of maintaining and holding. These reserves are an opportunity cost and it can be avoided as interest burden is high due to such reserves. The increase in foreign exchange reserves have not been accumulated because of a surplus balance of trade or positive current account. It has increased due to Non-resident Indian inflow of funds in the countries.

Capital Account Convertibility

The capital account convertibility is an issue which has been continuously debited. The Tarapore committees report defined capital account convertibility as the freedom to convert local financial assets into foreign financial assets and alternatively foreign financial assets into local assets at market determined rates of exchange. Capital account convertibility brings about mobility of capital amongst different countries and helps to maintain liquidity in capital in a country. It also assists in increasing the level of output and an equitable distribution in income level of people. The committee had suggested implementing of capital account convertibility if three specified preconditions could be attained with in a specified time frame work. The preconditions were that they should be a reduction in gross fiscal deficit as a percentage of gross domestic products to 3.5 in 1999 to 2000 and reduction of non productive assets to 12% in 1997-98, 9% by 1998-99 and 5% by 2000. The third condition refereed to the inflation rate of the country. It was suggested that between 1997 and 2000 the inflation rate would be between 3-5%. Since these preconditions could not be achieved, the capital account convertibility was not considered to be feasible.

Non-Resident Account

The RBI gave more freedom to non-resident Indians. They have been allowed full repatriation of current income in the form of rent, dividend, pension and interest with holding a Non-Resident Ordinary account (NRO). The NRO accounts could be repatriated to the USA for academic expenses up to $30,000 and up to $1,00,000 for medical expenses of the account holder or his family members and up to $1,00,000 could be transferred on the sale of immovable property which was held in India for at least 10 years.

Corporate Organizations

Indian companies can invest up to 25% of its net worth in companies oversees if they were listed on recognized stock market. They are also allowed to retain their American Depository Receipts (ADR's) and Global Depository Receipts (GDR's) amount for future foreign exchange requirements. Companies can also purchase immovable property outside India for business offices and residential houses.

Individuals

The resident individuals have been permitted to have Resident Foreign Currency Domestic account with Indian banks to deposit their foreign exchange earnings receipts through trading or honorarium. The account can be credited with foreign currency for services rendered in India or receipt as a gift. There is no ceiling on this account and the foreign exchange from this account can be used for personal purposes. The resident individuals who have a foreign currency account in India are also allowed to hold international credit cards which have been issued by banks abroad. They can also borrow on interest free loans up to US $2,50,000 from relatives and friends oversees.

Foreign Exchange Management Act (FEMA) 1999

The foreign exchange management Act was initiated in 1999 because FERA did not facilitate trade. This act was specially made to facilitated external trade and payments to bring about development in the foreign exchange market. This Act was also to bring about stability in transactions. This new Act brought about freedom for Authorized Dealers to transact genuine business transactions. FEMA has brought about many appellate authorities which provide adequate help to aggrieved parties in foreign exchange transactions.

Technical Group on Foreign Exchange Market 2005

In 2005 the RBI constituted an internal technical group to bring about further flexibility in foreign exchange transactions. This group brought about more freedom for carrying on business transactions. It made reforms in respect of resident entities for managing their exposures with respect to forward contracts. Reforms were also to be made for commercial banks where by trading volumes could increase. The reforms towards commercial banks were to provide them with more freedom in foreign exchange dealings.

Banks could extend their closing time in the foreign exchange market from 4 PM to 5 PM. They also are permitted to provide capital on actual overnight open exchange positions which was maintained by them rather than on their open position limits. The technical group also recommended that besides the popular US dollar, Pound sterling, Euro and Japanese yen foreign exchange non resident deposits should also be accepted in Canadian dollars, Australian dollars and New-Zealand dollars. The non-resident entities were allowed re-booking and cancellations of forward contracts booked by residents. They were permitted to hedge in international exchanges. Another reform was to raise the ceiling on investments made by Indians abroad. The Authorized Dealers were permitted to have foreign currency account of offices setup by foreign companies in India with any approval from the RBI.

Summary

➡ A market for the sale and purchase of foreign currencies is called as foreign exchange market.

➡ Foreign exchange market is an electronically linked network of banks, authorized dealers and bankers to being the buyers and sellers together.

➡ SWIFT is an international bank communication network that links electronically the traders and dealers together.

➡ The participants in the foreign exchange market are the Reserve Bank of India at the apex, banks, individuals, authorized dealers, financial institutions, speculators and brokers.

➡ The foreign exchange market can operate under the fixed rate system or market determined mechanism.

➡ A 'Nastro' account means 'our account with you'. A 'Vastro' accounts means 'your account with us'.

➡ The different kinds of transactions in a foreign exchange market are 'spot', 'forward' and 'swap' transactions.

➡ The bonds in the foreign exchange market shows that the rate fluctuates from year to year and the real rates are higher than nominal rates.

➡ The nominal rate is the rate preventing at a particles time. The real rate is the purchasing power rate of the currency.

➡ The trading mechanism takes place through inter bank quotations, direct quotation, indirect quotation, bid quotation, ask quotation and gross rates.

➡ The exchange rate system was made flexible in India through LERMS in 1992 and binefied market determined system 1993. There is full convertibility of the current account in India.

➡ RBI has made several changes in the foreign exchange market like developing the gold policy, reforms in banking transactions, introduction of foreign exchange management policy.

➡ There is a large reserve of foreign exchange in India. Some economists feel that reserves increase the interest burden and they should be reduced. Others however feel that reserves build up the confidence level of a developing economy.

Objective Type Questions, Answer True (T) or False (F)

(a) Swift is an electronic communication network in the foreign exchange market.

(b) Foreign exchange brokers are market makers

(c) Speculators are authorized foreign exchange dealers.

(d) The simultaneous purchase and sale of a give amount of foreign exchange is called a spot transaction.

(e) The liberalized exchange rate system replaced the pound staling replaced the US dollar as the intervention currency.

(f) The unified system of foreign exchange rate was conducted through Authorized Dealers.

(g) Conversion of one currency into another without restrictions is defined as currency convertibility.

(h) Nastro means 'your account with us'.

(i) The real exchange rate is the price of one currency in terms of another.

(j) The exchange rate which is fixed with the market forces is called the 'floating rate'.

Answer: (a) T, (b) F, (c) F, (d) F, (e) F, (f) T, (g) T, (h) F, (i) F, (j) T.

Multiple Choice Questions (Tick mark (✓) the right answer)

1. Gold standard is linked to:
    (a) Reserves of gold and currency
    (b) Notes and coins and promissory market
    (c) Currency cheques bank drafts and bills of exchange
    (d) Gold reserve owned by the bank

2. Speculators in the foreign exchange market are participants:
    (a) They make profit are Authorized Dealers
    (b) They are traders making profits
    (c) They make profits by anticipating future changes in price of foreign exchange
    (d) They make profit through inter bank dealings

3. A foreign exchange Authorized Dealer is a market maker:
    (a) A market maker
    (b) Buyer and seller of foreign currency
    (c) A foreign exchange broker
    (d) An inter bank foreign exchange operator

4. In the liberalized exchange rate system:
    (a) All foreign exchange receipts and payments were market determined
    (b) Receipts and payments were determined in the basis of 30% official rate and 70% market
    (c) Receipts and payments were based on 60% in the free market and 40% at official rate
    (d) 60% at official rates and 40% in the free market

5. The real exchange rate:
   (a) Measures purchasing power parity
   (b) Measures the price of one currency in terms of another
   (c) Measures the appreciated price of a foreign currency
   (d) Measures the devaluation of one currency against another

6. A Vastro account is:
   (a) Your account with us
   (b) Our account with us
   (c) Our account with each other
   (d) Your account with a foreign bank

   Answer: 1 (d), 2 (c), 3 (a), 4 (c), 5 (a), 6 (a).

Short Answer Questions

1. Distinguish between fixed and flexible exchange rate system.
2. Discuss the role of an Authorized Dealer of foreign exchange.
3. Write a brief note on:

   (a) Swift, (b) Spot rate, (c) Pegs and baskets.
4. What is LERMS?
5. Give the features of unified market determined systems 1993.
6. Write a short note on NASTRO and VASTRO.

Long Answer Questions

1. What is the nature of the foreign exchange market? Describe the participants of this market.

2. What are the different kinds of transactions taking place in a foreign exchange market?

3. What discuss the fixed and flexible exchange rates system in a foreign exchange market?

4. Distinguish between Normal Real and effective exchange rates.

5. What are the trends in the foreign exchange market in India?

6. Discuss the developments in the foreign exchange market in India.

7. How do you determine exchange rates? Discuss the advantages and limitations of fixed exchange rates.

8. Discuss the implications of a flexible exchange rate system.

Foreign Capital Flows

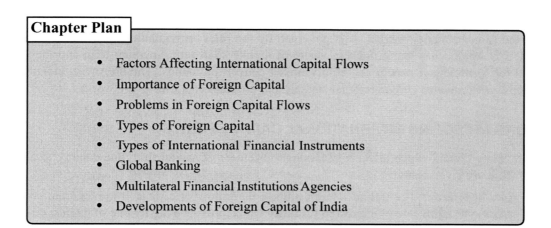

Chapter Plan

- Factors Affecting International Capital Flows
- Importance of Foreign Capital
- Problems in Foreign Capital Flows
- Types of Foreign Capital
- Types of International Financial Instruments
- Global Banking
- Multilateral Financial Institutions Agencies
- Developments of Foreign Capital of India

INTRODUCTION

Foreign capital flows have been significant in promoting international business and co-operation amongst different countries. Developing countries depend on developed countries for their technology, know how, human resources and superior knowledge to develop themselves. London, Amsterdam and Venice were known as significant financial markets. New York changed the complexion of international trade by becoming the leading global market in the 20th century. It provides facilities for financing foreign trade transactions of different countries and creates the environment for lending and borrowing internationally. The capital transactions take place through global integration of financial instruments and capital flows between different countries.

The financial market in USA is one of the most powerful international financial markets. It has many innovative instruments it is transparent in its financial dealings and ensures investor protection. It is regulated by the Securities Exchange Commission (SEC). The Euro market is a major global market. It deals with Euro dollar bonds developing countries like India trade through syndicated Eurodollar loans. The Japanese market has many funding instruments of which Samurai bonds are the most popular foreign Yen bonds. These bonds are offered through public issue to non-residents. They also encourage Shibosai bonds through private placements to institutional investors. They offer syndicated yen loans which are more reasonable than the foreign bonds. The Yen market dominates the international financial scenario. Indian organizations issued bonds in Japanese Yen market. The German market is another dominating financial market. Its bond market is very large. Non-resident borrowers like to borrow from this market. The German market has a strong banking system and has developed in universal banking but it has a small equity market. The Swiss financial market is an important international financial market. The borrowers in this market are banks, corporate organization, government and different countries. Their major segment of financing is bonds through public issues and private placement. Syndicated loans have small market. The Swiss market is attractive because it has political stability and a very high rate of savings. The Indian participation in the Swiss market is negligible. The Australian market is known for offshore bonds. Their Yankee Kangaroo bonds are well known in the international markets especially in the American, Asian and Euro market. The Australian market is popular with retail investors. The sterling market is one of the most significant financial markets in the world. It is better loan as the London money market. It is governed by the rules an regulations provided by Bank of England. The Market has many financial instruments like short term, medium term and long terms bonds. It has commercial papers and equity linked convertible bonds. The borrowers are financial institutions, governments, corporate organizations and different countries in the world.

FACTORS AFFECTING INTERNATIONAL CAPITAL FLOWS

There are many factors which affect international movement of capital from one country to another. Some of them are given below:

- *Rate of interest:* The rate of interest attracts the inflow of capital. It moves from countries which give a low rate of interest to countries which provide a higher rate of interest on capital flows.
- *Profit:* Profit motivates foreign capital movement. It moves to countries where it expects to earn a good rate of return on its investments. The return follows capital investments with a gestation period. Therefore, attractive returns will create an interest for inflows of capital.
- *Production costs:* Advanced countries look for opportunities to network with developing countries if the costs of production is low in that country. The cost of labour and raw materials is a decision factor for a country to make its investments. A low cost in production means that the earnings will be high and there will be profitability.
- *Government policies:* The policies relating to inflow of capital encourage or discourage foreign countries to take a decision to invest in a country. A flexible government policy which is interested in two way flows is a good precondition for creating a supportive environment for movement of capital. A controlled government with strict policies and closed door interests cannot encourage other countries to bring in capital to its country. The government policies towards tariffs, foreign exchange control, taxation and foreign collaboration should be carefully prepared. If a country is keen on international trade.
- *Political factors:* A country which has political stability can influence capital movements. Political stability creates an environment of freedom of occupation, security of life and reasonable

opportunity for making profits. This brings about an interest from foreign countries in making investments.

- *Infrastructural facilities:* The facilities provided with respect to movement of goods and human resources as well as an integrated banking and financial system helps to globalize and integrate global trade and capital movements.

IMPORTANCE OF FOREIGN CAPITAL

Foreign capital has many benefits. Primarily it integrates different countries together. There is an advantage for both the developed and the developing countries in assisting each other. The developed countries transfer their resources to develop the resources of the developing countries but in return they are earning a rate of interest for the services and the capital provided by them some of these advantages of developing foreign capital in a country.

- *Integration:* Foreign capital helps to internationalize a country from a closed economy to an open one. When a country has surplus funds to invest there is an outflow of capital from the country and an inflow into another country which has paucity for funds.

- *Technology:* Movement of capital creates a network where by production can be carried out at the country where labour is cheap and technology is backward. Transfer of technology from technologically superior country to a less developed country will upgrade the facilities and technologies of the developing country.

- *Penetration of products:* Foreign capital is able to bring about competition and increase in products by offering choices to the population. New products will create new markets and more business for different countries. Capital will flow from one country to another wherever it is desired.

- *Utilization of productive capacity:* When demand for a product is accelerated internationally the productive capacity of production units will be fully utilized. This will bring about a higher profit and will upgrade technologically sound products.

- *Risks sharing:* When two countries decide to do business together. They would be sharing of risks in capital financing. This will reduce the risk of both the countries.

- *Competition:* A protected market without any competition is unable to grow because of restrictions. In India government followed a restrictive policy with the state playing the main role in development. There were many barriers in trade due to restrictions and regulations. The non competition attitude became a restraining factor in India's development. In 1991 it had to liberalize its economic policies to let the market forces operate. Competition through demand and supply conditions opened up the market and encouraged growth in business and development in industries.

- *Economic growth:* The contribution of foreign investments encourages economic growth in a country through development of skills, technology, and communication and computer networks. It also brings about employment. The saving and investment process is accelerated with higher business and greater production.

PROBLEMS IN FOREIGN CAPITAL FLOWS

Foreign capital flows have many advantages for a country but there are many problems associated with foreign capital flows.

- *Legal Differences:* The legal environment of different countries cannot have a similarity because it is country specific. A law which is required in India may not be required in Singapore because the working system is very different. Before a country decides on capital in flows to another country, it must study the legal an economic environment of the country. If a capital flow has been made and it is not favourable at a later date it will result in a loss. Therefore, after carefully analyzing the legal situation of investment one party should decide in marking investment in another country. Sometimes within a country laws are region specific. In such a case the foreign investment has to be made after a careful scrutiny of the regional law.

- *Cultural differences:* The methodology of business depends on the culture of a country. For example, in some countries gifts and commissions are required for conducting business. Another country may not consider such commissions necessary for conducting business. Their policy may be to make direct contracts without any intermediary. Where as the host country may have the cultural system of working through intermediaries.

- *Currency units:* The currency units are different from one country to another. This creates problems of currency convertibility due to exchange rate fluctuations. The Euro currency binds 16 countries with one common currency. Hence, business dealings become simpler. Converting from one currency to another can bring about losses.

- *Trade restrictions:* Some countries impose high import duties and are liberal with export duties. Other countries have both high import and high export duties. This creates a problem of capital inflows especially in agreements on transfer payments and sale and purchase of specialized items between them.

Despite the problems of international capital flows, countries are keen on capital inflows and outflows. The main reasons which can be attributed to such flows are because of the 'pull' and 'push' factors. The pull factors are the forces of attraction which motivate a country to internationalize itself to earn profit and encourage growth within the country. The push factors are the compulsions of saturated markets within a country to internationalize it.

TYPES OF FOREIGN CAPITAL

There are different types of foreign capital. It can be from official sources as well as from private sources. There can be bilateral agreements, multilateral contracts and commercial arrangements.

- *Official Sources:* Foreign capital flows from official sources are mainly through loans, grants and gifts from different governments. They may also be sourced from government projects and from the private corporate sector. The funds would be routed through governments. The official funds would be preferred as the contract is clear in terms of cost of the project, maturity period and the payment schedule.

- *Private foreign capital:* Institutional investors and private individuals supply foreign capital through certain global financial instruments, foreign direct investment, multinational corporations, non-resident Indians and foreign financial institutions.

- *Joint ventures:* The flow of foreign capital is very useful through joint ventures. The host country provides the infrastructural facilities and the foreign country provides the technology other market or copyrights.

- *Multilateral sources:* The multilateral financial institutions are the World Bank and its affiliated institutions such as the Asian Development Bank, The International Monetary Funds and the Bank for International Settlements. The long term funds for development are supplied by the World Bank. The International Monetary Fund gives support during the short term period.

- *Non-resident Indian funds:* The NRIs have invested in India through bank deposits, financial instruments, portfolio investments and direct investment skills. They have established industries, export houses, hotels, nursing homes and business processing offices. They have also brought in capital flows through investment in housing and real estate development.

- *Foreign institutional investors:* The Indian stock market became liberal in 1992 to bring in the flow of capital in to the country. The new policy allowed portfolio investments by the foreign institutional investors. Global equity market attractive investment in developing countries with higher amount of interest in investments. India also gained support in flow of funds due to the activity in the equity markets in India.

- *Foreign direct investments:* The foreign direct investment has grown in India due to its liberal and global attitude towards development since 1992.

- *Mergers and acquisitions:* Large business has become important to be known in business. When a business is very small, it prefers to adopt other organizations through acquisitions and amalgamations. Mergers create an identity, increase volume of resources and bring about profitability.

The free flow of capital form one country to another depends on government policy and its attitude towards foreign capital and technology. In India foreign capital was very small from private sources. The main source of capital was from government because the public sector dominated the country. However, the economic policy in 1991 in India changed the complexion of business by opening up the economy and giving greater role for participation to the private corporate sector. It reduced the barriers of trade between countries by removing restrictions and licenses and reducing important and export duties. This has opened up the market and foreign capital flows have improved.

TYPES OF INTERNATIONAL FINANCIAL INSTRUMENTS

Foreign capital is brought into the country through various financial instruments. The instruments are Syndicated Bank Loans, Euro Currency Deposits, Foreign Bonds, Euro Bonds, Fixed Rate Notes (FRNs), American Depository Receipts (ADRs), Global Depository Receipts (GDRs) and International Depository Receipts (IDRs).

- *Syndicated Euro Currency Loans:* A syndicate of banks arranging a loan in Euro currency in the international financial market is called a *syndicated euro currency loan*. The syndicate of banks grand credit in the form of loans either for long term or medium term. The syndication begins by granting exclusive mandate to a lead manager the loans are normally of $10 million and have a maturity of 10 years. It is granted through a consortium of banks comprising of lead manager, manager, participant and agent. Defaults on these loans usually do not occur. If it does it is treated with a high penalty.

- *Euro bonds:* The euro bond market has different kinds of financial instruments. The Euro bonds are unsecured and have a fixed rate of interest. They are redeemable at their face value by the borrower on maturity of the bond. The income on these bonds is exempt from tax deducted at source but has to be reported as part of income within the countries regulations. Capital gains and losses are possible and they can be transferred easily form one percent to another. Euro bonds can be denominated in more than one currency. It is then called a multi currency bond. Euro bonds can also be equity linked bonds, euro convertible bonds, floating rate notes and euro callable bonds. Euro bonds are usually listed on London stock exchange.

- *Convertible bonds:* The straight bonds were innovated into convertible bonds. These bonds have the option of converting them into equity shares of the borrowing company. The conversion price is fixed above the market price of equity shares on the date of the bond issue. When they are converted the borrowing company issues new equity shares. Convertible bonds have a lower interest than the straight euro bonds. The instrument is safer than the straight euro bonds because investors get foreign exchange protection. The company issuing convertible bonds has the advantage of paying a low rate of interest and receives a premium on the price of shares. The issuing company also has the disadvantage of outflow of foreign capital if the bond is not converted into equity shares at the time of redemption.

- *Floating rate bonds:* These bonds are issued for short term period of time. They have a fixed rate of interest. They can be converted into another bond which has the same nominal value but a longer maturity period. These bonds become '*Drop Lock Bonds*' when they are automatically converted into fixed bonds with specified rate of interest.

- *Multiple tranche bonds:* These are another form of euro bonds and are issued in small parts of the total bond. The market conditions prevailing in the country provide the basis of decision making to the issuing company in the initial issue to the part amount to be issued on the bonds. The subsequent issues are based on the perception of the issuer of the bonds. These bonds are issued when the market conditions project a low rate of interest.

- *Currency option bonds:* The currency option bonds involve more than one currency at a time. The bonds give the investor the freedom of buying the bond in one currency and accepting the interest in another currency. The principal sum and the interest can be paid and received respectively in different countries.

- *Floating rate notes (FRNs):* These bonds are little different to the above bonds because they offer adjusted returns periodically. They reflect the changes in short term money markets by adjusting the rate of interest every six months. They resemble Euro dollar bonds in denomination of $1,000 each. The main difference is that they carry spread or margin above six months London Inter Bank Of Rate (LIBOR) for Euro dollar deposits. The spread is usually 1/4 points with in 1/8 % at one corner and 1½ % other corner. The pricing is done at a margin linked to the USA price rate or LIBOR bid rate. The maturity period of such bonds is between 5-7 years. Individual investors can purchase floating rate notes.

- Banks can lend through floating rate notes. It is the common practice of American and Non American banks for borrowing dollars without any problems of shrinking credit lines with other banks. They help banks for expending business in their country. They are traded easily and are attractive short term investments for banks as well as corporate units. The banks in United Kingdom used floating rate notes to raise capital from cheaper and reasonable sources for raising primary capital. Floating rate notes have been issued by Sweden for a maturity period of 40 years.

- *Floating rates certificate of deposits:* These financial instruments have a floating rate of interest. They are negotiable instruments and can be transferred from one person to another as they are bearer instruments. They have short term interest rates of six months which are adjusted through a spread above the inter bank rate of six months of US dollar deposits in London LIBOR.

- *Global bonds:* Global bonds were issued by the World Bank in 1990. These bonds were economical, had low transaction cost and high liquidity. These global bonds cost only 10 cents for deals of $25 million clearing and settlement cost are also low or lease bonds. The number of days for clearing such bonds are also few. It can be borrower by different currencies depending on the attractive rates of return.

- *Euro notes:* Euro notes are global bonds and are known as Euro commercial papers. These notes can be underwritten by banks. If they are underwritten there is a commitment by the banks to purchase the bonds. If they are not underwritten dealers sell them in the open market. These notes are of short term duration and do not have any guarantees. The underwritten as well as non underwritten notes supplement syndicated loans, commercial paper of USA as well as floating rate notes. In many countries Euro notes have been popular and they are legally underwritten by banks. Some countries which use the Euro notes are USA, Canada, Japan, United Kingdom and France. Interest is paid on these notes. The non bank investors of Euro notes are insurance companies and fund managers.

- *Participatory notes:* The Foreign institutional investors use accounts registered in tax havens like Mauritius or the Cayman Islands to trade in shares for their clients. These sub-accounts, issue participatory notes to the client as proof of purchase. Foreign institutional investors can be registered or non-registered. If it is not registered it can be used as a proxy by investors to play in the derivatives market. If it is registered, trade can be done legally. Stock futures are largely dominated by participatory notes and are used currently in India to hedge instruments to limit risk in cash markets.

- *Forward rate agreements (FRAs):* These are agreements between two counter parties to lend or borrow a principal sum of money. One party wants to protect itself against a future fall of interest rate. The other party is interested in protecting itself against a future rise of interest. Both parities agree to pay an interest rate for a period of three months which would begin after six months. On the maturity date the difference is paid between the agreed rate and current interest rate. This is similar to a financial future contract. It has a fixed settlement date. The FRAs have a maximum trade denominated in USA Dollars.

- *Note issuance facilities (NIFs):* This facility is for medium term commitments of 5-7 years. It provides a commitment or an underwriting of group of banks to enable the borrowers to have an access to funds. This facility is a combination of the floating rate notes and a syndicated bank loans. Through this arrangement a series of short term obligations are issued and they are rolled over continuously. It is also called a *revolving underwriting facility*.

There is a lot of development in global equity markets in the form of depository receipts. The most popular negotiable certificates adopted in the international equity markets are the American Depository Receipts (ADRs) in USA, European Depository Receipts (EDRs) in Europe and Global Depository Receipts (GDRs) internationally and USA.

- *American depository receipts:* The American depository receipts were started in America in 1920 to invest in oversees markets and to provide a base to non-USA companies who wanted to invest in the stock market in USA. When they were originally issued they were not '*fungible*'. They could be traded in the USA and the EDRs had to be settled in Euro but with the increasing volume of trade in 1990 the receipts became fungible which means that they could be traded settled and cleared with one receipt. ADRs can be sponsored or non-sponsored. Sponsored ADRs can be used for raising additional capital in USA. New ADRs can be listed on a national stock exchange and registered with the Securities Exchange Commission (SEC). The unsponsored ADRs a similar to stock exchange trading transfers and transactions with fixed outstanding equity.

- *European depository receipts:* The EDRs are issued in Europe and denominated in European currency. They resemble the ADRs but are not attractive instruments EDRs have a very small market. They are not well developed like the ADRs and GDRs.

- *Global depository receipts:* GDRs are an instrument for raising equity capital by organizations which are in Asian countries. They are placed in USA, Europe and Asia. They have a low cost and help in bringing liquidity. A company usually raises capital simultaneously from two counties. For example, the GDR may be issued in India and simultaneously placed in USA and Europe through one security. The issuer deals with a single depository bank which facilitates the secondary and inters market trading amongst investors which are situated in different counties. It is a fungible instruments and the issuer does not have any exchange risk. He can freely use the foreign exchange collected from this issue. Government of India allowed Indian companies to mobilized funds from foreign markets through Euro issues of global depository receipts and foreign currency convertible bonds. Companies with a good track record can issue GDRs for developing infrastructure projects in power, telecommunications, and petroleum and in construction and development of roads, airports and ports in India.

GLOBAL BANKING

International financial activities can take place through banks. Many private banks have been introduced to do business in development projects. Syndicated lending can be done through important multilateral agencies. Due to a large volume of trade offshore banking and tax havens have developed. Some of the developments in global banking are discussed below:

Inter Bank Transactions

The inter bank transactions take place through electronic international communication facility. The transfer of funds from one country to another is through the inter bank communications called CHIPS and SWIFT.

CHIPS: Chips was started in 1970 as clearing house in New York. It is an automated modern system of transferring funds from one bank to another. It has now become a global clearing house and it is based on an inter bank payment system.

SWIFT: Swift was introduced in 1973 in Belgium. It is the largest world financial telecommunication system. It is owned by a non profit cooperative society. It has its own communication lines from international carriers. It is owned by banks in 15 nations. The major share is with banks in Europe, North America and Japan. It links the banks world wide through an electronic network and transmission system. Swift means society for world wide inter bank financial communications.

Offshore Banking

Banking within a country but beyond its banking system is offshore banking. It operates through Offshore Banking Centres (OBC). Offshore banking provides international banking facilities. These centres are exempt from payment of income tax and corporate tax. They also have freedom from monetary controls. Offshore banking business is done only through external currencies with non-residents. These centres offer cross border banking business. Since, they have many concessions they give advantages in banking transactions to their clients. Besides banking they also undertake financial services like foreign exchange trading and becoming portfolio managers in international financial markets. Offshore banking sectors are located in large money centres like Singapore, Hong Kong and Bahrain.

Tax Havens

Tax havens provide a tax free environment. They are international financial centres developed in Netherlands, Panama, Bahamas, Luxemburg and Cayman Islands. Tax havens have the main objective of providing transactions for taking advantage of tax concessions and maintaining secrecy in transactions. Tax havens efficiently transact banking business.

MULTILATERAL FINANCING AGENCIES

The major sources of foreign capital from international institutions have been from the World Bank and its affiliates, Asian Development Banks, Then International Development Agencies and The International Monetary fund. These institutions are discussed briefly.

World Bank

The World Bank promotes development in member countries through projects for trade, infrastructure and reconstruction. The World Bank works with its affiliates. These are International Development Agency (IDA), International Financial Corporation (IFC) and Multilateral Investment Guarantee Agency (MIGA). It gives assistance to government, public sector units and autonomous bodies in developed and developing countries. The loan has to be guarantees by government of the borrowing country. Loans are provided for long term up to a period of 20 years at low rates of interest. The World Bank also provides guarantees while promoting private foreign investment. It participates in infrastructural development projects relating to electricity, power, education and environment. It is keen to develop long term balanced growth of international trade. It is also engaged in rural development projects. It helps member countries in meeting balance of payments problems and participates actively in discussions with countries to adopt good international trade practices to create the sprit of globalization and liberalization.

International Development Agency (IDA)

IDA provides assistance mainly to underdeveloped and developing countries which have a high rate of poverty. Its loan is at a very low cost with a low rate of return. The maturity period of its loan is 50 years. The IDA gives loans only to those institutions which can get a guarantee from government. Its modus operandi is to get the wealthy countries to contribute to the poor and developing countries. Its resources are provided by the high income group of countries. The IDA is an affiliate of the World Bank and it was established in 1960 with the purpose of providing loans with easy terms (soft loans) for development.

International Finance Corporation (IFC)

The International Finance Corporation was setup to promote private sector organizations by providing loans and equity capital to them in developing countries. Its purpose was to develop the capital markets and financial institutions of the developing countries. It sponsors, underwrites and distributes shares of individuals companies and funds which invest in international investments. It supplies to non-government organizations that are in the private corporate sector. It does not require any guarantees from government. It was established in 1956 and its capital has been funded by 135 countries.

Multilateral Investment Guarantee Agency (MIGA)

Multilateral Investment Guarantee Agency was setup as an affiliate of the World Bank in 1988. It gives insurance protection to foreign investors up to 90% of currency transfer risk, breach of contract risk and risk of war up to a period of 15 years. It encourages developing countries to provide a well developed investment environment for attracting foreign investors to make long term commitments in developing countries. It advises the developing countries on foreign policy matters.

Asian Development Bank

The Asian Development Bank deals with private corporate organizations in Asian and Pacific countries. Its purpose is to develop the capital markets of developing countries by lending support though underwriting of securities and guarantees for loans. New issues are underwritten by the bank to encourage private entrepreneurship in developing countries. It establishes private enterprises by backing them through guarantees for taking loans for setting up development projects.

International Monetary Fund

The International Monetary Fund in helps countries to obtain funds in advance for their requirements. It provides loans for problems in balance of payments and for temporary requirements of foreign exchange. Its purpose is to bring about harmony and co-operation in international trade through a multilateral trade and systematic payments system. The member countries can borrow from the international monetary fund for temporary requirements. The IMF can sell gold for providing special development loans. It has a special financing facility through which it can give temporary foreign exchange as a credit to a country which faces short term problems. It has also created a buffer stock facility for purchasing inventories. It can grant temporary loans to countries for inventories. The fund was established in 1944.

Bank for International Settlements (BIS)

This bank was setup in 1930 to be a Central Bank for the Central Bank of other countries in the world. It carries out the function of an agent between the different banks by creating an international network of Various Central Banks through their monetary reserves. The monetary reserve is then used in the world financial markets as deposits with commercial banks or for short term uses through treasury bills. The BIS tries to establish a forum for discussions between different banks brining in monetary co-operation.

DEVELOPMENTS OF FOREIGN CAPITAL OF INDIA

Foreign capital inflows: The composition of capital inflows for the period 1990-2007 is depicted in table 10.1. The table indicates the direction of capital inflow in the form of foreign direct investment, portfolio investment, External assistance, commercial borrowing, NRI deposits and Rupee debt services.

Table 10.1: Composition of capital inflows

Item	1990-91	1995-96	2001-02	2002-03	2003-04	2004-05	2005-06PR	2006-07P
1	2	3	4	5	6	7	8	9
Total Capital Inflows (Net) US $ million	7,056	4,089	8,551	10,840	16,736	28,022	23,400	44,944
of which:								(in per cent)
1. Nin-Debt Creating Inflows	1.5	117.5	95.2	55.5	93.7	54.6	86.1	58.8
(a) Foreign Direct Investment*	1.4	52.4	71.6	46.5	25.8	21.4	32.7	43.3
(b) Porifolio Investment	0.1	65.1	23.6	9.0	67.9	33.2	53.4	15.5
2. Debt Creating Inflows	83.3	57.7	12.4	−13.3	−6.0	35.2	37.0	56.1
(a) External Assistance	31.3	21.6	14.1	−28.6	−16.5	7.2	7.5	4.0
(b) External Commercial Borrowings @	31.9	31.2	−18.6	−15.7	−17.5	19.4	12.7	36.5
(c) Short term Credits	15.2	1.2	−9.3	8.9	8.5	13.5	7.3	7.3
(d) NRI Deposits @	21.8	27.0	32.2	27.5	21.8	−3.4	11.9	8.7
(e) Rupee Debt Service	−16.9	−23.3	−6.1	−4.4	−2.2	−1.5	−2.4	−0.4
3. Other Capital ±	15.2	−75.2	−7.6	56.8	12.3	10.2	−23.1	−14.9
4. total (1 to 3)	100.0	100.0	100.0	100.0	100.0	100.0	100.0	100.0
Memo: Stable flows *	84.7	33.7	85.6	82.0	23.7	53.2	39.3	77.1

PR : Partially Revised.

P : Provisional.

* : Data on FDI have been revised since 2000-01 with expanded coverage to approach international best practices. FDI data for previous years would not be comparable with these figures.

: Refers to medium and long-term borrowings.

@ : Including NR (NR) Rupee Deposits.

± : Includes leads and lags in exports (difference between the custom and the banking channel data). Banking Capital (assets and liabilities of banks excluding NRI deposits), loans to non-residents by residents, Indian investment abroad and India's subscription to international Institutions and quota payments to IMF.

± : Stable Flows are defined to represent all capital flows excluding portfolio flows and short-term trade credits.

Source: Reserve Bank of India Annual Report, Appendix Table 53, October 2007.

As per the data given the foreign direct investment in India it is estimated to be as high as 43.3% in 2006-2007. It has been quite high in India after the liberal policy was introduced in 1991. Portfolio investments increased from 23.6% in 2001-2002, it decrease to 9.0% in 2002-2003, again rose to 67.9% in 2003-2004 and fail to 33.2% in 2004-2005. In every year it has fluctuated widely and estimates are that it will fall to 15.5% in 2007. The maximum capital inflows in India are through external commercial borrowings for medium term and long term period of types. The NRI deposits have also been fluctuating but are still an important inflow of capital for India.

Table 10.2: Foreign investment inflows

Year	A. Direct investment		B. Portfolio investment		Total (A+B)	
	Rs. crore	US $ million	Rs. crore	US $ million	Rs. crore	US $ million
1	2	3	4	5	6	7
1990-91	174	97	11	6	185	103
1991-92	316	129	10	4	326	133
1992-93	965	315	748	244	1713	559
1993-94	1838	586	11188	3567	13026	4153
1994-95	4126	1314	12007	3824	16133	5138
1995-96*	7172	2144	9192	2748	16364	4892
1996-97*	10015	2821	11758	3312	21773	6133
1997-98*	13220	3557	6794	1828	20014	5385
1998-99*	10358	2462	-257	-61	10101	2401
1999-00*	9338	2155	13112	3026	22450	5181
2000-01*	18406	4029	12609	2760	31015	6789
2001-02*	29235	6130	9639	2021	38874	8151
2002-03*	24367	5035	4738	979	29105	6014
2003-04*	19860	4322	52279	11377	72139	15699
2004-05* P	27188	6051	41854	9315	69042	15366
2005-06* P	34188	7722	55306	12492	89494	20214
2006-07* P	88446	19531	31713	7003	120159	26534

P   :   Provisional.

*   :   Includes acquisition of shares of Indian companies by non-residents under Section 6 of FEMA, 1999. Data on such acquisitions are included as part of FDI since January 1996.

Notes 1. Data on FDI have been revised since 2000-01 with expanded coverage to approach international best practices. Data from 2000-01 onwards are not comparable with FDI data for earlier years.
2. Negative (–) sign indicates outflow.
3. Direct Investment data for 2006-07 include swap of shares of 3.1 billion.
   Also see Notes on Tables.

Source: RBI Handbook Table 161, 2007.

The foreign direct investment has been high in volume as depicted in table 10.2 in 2007 the volume of direct investment is Rs. 88,446 crores and portfolio investment is only Rs. 31,713 crores. This is due to the fact that a large number of projects are routed in India through Mauritius because of tax advantages. India has an agreement with Mauritius of avoiding double taxation. Many multinational corporations prefer to bring in their investments through Mauritius. The important sources of FDI into India are USA, Japan, UK, Germany, Netherlands, Singapore, France and South Korea. Since 1991, many more countries are investing into India. These are Thailand, South Africa, Israel and Saudi Arabia. The foreign direct investment in India has been mainly in the services sector like telecommunications. It has also been in oil and power, chemicals and food processing industries. India also opened up pharmaceuticals, cement and metal industries. Delhi, Maharashtra and Haryana had large inflows of capital in foreign direct investments well comparing India with China, India's foreign policy opened up in 1991 and it was also interested in expanding its industrial base. However, it has been reported that China is ahead of India in its investments. Another observation is that India has high inflow of foreign capital from external commercial borrowing. This is of high risk because international banks provide loans easily to support development of a country because they promote their own business. They also withdraw support whenever there are type money considerations.

Non-Resident Indian Deposits: The NRI deposits are a very important source of capital for India. There are different times of deposit schemes through which the funds are raised. They are high cost funds for India because high interest has to be paid on these deposits to make them attractive. The first scheme to be started was non-resident external rupee accounts in 1970. 2% premium was to be given on this to make it attractive. The second scheme which was introduced was Foreign Currency Non-Resident Account (FCNRA) in 1975. The rates of interest under the schemes were continuously adjusted according to international rates. The third scheme was the foreign currency deposits. This was started in 1990 but suspended because reserves became high. The non-resident (Non-Repatriable) rupee deposits scheme was introduced in 1992 but also discontinued in 2002. Balance under the scheme was allowed to be credited to non-resident accounts on maturity. Now, there are only two fully convertible deposit schemes. These are NR(E)RA and FCNR(B) non-resident volumes in 2007 is expected to be Rs. 1,06,786 crores in NR(E)RA accounts and Rs. 65,955 crores in FCNR(B) accounts. The impact of these funds due to its high volume brings about market volatility in India. The total volume of NRI funds is expected to be Rs. 1,72,741 crores as depicted in Table 10.3.

Table 10.3: NRI Deposits Outstanding - Rupees

(Rupees crore)

Year (end-March)	NR(E)RA	FCNR(A)	FCNR(B)	NR(NR)RD	FC(B&O)D	FC(O)N	Total
1	2	3	4	5	6	7	8
1991	7,040	19,845	–	–	515	–	27,400
1992	7,833	30,576	–	–	1,895	–	40,304
1993	8,616	33,163	–	1,952	3,261	–	46,992
1994	11,053	29,176	3,476	5,501	1,672	38	50,916
1995	14,348	22,207	9,648	7,831	–	32	54,066
1996	13,452	14,616	19,648	12,166	–	45	59,927
1997	17,886	8,282	26,906	20,116	–	14	73,204
1998	22,267	4	33,445	24,735	–	9	80,460
1999	25,629	–	33,222	28,058	–	–	86,909
2000	29,465	–	35,632	29,447	–	–	94,544
2001	33,357	–	42,357	31,966	–	–	1,07,680
2002	41,205	–	47,175	34,392	–	–	1,22,772
2003	71,184	–	48,651	16,253	–	–	1,36,088
2004	92,977	–	49,572	7,895	–	–	1,50,444
2005	93,159	–	50,108	1,015	–	–	1,44,282
						–	1,56,715
						–	1,72,741

PR   : Provisional.
FCNR(A) : Foreign currency non-resident (accounts).   NR(E)RA   : Non-resident (external) Rupee accounts.
FCNR(B)   : Foreign currency non-resident (banks).   NR(NR)RD : Non-resident (non-repatriable) Rupee deposits.
FC(B&O)D : Foreign currency (bank and other) deposits. FC(O)N   : Foreign currency (ordinary) non-repatriable deposits.
Source: RBI Handbook, 2007.

Table 10.4: Foreign Institutional Investments in India

Year	Gross Purchase (Rs. crore)	Gross Sales (Rs. crore)	Net Investment (Rs. crore)	Net Investment (US $ mn.)	Cumulative Net Investment (US $ mn.)
1	2	3	4	5	6
1992-93	17	4	13	4	4
1993-94	5,593	466	5,126	1,634	1,638
1994-95	7,631	2,835	4,796	1,528	3,167
1995-96	9,694	2,752	6,942	2,036	5,202
1996-97	15,554	6,979	8,574	2,432	7,634
1997-98	18,695	12,737	5,957	1,650	9,284
1998-99	16,115	17,699	−1,584	−386	8,898
1999-00	56,856	46,734	10,122	2,393	11,237
2000-01	74,051	64,116	9,934	2,159	13,395
2001-02	49,920	41,165	8,755	1,846	15,242
2002-03	47,061	44,373	2,689	564	15,805
2003-04	1,44,858	99,094	45,765	9,950	25,755
2004-05	2,16,953	1,71,072	45,881	10,172	35,927
2005-06	3,46,978	3,05,512	41,467	9,332	45,295

Source : RBI Handbook 2007.

Foreign Institutional Investment: The Indian financial market was opened to the foreign institutional investors in 1992 to widen and broaden the Indian capital market. The net investment by FIIs in India has been positive every year except in 1998-99. During the last three years, there has been a phenomenal increase in the portfolio investment by FIIs in the Indian market. The gross purchases of debt and equity together by FIIs increased by 59.9 per cent to Rs. 3,46,978 crore in 2005-06 from Rs. 2,16,953 crore in 2004-05. The gross sales by FIIs also rose by 78.6 per cent to Rs. 3,05,512 crore from Rs. 1,71,072 crore during the same period. However, the net investment by FIIs in 2005-06 declined by 9.6 per cent to Rs. 41,467 crore in 2005-06 from Rs. 45,881 crore in 2004-05 mainly due to large net outflows from the debt segment. The cumulative net investment by FIIs at acquisition cost, which was US$15.8 billion at the end of March 2003, rose to US$ 45.3 billion at the end of March 2006. Several factors are responsible for increasing confidence of FIIs on the Indian stock market which include, strong macro-economic fundamentals of the economy, transparent regulatory system, abolition of long-term capital gains tax and encouraging corporate results. Reflecting the congenial investment climate, the total number of FIIs registered with SEBI increased to 882 as on March 31, 2006 compared to 685 a year ago, an increase of 197 over the year. A distinctive feature of the profile of the newly registered FIIs relates to increase in registration from the unconventional countries such as Malaysia, Australia, Saudi Arabia, Trinidad and Tobago, Denmark, Italy, Belgium, Canada, Sweden, and Ireland etc. The FII investment in equity increased significantly since 2003-04. During 2005-06, FIIs increased their net investment in equities, but reduced their commitments in debt securities. The net FII investment in equity during 2005-06 was Rs. 48,801 crore, the highest ever in a single year. Buoyancy in the markets was sustained in 2005-06 on account of surge in net investment by the institutional investors with FIIs playing a major role. Month-wise, FII investment was negative in the months of April, May and October 2005 (Chart 2.14). However, during the remaining months of the financial year, there was large net equity investment by FIIs, particularly in the second half of 2005-06, which drove the benchmark indices to surpass the earlier record highs on several occasions. The net FII investment in December 2005 was the highest for 2005-06. The total net investment in the debt segment in 2005-06 declined by Rs.7,334 crore mainly due to firming up of the yield rate of G-sec across the entire maturity spectrum. The FIIs were permitted to trade in the derivatives market since February 2002. The cumulative FII investment in derivatives was Rs.1,94,437 crore as on March 31, 2006. Open interest position of FIIs in single stock futures was the highest at 59.9 per cent by end-March 2006, followed by index futures (34.7 per cent).

Summary

➠ The flow of foreign capital is through official government and private sources.

➠ The forms of foreign capital are through external borrowings loans equity capital portfolio investment foreign direct investment multination corporations, non resident Indians and foreign financial institutions.

➠ The major global markets are: United States financial Euro market, German market and Japanese financial markets.

➠ Foreign capital flows are through financial instruments, financial institutions, Inter-bank transactions, tax havens and offshore banking.

➠ The important instruments are Euro bonds, convertible bonds multiple trance bonds, currency option bonds, floating rate notes, floating rate certificates, global bonds, Euro notes and Note Issuance Facilities and Syndicated Euro Currency Notes.

➠ The global equity market issue depository receipts like American Depository receipts, European Depository receipts and global depository receipts.

➠ The multilateral financial institutions which provide foreign capital are World Bank and its affiliates the Asian development bank, International Monetary Fund and Bank for International Settlements.

➠ The share of foreign direct investment has been increasing in India since 1991.

➠ The borrowings in India have been denominated in dollars of America followed by Yen, Euro and Pound sterling in the post ninety one periods.

➠ The capital flows to India have increased as a result of which it has heavy reserves in foreign capital.

➠ The flow of FII funds have been increasing in India. This has boosted the capital market which is represented by a rise in sensex.

Objective Type Questions, Answer True (T) or False (F)

(a) The International Monetary Fund is an important source of foreign capital for India.

(b) Foreign direct investment has increased in India since 1991.

(c) A global depository receipt is a non-negotiable instrument.

(d) Foreign institutional investors are allowed to invest in mutual funds in India.

(e) If GDR's are converted into shares they cannot be converted bank into GDR's.

(f) CHIPS are an automatic system of transferring funds. It was introduced in Belgium.

(g) SWIFT is the world's largest financial telecommunication system for transferring funds from one country to another.

(h) Offshore Banking offers tax concessions and international financial services.

(i) The 'drop lock bonds' are floating rate bonds which can be converted into fixed rate bonds at a future date.

(j) Note issuance facility enables a borrower to issue a series of short term debt obligations with a commitment from banks.

Answer: (a) T, (b) T, (c) F, (d) T, (e) T, (f) F, (g) T, (h) T, (i) F, (j) T.

Multiple Choice Questions (Tick mark (✓) the right answer)

1. American Depository Receipt:

   (a) Is a Euro dominated negotiable instrument

   (b) Is a dollar denominated negotiable instrument

   (c) It is not a negotiable instrument but a stock in the capital market

   (d) Is a negotiable instrument traded settled and cleared in Europe

2. A Tax Haven:

   (a) Is an offshore banking centre.

   (b) Is an inter bank transaction for tax benefits.

   (c) It is a centre for international transactions especially for tax benefits and concessions.

   (d) It is a centre for international business services.

3. SWIFT:

   (a) It is a financial international telecommunication system with borrowed lines of communication.

   (b) It is a financial telecommunication system for electronic stock exchange business.

   (c) It is the largest financial international telecommunication system with own lines of communication.

   (d) It is a financial telecommunication system for 'Tax Havens' and tax concessions.

4. Multilateral sources of capital:

   (a) These sources are earnings from government projects in foreign countries.

   (b) These are sources from private earnings of foreign capital.

   (c) These financial sources are from joint ventures between a foreign country and the host country.

   (d) These financial sources are from World Bank, Asian Development Bank, International Monetary Fund and Bank for International Settlements.

5. Syndicated Euro currency loans:
    (a) These are loans in Euro currency arranged by a syndicate of banks.
    (b) These are unsecured bonds with fixed interest rates.
    (c) These are convertible bonds with a syndicate of banks arranging loans on it.
    (d) These are Euro bonds.

6. Floating rate bonds:
    (a) These bonds are issued in small parts of the total bond.
    (b) These bonds are American Depository Receipt.
    (c) These bonds are also called 'Drop Lock Bonds'.
    (d) These bonds are also called Floating rate notes.

7. International Development Agency:
    (a) It has the objective to fund developed and developing countries.
    (b) Its objective is to provide funds for private sector organization through loans.
    (c) Its objective is to provide loans for problems in international payments.
    (d) Its objective is to provide funds for developing and poor countries.

Answer: 1 (b), 2 (c), 3 (c), 4 (d), 5 (a), 6 (c) 7 (d).

Short Answer Questions

1. Why do you think foreign capital flows are important for India?
2. What are the different types of foreign capital available in India?
3. Distinguish between ADR's and GDR's.
4. Write notes on: (i) Note issuance facility, (ii) Floating Rate Notes, and (iii) Foreign Bonds.
5. Discuss the trend in NRI deposits in India after 1991.
6. What is the importance of foreign capital?

Long Answer Questions

1. What are the functions of multilateral financial institutions in foreign capital flows in India?
2. Discuss the international financial instruments which are instrumental in foreign capital flows in India.
3. What is a 'tax haven'? How does it help in international capital flows?
4. Analyze the trend in foreign capital inflows to India.
5. What is Offshore Banking? How is it in foreign capital flows?
6. Discuss the problems in foreign capital flows.
7. Discuss the factors affecting foreign capital flows.

Part – Five
Banking Institutions

11. Commercial Banks
12. Co-operative Banks

Chapter

Commercial Banks

Chapter Plan

- Types of Banks
- Functions of Banks
- Distinction between Banks and Financial Institutions
- Phases of Development
- Banking Sector Reforms
    - Deregulation of interest rates
    - Reducing reserve requirements
    - Diversification of services
    - Prudential norms
    - Banking supervision and discipline

- Transparency and disclosure
- Risk management
- Securitization of assets
- Non-performing assets
- Technology
- Debit credit cards
- Customer services
- Regional Rural Banks
- Maturity Pattern of Term Deposits
- Comprehensive Statistics of Commercial Banks

INTRODUCTION

Commercial banks are an integral part of the financial sector of an under developed and developing country. In India it has played a major role in mobilizing the savings of the individuals. It has helped in the transfer of resources from savers to borrowers. To promote savings in banks the Banking Regulation Act was passed in 1949 replacing the Banking Companies Act. This Act was passed in order to create sound banking practices in India. This Act was able to give powers to Reserve Bank of India to incorporate proper administration of banks and creating an environment of trust and confidence amongst the saving population.

TYPES OF BANKS

There are many types of banks. These are scheduled and non-scheduled, public and private sector, foreign banks and cooperative banks.

Scheduled and non-scheduled banks: Scheduled banks are those which are included in the Second Schedule of Banking Regulation Act 1965. Such banks should have a paid up capital and reserves of not less than Rs. 5 lakhs and should satisfy that their work is according to the interests of the depositors as included in the Second Schedule. Scheduled banks are required to maintain reserve with the RBI for the facility of financial accommodation and remittance facilities at a concession.

Public sector and private sector banks: The banking business conducted by government is called public sector banks. The major ownership of these banks is held by government. These can be classified into two categories state bank and its associates, and other nationalized banks. The state bank has 7 subsidiaries. These are State Bank of Bikaner and Jaipur, State Bank of Hyderabad, State Bank of Indore, State Bank of Mysore, State Bank of Patiala, State Bank of Saurashtra and State Bank of Travancore. The State Bank of India has 13,000 branches and 51 foreign branches. It is the world's largest commercial bank. It is also the largest commercial bank in India with 100 million accounts. The State Bank of India was initiated in 1921 with the name of Imperial Bank. It was created by amalgamating 3 Presidency banks. These are Bank of Bengal, Bank of Bombay and Bank of Madras. The Imperial bank was merged when the State Bank of India Act was passed in 1955. This bank the came the first nationalized Bank of India with the objective of expanding banking business in rural and urban areas and promoting the credit in priority areas such as agriculture and small industry. In 1993 the State Bank of India Act was amended to extend its operations to access funds from the capital market. In 1993 the State Bank of India raised funds through equity and bond issue. In 1996 it again raised funds from the capital market. It has now begun to extend its business in many new areas. In 1969 government nationalized 14 private sector banks and in 1980 further six commercial banks were nationalized. Now there are 27 nationalized banks. State Bank and its subsidiaries and 19 other nationalized banks. The New India Bank was merged with Punjab National Bank. Public sector banks have tried to focus on giving credit to priority sectors.

Since government nationalized banks in 1969 and new banks were not given the permission to begin their operations, there were only 24 private sector banks. The Narasimham Committee advised the government to allow banks to open up in the private sector to bring about competition in the banking sector and thereby increasing productivity. On the basis of this recommendation 8 new private banks were opened. There are 31 private sector banks currently (23 old and 8 new banks). All old banks as per the guidelines of January 1993 were to have at least 50 crores as their net worth by January 2001. They were also to increase their initial minimum paid up capital from a level of 100 crores to 200 crores and further 300 hundred crores within 3 years of commencing business. A non-banking finance company would also be permitted to convert into a commercial bank. If it had a AAA credit rating and a minimum net worth of 200 crores. It should also have a capital adequacy of a minimum of 12% and its net non-performing assets should not be more than 5%. Large industrial houses could not be permitted to have any controlling interest in commercial banks but they could participate as equity holders up to a maximum share of 10%. Banks were given the freedom for pricing their shares after they were listed on the stock market. However, Initial Public Offerings could be made to the public after due permission of the Reserve Bank of India. Foreign participation would be allowed to these private banks. The private sector banks which began their operations after 1994-95 have to bring about a customer centric approach.[1]

---

1. Bharti Pathak, *A Comparison of the Financial Performance of Private Sector Banks, Finance India*, Vol. XVII, No. 4, December, 2003, p. 1345-1356.

Indian and foreign banks: Indian banks are incorporated in India having their head office in India. Indian banks also have branches in foreign countries. Indian banks expanded their branches in foreign countries (Table 11.1) depicts the number of Indian banks which have been opened and are operating in foreign countries. In 2007, there were 16 Indian banks in countries like Hong Kong, Singapore, UAE, Malaysia, Belgium, China, Indonesia and United Kingdom. Out of these banks 11 were in the public sector banks and 5 were private sector banks. They had a network of 188 offices abroad.

In order to expand business of Indian banks in foreign countries, the prudential limit on credit and non-credit facilities extended by banks to Indian joint ventures having more than 51% holding/wholly owned subsidiaries abroad was increased from 10 per cent to 20 per cent of their unimpaired capital funds in both Tier I and II capital since November 2006.

Table 11.1: Offices of Indian Banks Opened Abroad: July 2006 to June 2007

Name of the Bank	Type of Presence	Country	Place
1	2	3	4
Allahabad Bank	Branch	Hong Kong	Hong Kong
Andhra Bank	RO	UAE	Dubai
Bank of Baroda	OBU	Singapore	Singapore
	Branch	Hong Kong	Hong Kong
	Branch	Hong Kong	Hong Kong
Bank of India	Branch*	China	Shenzen
	Branch	Belgium	Antwerp
Canara Bank	Branch	Hong Kong	Hong Kong
ICICI Bank	RO	Malaysia	Kuala Lumpur
	RO	Indonesia	Jakarta
Punjab National Bank	Subsidiary	United Kingdom	London
State Bank of India	Branch	UAE	DIFC
	Branch	Bahrain	Manama
	Branch	Israel	Tel Aviv
	Subsidiary**	Indonesia	
UCO Bank	RO	China	Guangzhou
	RO	China	Shanghai
Union Bank of India	Branch	Hong Kong	Hong Kong
	Branch	UAE	DIFC
UTI Bank Ltd.	RO	China	Shanghai

*   : Upgradation of a representative office to a branch.
** : 76 per cent stake in PBIM, an Indonesian Bank.
Note : RO   : Representative office.
        UAE   : United Arab Emirates.
        OBU   : Offshore Banking Unit.
        DIFC   : Dubai International Financial Centre.
Source: Reserve Bank of India, Annual Report: government of India publication, August 2007, p. 163.

Foreign banks have their offices in India but they are incorporated outside India and have their head office in foreign country. Foreign banks since 2002 have been allowed to setup their subsidiaries in India. They have to operate according to the banking regulations in India. The priority sector has to be given a special treatment in lending and the norms to be followed will be the same as those followed by the domestic banks. The foreign banks are allowed to operate in India only if they are financially sound. A foreign bank must have a minimum of 25 million US dollars in at least 3 branches. It must have 10 million US dollars in the first branch and 10 million in the second branch. The third branch should have at least 5 million. It can open more branches if its performance in India fulfills the criteria adopted in the Indian banks. There are 40 foreign banks from 21 different countries operating in India with more than 205 branches. They are located in 15 states (inclusive of union territories) in India. 12 countries have representative offices in India.

Table 11.2 depicts the offices of foreign bank in India between July 2006 and 2007. During that time RBI approved that foreign banks which were present in India could open their branches. 13 branches of foreign banks were approved. It also approved that six foreign banks could open one representative office each in Mumbai, while one foreign bank was allowed to open a representative office in New Delhi. Six foreign banks were approved to open their branches across India. 29 foreign banks with 268 branches were operating in India. Further 34 foreign banks were transacting business in India, through their representative offices.

Table 11.2: Offices of Foreign Banks Opened in India: July 2006 to June 2007

Name of the Bank	Type of Presence	Place
1	2	3
Hong Kong and Shanghai Banking Corporation (HSBC)	Branch	Raipur, Jodhpur, Lucknow
ABN Amro Bank NV	Branch	Kohlapur, Salem, Udaipur Ahmedabad
Barclays Bank	Branch	Kanchipuram, Bangalore
Shinhan Bank	Branch	New Delhi
Deutches Bank	Centralised Back Office	Mumbai
Standard Chartered Bank	AO	Chennai, Mumbai
National Australia Bank Ltd.	RO	Mumbai
Banca di Roma	RO	Mumbai
Depfa Bank PLC	RO	Mumbai
Banco Bilbao Vizcaya Argentina SA	RO	Mumbai

Note : AO : Administrative Office.
RO : Representative Office.
Source : RBI Annual Report, government of India publication: August 2007, p. 163.

Cooperative and regional rural banks (RRB's): The Co-operative banks are the collective effort of State Co-operative Banks, Central Co-operative Banks, Commercial Banks and Primary Agricultural Credit Society. Regional rural banks are the responsibility of the commercial banks in rural areas to provide finance for agriculture RRB's were formed to developed trade and agriculture and other productive activities in rural areas. It was specially organized to help the marginal farmers, small entrepreneur's agricultural labour and artisans. In 1975, there were six RRBs. They increased to 196. The sponsor banks and the RRBs were together involved in developing the rural sector. Where RRBs had deposits of Rs. 5 crores and above the sponsor banks involvement was 25%.

Universal Banks

These are new type of banks. They first began their operations in Germany. They do different types of business and also work as a bank. They are financial conglomerates or financial shops with different financial services. They are called multi-product firms. They target a large base of clients because they have a number of services. Universal banking refers to the combination of commercial banking with investments.[2] In the Indian context these banks have the objective of harmonizing the role of commercial banks and development financial institutions. Banks have short term assets and liabilities where as development financial institutions have long term assets and liabilities.[3] In India ICICI was the first financial institution to become a universal bank.

Types of Universal Banks: There are four different types of Universal Banks in the world. They are type (A) Fully Integrated Universal Banks are one institutional entities offering complete range of financial services that is banking securities and insurance. This system can take the best advantage of the Universal banking system such as the economies of scope optimal location of resources and stability in profits. This system has certain demerits such as conflict of interest bureaucratic inefficiencies and difficulty in auditing. In practice full integration is rare. (B) Partly integrated financial conglomerate are those which offers range of services but some of the range e.g., mortgage banking, leasing, asset management, factoring, management consulting and insurance are provided through wholly owned or partially owned subsidiaries. Duteshe Bank is a good example of this type of universal structure. This type of structure is called the German Type of financial system. It has been adopted in Germany, France, Italy, Netherlands and Switzerland. (C) In Type C Universal Bank the Commercial Banks focus on regular functions and have established separate subsidiaries for carrying out other functions such as Investment Banking and Insurance the U.K. type Universal Banks concentrate only on commercial banking operations and their subsidiaries deal with securities and insurance related services. Japanese banks as well as U.K. Banks have adopted this system, and (D) Is called the U.S. type of Universal Bank or holding company structure—where one financial holding company owns both banking and non-banking subsidiaries that are legally separate and individually capitalized insofar as financial services other than banking are permitted by law. Under this financial system bank subsidiaries and non-bank-subsidiaries are not closely related and so advantage cannot be taken of economies of scope. The U.S. type of bank has a strong point as well because the losses in one subsidiary do not spread to other subsidiaries.

---

2. For further information read Ingo Walter: Universal Banking: A share holder value perspective. European Management Journal, Vol. 15, No. 4, Printed in Great Britain, August 1997, p. 344-359.

3. C.M. Vasudev: Universal Banking of India, Economic Times, India, 24th Aug, 2002.

Generally the concept of Universal Bank is based on two financial models. One is German type in which banks carry comprehensive banking activities including commercial banking as well as other services such as securities related services and insurance. The other model is British-American type in which "Financial Conglomerates" offering full range of financial services in accordance with change of financial environment pursue diversification in securities and investment. In India, we find that "Financial Conglomerates" are emerging. One important difference among others between the Financial Conglomerates and Universal Banking is that while in respect of Financial Conglomerates the various activities are undertaken through different-subsidiaries, and in the case of Universal Banking, the bank is free to choose the activities it wanted to carry out subject to certain regulations.

Under the 1991 reforms, there was a need to devise an innovative financial mechanism to provide adequate financial support to the industries. Universal Banking has emerged as one of the alternatives that may lend some support to the ailing banking and financial institutions. By underwriting, investing and trading in securities ICICI bank made the first step in India to becoming a universal bank.

FUNCTIONS OF BANKS

Commercial banks have the main objective of creation of credit. To achieve this objective they carry out many functions. They encourage people to make deposits. Out of these deposits they supply *'money'* through short term and medium term lending. They extend their services in various directions. Out of the deposits made by individuals or corporate organizations, they lend to industry, give loans to individuals and provide services like underwriting, merchant banking, issue of credit and debit cards, and development finance for agriculture and priority sectors, portfolio management service, tax and investment counseling. In all services that they extend they charge commission or interest and in this way the bank always makes money. Banks have to be highly liquid for conducting their business. Out of its deposits it provides finance. The functions of commercial banks are the following:

- To open bank accounts like current, savings fixed and recurring deposits by individuals and corporate organizations as these accounts become a source of finance for the bank.

- To transfer the deposits of the customers in bank accounts by lending them to those who require funds.

- To undertake services for its clients. These can be classified into agency services, general utility services and trusteeship services.

Commercial Banks non-fund based activities do not require any financial outlay by them but they earn additional income. The *agency services* consist of collection of cheques, bills, drafts, dividends, payment of rent, electricity, telephone bills, credit card payment and payment of insurance premium. Their *general utility services* are issuing of letter of credit, merchant banking services, credit information and forfeiting services. Their *trusteeship services* include offering safety vaults for safe keeping of valuables and maintaining escrow accounts.

Banks provide *guarantees* in case of defaults in making payments. Guarantees can be financial or performance guarantee. Financial guarantee is a contract by the bank to pay the beneficiary if the customer does not make the payment. Performance guarantees are issued for projects. A bank guarantees and makes the payment if the customer does not perform. The bank however does not guarantee the customer performance nor does it perform the customers' duties in case of failure by the customer.

DISTINCTION BETWEEN BANKS AND FINANCIAL INSTITUTIONS

Commercial banks have the main function of creating deposits and lending to customers. They are different to financial institutions and the distinction is important. Banks are different to mutual funds and life insurance companies. They are also different to development financial institutions.

Banks and mutual funds: Banks can be distinguished from mutual funds as they provide deposits to their customers. Out of these deposits they lend to other customers and thus create credit. Mutual funds increase their resources by offering units to their customers. Such people are called unit holders when the mutual fund is able to collect a large pool of resources from many people it uses the fund to purchase securities from the market and to make viable investments. It gives an annual dividend to the unit holders and their principal remains safe with the mutual fund till the exit of the unit holder.

Banks and life insurance companies: While banks offer accounts to their customers, life insurance companies offer insurance policies to provide safety and security to the life of an individual. Out of the resources collected from insurance premiums, such companies invest wisely in viable securities and good investments according to their investment policies.

Banks and development financial institutions: The Industrial Development Bank of India, Industrial Finance Corporation of India, Industrial Credit and Investment Corporation of India and State Financial Corporations were the development banks. Unlike life insurance companies and mutual funds their major sources of funding were from government and Reserve Bank of India. They were engaged in providing term loans of long time duration. Commercial banks used to lend for shorter periods but they entered into term lending in 1980. The major source of finance was raised by commercial banks from individuals; the development institutions did not raise any funds themselves or offer units or policies against themselves. They were able to earn out of the funds that they gave on loan. Since 1985 they also began to raise bonds of different nature like *deep discount bonds* and *infrastructure bonds* to raise funds. The Narasimham committee recommended that the development institutions could convert themselves into commercial banks.

Thus, the working of the commercial banks is unique and quite different when compared to other institutions in India.

PHASES OF DEVELOPMENT

The Indian banking system has passed through four important phases. The period from 1950 to 1968 is called the foundation phase. From 1969 it was called the stage of expansion. From 1980-1990 banks passed through the phase of consolidation and diversification and post 1991 is the phase of financial reforms or prudential banking.

Foundation Phase

The foundation phase was the time when commercial banks were being developed in India through legislation, reorganization and consolidation of banks. Banks were small in size. The public did not have confidence in the banking system and deposits were very low. People were not educated into the banking habit. Cash was hoarded and considered to provide liquidity and useful. In 1961 the **Deposit Insurance Corporation** was setup to create confidence by providing protection to depositors through an insurance cover. India began its planning period with its first plan in 1951. Banks became an important source of finance to industry especially in the second plan which started in 1956. Since this plan was focused on development of large industries bank credit increased further. In the third plan as well, banks provided credit to industry. In 1963 banks entered into new areas of financing. In particular they began to lend through term lending to industry. They also underwrote new issues of companies. Banks provided loans to large industries that had collaterals. Agricultural sector and small scale and medium industries were unable to get loans from banks because of insufficiency of collateral. All through RBI had provided a policy through which banks could get concessions for providing loans to small industry, yet commercial banks were more favourable towards large industry. The Export Credit and Guarantee Corporation were started in 1964 to give guarantees to banks for giving finance and insurance cover to exporters. In 1968 RBI gave concessions to banks for giving loans to exporters as export credit at low rates of interest. In 1968 Reserve Bank of India passed the social control order where by banks were advised to give loans to priority sector in the country. However, despite control measures banks were unable to direct funds to the right channels where there was a paucity of funds. **The National Credit Council** was established in 1968 to indicate the priority sector for providing bank credit. The **Dehejia Committee** reviewed the credit needs of industry and trade in 1969 and stated that banks did not follow uniform policy in providing credit. According to the committee industry was dependant on bank credit which was provided according to the security provided by industry and not their requirements. Another committee called the **Gadgil Committee** was formed to find out the gaps in credit to industry.

Expansion Phase

In the expansion phase RBI setup several committees to provide an insight into the problems of various sectors requiring funds. In 1969 RBI setup a working committee to review the credit guarantee scheme of 1960 to provide loans to small industries. In 1970 a new **Credit Guarantee Scheme** was made through which banks began to lend to small industries as the loans were guaranteed by the credit guarantee organization. In 1969, **fourteen commercial banks were nationalized**. The objective was to mobilize savings of the people through increase in bank deposits and to benefit the rural and semi-urban areas by providing credit to agriculture, small and medium industries, artisans, self employed people and retail traders which were neglected areas and required improvement. In order to achieve this objective banks had to open new branches and extend their business by encouraging people to save. In 1969 **The Lead Bank Scheme** was decided to be adopted. The RBI indicated 336 districts in India which were to be distributed to the public sector banks to play a lead role. The allotment of the district was according to the size and volume of bank operations. The lead role of the bank was to coordinate between commercial banks, cooperative banks and financial institutions in the district in which they were to operate. There could be more bank one lead bank in state and the banks were expected to liaison with the district authorities to institute new banking centers. In 1969 RBI instituted the *All India Rural Credit Review Committee* to review agricultural programs. Its findings were that agriculture was expanding in India and it was necessary to think of requirements of finance for agriculture. It brought forth the need for commercial banks to play and active role in direct and indirect financing of agricultural marketing and processing of the produce.

In 1970 the *New Bill Market Scheme* was introduced on the recommendations of the Dehejia committee. This scheme was a measure to improve credit practices of banks to industry. The committee found that industry was taking short term loans from banks in excess of their requirements in production and in purchasing materials. Their modus oprendi was to take loans for short term requirements from banks and use it for other purposes like acquiring fixed assets. The New Bill Market Scheme would help to check this system. The *Narasimham Committee* was appointed in 1970 and for suggesting methods for developing and enlarging the bill market.

The *Tandon Committee* was constituted in 1974 to provide guidelines for follow up of bank credit. The findings of their report showed that bank finance was directed mainly to large industries and the priority sector was being ignored. The committee recommended that bank credit should be rationed to provide funds for all the sectors by fixing certain limits for use of credit. The *Chore Committee* was formed to review the implementation of *Tandon Committees* frame work of lending and the *Marathe Committee* recommended a credit monitoring arrangement by replacing the credit authorization scheme. Under the new scheme bank loans could be disbursed without prior approval of the RBI. In this scheme the RBI was to monitor loans after they were sanctioned to the borrowers.

The nationalization of banks brought about many changes in lending to industry. The banks were to increase loans to the priority sector by 33% until March 1979. They were also advised to ration credit to cover different sectors like large, medium and small industries both in the private sector and public sector.

Consolidation and Diversification Phase

From 1980-90 government took many steps to consolidate the banks and to diversify their operations. Six more banks were nationalized. This brought the number of nationalized banks to twenty. Banks were modernized to some extent by bringing in the computerization system. Banks were not keen to bring computers as they thought that there would be lying off staff from their jobs. An all India banks strike to a great extent hampered the development of banks modernization. In consolidation work banks tried to reduce gaps in credit to rural areas. They also brought about training of human resources in customer service and credit management. Services were diversified into new areas through bank branch expansion especially to rural areas through rural regional banks.

Since 1980 banks have become active participants in the capital market as providers of finance and promoters of industry on a turn key basis. They have leased out equipments and have been refinanced by IDBI. They also played and advisory role to seek units by providing services for their revival. They gave development loans at a rebate. The rate of interest was low on loans expected to bring about innovation and change in industries. Commercial banks also began to take an interest in starting mutual funds. They decided to enter into factoring where by banks undertook collection of debts of their clients by financing them on their credit sales and accounts receivables. Banks charge for the services provided by taking a discount from the bills. During this period banks began to offer credit to consumers for their purchases. State Bank of India started the consumer credit facility. Citi Bank in 1986 first offered loans for purchasing motor vehicles. The use of credit cards also started during this time. Plastic money or credit card was started by American Express Cards and Diner Cards.

Banks made some changes in their working but they suffered from lack of competition, high-cost, low productivity and a low capital bases. Banks did not give attention to risk management and did not follow prudential standards. This brought about low profitability, high non-performing assets and poor asset quality. Due to these reasons it was necessary to bring about economic reforms in the commercial banking sector in India.

BANKING SECTOR REFORMS

Reforms after 1990 were made in two phases. In 1992, on the basis of the Narasimham Committee report on financial system, reforms were made for *'enabling and strengthening'* the banking system. The second phase of reform was on the recommendations of the Narasimham Committee II in 1998, for *structural changes, improvements in transparency levels and standards of disclosure*. The objectives of these reforms have been to increase efficiency and stability in banks and to upgrade them to international standards. It was also to prescribe prudential norms to improve financial health and supervisory system, and institutional framework. Some of the following aspects of banking reforms were considered:

In November 2005 government was keen to extend banking services to different sections of the population. This included the poorer section of the society. Therefore banks were given directions to make a basic banking 'no-frills' system either with 'nil' or very low minimum balances and charges to make bank accounts accessible to a wide section of population. Public and private sector banks as well as foreign banks, were directed to introduce the basic banking 'no-frills' account. By the end of March 2007, 6.7 million 'no-frills' accounts were opened by banks.[4]

Deregulation of Interest Rates

The Narasimham committee I had made a recommendation that the controls on interest rates should be removed. The interest rates according to the reforms were to be preferably determined by the forces of demand and supply, to make it related to the market forces. The scheduled banks were allowed to bring about interest rates on deposits for their customers in the range of 4.5% and 11%. Ceilings were imposed on the maximum and minimum limits of rate of interest. The saving deposits were to be under the purview of government and interest to export credit was regulated. Besides these regulations banks were free to provide *prime lending rates* for commercial lending without any government interference.

Reducing Reserve Requirements

There are two reserves expected from commercial banks. These are the cash reserve ratio and the statutory liquidity ratio.

---

4. Reserve Bank of India, Annual Report: Government of India Publication, August 2007, p. 164.

Cash Reserve Ratio (CRR): Commercial banks had to compulsorily have a cash reserve with the RBI. The RBI used the Cash Reserve Ratio (CRR) as a measure of monetary control. It increased the CRR when it was required to reduce money supply in the economy and vice versa it decreased the CRR to increase money supply in the economy. This control mechanism was used by RBI since 1956. The Narasimham Committee I had recommended that CRR should be reduced to 3 to 5% as the level in 1989 was as high as 15%. This reduction in CRR would enable the banks to have more funds with them for increasing investments. Till the end of April 1993 the CRR was brought down to 8%, and further lowered to 5% by 2004. The 9th five year plan was keen to decrease the CRR to 3%.[5]

Statutory Liquidity Ratio (SLR): Another ratio which hampered the liquidity of banks was the statutory liquidity ratio. Commercial banks, Life Insurance Corporation of India, General Insurance Corporation and Provident Funds were required by law to invest a certain percentage in government and other approved securities. This provision provides that there is a quantitative control on funds. Narasimham Committee I recommended reduction of the SLR from 38.5% to 25% in 5 years. This would have the effect of increasing the volume of funds with the bank for the purpose of making investments. It would also increase their revenue. The borrowings of government from banks were also to be according to the market related rates of interest. This would enhance the income of the banks from the statutory investments in government securities.

Diversification of Services

It was a requirement for the commercial banks in the post reform period of 1991 to diversify their activity into challenging non traditional financial services like leasing, higher purchasing, factoring, mutual fund, merchant banking and venture capital funding. This would give a boost for maximizing profits, increasing customer base and create economies of scale. This would facilitate universal banking. The State Bank of India had taken the initiative to expand its activities into merchant banking in 1987 through its division called the SBI capital market. This service catered to capital market services such as issue management, project counseling, portfolio management, foreign currency loans and loans syndication.

Retail Banking: Since 1991 banks have diversified into retail banking. Banks provide housing loans, auto mobile loans, educational loans, credit and debit cards and purchases for consumer durables. ***Factoring:*** Another area is the service of factoring which is provided by SBI and Canara bank through their subsidiaries.

New Services: Financial services for financial guarantees, securitization of loans, stock broking and projects related to infrastructure. To enlarge their activities banks have setup subsidiaries to become the primary dealers of government securities. SBI and PNB have initiated this service. They have been interested in venture capital and have contributed to the funds of the Technology Development and Investment Corporation of India (TDICI).

Clearing and Settlement: Banks have setup the Clearing Corporation of India Ltd (CCIL) in 2001 for clearing and settlement of government securities and foreign exchange transactions. The SBI has contributed 51% of the equity to form this corporation. It has also been assisted by other banks as co-promoters. The remaining 49% of the equity has been contributed by LIC, IDBI, ICICI, HDFC Bank and Bank of Baroda.

---

5. Government of India, Planning Commission, Ninth Five Year Plan, 1997-2002, Vol. 1, p. 150.

Life insurance: In 2000 the government of India through Reserve Bank of India guidelines approved of banks to setup life insurance business. Many banks have begun life insurance business as a part of their activities in the post reform period.

Prudential Norms

Prudential norms were introduced by the Reserve Bank of India on the recommendation of the Narasimham Committee. Banks had been regulating the banks through interest rates and restriction on direct lending pattern. However, such methods were considered to be non productive as they brought about inefficiency in the banking system. The prudential norms were a measure to replace such restrictions. They were promotional in nature consisting of asset classification, capital adequacy and income recognition. The objective of such norms was to create a sound system which brought about solvency of banks, created financial safety and adaptable to international standards. The capital adequacy norms were to have a minimum amount of funds to create an atmosphere of security and safety. The capital adequacy ratio is the measure of a banks capital as a percentage of its risk weighted credit exposures. The capital adequacy norms were a proposal by Basel Committee in 1988. It proposed that banks should have *two tiers of capital*. Tier I proposed that banks could absorb losses without closing their trade and Tier II proposed that banks would absorb losses if they were in the winding up process. Basel Committee reforms were introduced in 1991 but the revised capital adequacy was brought out in 2001. Some of these provisions would be operational from 2005.

Capital adequacy norms: The Basel norms for capital adequacy were introduced in 1991 in India on the recommendations of the Narasimham Committee. It was based on some important principles. These were that a commercial bank should have a minimum 8% of its assets as its equity capital when it is multiplied by appropriate risk weights. The risk weights were given four limits by the Basel Committee. These were 0%, 1.6%, 4% and 8% for different types of assets. If capital was below this minimum requirement shareholders could be allowed to retain control only if the agreement is that they would recapitalize the bank. If it is not done, the regulatory authority has the discretion to liquidate or sell the bank. The Banking Sector Reforms Committee in 1998 had made the suggestion that banks should have a capital adequacy ratio. The RBI decided to follow this by initially directing the banks to maintain 8% reserve of their risk weighted assets. However this was revised in 2000 to 9% and further increased to 10% Basel II on the New Capital Adequacy Framework have to be adopted by Banks in India. Banks in India have to adopt the Standardized Approach for credit risk and the Basic Indicator Approach for operational risk for computing their capital requirements under the revised framework. Under the *Basic Indicator Approach* capital requirements for operational risk will be the average of a fixed percentage of positive annual gross income of the previous three completed financial years. The revised framework of *The Standardized Duration Approach* for computing capital requirement for market risk has to be adopted by March 31, 2008 by foreign banks in India and Indian banks having their operations outside India. All other commercial banks (excluding Local Area Banks and Regional Rural Banks) have to adhere to the Revised Framework by March 31, 2009.

Capital Risk-weighted Assets Ratio (CRAR)

Banks have to maintain a minimum capital to risk-weighted assets ratio (CRAR) of 9%. The RBI may direct a bank to have a higher level of minimum capital ratio to ensure that the capital held by a bank is in accordance with its overall risk profile. The RBI may take this decision after taking into account the relevant risk factor and internal capital adequacy assessments of each bank.

By 31st March, 2010, all Banks are required to maintain individually and at a consolidated level, a minimum Tier I ratio of at least 6 per cent. The minimum capital to be maintained by banks according to Basel II norms depends on the requirement as per Basel I framework for credit and market risks. The floor is fixed at 100%, 90%and 80% in the first three years for implementing of the revised guidelines. The risk weights for credit risk for capital adequacy (CRAR) have to be assigned by using credit ratings of four credit rating agencies in India and three international rating agencies. These are Credit Analysis and Research Ltd., CRISIL Ltd., Fitch India, and ICRA Ltd. Amongst the international agencies Fitch, Moody's and Standard & Poor's can be consulted for assigning risks to assets.

The claims of the Central Government will be assigned a zero risk weight while those guaranteed by State Governments will have 20 per cent risk weight. The scheduled banks will like wise be treated differently to other banks in assigning risk weights for claims on banks. Corporate Organization will have their claims risk weighted according to the ratings by credit rating agencies. Unrated claims will have a risk weight of 100 per cent. By April 1st, 2008, Claims sanctioned and renewed above Rs.50 crores will have a higher risk weight of 150% to be reduced to Rs. 10 crores from April 1, 2009.

There will be a preferential risk weight between 20% and 75% on consumption loans up to Rs.1 lakh against gold and silver ornaments, retail portfolio, mortgage residential property and loans to banks own staff members. On certain specified categories like venture capital funds, commercial real estate, consumer credit including personal loans and credit card receivables and capital market exposures there will be risk weights of 125% or 150% depending on the nature of the claims.

Venture capital funds: Venture Capital Funds (VCFs) play an important role in a country. In this respect disclosures with regard to the banks asset quality is necessary because it can increase risks. The prudential framework governing banks' exposure to VCFs was revised in August 2006. It was made at par with equity and had to be in compliance with the capital market exposure ceilings for direct investment in equity and equity linked instruments. It also had to be under the ceiling for overall capital market exposure. The quoted equity shares/bonds/units of VCFs in the banks' portfolio would be held under the 'available for sale' (AFS) category and would be marked to market, generally on a daily basis, or on a weekly basis in line with valuation norms for other equity shares. Banks' investments in unquoted shares/ bonds/units of VCFs made after issuance of these guidelines would be classified under the 'held to maturity' (HTM) category for an initial period of three years, and would be valued at cost. For the investments made before these guidelines the classification would be according to the existing norms. After three years, the unquoted units/shares/bonds would be transferred to the AFS category and valued according to the guidelines. Investments in shares/units/bonds of VCFs would be assigned 150 per cent risk weight for measuring the credit risk during the first three years when held in the HTM category. When these are either held under or transferred to the AFS, the capital charge for the specific risk component of the market for computation of capital charge (under existing guidelines) for market risk, would be fixed at 13.5 per cent to reflect the risk weight of 150 per cent. The charge for general market risk component would be at 9 per cent for investments in shares/units, as in the case of other equities. For investments in bonds, the charge for general market risk would be computed as in the case of investment in any other kind of bonds. The exposures to VCFs other than investments would also be assigned a risk weight of 150 per cent. The total investments in VCFs will not be covered under the guidelines related to non-SLR securities.[6]

---

6. Information from RBI Annual Report, Government of India Publication, August 2007, p. 161.

Investment norms: Banks have certain norms with respect to investments. Since 2004, the banks could exceed their total 25% investment level in held to maturity category when the excess consisted of securities beyond the statutory liquidity ratio. The total statutory liquidity ratio securities which were held in the held to maturity category could not exceed 25% of their demand and time liabilities.

These norms were decided due to valuation issues of investments. All investments would be valued at cost or realizable value which ever is lower. The market value would be normally the realizable value but where such rates are not available; the realizable value would be fair value.

Banking Supervision and Discipline

The Basel Committee recommended setting up a group on banking supervision to monitor the capital adequacy norms, to promote soundness of banks, enhance competition and to evaluate risks of banks. The internal work processes of banks would be constantly reviewed and intervention would take place to improve the situation. India became a member of the Financial Stability Forum (FSF) of 20 countries and it is called G20. Basel Committee was established by the Bank for International Settlements and it has a meeting four times a year for review and supervision. The prompt corrective action is an effective tool of supervision because it is a legal measure through which corrective action can be taken immediately. In India this corrective measure is taken when there are NPA's and capital to risk weighted assets ratio falls below the expected level at that particular time. The corrective action can be taken by the board of financial supervision.

The Basel Committee on Banking Supervision (BCBS) decided to introduce Basel II reforms with a consultative approach and without any disruption in the working environment. Towards these reforms they brought out a document called 'International Convergence of Capital Measurement and Capital Standard: A Revised Framework' on June 26, 2004. To bring in the reforms on capital adequacy a Steering Committee was formed. The members of this committee were appointed from capable senior staff members of banks, the Indian Banks' Association (IBA) and the Reserve Bank. The steering committee prepared certain guidelines on the basis of feedback on draft recommendations of the committees for implementation of the New Capital Adequacy revised Framework on April 27, 2007.

The strengthening of supervisory framework has also been on the agenda of reforms in India due to banks becoming large financial conglomerates. Since the emergence of universal banks, the RBI is keen to have an efficient supervisory system for avoidance of corruption and frauds as well as smooth movement of funds. Since banks with multi-functions is a new concept in India, RBI wanted to find out the methodology of supervision in other countries before initiating it in India. In 2007 it has been actively participating in discussions towards a good supervisory system to be adopted in the Indian banking system.

Market Discipline

The RBI has taken an interest in encouraging market discipline and good governance. The discipline will be possible through greater disclosure system of banks. The disclosure would specially provide capital adequacy and risk assessment. The Reserve Bank of India has focused on the compliance of international standards by banks. It has directed the banks to follow International Rating Based approach when they are internationally linked with business and banks. For other banks it has permitted a simple and standard approach. The RBI is also keen on implementing the new adequacy Basel II framework of reducing risk to the minimum, to avoid internal and external frauds, to create a safe work place, to avoid system failures and to execute business efficiently. It is keen to disseminate the flow of information between banks to bring about market discipline.

Transparency and Disclosures

The flow of information and a transparent system would minimize risks. Transparency in banks is possible only when there is adequate information so that it can be monitored according to international standards. RBI has provided guidelines to banks on both qualitative and quantitative aspects to create an effective and efficient system of banking as per Basel Committee suggested reforms. To strengthen the banking system through the adoption of policies aimed at both improving the financial strength of banks as well as bringing about greater transparency in their operations, several policy measures were initiated during 2006-07. Income recognition and asset classification was important to avoid sub-prime losses of banks like in the case of USA. Banks in India would indirectly suffer from sub-prime losses but directly they would become safe through adequate transparency and disclosures and laws enforced by market regulators.

Income recognition and asset classification: The prudential norms prescribed that assets should be classified into standard assets and Non-Performing Assets (NPAs). Under the NPAs category there are sub-standard assets, doubtful assets and loss assets. The substandard assets are those which are NPA's for less than 12 months. Doubtful assets are sub standards assets which exceed the 12 month period of being NPA's. Loss assets are those which have not performed for more than 36 months. They are identified as non recoverable assets. Banks have to make a provision out of its total outstanding. For substandard assets 10% of total outstanding, if assets are doubtful 100% of the unsecured portion and 20 to 50% of secured portion over a period of three years and in loss assets the total loss should either be written off or hundred percent provisions should be made.

Income recognition is based on the guidelines and directions of the Institute of Chartered Accountants of India. This should be consistent with the recognized principles of accounting.

Asset classification norms for infrastructure projects were modified with effect from March 31, 2007. Since implementation of infrastructure projects normally gets delayed due to factors beyond the control of the promoters, it required restructuring by the banks. Infrastructure projects would be treated as sub-standard if the date of commencement of commercial production extended beyond a period of one year after the original date of completion of the project. The earlier provision for infrastructure asset classification was six months from the date of completion of six months.[7]

Risk Management

Risk management is an important area in banking. The Basel norms stated that the banking supervisors have to monitor and control all the risks in banks. In 1999, RBI directed banks to have an effective Asset Liability Management (ALM) system. In this system the risks have to be identified measured and monitored to control them effectively. Each bank is required to have an asset liability committee which would monitor the liquidity of the bank through cash flow or maturity miss-matches. The committee has to

---

7. See further information from RBI Annual Report, Government of India Publication, August 2007, p. 160.

periodically submit their return of liquidity which will be basis of the monitoring process by the Reserve Bank of India. The banks also had to provide data on Interest Rate Risk Management and Currency Risk Management periodically. Since 1999 risk management has been an important step for good management practices in banks. Risk management has been conducted according to Basel principles which state the importance of on-site and off-site supervision.

On-site supervision has mainly been used in India as a control mechanism. It has been improved in the form of Capital adequacy, Asset quality, Management, Earning, Liquidity and Systems and Control model (CAMELS). Off-site supervision is to submit the statistical data of returns by banks to the central bank of the country. In 1995 RBI took up this system of monitoring with the commercial banks. This system is considered to be beneficial for the banking organization. Therefore in India there is both on-site and off-site monitoring but it requires constant review for the supervisory system to be modern and up to date.

In 2006-2007 the supervisory rating model based on CAMELS used for the purpose of rating the commercial banks in India during the Annual Financial Inspection (AFI) was revised comprehensively to ensure greater objectivity in assessment by introducing benchmarks based on industry averages/ frequency distributions. It was also decided that the rating model would be assessed for its viability and effectiveness on an ongoing basis and updated regularly to factor in the evolving dynamics and requirements to reflect the most objective scenario.[8]

Consolidated Supervision

Banking supervision not only consist of the banks on-site and off-site monitoring but also supervision of subsidiaries and joint venture of banks for better control over them. Banks have to submit to RBI not only their own financial data periodically but also the data of their subsidiaries. The annual reports of banks are expected to provide information and consolidated data of both the bank and its subsidiaries.

Securitization of Assets

An Act was made on the recommendations of Narasimham Committee II in 1998 for setting up a mechanism for tackling the problem of non-performing assets. It suggested the setting up of an Asset Reconstruction Company (ARC) for operational restructuring, staff rationalization and branch revitalization so that after clearing the NPAs, no new NPAs are created. The financial restructuring would help in strengthening the banks and providing them with a good background to begin on the reforms for progress in internationalization. The Assets should first be identified and their realizable value determined. These assets should be transferred to an asset reconstruction company. The ARC could be setup by one bank or a set off banks and could even include a private sector bank. Another approach to securitization was recapitalization of banks with budgetary support so that they could issue bonds to form part of Tier II capital to improve their capital adequacy. However the issue of bonds would be helpful only if Tier I capital had adequate capital to make such provisions possible. It would also be difficult to sell bonds until a proper guarantee is given to them by approved government or financial institutions instruments. The NPAs of banks would however remain in the books in both alternate methods until they were written off or realized by banks. To have a control system for securitization an

8. Information from RBI Report: Government of India Publication, August 2007, p. 159.

Act was passed in 2002 to regulate securitization reconstruction of financial assets and enforcement of security interest and connected matters. It was called SARFAESI.

This Act proposed to setup a Central Registry with its own seal for registration of transaction of securitization and reconstruction of financial assets and creation of security interest. The central government would specify the location of the head office of the Central Registry and the Registry will be located in a place decided by government. The Central Registry will maintain a Central Register at its head office for securitization of financial assets, reconstruction of financial assets and creation of security interest. Every transaction of securitization or asset construction has to be reported with in 30 days of taking a security interest.

In 2005 RBI prepared guidelines for securitization of standard assets. The methodology of securitization was to adopt it in a two stage manner. The first stage was responsible for pooling and transferring of assets to a bankruptcy remote Special Purpose Vehicle (SPV). The second stage was to sell the security through repackaging. This would represent claims in incoming cash flows from the pool of assets to third party investors. The transferred assets would be removed from the balance sheets after the true sale criteria have been established. The sale has to comply with the prudential requirements of the assets. The securities issued by SPV have to be rated by an external credit rating agency.

Non-Performing Assets (NPAs)

A non-performing asset is one in which income is overdue for more than six months as per the Narasimham Committee Report. The NPAs have caused the financial downfall of the banking system especially in the public sector banks. As banks expanded into different regions, the standards of asset quality did not meet the required standards. They gave loans for social objectives without the appraisal of economic considerations. This reduced their profitability because the NPAs increased. According to the SARFAESI a non-performing asset can be securitized. It can be acquired by a securitization or reconstruction company whose funds are not less then Rs. 2 crores. Commercial banks have to prepare a report as on 31st march, after completion of audit, showing NPAs. They amount which is held in the interest suspense account should be depicted as a deduction from gross NPAs and gross advances when net NPAs are illustrated. Income on interest relating to bad and doubtful debts is chargeable to tax of the previous year in which it is shown in the profit and loss account. Banks should write of the NPAs to claim tax benefits or make provisions for NPAs. However provisions are not eligible for tax deductions. Banks have the option to write off bad and doubtful debts at head offices even though the advance is shown as outstanding in branches but provision should be made against the loss asset.

The net NPAs to net advances ratio is given in the Table 11.3. It shows the NPAs from 2002-03 to 2006-07. The data relating to public sector banks depicts that there is a change between 2002-03 and 2007. In 2002-03 there were 10% NPAs above 5%. In 2003-04 there were 5% NPAs above 5%. In 2005-06 and 2006-07 the NPAs had improved the statistics show that NPAs were 0 above 5%. When private sector old and new banks are analyzed the same situation can be seen. From 15% NPAs above 5% there are only 1% NPAs above 5% both in old and new banks. The foreign banks also show a similar situation. However, when NPAs are analyzed upto 2% of net advances ratio there are still quite high in 2006-07. The Public sector banks have 18% NPAs private sector old banks 14% and new banks 7% and foreign banks 27% respectively. This is still a very high amount of NPAs.

Table 11.3: Non-performing Assets of Commercial Banks

Year/Net NPAs to Net Advances Ratio	Public Sector Banks		Private Sector Banks		Foreign Banks
	SBI Group	Nationalized Banks	Old	New	
1	2	3	4	5	6
Number of Banks					
2002-03					
Up to 2 per cent	1	3	1	3	21
Above 2 per cent and up to 5 per cent	6	6	4	2	2
Above 5 per cent and up to 10 per cent	1	8	13	4	5
Above 10 per cent	0	2	2	1	8
2003-04					
Up to 2 per cent	6	5	2	4	19
Above 2 per cent and up to 5 per cent	2	9	9	5	4
Above 5 per cent and up to 10 per cent	0	4	7	0	3
Above 10 per cent	0	1	2	1	7
2004-05					
Up to 2 per cent	7	10	4	6	22
Above 2 per cent and up to 5 per cent	1	8	12	3	2
Above 5 per cent and up to 10 per cent	0	2	4	1	2
Above 10 per cent	0	0	0	0	4
2005-06					
Up to 2 per cent	7	15	11	6	26
Above 2 per cent and up to 5 per cent	1	5	7	2	0
Above 5 per cent and up to 10 per cent	0	0	2	0	0
Above 10 per cent	0	0	0	0	3
2006-07 *					
Up to 2 per cent	8	18	14	7	27
Above 2 per cent and up to 5 per cent	0	2	2	1	1
Above 5 per cent and up to 10 per cent	0	0	0	0	0
Above 10 per cent	0	0	1	0	1

* Data as on March 31, 2007 are unaudited and provisional.
Source: RBI Annual Report, Government of India Publication, 2007, Table 5.8, Off-site supervisory returns submitted by banks pertaining to their domestic operations only.

Lok Adalat

Banks had very high NPAs due to disputes with their customers. Lok Adalats were forums which could settle banking disputes to recover amounts up to Rs. 5 lakhs. The monitory ceiling was increased to 20 lakhs in 2004. The Lok Adalats were organized by civil courts. Those which were convened by Debt Recovery Appellate Tribunals could take up cases up to Rs. 10 lakhs. At the end of March 2007 a large number of cases were filed by commercial banks with Lok Adalats the number of cases which were to be settled were 9,76,101 and the amount was Rs. 5,833 crores. The settlement of these cases would help in reducing NPAs to some extent.

The Recovery of Debts Due to Banks and Financial Institutions Act, 1993 provided for the establishment of tribunals for quick recovery of debts owed to banks and Financial Institutions (FIs). Several amendments were made in 2000 and 2003 to the Act and the new rules which were framed have strengthened the functioning of the Debt Recovery Tribunals (DRTs). A number of pending cases have been settled by the end of March 2007.

Technology

Since 1991, the Reserve Bank of India recognized the importance of improvement in technology for the flow of information between banks. Modernization was necessary to bring the banks to international standards. One of the issues was to bring in computerization in all the private sector banks. The RBI focused on customer centered efficiency through technology. It brought out a financial sector technology vision document for banks to plan computerization and e-banking. These technological instruments would bring about telephone banking, mobile banking and internet banking. In 1998 the RBI took technical assistance for upgrading technology from the Department for Financial International Development (DFID) United Kingdom. It stressed on Information Technology (IT) environment risks, operations risk and product risks and it advised the banks on control mechanisms relating to risk through the new technology. In 2000 government enacted the IT Act to give a legal backing for electronic transactions. Banks were given the freedom to operate on inter-banking system through computers without the permission of RBI. In 2001 a working group under the chairmanship of S.R. Mittal, was setup to decide on a policy for internet banking, to bring about some structure and broad parameters in the modern technological system. The working group made some recommendations on legal and operational standards and securities systems as per international standards.

The working group took a decision on licensed software to be installed with a proper system of backup data and its continuity in upgrading to the latest technology. It also brought out the gaps in the security system of computers and methods to evolve a good and strong security control programme. The control would be specifically designed for software, telecommunication lines, libraries, system software and application software. For sensitive information it recommended a firewall system. The group was of the view that there should be a LAN system installed to support the dial up services into the network. The telnet services should be disabled and the application server should be isolated from the email server. The massages received and computer access of people should be logged and security violations should be immediately checked.

The working group recommended that there should be a method of testing. Periodic penetration test of the system should be undertaken to find out if any data has been hacked. Controls should be immediately enforced. The bank should also have backup data and develop tools for recovery of data, if data is lost due to transmission process. Only certified products should be used for security system.

Ones installed the system should be well maintained. The security system should be constantly reviewed for effectively controlling it.

Internet banking services requires the approval from RBI. Commercial banks have to send an application to RBI with complete information of its infrastructure and security system. It should also include its business plan, cost and benefit analysis and control procedure for managing risks. The RBI would send its auditors to inspect the infrastructure and the facilities provided by the bank. In some cases banks may require an inter-bank payment gateway for internet payments. RBI has to inspect and give its approval of data integrity before such a practice can be taken up by commercial banks.

In May 2007 RBI discussed the options of providing Information Technology (IT)- services in remote and rural areas. One of the important aspects was to bring about technology in such areas with low transaction costs, Banks were directed to provide high security to technology enable services accepted Banks started the IT services with pilot projects through smart cards to extend such services.

Electronic Money—Debit and Credit Cards

In 2002 a working group was formed with Zaire. J. Camas as chairman, to give their recommendations on electronic money. Electronic money can be classified as a store of monetary value on a technical device. It uses computer networks for digital cash. The stored value may be a single purpose card, a limited purpose card, a general purpose card. The single purpose card can be used only for one kind of transaction. In India such cards are currently being issued by retail outlets. They can be used only to purchase items at that store. The closed system is limited to a particular area of sale. A general card is a multi purpose card which can be used in many different situations. It can be used in restaurants, hospitals, retail outlets, for payment of bills of electricity and telephone as well as internationally for transactions in different countries. These can be issued as debit cards and credit cards. These cards can also be used to withdraw cash from *Automatic Teller Machines (ATM's).*

Debit cards can be distinguished from credit cards when a person pays by a debit card the money gets debited directly from the customers bank A/c. The customer does not receive any fuither bill for settlement in a credit card the ank sends a statement to the customer and raises a bill through which is paid by cheque.

The group recommended that e-money should be permitted but RBI would periodically review the legal issues of ensuring security to the customers. *The ATM's have become an important source of money and it has extended both in the public sector banks as well as private bank. Now there are credit cards, debit cards, smart cards, internet banking and phone banking facilities provided by banks.*

Anti-Money Laundering

The Financial Action Task Force (FATF) on Anti-Money Laundering Standards and on Combating Financing of Terrorism issued guidelines to banks in November 2004 to formulate a policy framework on 'Know Your Customer' and Anti-Money Laundering (ALM) measures. These guidelines were specifically made to implement Special Recommendation VII (SR VII) of the FATF, to prevent terrorists and other criminals from having free access to wire transfers for moving their funds. In April 2007 RBI directed banks that domestic wire transfers of Rs.50,000 and above and all cross-border wire transfers could be sent through detailed information giving name, address and account number of a person and the details should be retained throughout the payment chain for 10 years. This was required under the Prevention of Money Laundering Act (PMLA), 2002. The beneficiary banks would have to make effective risk-based procedures to identify wire transfers which did not have complete originator's information. If such information was not provided banks would be liable for penal action to the extent of closure of business.

Mergers and Amalgamations of Banks

One of the important aspects of reforms was that banks should be able to perform and do well in business. Since there were problems of deteriorating financial condition in certain banks, the Reserve Bank of India actively tried to sort out the problems of such banks. It was only if the problems continued and there was no way that the banks could continue business that steps like mergers of banks and amalgamations were taken. The modus operandi was to put the bank facing problems in a moratorium period for 3 months and then decide whether the merger or amalgamation applied by the bank was feasible.

The notable cases in respect of amalgamation and mergers in 2006-2007 are that of: (i) Ganesh Bank of Kurundwad Ltd. (GBK) to be amalgamated with Federal Bank Ltd., (ii) United Western Bank Ltd. (UWB) with the Industrial Development Bank of India (IDBI), (iii) Sangli Bank Ltd. with the ICICI Bank Ltd., and (iv) Scheme of Transfer of Undertaking of Bharat Overseas Bank Ltd. to Indian Overseas Bank.

Government of India, on the recommendation the Reserve Bank, put the Ganesh Bank of Kurundwad Ltd. (GBK), bank under an Order of Moratorium for a period of three months. Federal Bank Ltd. was keen to amalgamate the business of GBK with it. Government of India sanctioned the amalgamation after RBI made observations and prepared the Scheme of Amalgamation. However, the amalgamation was challenged by GBK and others before the High Court of Bombay and later in the Supreme Court. The case was dismissed in the Supreme Court. GBK was finally amalgamated with the Federal Bank Ltd. and started its operations on September 2, 2006.

The United Western Bank Ltd. (UWB) was suffering with financial problems. They were issued a moratorium period of 3 months by Government on the application made by the Reserve Bank of India on September 2nd, 2006. There were 17 different organizations interested in there amalgamation with them. The UWB was amalgamated with the Industrial Development Bank of India (IDBI) Ltd. on October 3, 2006.

ICICI Bank Ltd. and Sangli Bank Ltd. applied to the Reserve Bank, for amalgamation after obtaining the approval from their shareholders. The scheme of amalgamation was sanctioned by the Reserve Bank Banking and it became effective for starting business, from April 19, 2007.

The Government of India sanctioned the Transfer of Undertaking of Bharat Overseas Bank Ltd. to Indian Overseas Bank which was made effective from March 31, 2007. In February 2008 Centurian Bank merged with HDFC.

These measures provided an improvement in the financial health of banks.

Protected Disclosures Scheme for Private Sector and Foreign Banks

In April 2004, government authorized the Central Vigilance Commission (CVC) to investigate into corruption and misuse of office of employees. Such a scheme was in force for government companies and employees working in them. This was extended to private sector and foreign banks operating in

India. The scheme was formalized in April 2007 to safeguard public interest. It was based on the Whistleblower Protection Act in United States of America (USA). Written complaints would be received by the Central Vigilance Commission for corruption, criminal offences, suspected/actual fraud, and loss of reputation and detrimental to depositors/public interest. Action would be taken after finding out the correctness of such complaints.

The complainants may be individuals, employees of the bank, customers, stakeholders, NGOs and member of the public.

Settlement of Deceased Depositors Claims

In 2003 the Tarapore Committee on Procedures and Performance Audit on Public Services recommended that deceased depositors claimed should be settled as quickly as possible. Based on this recommendation, the RBI in 2005 directed the banks to make a timely settlement of dues with the surviving family members of the deceased depositor. In those cases where they were single or jointly operated accounts and they were styled as 'either or survivor'. The survivor should be made the payments through simplified procedures. The termination of term deposits should be allowed even though the closure was premature. Banks were advised to settle the accounts with the survivor within 15 days from the date of claim. Since it is difficult for the nominee to produce many records pertaining to the deceased person banks should not insist on producing succession certificate or any bond of indemnity. A simple identification to satisfy the bank would enable the bank to clear the payments on the account of the deceased person.

Non-Resident Indian Accounts

The Indian government has supported the Non-Residents Indians (NRIs) inflow of funds into the country. To facilitate the NRIs to deposit their funds in banks the RBI extended their rights in 2005.

The NRIs were allowed to have NRO accounts remittances up to US $1 million per calendar year.

Door Step Banking

In February 2007, banks were permitted to offer 'doorstep banking' services to their customers, with the approval of their boards, without the requirement of permission from Reserve Bank of India. Doorstep services involve pick up of cash/instruments, delivery of cash against cheques received at the counter and delivery of demand drafts to corporate organizations, government departments and public sector units. This service was also available for individual customers. In May 2007, banks were allowed to give delivery of cash and demand draft to individuals.

Customer Service

The Reserve Bank was keen to empower the people in getting banking services and strengthening customer-service delivery by adopting a consultative process with banks through the Indian Banks' Association (IBA). The focus was to sensitize banks to customer service and to involve the boards of banks, in matters relating to banks' own grievance redressal machinery. RBI was interested in bringing about transparency in dealings and commitment to customers. Banking Codes and Standards Board of India (BCSBI) would create good standards as they would be an independent agency in monitoring the banks. Since disputes and disparities occur while transactions take place RBI wanted to strengthen and empower institutional mechanism for dispute resolution by encouraging the IBA to take an initiative in solving problems and only in extreme cases to look for legal procedures. Finally RBI wanted to rationalize its own systems and procedures to enhance customer service. On July 1, 2006 the Customer Service Department was setup in the Reserve Bank.

Customer Service Department

The Reserve Bank has tried to improve the customer service in the banking sector. It has taken several measures for protection of customers' rights, enhancing the quality of customer services and strengthening the grievance redressal mechanism in banks. It has also made changes to improve the customer service department. In order to improve customer services, it has brought together all activities relating to customer service in banks and the Reserve Bank in a single department. The new department started in 2006 was to focus exclusively on delivery of customer services. The functions of the Customer Service Department were to include dissemination of information relating to customer service and grievance redressal by banks. It was to act as a nodal department for the Banking Codes and Standards Board of India (BCSBI). It was to act as an intermediary between banks, the Indian Banks' Association, the BCSBI, the BO offices and the regulatory departments in the Reserve Bank.

'Code of Banks' Commitment

On July 1, 2006 'Code of Banks Commitment' towards customers' was released. The Code is the first formal collaboration by the Reserve Bank, the banks and the Banking Codes and Standards Board of India (BCSBI) to provide a minimum standard for banking services to customers. This code would endeavor to bring about reliability, transparency and accountability in transactions with customers. The code would provide the methodology of the banks day-to-day dealings with the customers and what each customer should expect from his/her bank.

Banking Ombudsman

Ombudsman means a 'grievance man', a public official who is appointed to investigate complaints against the administration. In India, any person whose grievance against a bank is not resolved within one month can approach the Banking Ombudsman, if his complaint pertains to any of the matters specified in the Scheme. This scheme deals with complaints in deficiency of banking service, loans and advances and non observance of RBI rules relating to interest rates. Banking Ombudsman helps in settlement of complaints between the customer and banks.

The Banking Ombudsman Scheme, 1995 was notified by RBI on June 14, 1995 to provide for a system of redressal of grievances against banks. It was inexpensive scheme for resolving customer complaints. It has been revised twice in the years 2002 and 2006. The Scheme is being administered by Banking Ombudsmen appointed by RBI.

On 1st January, 2006 new features were added to the scheme concerning complaints, easier complaint submission facility and appeal option to the complainants was included. During 2006-07, the complaint tracking software was updated to enable complainants to file their complaints online. On May 24, 2007, the Scheme was amended to enable bank customers to appeal to the Reserve Bank against awards passed by the Banking Ombudsmen and also other decisions given by it under this Scheme.

Fair Practices Code

In May, 2003 the Reserve Bank issued guidelines on Fair Practices Code for Lenders. This code was to protect the interest and rights of borrowers against harassment by lenders. Banks were required to provide information about fees, charges and important matters affecting the interest of borrowers regarding loan application forms of priority sector advances up to Rs. 2 lakh. If banks rejected the loan application of small borrowers up to Rs. 2 lakhs. They had to convey in writing the reasons for rejection of loan applications. In March 2007, these guidelines became applicable for all categories of loans even beyond Rs. 2 lakhs. The guidelines became comprehensive to include credit card applications. In case credit card applications were rejected banks had to give their reasons for it.

Do Not Call Registry

In November 2005 all scheduled commercial banks in credit card operations were advised in to maintain a '*Do Not Call Registry*'. The right of privacy of people was to be maintained and telemarketing was to be avoided with those people who wanted to maintain privacy relating to unsolicited commercial communications being received by banks. Complaints continued to be received from credit card subscribers despite directives sent to banks. The Telecom Regulatory Authority of India (TRAI) has framed the Telecom Unsolicited Commercial Communications (UCC) Regulations, 2007. The Regulations have planned a mechanism with all telecom service providers to receive requests from subscribers who do not want to receive calls and maintain a private 'do not call' list. This would be maintained by National Informatics Centre. Telemarketers will have to register the with it and update themselves with the latest instructions received on '*do not call*' subscribers.

Pass Book Service

In October 2006 RBI advised the banks to offer pass book facility to all their savings bank account holders. If a bank has the policy of sending statement of account to their customers it must be provided to the customer every month. Banks were not to charge the customers the cost of providing a pass book or monthly statements. Banks had to write the full address and telephone numbers of branches are as given in the passbook or statement of accounts which is issued to the account holders to improve the quality of customer service in branches. In December 2006 banks had to provide both the drop box facility and the facility for acknowledgement of the cheques at the regular collection counters. In 2006 to improve transparency, banks were advised place their service charges and fees on their websites under the title of 'Service Charges and Fees'. A link to the websites of the banks has been provided on the Reserve Bank's website.

Human Resource Development

One of the important issues in the reform process of banks was to bring about professionalism and quality of governance in their operations. In this respects the Reserve Bank provides training for skill up-gradation in all important areas of banking operations. Human resource development, recruitment of staff and training programmes for existing staff are integral part of this process. The RBI has been trying to bring about new training methods and management development programs to upgrade the skills of their human resources.

Higher Education Finance

Loans have been provided by commercial banks for higher education. An educational loan scheme was included in the priority sector lending. The criteria for giving these loans are that the person has a good academic record and is keen to study either in India or abroad. Despite the fact that it was in the priority sector, the sanctioned loans for education were very small. In 2000 a study group under the chairmanship of R.J. Kamath was formed to review the educational loan scheme of different banks and to form a uniform procedure for granting these loans. The group recommended loans for education to be raised from Rs. 3 lakhs to a maximum of Rs. 7.5 lakhs for studies in India. It was to be raised from Rs. 5 lakhs to Rs. 15 lakhs for studies in foreign countries. Repayment of the loan was to be made between 5 to 7 years. Repayment was to start 1 year after completion of the course or 6 months after getting a job whichever is earlier.[9]

REGIONAL RURAL BANKS

The RBI constituted the Bhandari committee in 1994-95 for restructuring and reviving RRBs. The committee suggested the amalgamation and recapitalization of a large number of RRBs. In September 2005, the process of amalgamation of regional rural banks (RRBs) was initiated to strengthen them. In 2006-2007 this was continued. The amalgamation of 145 RRBs into 45 new RRBs, brought down the total number of RRBs from 196 in March 2005 to 133 in March 2006 and to 96 by March 2007.

The sponsor banks were guided by RBI to continue development work by developing human resources, information technology and operations of the RRBs sponsored by them. A Task Force was constituted by the RBI for greater participation of the RRBs in decision making. K.G. Karmakar was the first chairman to be appointed in September 2007 for suggesting areas where more autonomy could be given to the boards of the RRBs, in matters of investments, business development and staffing. In January 2007, the Task Force submitted its Report. It recommended the selection of the chairman for a minimum period of 3 years on merit from a panel of qualifying officers from large sized banks and an increase in number of directors on the boards of the RRBs. It also advised the extension of capital adequacy norms to RRBs. Government of India in consultation with the State Governments and sponsor banks are working out the methodology for recapitalization of RRBs.

MATURITY PATTERN OF TERM DEPOSITS

The maturity pattern of term deposits of scheduled commercial banks for the years 2004-06 is given in Table 11.4. The share of short term deposits upto 90 days is higher than the deposits of above 91 days and less than 6 months in all the 3 years. In 2004 the number of accounts were 8.5% where as those upto 1 year were only 6.7%. The same trend can be seen in 2005 and 2006. The upto 90 days the number of accounts were 8.2% and 7.9% where as less than 6 months were 5.9% and 5.7% respectively. While analyzing the data a similar trend can be seen for deposits above 5 years. There is a sudden decline in the percentage of accounts between more than 5 years and between 3 to 5 years. This trend can be noticed in all the 3 years. In 2004 it was 24.2% between 3 and 5 years but there is a sharp fall at 13.5% account. In 2006 it is 23.9% and 16% respectively between 3 to 5 years and above 5 years. The analysis shows that the most popular term deposits are between 1 year maturity and upto 5 years. This accounts for more than 50% of the term deposits of scheduled banks in India. A similar trend was analyzed between the years 1969-2002 by Bhole who found that the medium term deposits were most popular.[10] This shows that the government policy does not encouraged long term bank deposits.

---

9. For further information on education loans, see B.S. Sreekantaradhya, *Banking and Finance*, Deep & Deep Publication Pvt. Ltd. New Delhi 2004, p. 50-61.
10. L.M. Bhole, *Financial Institutions and Markets*, Tata McGraw Hill Publishing Company Ltd. New Delhi, 4th Edition 2004, p. 8.17.

Table 11.4 : Maturity Pattern of Term Deposits of Scheduled Commercial Banks—2004-06

(Amount in Rs. crore)

Period of maturity	As on March 31					
	2004		2005		2006	
	No. of Accounts	Amount Outstanding	No. of Accounts	Amount Outstanding	No. of Accounts	Amount Outstanding
	(1)	(2)	(3)	(4)	(5)	(6)
Upto 90 days	1,15,56,666.0	1,21,059.0	1,05,79,624.0	147979.0	9674413.0	168248.0
	(8.5)	(12.9)	(8.2)	(13.9)	(7.9)	(13.5)
91 days & above but	91,51,282.0	1,01,885.0	75,98,758.0	111888.0	6954578.0	117928.0
less than 6 months	(6.7)	(10.9)	(5.9)	(10.5)	(5.7)	(9.5)
6 months & above but	1,54,72,612.0	1,33,177.0	14,2,64,304.0	159124.0	13021077.0	206329.0
less than 1 year	(11.4)	(14.2)	(11.1)	(15.0)	(10.7)	(16.6)
1 year & above but	2,86,51012.0	2,10,174.0	2,77,43,289.0	249091.0	25817363.0	330376.0
less than 2 years	(21.0)	(22.5)	(21.5)	(23.4)	(21.2)	(26.5)
2 years & above but	2,00,74,114.0	1,09,149.0	1,99,85,869.0	113742.0	17695362.0	118283.0
less than 3 years	(14.7)	(11.7)	(15.5)	(10.7)	(14.5)	(9.5)
3 years & above but	3,30,03,866.0	1,83,364.0	3,03,29,238.0	192613.0	29128550.0	201227.0
less than 5 years	(24.2)	(19.6)	(23.5)	(18.1)	(23.9)	(16.1)
5 years & above	1,83,46,112.0	77,048.0	1,85,73,161.0	89709.0	19439312.0	103963.0
	(13.5)	(8.2)	(14.4)	(8.4)	(16.0)	(8.3)
Total	**13,62,55,664.0**	**9,35,856.0**	**12,90,74,243.0**	**1064146.0**	**121730655.0**	**1246354.0**
	(100.0)	**(100.0)**	**(100.0)**	**(100.0)**	**(100.0)**	**(100.0)**

Note : Figures in brackets represent per cent share in total.
Source : Basic Statistical Returns of Scheduled Commercial Banks in India, Volumes 33-35.

Comprehensive Statistics of Commercial Banks

The data in Table 11.5 given below depicts at a glance the details.

It gives the data of growth of schedule banks from 1969 to 2007. In 1969 the number of schedule banks were 89. They increased to 300 in 2001. It then declined due to changes in policy. There were a large number of mergers and amalgamations of banks and by March 2007, the number of banks decreased to 183. The number of bank offices in India increased as government was keen to enlarge business operations to every area in the country. Thus from 8,262 banks in 1969 the number of offices rose to 73,836. As can be seen from the data in Table 11.5 the rural areas have specially benefited as bank offices increased from 1,833 to 30,560. However, the population per office has remained between 15,000 and 16,000. The aggregate deposits of scheduled commercial banks have increased from Rs. 4,646 crores to Rs. 26,08,309. The deposits in scheduled commercial banks are still low. Although there is a significant increase from 1969 from 2000-07 it could be increased further if government policy favoured the commercial banks. Since interest was low the depositor was not attracted towards commercial bank deposits for long term period of time. Short term deposits were preferred to long term deposits as seen in table 11.4. The share of priority sector advances in total credit does not show much change between 2000 and 2007. However, banks are giving advances of about 33% to the priority sector.

Table11.5: Statistics Relating To Scheduled Commercial Banks at a Glance

Indicators	June 1969	March 2000	March 2001	March 2002	March 2003	March 2004	March 2005	March 2006	March 2007
Number of Commercial Banks	89	298	300	297	292	290	289	222	183
(a) Scheduled Commercial Banks	73	297	296	293	288	286	285	218	179
of which: Regional Rural Banks	—	196	196	196	196	196	196	133	96
(b) Non-Scheduled Commercial Banks	16	2	5	4	4	5	4	4	4
Number of Bank Offices in India	8262	67868	67937	68195	68500	69170	70373	71685	73836
(a) Rural	1833	32852	32585	32503	32283	32227	30790	30436	30560
(b) Semi-Urban	3342	14841	14843	14962	15135	15288	15325	15811	16484
(c) Urban	1584	10994	11193	11328	11566	11806	12419	13034	13840
(d) Metropolitan	1503	9181	9316	9402	9516	9750	11839	12404	12952
Population per Office (in thousands)	64	15	15	15	16	16	16	16	16
Aggregate deposits of Scheduled Commercial Banks in India (Rs. crore)	4646	851593	989141	1131188	1311761	1504416	1700198	2109049	2608309
(a) Demand deposits	2104	145283	159407	169103	187837	225022	248028	364640	429137
(b) Time deposits	2542	706310	829734	962085	1123924	1279394	1452171	1744409	2179172
Credit of Scheduled Commercial Banks in India (Rs. crore)	3599	454069	529271	609053	746432	840785	1100428	1507077	1928913
Investments of Scheduled Commercial Banks in India (Rs. crore)	1361	311697	367184	437482	547546	677588	739154	717454	790431
Deposits of Scheduled Commercial Banks per office (Rs. lakh)	56	1255	1456	1659	1925	2265	2574	3047	3675
Credit of Scheduled Commercial Banks per office (Rs. lakh)	44	669	779	893	1143	1330	1700	2209	2757
Per capita Deposit of Scheduled Commercial Banks (Rs.)	88	8542	9770	11008	12253	14089	16281	19130	23382
Per capita Credit of Scheduled Commercial Banks (Rs.)	68	4555	5228	5927	7275	8273	10752	13869	17541
Deposits of Scheduled Commercial Banks as percentage to Gross National Product at factor cost (at current prices)	15.5	53.5	56	54.4	58.8	59.4	60	65.4	70.1
Scheduled Commercial Banks' Advances to Priority Sectors (Rs. crore)	504	155779	182255	205606	254648	263834	381476	510175	632647
Share of Priority Sector Advances in total credit of Scheduled Commercial Banks (per cent)	14	35.4	31	34.8	35.1	34.5	36.7	35.3	34.3
Credit-Deposit Ratio (per cent)	77.5	53.3	53.5	53.8	56.9	55.9	62.6	70.1	73.5
Investment-Deposit Ratio (per cent)	29.3	36.6	37.1	38.7	41.3	45	47.3	40	35.3
Cash-Deposit Ratio (per cent)	8.2	9.8	8.4	7.1	6.3	7.2	6.4	6.7	7.2

Notes :

1. Number of bank offices includes Administrative Offices.
2. Classification of bank offices according to population for the year 1969 is based on 1961 census and for the subsequent years up to March 2004, it is based on 1991 census. For March 2005 upto March 2007, classification of bank offices were based on 2001 census.
3. Population per office, per capita deposits and per capita credit are based on the estimated mid-year population figures, supplied by the Office of the Registrar General, India.
4. Deposits, credit and investments of Scheduled Commercial Banks in India are as per "Form-A" return under Section 42(2) of the Reserve Bank of India Act, 1934 and relate to the last Friday of the reference period.
5. Scheduled Commercial Banks' advances to priority sectors and the related ratios are exclusive of Regional Rural Banks.
6. For working out cash-deposit ratio, cash is taken as the total of 'cash in hand' and 'balances with the Reserve Bank of India'. The data for 'cash in hand' are taken from "Form-A" return as per Section 42(2) of the Reserve Bank of India Act, 1934 and 'balances with the Reserve Bank of India' are taken from the "Weekly Statement of Affairs of the Reserve Bank of India".
7. Investments of Scheduled Commercial Banks in India include only investments in government securities and other approved securities.

Summary

➡ Commercial banks have played a major role in mobilizing the savings of the individuals. They have participated in the transfer of resources from savers to borrowers.

➡ There are many types of banks. These are scheduled and non-scheduled, public and private sector, foreign banks and cooperative banks.

➡ The Imperial Bank was started in 1921. It was merged with the State Bank of India through an Act passed in 1955. This bank was the first nationalized Bank of India. Its objective was to expand banking business in rural and urban areas and to promote credit in priority areas like agriculture and small industry.

➡ Indian banks have their head office in India. They have been permitted to do business in foreign countries. In 2007, there were 16 Indian banks in countries like Hong Kong, Singapore, UAE, Malaysia, Belgium, China, Indonesia and United Kingdom. 11 banks were in the public sector and 5 in the private sector. They had a network of 188 offices abroad.

➡ Foreign Banks have started the business in India since 2002. They have their offices in India but their head offices are in a foreign country.

➡ The regional rural banks have been setup by commercial banks in rural areas for agricultural and trade financing from those areas.

➡ Universal banks are new in India. They are called multi product forms. They have a combination of banking with investments. The ICICI was the first financial institution to become a universal bank.

➡ The functions of commercial banks are to open bank accounts of individuals and corporate organizations and to transfer this accounts into loans to those units which are deficit in finance. To increase funds they are engaged in many kinds of services to the clients. The services may be agency, general utility and trusteeship.

➡ Banks should be distinguished from financial institutions and development institutions. Although both are intermediary institutions yet their methodology and working is different. The financial institutions give claims against themselves through a financial paper. Banks provide deposits and through them they create credit by offering loans to deficit units. Development banks raise funds through bonds. They give loans for development.

➡ Commercial banks have developed themselves in different phases. In the foundation phase they tried to develop themselves between 1949 and 1969. In the expansion phase in 1969, 14 commercial banks were nationalized to give loans to the priority sector since 1970 the banks tried to expend into new areas of lending. Their focus however continued to be towards development of large industries. From 1980 to 1990 government took steps for consolidation. It nationalized six more banks. It also diversified into priority sector lending, mutual fund, credit cards and loans for purchase of motor vehicles.

➡ Banking sector reforms were passed in 1992 and in 1998 on the basis of Narasimham Committee I and II to increase efficiency levels, improvement and transparency and standards of disclosures.

Contd....

➡ Deregulations were brought about on interest rates and the reserve requirements of cash and statutory liquidity ratio was reduced.

➡ There were diversification of services into non-traditional areas like leasing, higher purchase, factoring, merchant banking, mutual fund and venture capital.

➡ Prudential norms were introduced by the Reserve Bank of India on the recommendation of Narasimham Committee. The capital adequacy ratio norms as approved by Basel Committee were also implemented in difference stages. The capital risk weighted asset ratio was require to the maintained to 6% by the year 2010. The risk weights were to be assigned by using credit ratings of for rating agencies.

➡ The venture capital funds were made at par with equity shares. Market risk and other exposures had to be covered according to the guidelines and changes as on August 2006.

➡ Investment norms of banks have been revised since 2004.

➡ Banking supervision was recommended by Basel Committee to monitor capital adequacy norms and evaluate risks of banks. Since April 2007 the supervisory system has been further strengthened to avoid frauds and for smooth movement of funds.

➡ The RBI has taken a great interest on encouraging market discipline and good governance. It also focused on transparency and disclosure.

➡ Income recognition, risk management and asset classification was done by banks to monitor NPAs. In 2006-07 the supervisory rating model based on CAMELS or capital adequacy, asset quality, management, earning, liquidity and systems and control model was adopted.

➡ Consolidated supervision for monitoring the banks was extended to its subsidiaries and joint venture banks. According to this guideline banks have to provide information of consolidated data of banks and subsidiaries.

➡ Securitization of assets was considered to be important for reducing non-performing assets. The Securitization Act was passed in 2002 for setting up a central registry and reconstruction of financial assets. In 2005 RBI prepared guidelines for securitization of standard non-performing assets.

➡ The non-performing assets have been reduced to 2% of its net advances by 2007 through the various majors taken up by the commercial banks.

➡ Disputes relating to non-performing assets were to be settled through Lok Adalats. The functioning of Debt Recovery Tribunals was also strengthened for settling disputes.

➡ Modernization of banks was done through improvement in technology by brining about computerization and E-banking.

➡ In 2002 technology was upgraded through debit and credit cards and induction of Automatic Teller Machines which have been extended to public sector and private sector banks.

➡ Anti money laundering standards were formulated in November 2004.

➡ Mergers and amalgamation of banks took place in 2006-07.

Contd.....

➡ Improvements were made in customer services. The accounts of a deceased depositor were to be settled quickly. Door step banking was provided and non-resident Indians were given privileges in banking.

➡ Customer service and redressel measures were taken up by instituting a special customer service department for protecting the rights of the customers and the code of banks commitment was released in 2006.

➡ Banking OMBUDSMAN Scheme of 1995 was revised to enable customers to file their grievances.

➡ A Fair practices code for lenders was issued to protect the rights of borrowers against harassment by lenders.

➡ A do not call registry was maintained for privacy of people from telemarketing operators since 2005.

➡ In 2006 pass book service was extended to customers by banks without any charge.

➡ Human resource development was given attention through training programmes.

➡ Higher education finance was revised to raise the limits both for studies in India and a broad.

➡ Regional rural banks were restructured and revived following the recommendations of the Bhandari Committee in 1994-95.

➡ The maturity pattern of term deposits shows that the popularity of deposits were in deposits between 3 to 5 years.

Objective Type Auestions, Answer True (T) or False (F)

(a) The imperial bank was established in 1955.

(b) The maturity pattern of term deposits in India shows that they are popular between the 3-5 year periods.

(c) K.G. Karmakar is the first chairman appointed in 2007 for brining about improvements and changes in RRBs.

(d) There are no higher education loans in India.

(e) The RBI has provided training to human resources since 1970.

(f) The pass book services are very expensive in India.

(g) The do not call registry is the right of privacy of people from telecom operators.

(h) The fair practices code is a guideline issued for do not call registry.

(i) The banking ombudsman is appointed to investigate the complaints against the administration.

(j) The code of banks commitment is to bring about transparency of services.

(k) The protected disclosure scheme is for government employees.

Answers: (a) F, (b) T, (c) T, (d) F, (e) F, (f) F, (g) T, (h) F, (i) T, (j) T, (k) F.

Multiple Choice Questions (Tick mark (✓) the right answer)

1. Scheduled banks are:
   (a) Public sector banks which adhere to the banking regulation Act.
   (b) Scheduled banks are included in the second schedule of banking regulation Act of 1965.
   (c) Scheduled banks are private sector banks in the first scheduled of banking regulation Act of 1965.
   (d) Public sector banks are nationalized banks with the State Bank and associates.

2. Foreign banks are incorporated:
   (a) In India with head office abroad.
   (b) Outside India but with its offices in India.
   (c) In India with head office in India.
   (d) Outside India with offices outside India but business in India.

3. Regional Rural Banks were formed:
   (a) To develop exports of large companies.
   (b) To help marginal farmers and small entrepreneurs.
   (c) To provide loans for helping the leaders in rural areas.
   (d) To establish large banks in rural areas.

4. Universal banks were first started in:
   (a) India
   (b) USA
   (c) Japan
   (d) Germany

5. The Narasimham Committee brought about the reforms for:
   (a) Structural changes and transparency levels in commercial banks.
   (b) Revision of Ombudsman Act for settlement of disputes.
   (c) Features of Universal banks and extension of their services.
   (d) Reduction of statutory liquidity ratio with banks.

6. The trusteeship services of banks are:
   (a) Collection of cheques and credit card payments.
   (b) To provide guarantees in case of defaults.
   (c) To issue letter of credit, merchant banking services and credit information.
   (d) To provide safety vaults and maintaining escrow accounts.

7. Banks can be distinguished from mutual funds:
   (a) Banks provide deposits, mutual funds create credit.
   (b) Banks offer accounts to customers' mutual funds provide safety to their customers.
   (c) Banks offer deposits, mutual funds offer units to their customers.
   (d) Banks offer deposits and loans but mutual funds offer bonds.

Answers: 1 (b), 2 (a), 3 (b), 4 (d), 5 (a), 6 (d), 7 (c).

Short Answer Questions

1. What are the different types of banks operating in India?

2. Distinguish between commercial banks, financial institutions and development banks in India?

3. What is universal banking? How is it different from a commercial bank?

4. What is a non-performing asset? Discuss briefly some of the measures adopted by government for reducing such assets.

5. What are the measures taken in the reform period for effective supervision of banks?

6. What is banking Ombudsman? How does it help the commercial banks?

7. What are the different types of bank accounts? What is the maturity pattern of bank accounts in India?

Long Answer Questions

1. How do you think that the reform period has brought about transparency and disclosures in commercial banking?

2. What is the methodology of risk management by commercial banks in the post reform period after 1991?

3. What is securitization of assets? Why are assets securitized? How can the level of non-performing assets be reduced?

4. What steps have banks taken in modernization and new technology development in India?

5. Why have mergers and amalgamations taken place in commercial banks in India? Give some examples.

6. *'Banks have brought about changes in customer services'*. Do you agree with this statement? Discuss of the some of the important changes for creating customer service.

Chapter  **12**

Co-operative Banks

Chapter Plan

- Structure of Co-operative Banks
- Urban Co-operative Banks
- Rural Co-operative Banks

INTRODUCTION

Co-operative credit institutions play an important role in the financial system of a country. Their main objective is to fill in the gaps of providing finance to people of small and medium income. In a way co-operative banks supplement the work of commercial banks in mobilize savings and credit requirements of the local population. Co-operative banks were introduced in India in 1904 by enacting the co-operative Credit Society Act. In 1912 a new Act was passed to establish co-operative central banks. Co-operative Banks in India are registered under the Co-operative Societies Act. The cooperative bank is also regulated by the RBI. They are governed by the Banking Regulations Act 1949 and Banking Laws (Co-operative Societies) Act, 1965. The co-operative bank has to be registered with the State Registrar of Co-operative societies. It is promoted by members. Each member has one vote and the bank works on the principle of '*no profit, no loss*'.

STRUCTURE OF CO-OPERATIVE BANKS

In India there are **urban** co-operative banks and **rural** co-operative credit institutions. While urban co-operative banks have a single tier structure, rural cooperatives have a complex structure. Rural co-operative credit institutions have two structures. These are the short-term co-operative credit structure (STCCS) and the long-term cooperative credit structure (LTCCS). The rural institutions are categorized into State Co-operative Banks (SCBs), District Central Co-operative Banks and Primary Agricultural Credit Societies which provide short term credit. State Co-operative agriculture, rural development banks and primary co-operative agriculture deal with long term credit requirements. The primary agricultural co-operatives were instituted at the grass root level, Co-operative Central Banks in the intermediate level and State Co-operative Banks in the apex level. Thus forming a three tier approach, for short term and medium term lending. It was considered that long term lending should be separated from short term lending to make it more effective. The State Co-operative Banks are at the apex for long term loans and are engaged in co-ordinating the Central Co-operative Banks with the money market as well as the Reserve Bank of India and the entire co-operative system. The Primary Credit Societies are at the base of the co-operative credit system. The structure of rural co-operative banks is not uniform across the States of the country. It varies from one State to another. Some States have a unitary structure with the State level banks operating through their own branches, while others have a mixed structure incorporating both unitary and federal systems.

The All India Rural Credit Review Committee in 1969 recommended that RBI should be assigned the role of building co-operative credit. As a follow up of the recommendations, the RBI contributed in a major way by giving directions and making policies to increase the share of co-operative credit in rural areas. It adopted a multi agency approach by creating a link between the commercial banks and co-operative banks in supplementing credit wherever it was required. It also brought in the Regional Rural Banks (RRBs) to provide credit along with the commercial banks and co-operative banks. Co-operative banks in India finance rural areas under farming, cattle, milk, hatchery and personal finance. Co-operative banks in India finance urban areas under self-employment, industries, small scale units, home finance, consumer finance and personal finance. The problems of rural co-operatives was reviewed by the Task Force (2004) constituted by the Government of India and the Vision Document on urban co-operative banks (UCBs) was released in March 2005 by the Reserve Bank. They have provided a new practical approach to rejuvenate the Indian co-operative banking structure. The focus is to revitalise these institutions for creating and building the confidence of the public in the co-operative banking system. The new regulatory and supervisory framework was to maintain their co-operative character and institutional specifics. The structure of co-operative banks is depicted in Fig. 12.1.

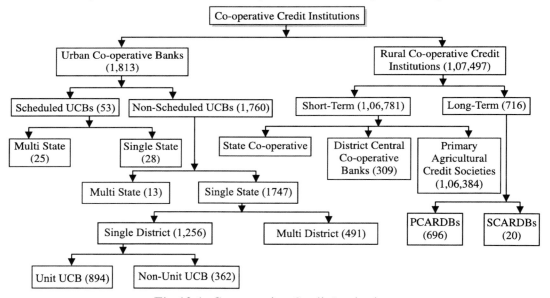

Fig.12.1: Co-operative Credit Institution.

SCARDBs : State Co-operative Agriculture and Rural Development Banks.
PCARDBs : Primary Co-operative Agriculture and Rural Development Banks.
Note : Figure in parentheses indicate the number of institutions at end March 2007 for UCBs and at end-March 2006 for rural co-operative credit institutions.
Source: RBI Report on Trend and Progress of Banking in India, Government of India Publication, 2006-07.

URBAN CO-OPERATIVE BANKS

The Urban Co-operative Banks were setup for mobilizing the savings of the low and middle income group of people. Its objective is to give emphasis to the weaker section of the society. Urban Co-operative Banks can be started by applying for a license from the Reserve Bank of India. In 2000 the Reserve Bank of India made four categories of co-operative banks based on population.

Category 1: Population above 10 lakhs. The membership requirement is of 3,000 people with a share capital of a minimum of Rs. 4 crores.

Category 2: Population between 5 to 10 lakhs. The membership should be of 2,000 people with a share capital of a minimum of Rs. 2 crores.

Category 3: Population 1 to 5 lakhs. The banks should have a membership of 1,500 people and a minimum capital of Rs. 1 crore.

Category 4: Population upto 1 lakh. The minimum share capital should be 25 lakhs and the number of member should be at least 500.

Vision Document

The urban co-operative banks played a significant role in providing banking services to the middle and lower income people, for this reason, the RBI made an attempt to strengthen these banks. In June 2004, the RBI put a ban on the issue of licenses to UCBs for setting up new banks or for opening new branches, because it was preparing a revised framework for regulation and supervision of the existing UCBs. In March 2005, the Reserve Bank prepared a draft Vision document for UCBs which cited some of the problems of this sector. It also brought into focus the issue of dual regulatory mechanism which restricted the ability of the Reserve Bank in handling the weaknesses of the UCBs. The Vision document proposed to have a consultative approach for deciding the future set up of weak and sick banks in each State. The Reserve Bank approached the State Governments for signing MOU between the two agencies entrusted with the regulation and supervision of UCBs. As part of the MOU, it was decided to set up State level Task Force for Co-operative Urban Banks (TAFCUBs) having some representatives of the Reserve Bank, State Government and federation/association of UCBs. The Task Force was given the work of identifying viable and non viable UCBs in the State and the steps for their revival. Banks which were not remunerative should go through the exit route which could be implemented by mergers or amalgamation with financially sound and larger banks.

New Branches

In 2006-07 in its Annual Policy statement RBI directions that financially sound banks in the States would be permitted to open new branches. The focus for the sector would be on development of Human Resources (HR) and Information Technology (IT) infrastructure and governance. The mergers of UCBs have also begun to consolidate them. The UCBs have to get 'no objection' certificate to their merger proposals. As on October 30, 2007, a total of 33 mergers had been made on the issue of statutory orders by the Central Registrar of Cooperative Societies/Registrar of Co-operative Societies (CRCS/RCS). In addition to the existing 1,813 UCBs at end-March 2007, 259 UCBs were under various stages of liquidation. The reduction in the number of UCBs helped to expand their business operations and bring an improvement in their asset quality.[1] The RBI has extended the development of new branches to eligible banks in States and multi-State UCBs.

Policy Development

The Reserve Bank formulated a policy for the UCBs. The tier I UCBs which had a deposit base of less than Rs.100 crore and having branches limited to a single district were given the Vision Document for UCBs comprising of guidelines relating to interest rates, prudential norms, disclosure and exposure norms and risk management. Tier I UCBs had to give preference to the urban poor. Therefore RBI gave specific directions on credit delivery, customer service and financial inclusion.

The problems of Tier I UCBs were outlined in the vision document. Suggestions were also made to adopt measures to become sound and strong to provide need based quality banking services, especially to the middle and lowers middle classes and marginalized sections of the society.

Relaxations in Norms

The UCBs were classified as Tier I banks if they had branches within a single district and had deposits below Rs.100 crores. This classification was important to strengthen these banks to be able to achieve their targets. Prudential norms for Tier I and Tier II banks were also revised. Tier I and II banks with the 90-days delinquency norm and the 180-day loan delinquency norm for Tier I banks was extended up to March 31, 2008 to give relief to small UCBs. This relief was given to make profits and to build a capital base in them with the expectation of reverting it to 90 days norm.

Tier I UCBs have been given exemption from maintaining SLR in government securities to the extent of funds which were deposited in interest bearing deposits with State Bank of India and its subsidiary banks and the public sector banks including Industrial Development Bank of India Ltd. The composite off-site surveillance has also been avoided for Tier I banks. Banks between 50 crores and 100 crores limited to a single district are under a simplified system of reporting.

Supervision and Surveillance

Large UCBs have strict supervision and surveillance norms. They are placed under a composite off-site surveillance (OSS) reporting system comprising a set of eight prudential supervisory returns,

Memorandum of Understanding

The RBI signed a memorandum of understanding in 13 different States for a consultative approach between state Central and State Governments and federation concerning problems of Urban co-operative banks. It signed MOU with 13 States. These are Gujarat, Andhra Pradesh, Karnataka, Madhya Pradesh, Uttarakhand, Rajasthan, Chhattisgarh, Goa, Maharastra, Haryana, National Capital Territory of Delhi, West Bengal and Assam. The MOUs were signed in 1,511 out of 1,813 existing banks at the end of March 2007. This accounts for 81.5 per cent of the existing UCBs and it covers 67 per cent of total deposits. The Reserve Bank and the Central Government have jointly signed an MOU in the case of Multi-State UCBs which consist of 25.5 per cent of deposits of the sector.

The Task Force for Co-operative Urban Banks (TAFCUBs) consisting of representatives of the Reserve Bank, State Government and Urban Co-operative Banks have been constituted in all States

---

1. RBI Report on Trend and Progress of Banking in India, Government of India Publication, 2006-07.

with which MOUs have been signed. A Central TAFCUBs has been initiated for the Multi-State UCBs. The work of the Task Force is to identify both potentially viable and non-viable UCBs in the State. Identification of viable UCBs would be useful for reviving them. The non-viable UCBs could plan an exit route through mergers and amalgamations or through liquidation.

New Areas of Business

In States and multi-states in which the RBI has signed MOUs, the UCBs have been allowed to undertake new business opportunities in the eligible banks. The UCBs are permitted to set up currency chests, sell mutual fund products, grant of Authorized Dealer category I and II license, permission to open new ATMs. In addition they have relaxed norms for conducting insurance business on non-risk participation basis and can convert their extension counters into branches.

Mergers and Amalgamations

Merger and amalgamation of UCBs is done through a certain specified process. A proposal has to be submitted by the acquirer bank to Central Registrar of Co-operative Societies/Registrar of Co-operative Societies CRCS/RCS. Since the RBI is an apex bank it is necessary to forward a copy of the proposal with complete information. After examining the proposal it sends it to an expert group for giving their comments and recommendations. If the proposal seems good to the RBI it issues a No Objection Certificate to the RCS/CRCS and to the applicant banks. The order of amalgamation is then issued by CRCS/RCS issues the order of amalgamation compliance with the provisions of the Co-operative Societies Act under which the bank is registered.

Non-resident External (NRE) Accounts

The NRE accounts were to be paid interest on their deposits according to the ceiling rate of LIBOR/ SWAP rules from January 31, 2007. This would be according to the FCNR currency or corresponding maturities minus 25 basis points. In April 2007 the ceiling rates were revised and the corresponding maturity minus 75 basis points was considered.

Urban co-operative banks were prohibited from granting new loans beyond Rs.20 lakhs against NRE and FCNR(B) deposits, either to depositors or to third parties. UCBs were directed that from April 24, 2007, the interest rates on fresh Non-Resident (External) Rupee term deposits for one to three years maturity should not exceed the LIBOR/SWAP rates, as on the last working day of the previous month, for US dollar of corresponding maturities Banks were sent guidelines to prohibit them to slice the loan amount to change the effect of ceiling.. On floating rate deposits, interest could be reset after every 6 months. Within the ceiling of SWAP rates for the respective currency/maturity minus 25 basis points. These rates were revised to currency/maturity minus 75 basis points.

Cash Reserve Ratio

The cash reserve ratio was revised by Government of India on March 2nd, 2007 to be effected from April 1st, 2007 through an extraordinary Gazette and amendment by the RBI Act. The cash reserve ratio (CRR) for scheduled primary (urban) co-operative banks as a percentage of net demand and time liabilities was increased from 5 per cent to 7.0 per cent in seven stages. The Reserve Bank exempted those UCBs which had breached the statutory minimum CRR level of 3.0 per cent during the period June 22, 2006 to March 2, 2007.

Risk Management

Tier II banks were directed to increase the general provisioning requirement on standard advances in specific sectors such as in the case of personal loans, loans and advances qualifying as capital market exposures and commercial real estate loans from the existing level of one per cent to two per cent. Risk weight on exposure to commercial real estate was increased from 100 per cent to 150 per cent. The UCBs were notified that they had to continuously monitor the end use of the loans given by them. They were to give a detailed report of all loans given by them to avoid risks.

The UCBs had to value the fixed assets owned by them and its should also value those fixed assets which have been received by them as collateral on advances given by them. This would give a correct picture of their capital adequacy position. The RBI would issue guidelines for valuation of properties of and appointment of valuer's.

Forged Note Vigilance Cell

The Government of India and the National Security Council have given directions that they should establish a 'Forged Note Vigilance Cell' at their Head Office ATMs should have good quality notes and should not circulate any forged notes. Every UCB was to disseminate instructions of the RBI on forged notes to their branches. They had to monitor its implementation and compile data if forged notes are found. The UCBs have to file a report with the police if such forged notes are detected.

Housing Loans

The UCBs were directed to sanction housing loans only on authorized structures because it was based on directions of Delhi High Court. The UCBs can only give loans if the applicant obtains an undertaking on an affidavit that the buildings will be constructed as per sanctioned plans. UCBs have been permitted to sanction individual housing loans up to the limit of Rs. 25 lakh per beneficiary of a dwelling unit.

Priority Sector Lending

The UCBs were advised to lend to the weaker sections of the society and the minority community as part of the Prime Minister's 15 Point Programme for the Welfare of Minorities to ensure an appropriate percentage of priority sector lending. The main essence of priority sector lending is that the benefits of various government sponsored schemes reach the under-privileged. UCBs had to target 25 per cent of the overall lending towards the weaker sections. Housing finance upto Rs. 15 lakhs was to be treated as priority sector lending. The following table 12.1 depicts the different forms of financing by UCBs to the priority sector.

UCBs provided finance to agriculture, small scale industries, road and water transport operators, private retail trade, small business enterprises, self employment, educational loans, housing loans, consumption loans and software industries. Out of these, 3 areas got substantial financing from UCBs in 2006-07. The highest share of financing was to cottage and small scale industries of Rs. 12,125 crores. The share of housing loans was second of the amount of Rs. 10,247 crores and small business enterprises of Rs. 6,079 crores. This accounts to Rs. 28,451 crores out of a total of Rs. 44,058 crores which is 64.57% of the total amount of financing. ***UCBs extended 56.0 per cent of its total credit to the priority sector and 25.9 per cent of total priority sector loans to the weaker section.***

**Table 12.1: Priority Sector and Weaker Section Advances by Urban
Co-operative Banks - 2006-07**

Segment	Priority Sector		Weaker Sections	
	Amount	Share in	Amount	Share in
	(Rs. crore)	Total Advances (Per cent)	(Rs. crore)	Total Advances (Per cent)
1	2	3	4	5
Agriculture and Allied Activities	2,190	2.8	1,010	1.3
Cottage and Small Scale Industries	12,125	15.4	1,397	1.8
Road and Water Transport Operators	2,147	2.7	497	0.6
Private Retail Trade (Essential Commodities)	2,034	2.6	761	1.0
Retail Trade (Others)	4,699	6.0	1,069	1.3
Small Business Enterprises	6,079	7.7	1,698	2.2
Professional and Self Employed	2,685	3.4	927	1.2
Educational Loans	628	0.8	232	0.3
Housing Loans	10,247	13.0	3,092	3.9
Consumption Loans	1,169	1.5	709	0.9
Software Industries	55	0.1	7	0.0
Total	**44,058**	**56.0**	**11,399**	**14.5**

Note : Data are provisional.
Source: RBI Report on Trend and Progress of Banking in India, Government of India Publication, 2006-07.

Relief to Poultry Industry

The poultry industry was given relief by the UCBs since March 31, 2006. They were directed to give loans to poultry farmers due to the Avian Influenza (bird flu) in some parts of India. The principal and interest on working capital loans were to be converted into term loans which would be recovered in instalments based on projected future inflows over a period of three years with an initial moratorium of up to one year. The relief was extended to all poultry accounts classified as standard as on March 31, 2006.

Anti-Money Laundering

The UCBs were required to be compliant with anti money laundering standards. They have to monitor guidelines and procedures regarding transfer of funds from one country to another. The Chief Executive Officer of each bank was personally liable and had to oversee that funds were transferred legally to prevent terrorist and criminals from misusing funds internationally. In order to achieve this objective it was important that all transfers were made with full and accurate information about the originator. The details of name, address, unique reference number and the beneficial banks to which the transfers are made above Rs. 50,000 must be furnished. Inter-bank transfers and settlements where both the originator and beneficiary are banks or financial institutions are exempted from providing detailed information. Sometimes customers deliberately send transfers below 50,000 to avoid reporting and monitoring. In these cases banks should be extra careful. In any suspicious transactions the UCBs should report to Financial Intelligence Unit – India (FIU-IND).

All transfers of funds must have complete information of the originator. The intermediary bank should retain the information and the record should be preserved for a period of 10 years. A beneficiary bank should have effective risk-based procedures to identify transfers. The transfer of funds which lack complete originator information may be considered to be suspicious transactions and UCBs may report the matter to the FIU-IND.

Corporate Governance

The UCBs were prohibited to extend loans and advances whether secured or unsecured as a follow up of the Joint Parliamentary Committee Report on Stock Market Scam to the directors, their relatives and the firms/concerns/companies in which they are interested. On October 6, 2005, with the approval of Government of India certain revisions were incorporated. The changes were made to give certain concessions to directors and other members of UCBs. It allowed loans to staff directors on the board of UCBs, normal loans, as applicable to members, to the directors on the boards of salary earners' co-operative banks, and normal employee-related loans to managing directors of multi-state co-operative banks. UCBs were allowed to give loans to the directors and their relatives against their fixed deposits and life insurance policies.

Classification of Micro Small and Medium Enterprises

The classification of micro, small and medium enterprises was made according to investment manufacturing and services.

The enterprises producing processing or preserving of goods with an investment in plant and machinery of upto Rs. 25 lakhs is a micro enterprise. An investment in plant and machinery of more than Rs. 25 lakhs but not exceeding Rs.5 crores is a small enterprise. An investment in plant and machinery which is more than Rs. 5 crores but does not exceed Rs. 10 crores is a medium enterprise.

Services providing enterprises were to be classified according to the investment pattern. When the investment in equipments is less than Rs. 10 lakhs it is a micro enterprise. When investment in equipment is more than Rs. 10 lakhs but does not exceed Rs.2 crores it is a small enterprise. And when the investment in equipment is more than Rs. 2 crore but does not exceed Rs. 5 crores is a medium enterprise.

Customer Services

The UCBs were encouraged to provide good services to their customers. A large number of services ware extended at their extension counters. They were permitted to take deposits and allow the customer the facility of withdrawal from their accounts. They could Issue and en-cash drafts and mail transfers, issue and en-cash travellers' cheques. They could also provide services such as collection of bills; advances against fixed deposits of their customers at the extension counters. Their services include disbursement of loans sanctioned by the head office/base branch up to the limit of Rs. 10 lakhs.

The UCBs made their charges very reasonable following the recommendations of the Working Group on 'Formulating a Scheme for Ensuring Reasonableness of Bank Charges'. They also make the customer aware of service charges before accepting their deposits or conducting any services towards them. The customers with low value are honoured like other customers of the bank.

UCBs display and update in their offices/branches, and their website, the details of various service charges in the prescribed format. They also display information in local languages.

The Scheduled UCBs display and update on the homepage of their websites the details of service charges and fees prominently under the title of 'Service Charges and Fees'. On the homepage a complaint form is provided with the name of the nodal officer for complaint redressal. The form indicates the first point for redressal of complaint is the bank itself and that the complainant may approach Banking Ombudsman only if the complaint is not solved within one month.

UCBs customer services extend to demand drafts. If their customers require a duplicate demand draft it should be issued within a fortnight from the receipt of the request. For delays beyond this period, UCBs would pay interest to compensate the customers for delay in service.

Another service provided by UCBs is to offer passbook facility to all their individual savings bank account holders without any cost as it is more convenient than statement of account for small customers. The full address/telephone numbers of the branch is written in the pass book/statement of accounts issued to account holders to provide quality service to the customers. To facilitate the customer services Allahabad High Court made a judgment which was to be followed by UCBs. Every person opening a deposit account has to make a nomination.

As part of quality towards customer services the scheduled and non-scheduled UCBs were permitted to open Automated Teller Machines and issue debit cards. The cheque clearing service, of UCBs was made through 'on-city back-up centres' in 20 large cities and effective low-cost settlement solutions for the remaining cities. Banks undertook cheques for higher amounts to meet customers' requirement of funds. They could also consider waiving fees or facilitate inward transfer of funds to accounts of persons who were affected by natural calamities.

The Reserve Bank would consider permitting some of the financially sound UCBs registered in States and Multi-State Co-operative Societies Act, 2002 to convert existing extension counters into full-fledged branches, subject to certain conditions.

If UCBs did not provide good customer services they would be liable to be penalized under the provisions of Banking Regulation Act, 1949 as applicable to co-operative societies.

Loans to Farmers in Distress

To make their existence meaningful UCBs have tried to support farmers. They have enhanced loans without sanctions, collateral and risk funds to Rs. 5,000. The principal amount outstanding and accrued interest in the crop loans and agricultural term loans interest may be converted into term loans to facilitate farmers. The restructured period for repayment may be 3 to 5 years. If there is a great damage to crops banks may extend the repayment period up to 7 to 10 years without additional collateral security.

The UCBs provided relief for stressed farmers in Andhra Pradesh, Karnataka and Kerala and in 25 specified districts. They farmers loan accounts in UCBs and multi-state co-operative banks as on July 1, 2006 were rescheduled for a period of 3-5 years with one year moratorium and interest was waived. Such farmers were also given new loans. One time settlement was made for certain distressed farmers after the announcement in the Mid-term Review of Annual Policy Statement of 2006-07.

Marketing of Units

UCBs registered in States which signed MOUs and those registered under Multi-State Co-operative Societies Act, 2002 were allowed to make agreements with mutual funds for marketing their units. This facility was to enable the UCBs to encourage small savers. However, the prescribed norms had to be followed.

Insurance Business

UCBs registered in States and having an MOU with the Reserve Bank or those registered under Multi-State Co-operative Societies Act, 2002 were allowed to undertake insurance agency business as corporate agents without risk participation. This announcement was made in the Annual Policy Statement for the year 2007-08. However, UCBs had to follow certain eligibility norms. Their minimum net worth should be of Rs. 10 crores and it should not be under the classification of Grade III or IV. For unregistered UCBs there would be no change in the norms for insurance business.

Non-Performing Assets

One of the important aspects of Urban Co-operative banks is the asset quality taken against advances and loans sanctioned Table 12.2 depicts the gross and net non-performing assets as percentage of total advances. The asset quality of the UCBs improved in 2007 as the gross and net have declined in absolute as well as percentage terms. However, NPA ratios of UCBs at 17.0 per cent (gross) and 7.7 per cent (net) at end-March 2007 were still very high and it is required to bring them down.

Table 12.2 : Gross Non-Performing Assets of Urban Co-operative Banks

(Amount in Rs. crore)

End-March	No. of Reporting UCBs	Gross NPAs (Rs. crore)	Gross NPAs as percentage of total Advances	Net NPAs (Rs. crore)	Net NPAs as percentage of total Advances
1	2	3	4	5	6
2004	1,926	15,406	22.7	8,242	2.1
2005	1,872	15,486	23.2	8,257	12.3
2006	1,853	13,506	18.9	6,335	8.8
2007P	1,813	13,363	17.0	6,044	7.7

P: Provisional.
Source: RBI Report on Trend and Progress of Banking in India, Government of India Publication, 2006-07.

Operations and Financial Position of Urban Co-operative Banks

Table 12.3: Liabilities and Assets of Urban Co-operative Banks

(Amount in Rs. crore)

Item	As at end-March		Percentage Variations
	2006	2007 P	2006-07
1	2	3	4
Liabilities			
1. Capital	3,488	3,884	11.4
	(2.3)	(2.4)	
2. Reserves	10,485	10,867	3.6
	(6.9)	(6.8)	
3. Deposits	1,14,060	1,20,983	6.1
	(75.6)	(75.7)	
4. Borrowings	1,781	2,602	46.1
	(1.2)	(1.6)	
5. Other Liabilities	21,140	21,515	1.8
	(14.0)	(13.5)	
Total Liabilities/Assets	**1,50,954**	**1,59,851**	**5.9**
	(100.0)	**(100.0)**	
Assets			
1. Cash in Hand	1,558	1,639	5.2
	(1.0)	(1.0)	
2. Balances with Banks	9,037	9,806	8.5
	(6.0)	(6.1)	
3. Money at Call and Short Notice	1,835	1,859	1.3
	(1.2)	(1.2)	
4. Investments	50,395	47,316	– 6.1
	(33.4)	(29.6)	
5. Loans and Advances	71,641	78,660	9.8
	(47.5)	(49.2)	
6. Other Assets	16,488	20,571	24.8
	(10.9)	(12.9)	

P : Provisional.
Note : Figures in parenthesis are percentages to total liabilities/assets.
Source: RBI Report on Trend and Progress of Banking in India, Government of India Publication, 2006-07.

The business operations of UCBs expanded very slowly. The composition of the assets and liabilities of the UCBs were quite similar in both the years 2006 and 2007. Borrowings increased to 46.1 per cent while 'other liabilities' increased moderately by 1.8 per cent during 2007. Capital and reserves increased at a rate of 11.4 per cent. Loans and advances and investments, which form the major items on the asset side, constituted 49.2 per cent and 29.6 per cent of the total assets, respectively. Deposits grew by 6.1 per cent during the year, loans and advances increased by 9.8 per cent and investments declined by 6.1 per cent during 2006-07.

RURAL CO-OPERATIVE BANKS

Rural credit co-operative institutions have been formed to extend credit and mobilize deposits to rural areas. Rural co-operatives were running into losses and had high NPAs. The task force appointed in 2004 with Prof. A.Vaidyanathan as chairman recommended that an action plan should be made for reviving the short-term rural cooperative credit structure. A revival package was prepared for state co-operative credit societies. The revival package would be implemented by NABARD in all the States. The package has to be signed through and MOU among the participating State Government and NABARD. A special audit of all Primary Agricultural Credit Societies, District Credit Cooperative Banks and State Co-operative Banks was undertaken to assess the losses as on March 31, 2004. After the initial assessment the institutional and legal reforms in the revival package would go through with legislation. The package to implement the reforms has begun in thirteen States. These are Andhra Pradesh, Arunachal Pradesh, Bihar, Chhattisgarh, Gujarat, Haryana, Madhya Pradesh, Maharashtra, Orissa, Rajasthan, Uttarakhand, Uttar Pradesh and West Bengal.

The financial performance of the rural co-operatives did not improve with the legal enactment. There were variations in the financial performance of different regional areas of the rural co-operative banking sector. The upper tier of both short-term and long-term rural co -operative credit institutions made profits during 2005-06 but the lower tier consisting of Primary Agricultural Credit Societies made overall losses. The Asset quality of rural co-operative banks also declined. The Reserve Bank and NABARD focused their attention towards growth and development of rural credit institutions to make reforms so that the asset quality improves and recovery of loans is done at a fast pace.

Reforms in Customer Services

The Reserve Bank and the Banking OMBUDSMAN received many complaints about customer services. They initiated several reforms in this area to make banking more useful for customers.

Deposit of Cheques: State co-operative and district co-operative banks had cheques drop box system. For the convenience of the customers, deposit of cheques was acknowledged at the regular collection counter in addition to drop boxes. Banks used to refuse acknowledgement of cheques but with the reforms, no branch could refuse to give an acknowledgement the cheques. However, banks would make their customers aware that drop box facility could be used. The bank would install a drop box at its branch and display cheque-drop box in English, Hindi and the concerned regional language of the State.

Note Packets: The note packets from banks were stapled and soiled notes were inserted in the stapled packets. All State co-operative and district co-operative banks improved their service by sorting out neat and soiled notes. They could issue only clean notes to public. The note packets had to be secured with paper bands and stapling was prohibited. Soiled notes in unstapled condition could be remitted to the Reserve Bank. The co-operative banks were also advised that they should stop writing of any kind on watermark window of bank notes.

Interest Charges: All State co-operative and district co-operative banks announcement in the from 2007-08, had to lay down appropriate internal principles and procedures so that interest, processing and other charges were not levied on customers on loans and advances taken by them towards personal loans.

Procedure for Extending Loans to Customers

Banks have to follow broad guidelines for extending loans to customers. The process of granting loans is through the following steps:

Step 1: Banks have to first go through a prior-approval process for sanctioning loans, which has to take into account, the cash flows of the prospective borrower.

Step 2: The interest rates charged by banks must incorporate risk premium, which is reasonable and justified, but based on the internal rating of the borrower.

Step 3: To analyze the security and the total cost to the borrower, including interest and all other charges to be levied on the loan.

Step 4: Took calculate the interest, including processing and other charges to be taken on the loan. Finally the loans is sanctioned with the term and conditions well defined.

Supervision of the Rural Co-operative Structure

National Agricultural Bank for Rural Development (NABARD) has to undertake inspection of Rural Regional Banks, State Co-operative Banks and District Co-operative Banks Banking. The objective of NABARD's supervision is to assess the financial and operational soundness and managerial efficiency of co-operative banks in conformity with the provisions of the relevant Acts/Rules, Regulations and Bye-laws, to protect the interests of their depositors. It also makes suggestions for strengthening the institutions to play and effective role in disbursing rural credit. The inspection is to focus on the core areas of the operations of banks towards performance in capital adequacy, asset quality, management, earnings, liquidity, systems and compliance (CAMELSC).

Transparency in Dealings

Transparency in dealings with customers can be gained by providing proper information about their operations. Therefore, the balance sheets of co-operative banks giving full information are put on the website of NABARD with a suitable disclaimer. Co-operative banks also display the abridged balance sheets in their branches.

Self Help Groups (SHG)

The SHG programme has been linked to cover different states and union territories through this programme. The need for credit is being realized and a large number of non-government organizations (NGOs) are participating in this program to provide micro finance to rural families in different districts. In every district there are pilot projects for providing micro finance to micro enterprises. NGOs have in each district worked towards the implementation of the projects.

Micro Finance by Government

Micro finance is being promoted by government. It has given a development fund for this purpose. It is called micro finance development and equity fund. It has a corpus fund of 200 crores and its chief role is to extend loans. The RBI had set an internal group on rural credit and micro finance under the chairmanship of H.R. Khan in 2005 for suggesting development, regulation and supervision of micro finance services.

Kisan Credit Cards

Kisan credit cards were issued in 1998-99 for providing crop loans to farmers. The beneficiaries of this scheme receive a credit card a pass book with name address and particular of their borrowing limit and validity period. The production credit limits are fixed by taking into consideration the production of crops for the whole year. The short term credit is in the form of revolving cash credit facility.

NABARD and Co-operative Credit

NABARD refinances state co-operative agriculture and rural development banks, state co-operative banks, regional rural banks and institutions which have taken the approval of the RBI. It extends short term refinance to state co-operative banks and RRBs. It has setup a Rural Infrastructure Development Fund since 1995-96 to give loans for rural infrastructure projects. It provides short term credit to state co-operative banks. NABARD has provided refinance in all areas which required development. It had funded rural irrigation projects, drinking water, soil conversation, plantation, fisheries then construction of toilets and marketing of products.

Profile of Rural Co-operative Banks

Table 12.4 indicates the details of rural banks relating to balance sheet items. It gives a complete picture of the rural co-operative banks. Based on this table, the number of existing rural co-operative banks is given at 1,07,497. Rural co-operative credit institutions including primary agricultural credit societies as on March 31, 2006, together held Rs.3,38,927 crores of assets, Rs.1,53,516 crores of deposits and a loan portfolio of Rs.2,01,118 crores. Their financial performance was not good. There was an overall loss during 2005-06. The loss was Rs. 9,139 crores. The number of loss making banks exceeded the number of profit making centres. The upper-tier of the short-term and long-term structure made profit, the lower-tier Primary Agricultural Credit Co-operative and Primary Co-operative Agricultural Rural Development Banks made losses. The problem of high non-performing assets and low recovery performance of rural co-operative banks reduced their efficiency. The non-performing assets in long term loans, in State co-operatives and Primary co-operatives was as high as 32.7 and 35.4% as percentage of loans outstanding. In respect of recovery of loans the long term loans fared better than short term loans.

Table 12.4: A Profile of Rural Co-operative Banks

(At end-March 2006)						
(Amount in Rs. crore)						
Item	Short-Term			Long-Term		Total
	StCBs	DCCBs	PACS	SCARDBs	PCARDBs	
1	2	3	4	5	6	7
A. No. of Co-operative Banks	31	366*	1,06,384	20	696**	1,07,497
B. Balance Sheet Indicators^						
(i) Owned Fund (Capital + Reserves)	10,545	23,450	9,292	3,352	3,380	50,019
(ii) Deposits	45,405	87,532	19,561	636	382	1,53,516

(iii) Borrowings	16,989	24,217	41,018	17,075	13,066	**1,12,365**
(iv) Loans and Advances Issued	48,260	73,583	42,920	2,907	2,254	**1,69,924**
(v) Loans and Advances Outstanding	39,684	79,202	51,779	17,713	12,740	**2,01,118**
(vi) Total Liabilities/Assets	76,481	143,090	73,387+	24,604	21,365	**3,38,927**
C. Financial Performance^						
(i) Institutions in Profit						
(a) No.	27	278	44,321	11	331	**44,968**
(b) Amount of Profit	408	1,116	1,064	335	328	**3,251**
(ii) Institutions in Loss						
(a) No.	4	88	53,050	8	194	**53,344**
(b) Amount of Loss	30	913	1,920	247	411	**3,521**
(iii) Overall Profit/Loss (–)	378	203	– 856	88	– 83	**-271**
(iv) Accumulated Loss	274	5,275	N.A.	918	2,672	**9,139**
D. Non-performing Assets^						
(i) Amount	6,360	15,712	15,476@	5,786	4,554	**47,888**
(ii) As Percentage of Loans Outstanding	16.0	19.8	30.4#	32.7	35.4	**23.8**
(iii) Recovery of Loans to Demand (%)	87	69	62.1	47	48	

N.A. Not available.

* : Taran Taran DCCB in Punjab excluded as the scheme of bifurcation was not approved by the Reserve Bank.

** : Number reduced due to recognition of 48 PCARDBs in Haryana to 19 District PCARDBs and two PCARDBs in Orissa.

\+ : Working Capital.

@ : Total Overdues.

^ : Figures based on reporting co-operative banks and may not tally with the appendix tables.

\# : Percentage of Overdues to Demand.

Source: RBI Report on Trend and Progress of Banking in India, Government of India Publication, 2006-07.

Review of Co-operative Banks

The co-operative banks have made several reforms. Yet, there are many problems. There are a high volume of non-performing assets. Due to this reason it does not have any profitability. It has high transaction costs and very low margins because it caters to the weaker sections of the society and to rural India. The essence of the co-operative banks is to participate in the development process of the country. With this objective, profitability cannot be its main criteria of functioning.

The structure of the co-operative banking system should be integrated to reduce transaction costs and delays in implementations of loans. The concept is good but it is unable to be successful. Finally, the co-operative banks have many challenges before them. They have a very low resource base and are highly dependant on refinancing agencies. In order to expand they have to increase their resources and diversify into new areas.

Summary

➡ The main objective of cooperative banks is to provide finance to people small and medium income

➡ Co-operative banks supplement the work of the commercial banks. They work on no profit no loss basis.

➡ There are urban co-operatives and rural co-operatives. There are different co-operative institutions for Short-term and long term loans.

➡ The problems of rural co-operatives were reviewed by the Task Force 2004 and the urban co-operatives through a vision document released in March 2005 and a task force to identify viable and non-viable UCBs and the process for their revival or exit.

➡ The urban co-operative banks were classified according to population and capital invested in it.

➡ Mergers and amalgamations were proposed to streamline the urban co-operative banks. New branches could also be developed by existing co-operative.

➡ An MOU was signed with 13 different states for a consultative approach between central and state governments and federation relating to problems of the UCBs.

➡ UCBs had to develop human resources, technology and new opportunities of business operations.

➡ RBI focused on risk management especially in tier II co-operative banks.

➡ Some new areas were housing loan upto the limit of 25 lakhs per beneficiary, priority second lending towards under privileged sections of the society.

➡ UCBs setup forged note vigilance cells and made certain standards for anti money laundering. They also made an effort towards corporate governance.

➡ The UCBs classified the enterprises into micro small and medium for purposes of funding.

➡ The UCBs gave a lot of attention towards customer service by introducing new services like travellers cheques, issuing and en-cashing drafts, installing ATMs making bank charges and interest reasonable.

➡ There were very high NPAs in UCBs and this lead to the downfall of UCBs. However, their objective is not to make profit but to finance people of medium and small income.

➡ Rural co-operatives have also been revived through an action plan by Vaidyanathan. Committee by signing MOUs with the participating state governments and NABARD.

➡ Rural Co-operatives made many reforms towards customer service regarding deposit of cheques, making note packets without staples, sorting out neat and soiled notes and making interest charges reasonable.

➡ Supervision and inspection of rural banks protects the interest of their depositors.

➡ Transparency in dealings with customers is encouraged.

➡ Micro Finance and Kisan Credit Card help the farmers in improving their financial position.

➡ Self help groups are participating with rural banks to provide micro finance to rural families.

Objective Type Questions, Answer True (T) or False (F)

(a) A co-operative bank functions as a part of a commercial bank in India.

(b) There are co-operative banks situated only in rural areas.

(c) The co-operative banks are all making profits.

(d) Co-operative banks were amalgamated to make them powerful and more profitable.

(e) The rural co-operative banks follow a three tier system with the primary agricultural credit societies at the lowest tier.

(f) There are separate co-operative banks for long term and short term finance.

(g) The urban co-operative banks have to establish a forged note vigilance cell.

(h) The urban co-operative banks sanction housing loans to a limit of 25 lakhs per beneficiary.

(i) A micro enterprise is classified as one having less then Rs. 10 lakhs investment in equipments for eligibility to apply for loan from UCBs.

(j) Payments made above Rs. 50,000 require details of the depositor to be furnished in the case of money transfers.

(k) UCBs have provided loans of Rs. 5,000 each to farmers in distress.

Answers: (a) F, (b) F, (c) F, (d) F, (e) T, (f) T, (g) T, (h) T, (i) T, (j) T, (k) T.

Multiple Choice Questions (Tick mark (✓) the right answer)

1. Rural co-operative banks have the following structure:
   (a) Three tier structure
   (b) Split structure
   (c) Commercial banking division structure
   (d) Structure between RBI State Governments and State Bank of India.

2. The long term loans are given by the following rural co-operatives:
   (a) State co-operative banks
   (b) Central co-operative banks
   (c) State Co-operative Agriculture and Rural Development Banks
   (d) NABARD

3. The micro credit program was made by linking:
   (a) State Bank of India
   (b) Self help groups
   (c) Government of India
   (d) Commercial banks

4.   The kisan credit cards provide:

(a)   Long term loans for farmers

(b)   Short term loans for working capital

(c)   Membership to co-operative banks

(d)   Loan from NABARD

5.   NABARD provides the following function towards co-operative banks:

(a)   Financing micro enterprises loans sanctioned by co-operative banks

(b)   Making reforms for efficiency in the co-operative banking sector

(c)   Making co-operative banks 'no profit no loss centres'

(d)   Refinancing the loans of the co-operative banks

Answers: 1 (a), 2 (c), 3 (b), 4 (b), 5 (d)

Short Answer Questions

1.   Give the classification of the rural co-operative banks.

2.   Discuss the measures taken by rural co-operative banks towards customer service.

3.   Give the process of granting credit to farmers in rural areas.

Long Answer Questions

1.   Discuss the structure of rural and urban co-operative banks and illustrate it with a diagram.

2.   State the weakness of the co-operative banks in India. What are the measures taken for improving the situations?

3.   Discuss the changes in co-operative banks to make them more efficient and transparent.

Part – Six
Non-banking Financial Intermediaries

13. Non-bank Financial Companies
14. Small Savings, Provident Funds & Pension Funds
15. Insurance Companies
16. Unit Trust of India and Mutual Funds
17. Development Banks

Chapter 13

Non-Bank Financial Companies

Chapter Plan

- Introduction
- Classification of NBFCs
- Mutual Benefit Finance Companies (MBFCs)
- Fair Practices Code
- Corporate Governance
- Diversification of Activities
- Certificate of Registration
- Change of Management
- Financial Regulation of Systemically Important NBFCs
- Securitization
- Prudential Norms of NBFCs
- Norms for NBFCs Accepting Public Deposits

INTRODUCTION

Non-bank financial companies (NBFCs) provide financial services like hire-purchase, leasing, loans, investments and chit fund services. These intermediaries are small in size and they are owned privately. They provide credit to the un-organized sector and to small borrowers. The NBFCs have grown rapidly since 1990. They offer attractive rates of return and are categorized as non-bank financial companies (NBFC) and non-bank financial services companies (NBFCSI). They are fund based as well as service oriented companies. Their main competitors are banks and financial institutions. It is mandatory to register the NBFCs with the RBI if they carry on any business relating to equipment leasing, hire-purchase, loans and investments. *These companies can be classified into deposit accepting companies and non deposit accepting companies*. Apart from these companies there are Residuary Non-banking Companies (RNBC's) which have their principal business of accepting deposits (but are not leasing, hire-purchase, investment or loan companies). These companies work under the guidelines of RBI with reference to their investments. The NBFCs which are regulated by other regulators are exempted from registration with RBI. Such NBFCs include venture capital funds, merchant banking companies; stock broking companies register with Securities Exchange Board of India (SEBI), insurance companies which have a certificate of registration with Insurance Regulatory Development Authority (IRDA). Nidhi companies under section 620A of the Companies Act of 1956, housing finance companies regulated by National Housing Bank (NHB) and Chit Fund Companies registered under section 2 clause (b) of the Chit Fund Act of 1982. Such companies are regulated by Government of India, Ministry of Company Affairs.

The main points of the above discussion can be explained in the following manner:

- A non-bank financial company according to the Reserve Bank amendment act of 1997 means a financial institution which is a company having is principal business of receiving of deposits and lending of funds and approved by Central Government.

- An equipment leasing company is financial institution which is carrying on the principal business of leasing of equipments.

- A hire purchase finance company is an institution with the principal business of financing physical assets through the system of hire purchase.

- An investment company is the financial institution has the principal business of dealing in securities through acquisition and sale thereof.

- A loan company is a financial institution the business of providing finance through loans and advances.

- A Mutual Benefit Finance Company (MBFC) is a financial institution under section 620A of the companies Act 1956.

- A Miscellaneous Non-Bank Company (MNBC) is a company which transacts business of collection of money and its utilization collected through sale of units and other instruments, chit funds, lotteries and giving of prizes and awards.

- A Residuary Non-Banking Companies (RNBCs) is a non banking institution which receives deposits from public either through lump-sum contribution or instalments or through sale of units or certificates. The NBFCs and MNBCs are excluded from RNBCs.

Non-banking financial companies (NBFCs) play an important role in broadening the access to financial services, diversification of the financial sector and competitive spirit in business. Some NBFCs have grown to become a conglomerate, as they are engaged in many different types of activities. Their services are under more than one financial sector regulator. Due to a large number of services and the volume of business the need to strengthen these intermediaries and to monitor their activities has become necessary in the Indian financial system. The Reserve Bank of India has since 1997 worked towards making a regulatory and supervisory framework for NBFCs. The main objective of these regulations is to make the NBFCs sector healthy, vibrant and dynamic. In 2006-07, many more policies were prepared towards financial supervision.

NBFCs have played an important part since the financial reforms in 1991 in India. In fact their services have become complementary to the banking system. In times of financial difficulties they support and diversify financial activities and reduce risks. An internal group was setup to examine regulatory and supervisory issues relating to NBFCs. Based on their recommendations a revised framework was drawn up.

CLASSIFICATION OF NBFCs

In December 2006, the classification of NBFCs was modified. The new classification was given to asset financing companies whose principal business was to finance physical assets which brought about economic activity which was productive in nature.

If NBFCs had an investment of 60% of their total assets and total income from financing of real/physical assets supporting economic activity such as automobiles, general purpose industrial machinery they would be classified as asset finance companies. *The equipment leasing companies and hire-purchase companies would according to the new classification become asset finance companies.* The classification for the purpose of income recognition, asset classification and provisioning norms is based on asset specification. The exposure norms relating to restriction on investments in land and buildings and unquoted shares would be modified to bring the asset finance companies in uniformity with the rules and provisions that are applicable to hire purchase and leasing companies.

The definition of NBFCs has been revised in non-deposit taking companies. According to the new classification, NBFCs with asset size of Rs. 100 crores and above have been defined as *'systemically important NBFCs'*. These large NBFCs have to follow certain guidelines to function. They have certain requirements to be fulfilled.

- They have to maintain a minimum capital to risk-weighted asset ratio (CRAR) of 10% to lend surety to its customers that it has good and standard assets within the company.

- A company of this category should be sure of its borrowers. It should be careful by finding out the credibility of a borrower. In its own interest it should not lend to any single borrower/any single group of borrowers more than 15% and 25% of their owned funds, respectively.

- The company should also not invest in the shares of another company/any single group of companies more than 15% and 25% of their owned funds, respectively; and

- The company is not permitted lend more than 25% or invest more than 40% of their owned funds to a single party/a single group of parties, respectively.

- The above credit/investment norms can be in excess of 5% points for any single party and by 10% points for a single group of parties, if the additional exposure is on account of infrastructure loan and/or investment.

- Asset finance companies (AFCs) are permitted to exceed the exposure norms further by 5% points of their owned funds only when it is necessary but it must be approved by their boards.

The revised guideline came into force from April 1st, 2007. The ceiling on investments was not made applicable to insurance companies in their equity capital upto the permissible level required by the Reserve Bank. Other non-banking companies and primary dealers would be governed by the existing guidelines.

MUTUAL BENEFIT FINANCE COMPANIES (MBFCs)

Such companies were exempt from the provisions of the RBI. In 1996 RBI directed the MBFCs to restrict their interest rate on deposits and a ceiling of 15% was imposed. This would be revised from time to time. They were also prohibited from paying brokerage for collection of deposits or issuing advertisements for attracting deposits. These companies can accept and renew deposits only from their shareholders. They cannot accept current account deposits.

The Ministry of Corporate Affairs has taken over the regulation of Mutual Benefit Financial Companies (Notified Nidhis) (MBFCs) and Mutual Benefit Companies (Potential Nidhis) (MBCs). It took a decision that MBFCs and MBCs would not have to file their annual returns statement but if the application of MBCs (Potential Nidhis) for the granting a nidhi status is rejected by the Ministry, the provisions as applicable to NBFCs would apply to such companies.

FAIR PRACTICES CODE

In September 2006 The Fair Practices Code was issued by the RBI to provide customer satisfaction and transparency in the NBFCs lending operations. According to these guidelines require the NBFCs were to furnish specified information in loan application forms. All loan applications would necessarily have a system of acknowledgement through a receipt of the application. The loan agreement would indicate a timeframe for disposal of loan applications and convey in writing to the amount of loan sanctioned to the borrower. The terms and conditions of the loan would be specified giving details of annualised rate of interest. The NBFCs would in no condition harass any borrower. If any change in terms and conditions occur the borrower will have to been informed. The NBFCs would not interfere in the affairs of the borrower; or create problems in the recovery of loans. The boards of directors of NBFCs would also have a proper grievance redressal mechanism within the organisation to resolve disputes between the borrower and the company.

CORPORATE GOVERNANCE

Corporate governance was given importance in non-bank financial companies to gain investor confidence by adopting good corporate practices. NBFCs of Rs. 20 crores and above and systemically important NBFCs were directed to frame internal guidelines on corporate governance by constituting an audit committee, nomination committee, risk management committee, and disclosure and transparency practices.

DIVERSIFICATION OF ACTIVITIES

In December 2006 NBFCs were allowed to diversify their area of business. The new activities were the following.

- Distribution and marketing of mutual fund products as agents of mutual funds.
- NDBCs were permitted to issue co-branded credit cards with commercial banks, without risk sharing with the prior approval of the Reserve Bank for an initial period of two years.
- The credit cards could be extended after a review and fulfilment of the minimum requirements by the NBFCs. The minimum requirements are of net owned fund of Rs.100 crores, and net

profits as per last two years' audited balance sheet. In addition the net NPAs were not to exceed 3% of net advances, as per the last audited balance sheet. The CRAR of 10% for non-deposit-taking NBFCs and 12%/15% for deposit-taking NBFCs should be maintained.

- The mutual fund business, NBFCs should, comply with SEBI guidelines and regulations. The NBFCs should act as agents and were not permitted to acquire units of mutual funds.
- In credit card business, the role of NBFC was limited only to marketing and distribution.

CERTIFICATE OF REGISTRATION

Since January 1997, the NBFCs have to obtain a certificate of registration from the Reserve Bank of India to commence their business. The net owned funds should be Rs. 25 lakhs and should have the maximum limit of Rs. 200 lakhs. The net owned funds are made up of paid of capital and free reserves minus the accumulated losses as per the latest balance sheets. It reduces the value of investment in shares and it includes the book value of debentures, bonds and outstanding loans and advances. In September 2006, every NBFCs which was engaged in the business of non-banking financial institution (NBFI) had to submit a certificate from their Statutory Auditors every year to the effect that they were continuing business. NBFCs which no longer conducted business had to withdraw their certificate of business as they no longer participated actively in business.

The NBFCs would be granted a registration by the RBI if they were able to pay the claims of their future depositors. It had adequate capital structure and earning prospects. The RBI would also evaluate the general character and conduct of the management towards public interest before granting the certificate of registration. After the issue of the certificate it is the discretion of the RBI to continue or cancel the registration depending on the conduct of the company and compliance of the provisions of the RBI.

CHANGE OF MANAGEMENT

If an NBFC is interested in changing its management and control pattern it has to give a prior public notice of 30 days before the sale or transfer of the ownership. The change can take place either by sale of shares, or transfer of control. It can also take place without sale of shares. The change of control or management pattern is possible through various kinds of amalgamations or mergers. The merger of an NBFC can take place with another NBFC. A change of control can take place by merger of a non-financial company by the NBFC. Since October 2006, the RBI directed the NBFCs to give prior public notice. The notice can also be given by the transferor or the transferee or jointly by the parties concerned.

FINANCIAL REGULATION OF SYSTEMICALLY IMPORTANT NBFCs

The NBFCs operations were reviewed to reduce gaps in their functioning. Some of the principles adopted in the review procedure were that the systemically relevant NBFCs which were engaged in the business of financial services should be under a regulatory framework to contain systemic risks. The important aspect of the review was that it was to be activity-centric regulation and not institution-centric regulation to reduce or eliminate scope for regulatory arbitrage.

If the NBFCs operate as a group the ownership pattern of NBFCs should have only one entity in the Group for public deposits and it's the ownership structure would not be the determining factor to decide on the products of the group. The foreign entities would do their business within the permitted scope of activities. If such companies were interested in foreign direct investment they would have to go through an authorisation process. The NBFCs would not have regulatory arbitrage opportunities or bypass bank regulations.

On the basis of the review procedure based on the above conditions certain regulations were imposed on the non-bank financial companies to reduce risks. The regulations were made on lending and investment including off-balance sheet exposures. A bank could lend to a single NBFC/NBFC-Asset Finance Companies to the extent of 10%/15% of the bank's capital funds as per its last audited balance sheet.

The exposure ceilings would be 15 per cent/20 per cent of the capital funds, in case the exposure is in excess of 10%/15% by the NBFC asset finance company to infrastructure sectors then the NBFCs if promoted by a parent or group, or a subsidiary of a foreign bank which has a presence or management control in India, it would be brought under consolidated supervision.

The NBFCs which are sponsored by banks and are currently not permitted to offer portfolio management services would be permitted to offer such services to their clients but it would be reviewed and based on the performance and requirement of each NBFC.

The Banks in India and the foreign banks which are operating in India are not permitted to have more than 10 per cent of the paid-up equity capital of a deposit taking NBFC. This rule does not apply to housing finance companies. This regulation would come in force from April 1, 2007.

SECURITIZATION

In September 2006, the Securitisation companies/reconstruction companies (SCs/RCs) had to invest in security receipts, issued by the trust set up for the purpose of securitisation 5% in each prescribed scheme. In October 2006, the SCs/RCs which had applied and were given a Certificate of Regulation from the Reserve Bank under the SARFAESI Act, 2002, had to begin their business within 6 months. If they required any extension of time for commencing business beyond six months, they had to apply to the Reserve Bank of India. However, the extension for commencing business could not exceed 12 months from the date of grant of the certificate of regulation. This certificate has been granted to only six SCs/RCs. 3 such organizations have began operating their business of securitization of assets.

The RBI has strictly enforced the securitization companies to comply with regulations. In May 2007, SCs/RCs had to declare net asset value of the security receipts issued by them at periodic intervals.

PRUDENTIAL NORMS OF NBFCs[1]

The NBFCs including RNBCs which accept public deposits are required to comply with prudential norms such as income recognition, accounting standard, asset classification, providing for bad and

---

1.   **Reserve Bank of India, Government of India Publication, Annual Report 2007.**

doubtful debts, capital adequacy and credit investment directions. The prudential guidelines were issued in June 1994. As an introductory measure the minimum capital adequacy norm was placed at 6% by 31st March, 1995. This was revise to 8% by March 31st, 1996. Liberalization measures were announced on 24th July, 1996. Further amendments were made in 1997 and 1998. In 1998, the Reserve Bank directed that the supervisory mechanism would be according to the size, activity and acceptance or non acceptance of deposits from public. For introducing norms the companies were placed in 3 categories.

- **Category 1 :** Companies accepting public deposit.
- **Category 2 :** NBFCs engaged in loan, investment, hire purchase finance and leasing equipments. Such companies do not accept public deposits.
- **Category 3 :** NBFCs which do not accept public deposits but they have acquired shares and securities in their own group as a holding or a subsidiary company having not less than 90% of their total assets. Such companies are not trading in these shares or securities.

NORMS FOR NBFCs ACCEPTING PUBLIC DEPOSITS

Public deposit includes fixed or recurring deposits which are received from friends, relatives, shareholders of a public limited company and money raised on issue of unsecured debentures or bonds. It would exclude money raised from issue of secured debentures and bonds or from borrowings of banks of financial institutions, deposits from directors or inter-corporate deposits received from foreign national citizens and from shareholders of private limited companies. The NBFCs which have net owned capital of less than Rs. 25 lakhs will not be permitted to accept deposit from public. In order to raise funds the can borrow from some other resources. All NBFCs will have to submit their annual financial statements and returns if they accept public deposits.

The RBI has given directions to NBFCs accepting public deposits to regulate the amount of deposit, rates of interest, time period of deposit, brokerage and borrowings received by them. The directions do not include amount received or guaranteed by central or state governments, local authorities of foreign governments. Amounts received from IDBI, LIC, NABARD, Electricity Board and IFCI are also excluded. Amounts received from mutual funds, directors of a firm and shareholders also do not come under the category of amount received for regulation from RBI.

Ceiling on Interest: There is ceiling on the rate of interest of deposits. This ceiling changes with the RBI directions.

Period of Deposits: The deposits can be accepted for a minimum period of 12 months and a maximum period 60 months.

Register of Depositors: The NBFCs have to maintain a register of depositors with details like name, address, amount, date of each deposit, maturity period and any other details according to those required by RBI.

Floating Charge: In January 2007, all NBFCs which accept or hold public deposits were required to create floating charge on the statutory liquid assets invested in favour of their depositors. Since this task had practical problems NBFCs accepting/holding public deposits were allowed to create the floating charge through a 'Trust Deed', by March 31, 2007.

Credit Rating: To protect the public NBFCs are required to have themselves approved by the RBI through credit rating agencies. The non bank financial companies which have net owned funds of Rs. 25 lakhs can obtain public deposits if they are credit rated and they receive a minimum investment grade for their fixed deposits from an approved rating agency. This rating has to be submitted to the RBI every year with a return on prudential norms. Equipment leasing and hire purchase finance companies. When the rating is made within 15 days the RBI has to be informed of the great that is given to the NBFC. The credit rating from the different agencies is as follows:

- The Credit Analysis and Research Limited (CARE) give the minimum rating of BBB in or triple B rating.
- The Investment Information and Crating Agency of India Ltd. (ICRA) gives the minimum rating of (MA –).
- The Credit Rating Information Services of India Ltd. (CRISIL) has the minimum acceptable rating of (FA –).
- FITCH Rating India Pvt. Ltd. Provides (BBB –) as its acceptable rating.

If the credit rating is below the minimum investment grade the NBFCs have to send report to the RBI within 15 days of receiving the grading. During that time it must stop accepting deposits and within 3 years make the repayment to the depositors.

The prudential norms for NBFCs and RNBCs accepting public deposits are the following:

Income Recognition: Income recognition is based on recognized accounting principles. The income can be recognized when it is actually realized. A lease, hire purchase or a rent which is due for more than 12 months can be recognized when it is actually received. The net lease rental is gross lease minus the depreciation and other adjustments on it. The NPAs of the assets will be identified when the interest is due for more than 6 months. This has been increased to 12 months in the new norms.

Capital Adequacy Ratio: The capital adequacy ratio for NBFCs with net owned funds of 25 lakhs is 12% since March 31st 1999. The net owned fund for capital adequacy has been revised and now includes preference shares which are convertible into equity shares.

Asset Classification: The NBFCs have to classify their lease or hire purchase assets according to standard assets, sub standard assets, doubtful assets and loss assets.

A standard asset is classified as one which does not have any default in paying interest and does not have more than a normal risk attached to the business.

A substandard asset is classified as one which has NPAs that exceed 2 years and its terms and agreements on principal and interest had to be renegotiated. A 10% provision of the total outstanding is to be made by the NBFCs.

A doubtful asset is one which is a substandard asset exceeding a period of 2 years. 100% provided has to be made if the advance is not covered by the realizable value of the security. Further, if the asset continued to be doubtful provision has to be made of 20% for 1 year, 30% upto 3 years and 50% more than 3 years of the secured portion of the realizable value of the asset should be made.

Loss assets are those which have a threat of non recoverability of the value of the assets. This has been valued by internal or external auditors or NBFCs and RBI inspection and it has been written off.

Disclosure of Balance Sheet: The NBFCs have to disclose NPAs, bad and doubtful debts, provision of depreciation in investments in the balance sheet. The provision for each year should be debited profit and loss account.

Concentration of investment: The NBFCs are not permitted to lend to a single group of borrowers in excess of 15% to a single borrower and 25% to a group of borrowers. The ceiling on loans and investments of composite limits of credit and investments in a single entity is prescribed at 25% and to a group of entities to 40% of its net owned funds.

Regulation of NBFCs Not Accepting Public Deposits: The NBFCs not accepting public deposits are exempted from regulation of capital adequacy and concentration norms. To get exemptions from regulation the directors have to pass a regulation that they will not accept any deposit from public. Those companies which have less than 90% of their assets in their group/holding/subsidiaries companies will have to give the names of those companies who shares they are holding or are proposing to hold or invest. The statuary auditors have to give their remarks and comments that the company has complied with specific norms. The auditor has to certify that there has been no violation of regulations.

Summary

➟ Non-bank financial companies (NBFCs) provide financial services like hire-purchase, leasing, loans, investments and chit fund services.

➟ These financial companies are small in size and they are owned privately.

➟ Their main competitors are banks and financial institutions.

➟ NBFC's are both fund based and service based companies.

➟ They can be classified into deposit accepting companies and non deposit accepting companies

➟ The NBFC's are regulated by Reserve Bank of India. Some of them are exempted because they are regulated by other regulators like Government or Insurance Regulatory Authority, Companies Act or Securities Exchange Board of India.

➟ According to the modified and new classification in 2007 NBFCs having an investment of 60% of their total assets and total income from financing of real/physical assets supporting economic activity such as automobiles, general purpose industrial machinery would be classified as asset finance companies.

➟ NBFCs with asset size of Rs. 100 crores and above have been defined as systemically important NBFCs. They have to maintain a minimum capital to risk-weighted asset ratio (CRAR) of 10% to lend surety to its customers that it has good and standard assets within the company.

➟ The Mutual Benefit Finance Companies are permitted to accept deposits only from their shareholders. They do not accept current account deposits.

➟ A fair practices code was incorporated for transparency in loan applications.

➟ Corporate governance was given a lot of importance for systematically important NBFC's.

➟ Since December 2006 NBFC's have been permitted to diversify into new areas of business. They can now issue co branded credit cards and distribute and market mutual fund products.

Contd....

> ➡ NBFCs have to obtain a certificate of registration from the Reserve Bank of India to commence their business. The net owned funds should be Rs. 25 lakhs and should have the maximum limit of Rs. 200 lakhs.
>
> ➡ Management and control pattern of an NBFC can change by giving a prior public notice of 30 days before the sale or transfer of shares, or transfer of control of ownership.
>
> ➡ The financial regulation of Systematically Important NBFC's would be activity-centric and not institution-centric to reduce or eliminate scope for regulatory arbitrage. Regulations were made on lending and investment including off balance sheet exposures.
>
> ➡ There are specific prudential norms for NBFC's which accept public deposits. These norms relate to income recognition, accounting standards, asset classification, capital adequacy, credit investment direction and provision for bad and doubtful debts. There are several relaxations for companies not accepting public deposits.

Objective Type Questions, Answer True (T) or False (F)

(a) Residuary Non-banking Companies (RNBC's) have their principal business of accepting deposits.

(b) NBFCs with asset size of Rs. 50 crores and above have been defined as 'systemically important NBFCs'.

(c) The Ministry of Corporate Affairs regulates the Mutual Benefit Financial Companies.

(d) Housing finance companies are regulated by chit fund Act of 1982.

(e) The chit fund Act of 1982 is regulated by Ministry of Company Affairs.

(f) An equipment leasing companies has the main business of leasing of equipments.

(g) An investment company buys and sells property as its main business.

(h) The credit rating companies have to give a grade to the NBFCs for obtaining public deposits.

(i) The financial regulation of Systemically Important NBFCs was reviewed to have institution centric regulation.

(j) Change of control of management in NBFCs can take place by sale of shares or transfer of control.

Answer : (a) T, (b) F, (c) T, (d) F, (e) T, (f) T, (g) F, (h) T, (i) F, (j) T.

Multiple Choice Questions (Tick mark (✓) the right answer)

1. An NBFCs is a company:
   (a) Which is engaged in telecommunication
   (b) Which has the business of chit funds
   (c) Which is a commercial bank
   (d) Which buys and sells retail marketing goods

2. A Systematically Important NBFCs is defined as:
   (a) An NBFCs with asset size of Rs. 25 Crores
   (b) An NBFCs with asset size of Rs. 50 Crores
   (c) An NBFCs with asset size of Rs. 150 Crores
   (d) An NBFCs with asset size of Rs. 100 Crores

3. The prudential norms are related to:
   (a) Capital adequacy ratio
   (b) Certification of registration
   (c) Fair practices code
   (d) Diversification in to new years

4. Credit rating can be done by:
   (a) CRISIL
   (b) An insurance company
   (c) A mutual fund company
   (d) A chit fund company

5. A fair practices code was issued by the RBI:
   (a) For the purpose of diversification
   (b) For the purpose of mutual fund business
   (c) For the purpose of transparency in lending operations
   (d) For the purpose of transparency in accepting deposits from public

   Answer: 1 (b), 2 (d), 3 (a), 4 (a), 5 (c).

Short Answer Questions

1. What is a non-bank finance company? Discuss some of their areas of business.
2. What are the prudential norms to be complied with by companies accepting deposits from public?
3. What are the new areas of business of non-bank financial companies?
4. What are the steps to be taken by NBFCs for change in the management control pattern of the company?

Long Answer Questions

1. Discuss the prudential norms which the non-bank finance companies (NBFCs) have to follow.
2. What are the different types of non-bank financial companies? How are they important? Give their classification.
3. What is the pattern of financial regulation of 'Systemically Important' NBFCs?
4. What is credit rating? In which circumstances do the NBFCs have to rate themselves?

Chapter 14

Small Savings, Provident Funds & Pension Funds

Chapter Plan

- Post Office Saving Instruments
- Pension Fund
- Provident Funds

INTRODUCTION

This chapter discusses the savings media of the small savers. The small savings organizations mobilize a large volume of savings in India. These small savings have a great importance in India. These are canalized through post offices and through savings certificates and bonds. The provident funds are usually for salaried earners. Self employed people can save through the Public Provident Fund. Pension funds are very useful in foreign countries as there are different kinds of pension plans available for people to make a retirement plan. In India pension funds have been primarily by government for its employees. It is proposed to reform the pension plan and to allow private operators to participate in it. Small savings and provident funds are useful as they contribute to budgetary resources of the Government of India. Central government and state government share the resources received from these sources.

POST OFFICE SAVINGS INSTRUMENTS

Post office savings are desired by the small savers because of the following qualities.

Liquidity: The post office savings offer liquidity to the small savers. It has Cumulative Time Deposits in which the outstanding balance can be drawn twice to the extent of 50% of the outstanding balance and it can be repaid in instalments or as a lump-sum. The post office also has Recurring Deposits in which it permits one withdrawal of 50% of the deposit. However, it charges an interest rate of 9.6% on the amount withdrawn. Another advantage is in the case of time deposits which can be used as a pledge for taking a loan from a bank for a temporary requirement. After a fixed period of one year the depositor is permitted to close his account prematurely if required. In such a case the depositor will still earn an interest rate but it will be 2% lower than the applicable rate of the deposit. However, post offices do not allow borrowing against their deposits. The National Saving Certificates (NSCs) can also be used to obtain loans from banks.

Time framework: The post office savings are usually for medium term and long term. Those investors who are unable to understand the complex character of equity shares, bonds or mutual funds find the post office a very useful media for savings. The lower income and middle income group of people are attracted to post office savings. There are several new plans for retired people. The simplicity and ease of investment in post office savings are able to draw people into the time framework of post office savings.

Re-investment Plans: Post offices have many plans in which the investor can re-invest after completion of the maturity period of the plans. Such plans provide a cover against inflation.

Savings Plans: Post office acts like a commercial bank as it attracts funds from small savers as saving accounts. These accounts are liquid and as near as cash. There are no restrictions on withdrawals. They can be withdraw and demand.

Insurance Cover: The recurring deposit and cumulative time deposits offer the advantages of providing insurance cover to the small saver in addition to the other benefits already explained. In the event of death his nominee is entitled to the full amount of the depositors account.

Therefore post office savings have many advantages for people to save their funds.

Types of Post Office Instruments

The post offices have different kinds of instruments to suit the requirements of the people.

Savings Bank Deposits: The savings bank deposits can be opened individually or jointly. It was started in post offices in the year 1896. It has a very low rate of interest. It has a limit to investment. A single account has a maximum limit of Rs. 1 lakh and joint account is limited to Rs. 2 lakhs. The minimum amount to be deposited is Rs. 20. The interest on this deposit is tax free. It has an exemption from wealth tax since 1993-94.

Time Deposits: Any person is permitted to have a time deposit in a post office. The maturity period of these deposits may be 1, 2, 3 and 5 years. The rates of interest on these deposits are between 6 and 7.5%. Its income from interest is exempt from tax. It is also eligible for wealth tax exemption. However, is doesn't have any tax rebates. There is no limit to the amount of investment of a person contribution to it.

Cumulative Time Deposits: The time deposits were introduced by the post offices in 1959 but it has been discontinued since 1973. These accounts had a maximum maturity period of 15 years and a minimum period of 5 years. It gave a compound interest of 6.25% and the interest was paid on maturity. The interest was tax free and the deposit amount qualified for income tax rebate and wealth tax exemption.

Post Office Recurring Deposits: This scheme was introduced in 1970. It has an interest rate of 12.5% per annum and it has a maturity period of 5 years. There is no maximum limit in this account. An individual is free to invest any amount. The deposit amount qualifies for exemption from wealth tax. It is tax free but it is not deductible for purposes of tax.

National Savings Certificates: These certificates have been issued in different series. They are in 7 years and 6 years series. The interest from these certificates is tax free. The amount of the certificate is eligible for deduction for calculating taxable income. The certificates were first issued in 1970 when II, III and IV series of 7 years were issued. Series II were discontinued in April 1989. Another issue series V was issued for 7 years duration in April 1974. In 1981-82 two 6 years series VI and VII were issued but again discontinued 1989. Series VIII was introduced for 6 years duration in 1989. On this certificate there was compound rate of interest of 8% and Individual can purchase any number of National Saving Certificates. The interest on these certificates is tax free. It qualifies for deduction in calculating taxable income.

Kisan Vikas Patra: These certificates have a maturity period of 7 years and 8 months. They were introduced in April 1988. There are no tax benefits but it carries an interest of 10.03%. There is no maximum limit to investing in it. These certificates are very popular. They can be taken in denominations of Rs. 500 each.

Indira Vikas Patra: These certificates are like bearer bonds. They are not registered instruments. They can be transferred from one person to another without any registration. It is transferable by delivery. They were introduce in 1986 but discontinued in 1999. These certificates doubled in 5.5 years and had a compound rate of interest at 13.43 % per annum. An individual could invest in any number of certificates and since it could be transferred easily it was very popular even though it was not eligible for any tax benefits. They were misused by people as unaccounted cash was being used to buy these certificates. For this reason they were discontinued.

National Saving Schemes: This is in the form of a deposit in which a person can invest a maximum sum of Rs. 40,000. It gives an interest of 11% per annum and the full amount which is deposited in a year is eligible for deduction from income of the depositor for purposes of income tax. However, when the deposit is withdrawn, the full amount inclusive of interest is added to the income of the depositor in the year of withdrawal of the deposit.

Post Office Monthly Income Scheme: In this scheme a fixed deposit is made by individual. The maximum sum that a person can invest in as an individual is Rs. 3 lakhs. If a joint accounted open then the maximum amount is Rs. 6 lakhs. The minimum investment for such accounts is Rs. 6 thousands. The account has a maturity period of 6 years. The depositor receives an interest rate of 8% per annum. Since this is called a monthly income scheme, interest is paid every month. It qualifies for a bonus of 10% on the deposit made in this account. However, this is paid at the end of 6 years at the time of maturity of the account. The interest income is eligible for tax rebate.

Scheme for Retiring People: Post offices have a special scheme for people when they attain the age of 60 years. They call this scheme the senior citizens scheme. The post office offers 9% rate of interest. A maximum sum of Rs. 15 lakhs can be deposited with the post office in this account. This scheme is very popular as the interest rate is high compared to other savings plans.

Let us now discuss provident funds as a means of savings for people with salaried and non salaried income.

PROVIDENT FUNDS

There are different types of provident funds in India. These are Employees Provident Fund for Central Government and State Government, Employees Provident Fund exempted and for non-exempted industrial organizations, Coal Mines Provident Fund and Assam Tea Plantations Provident Fund. The non-salaried people have a provident fund called Public Provident Fund. The provident funds can be further classified into Statutory Provident Fund, Recognized Provident Fund, Unrecognized Provident Fund and Public Provident Fund.

Employees Provident Fund

Employees Provident Fund Organization in India is an autonomous tripartite body under the control of Ministry of Labour, Government of India with its head office In NEW DELHI. The Central Board of Trustees has been constituted. It consists of Central/State Government representatives, representatives of employers and Establishments and representatives of the employees in the establishments. EPFO has 17 Regional offices and their sub regional offices to its 23 million members.

Employees Provident Fund Covers Establishments employing 20 or more persons and engaged in any of the 180 industries/Classes of Businesses specified. Co-operative Societies, employing 50 or more persons and working without the aid of power. The employers are required to file the particulars in the specified format for registration and allotment of business number.

The statutory rate of contribution is 12% of emoluments (basic wages, dearness allowance, cash value of food concession and retaining allowances if any,) in the case of 175 establishments.

Rate of contribution is 10% in the case of the following: Brick, beedi, jute, guar gum factories, coir industry other than spinning sector. For establishments which are declared as sick undertakings by BIFR. A matching contribution is to be collected from the emoluments of the employees. Out of 12% (or 10% as the case may be) of the employer's share of contribution, 8.33% is to be remitted towards pension fund.[1]

In India provident funds have had a phenomenal growth. The reason for this is that they have become compulsory by statute for industrial organizations. Since, there has been a vast increase in the number of business organizations; the number of working force has also increased. Their contribution has thus increased. There are tax benefits provided to the savers in this scheme.

Statutory Provident Fund

Statutory Provident Fund was set up in 1925. This fund is maintained by Government, Semi-Government Organization, local authorities, railways, universities and educational institutions. In statutory

---

1. This information is from Employees Provident Fund Organization, India.

provident fund contribution from the employer is exempt from tax. Relief under Section 88 of employee's contribution is available to the interest credited to the provident fund which is exempt from tax and the lump sum amount which is paid at the time of retirement is also exempt from tax.

Recognized Provident Fund

Recognized Provident Fund is given this name because it is recognized by the Commissioner of Income Tax according to the rules which are contained in Part-A, Schedule-IV of the Income Tax Act. When the Commissioner of Income Tax recognizes this fund it becomes recognized also by the Provident Fund Commissioner. Recognized provident fund is also contributed in the same way as Statutory Provident Fund, i.e., both by the employer and the employee. Recognized provident fund has an interest rate of 8%

The recognized provident fund and statutory provident funds have another advantage. Loans may be taken from this account without payment of any interest. This, therefore, forms a very cheap means of taking loans for the purposes of making a house, making additions to a house, house repairs, and wedding in the family or illness.

Unrecognized Provident Fund

Unrecognized Provident Fund is exempt from tax when the employer contributes to it but relief under Section 88 is not available to the investor. The interest which is credited to this account is, however, exempt from tax and the payment which is received in respect of employee's own contribution at the time of retirement is also exempt from tax.

Public Provident Fund

Public Provident Fund is a fund provided for self employed people to mobilize personal savings. Any person from the public, whether salaried or self-employed, can open a Public Provident Fund Account at any branch of State Bank of India. Any amount up to a maximum of Rs. 70,000 per annum can, be deposited under this account but the amount so accumulated will be paid only at the end of maturity. In this fund employer does not contribute, but relief Under Section 88 is available and the interest credited to this fund is exempt from tax. The amount received at the time of termination of this contract is also exempt from tax. The Public Provident Fund has a maturity period of 15 years. An individual can withdraw to the extent of 50% of the outstanding amount at the end of 7 years, 11 years and 15 years. In the first 6 years of the scheme the depositor can take a lone upto 25% of his balance. But the deposit has a closed period of 2 years from the date of deposits. The scheme was started in India in 1968 and is popular as it gives the advantage of deduction of tax.

PENSION FUND

A pension fund is a retirement benefit in India. The government employees receive a monthly payment for their old age. The maximum benefit is attained after 33 years of service in a government organization. Some companies in the private sector also give a pension to their retired employees but the number of such companies is very low. In India it has been mainly a subject in government organizations. Most of the public sector enterprises offer a defined benefit pension plan.

Defined Benefits Pension Plan: This plan is based on the last salary and the time period of service of the employee in an organization. It is guaranteed by government and it is paid every month after retirement. Government establishes a legal trust fund and the amount it contributes to the employee is invested in a lump-sum. The investments receive interest which is used by government to pay pension to their retired employees.

Defined Contribution Pension Plan: In this plan the employer and the employee make a defined amount of contribution every year. This is invested and when the employee retires the value of the investments is made and a lump-sum amount is given to the employee on retirement. This scheme is popular in the United State of America but in India it has not gained the same popularity.

Pay as You Go Pension Plan: This pension plan is being used in Germany and France under this plan government contributes for old people. The people in service also contribute a percentage of their current income for retired people. Out of these funds a sustenance level is fixed for looking after the old people.

Investment Based Pension Fund: The first Investment based pension fund was approved by government in October 1994 to be started as a fund by the Unit Trust of India. It was meant to be a retirement benefit plan for self employed people. Since self employed people did not have any provident fund except the public provident fund. The pension fund was designed for their security at old age. This was an open ended program for people between the age of 18 and 52 years. The contributors would receive a regular monthly income after attaining 58 years of age. This scheme was to work by investing in equity shares and debt. The ratio of 40 : 60 was considered to be a workable solution. In this scheme the minimum amount to be subscribed would be Rs. 10,000 which would be paid in 20 installments and it would have a minimum payment of Rs. 500. The contributor would have the option withdrawing from the scheme after attaining the age of 70 years. He would be permitted to withdraw prematurely but with a discount.

Pension Plan in India

Government Pension Plan: The pension market in India is very small. It covers people employed in government in India. Government contributes to 8.33% of the employees' salary. It contributed to 1.16% of the employees salary. It pays a minimum amount of Rs. 500 per month. The maximum pension is 60% of the salary. It also pays a disability pension and in the event of death of the employee the pension is given to the widow or widower in case the employee is married. If both husband and wife are dead then the orphan gets pension.

Bank Officer and Insurance Employees Pension Plan: The bank officers and the insurance employees are governed by the pension scheme of 1993. The employer pays 10% of the basic salary. In this scheme after 60 years of age and 33 years of service the employee gets a pension of 50% of the average basic salary of last 10 months of employment. The also get 50% of the average of their allowances excluding Dearness Allowance in the last 10 months of their service.

New Pension Plans: In India two new pension plans were brought about. One plan was started in 1999, recommended by Dave Committee and the other one in 2003 was introduced as the new pension scheme.

The Old Age Social Income Security (OASIS) was recommended by the Dave Committee. The pension funds would be permitted to invest in secondary financial markets in different securities. Accordingly the annual increase in pension funds would be permitted to be invested in equity shares and 20% of the annual increase in debt securities. Private pension funds would be allowed and a regulatory authority would be setup. They would be a favourable tax treatment for contributions. The earnings from investments would be managed by professional fund managers.

The OASIS made other suggestions as well relating to individuals who could make voluntary contributions into their own retirement accounts through their work life but contributions should be of small amounts. They would be a central depository for transferring block of funds to pension fund managers and record keeping of the individual retired accounts would be centralized through a central depository.

The new pension scheme of 2003 announced the following new aspects of the scheme.

- The new government employees and self employee professionals in the organized sector could take the option of joining the contributory pension scheme. An individual in the existing provident fund scheme could in addition to that scheme participate in the new pension scheme. The existing provident fund would be withdrawn for the new employees.

- The contribution of pension would be 10% of employees' salary Plus Dearness Allowance and a matching contribution from government.

- At the age of 60 the individuals could exit from this scheme but they have to invest compulsorily 40% of their pension amount to purchase an annuity from IRDA regulated life insurance.

- The banks and post offices would collect contribution of the participants.

- Pension fund managers would be permitted to make investments in international markets subject to the regulations of the government.

- Pension fund managers could invest: (a) 60% in government securities, 30% in government bonds and 10% is equities, (b) 40% in government securities, 40% in corporate bonds and 20% in equities, (c) 50% is equities and 50% in government and corporate bonds. Any one of the three options could be selected by fund managers.

The provident and pension funds in the year 2004-05, 2005-06, 2006-07 had a contribution of 13%, 10.5% and 9.2% of the total financial savings of household sector. In amount it was Rs. 56,552 crores, Rs. 62,704 cores and Rs. 69,571 crores respectively. Since the workforce is increasing, it is expected that savings will increase further. Currently it is fallen as the figures in the 3 years are depicted above. In India the problem of old age is being experienced by nuclear families, provident fund and pension schemes are becoming increasingly important for people.[2]

---

2. Reserve Bank of India Annual Report, Government of India Publication 2007.

Summary

➡ Small savings are very important in India as they cover the low income and medium income group of people. Post offices encourage small savings through different kinds of plans.

➡ Provident funds in India have been for salaried people. Public Provident Fund is a unique scheme for self employed people.

➡ Pension funds in India have been mainly in the government sector. Since 2003, private pension funds have also been allowed to operate.

➡ Post offices are favoured by the people because of the convenience of operation. They have the facility of savings account, recurring deposits, medium term and long term deposits. They also issue certificates like Kisan Vikas Patra and National Savings Certificate. Indira Vikas Patra has become a closed scheme. They also have schemes for retiring people and offer better rates of interest on them in comparison with bank savings.

➡ Provident fund covers establishments which employee 20 or more people. 180 industries are specified underrate. It is applicable to co-operative society which employee 50 or more people working without the aid of power.

➡ There are different kinds of provident funds for employed people. These are Statutory Provident Fund, Recognized Provident Fund and Un-recognized Provident Fund.

➡ Pension fund is a retirement benefit in India. There are different kinds of pension schemes Defined Benefits Pension Plan , Defined Contribution Pension Plan Pay as You Go Pension Plan, Investment Based Pension Fund.

➡ The old age income security OASIS was recommended by the Dave Committee in 1999. Private operators were permitted to start pension funds.

➡ The new pension scheme was started in 2003. In this scheme all new government employee and self employee professionals in the organize sector could the take option of becoming a member of the contributory pension scheme.

Objective Type Questions, Answer True (T) or False (F)

(a) There are recognized and unrecognized pension funds in India.

(b) All government employees have to compulsorily join the contributory pension fund.

(c) Provident funds have been specified in 180 different kinds of industries.

(d) In new pension scheme of 2003 the contribution of the employee would be 10% of basic salary plus Dearness Allowance with a matching grant by government

(e) In the new pension scheme the employees' contribution will be deducted by private organizations.

(f) The first investment based provident fund was given permission in 1994.

(g) In the new pension scheme it is purposed to have a central depository for transferring block of funds.

(h) In a Recognized Provident Fund both the employee and the employer have to contribute towards the fund.

(i) In a Statutory Provident Fund loans can be taken by the employee without paying any interest but in a Recognized Provident Fund the employee has to pay interest on amounts withdrawn by him.

(j) In an Unrecognized Provident Fund the benefits of section 88 is not available to the employee.

Answer: (a) F, (b) F, (c) T, (d) T, (e) F, (f) T, (g) T, (h) T, (i) F, (j) T.

Multiple Choice Questions (Tick mark (✓) the right answer)

1. The recurring deposit offer:
    (a) tax benefits to the contributor
    (b) insurance cover to the depositor
    (c) loans on the deposit amount
    (d) investment in shares and bonds

2. National Savings Certificates are:
    (a) tax free
    (b) are not tax free
    (c) were tax free but now it is taxable
    (d) They are tax free and also qualify for deduction in calculating taxable income

3. National Saving Scheme is:
    (a) tax free
    (b) it is not tax free
    (c) it is deductible from income at the time of deposit
    (d) deductible but interest has to be paid

4. Provident fund in government organizations is paid in:
    (a) Statutory Provident Fund
    (b) Recognized Provident Fund
    (c) Unrecognized Provident Fund
    (d) Public Provident Fund

5. In a Pension Fund:
    (a) The maximum benefit is after 33 years of service
    (b) After 30 years of service
    (c) Maximum benefit after 25 years of service
    (d) Maximum benefit after 20 years of service

Answer : 1 (b), 2 (d), 3 (c), 4 (a), 5 (a).

Short Answer Questions

1. Name the different types of Provident Funds in India. Which of these funds is applicable for self employed people?

2. What is a Pension Fund? Outline the new pension fund of 2003.

Long Answer Questions

1. What is a Provident Fund? Explain the difference between Recognized Provident Funds and Statutory Provident Funds.

2. What are the different kinds of schemes in pension funds? Which is applicable to India? How does the Pension fund scheme of 2003 bring in a reform in the Pension Fund in India?

Insurance Companies

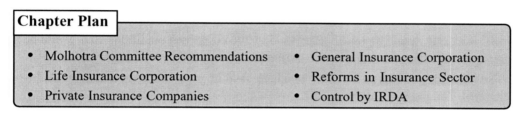

Chapter Plan

- Molhotra Committee Recommendations
- Life Insurance Corporation
- Private Insurance Companies
- General Insurance Corporation
- Reforms in Insurance Sector
- Control by IRDA

INTRODUCTION

Insurance institutions have the main function of offering social security and investing the savings of individuals. It provides protection against risks. Insurance companies in India have until 1999 essentially consisted of the Life Insurance Corporation of India (LIC) and the General Insurance Corporation of India (GIC) with its four subsidiaries. Both these institutions were monolithic in nature. After the new economic policy in 1991 the Malhotra Committee was appointed in 1993 by government to recommend insurance sector reforms.

Malhotra Committee Recommendations

- Malhotra Committee recommended that government should reduce its stake to 50% holding in insurance companies.

- Insurance companies should be given freedom from control in their operations.

- Private Insurance companies should be allowed to begin its business in India. Those companies which have a minimum paid of capital of Rs. 100 crores should be given an entry into insurance industry. In the private company the promoter's role would be defined. The promoter's contribution would be between 26 and 40% of the paid up capital of the company. No other individual would be allowed to hold more than 1% equity of the company.

- Foreign companies should also be allowed to enter the Indian market but in collaboration with the Indian companies. The license should be given carefully to foreign companies. Only those companies which are able to condition themselves with the requirement of the Indian financial system would be allowed to enter in the insurance industries.

- An insurance regulatory body should be setup independently to regulate insurance business and bring about prudential and regulatory norms. It should have a separate identity from the Finance Ministry.

- The Life Insurance Corporation should be restructured. The central and zonal offices should be reorganized. The central office should focus on formulating its policies and the engaged in development and pricing measures. It should also give due attention to investments, valuation and review. The zonal offices should collect insurance business and disbursements.

- Government to take over the holding of GIC and its subsidiaries and GIC should act as independent from its subsidiaries. All of them should become corporations. GIC should become a reinsurance company.

- Life Insurance and General Insurance would be separate companies. No companies would be allowed to do both the business.

- Postal Life Insurance should operate in rural areas.

- LIC is capital should be raised from Rs. 5 to 200 crores and out of this 50% would be held by government. The rest would be a contribution held by public and employees of LIC.

- The mandatory investment of LIC which are held in government securities should be reduced to 50%. The present level it is 75%.

- The capital of GIC was to be increased from Rs. 107.5 to 200 crores out of which 50% would be held by government and the rest by public and employees of GIC.

- GIC and its subsidiaries would not be allowed to hold more than 5% of paid up capital and of any company.

- Government should acquire the capital of all the subsidiaries of GIC. At the present level it was Rs. 40 crores in each subsidiary. Government should after acquisition raise the amount to Rs. 100 crores. 50% would be government holding and the rest would be in some proportion between public and employees.

- In the interest of the policy holders LIC should not delay their payments beyond 30 days. If they do, then they are liable to pay interest.

- LIC and GIC should have a proper management board to run it on business lines.

- OMBUDSMAN should be setup by the General Insurance Companies to solve disputes and other complaints.

LIFE INSURANCE CORPORATION (LIC)

Life Insurance was brought into India from United Kingdom with the establishment of a British firm Oriental Life Insurance Company in Calcutta in 1818 followed by Bombay Life Assurance Company in 1823.In 1912 the Indian Life Assurance Companies Act was passed to regulate the life insurance business. In 1928 the Indian Insurance Companies Act was brought about so that Government was able collect statistical information about both life and non-life insurance business transacted in India by Indian and foreign insurers including provident insurance societies. In 1938 a comprehensive insurance Act was enacted with detailed provisions to effectively control the activities of insurers. The Act was amended in 1950. In1956, 154 Indian insurers, 16 foreign insurers and 75 provident societies were carrying on life insurance business in India. On January 19, 1956, the management of life insurance business of 245 Indian and foreign insurers and provident societies then operating in India was taken over by the Central Government. Life Insurance Corporation was formed in September 1956 by LIC Act 1956 of Parliament.

The then Finance Minister Mr. C.D. Deshmukh outlined the objectives of LIC. In his words the objectives of LIC are the following

"To conduct the business with utmost economy with the spirit of trusteeship; to charge premium no higher than warranted by strict actuarial considerations; to invest the funds for obtaining maximum yield for the policy holders consistent with safety of capital; to render prompt and efficient service to policy holders thereby making Insurance widely popular."

LIC,s future endevour is to become 'A trans-nationally competitive financial conglomerate of significance to societies and Pride of India.'

Objectives of LIC

The objectives of LIC are listed below:

* To spread life insurance extensively with a focus on rural areas and socially and economically backward classes and providing them adequate financial cover against death at a reasonable cost.

* To mobilize the savings of the people by making insurance-linked savings adequately attractive.

* To hold the money of the policyholders as its primary obligation and to invest the funds in the best interest of the investors with attractive returns to the policyholder.

* To conduct business carefully and economically as the money belongs to the policyholders.

* To act as trustees of the insured public in their individual and collective capacities.

* To make need based changes in policies depending on social and economic environment of the country.

* To provide service to the policyholders.

* To involve the agents and employees so that they participate, actively in development of the objectives of the corporation and discharge their duties with dedication.

Restructure of LIC

In 1980, this monolithic institution was again sought to be broken up into four units because of its unwieldy structure and vast increase in business during the last 24 years. It was also felt that there was a lack of spirit of competition and more effort was required to tap the savings surpluses from households both in rural and in urban areas. Under these circumstances, it was finally decided to divide its operations into four units in 1983 during the Parliamentary session. Reforms in the Insurance sector were however not initiated until the IRDA Bill in Parliament in December 1999. The IRDA was incorporated as a statutory body in April 2000. Since then it has framed regulations and registered private sector insurance companies. The IRDA has framed globally compatible regulations to provide the supporting systems to the insurance sector and in particular the life insurance companies. It has launched the IRDA online service for issue and renewal of licenses to agents. It also has approved institutions for imparting training to agents. The insurance companies would have a trained workforce of insurance agents to sell their products.

LIC has set up a network of branches, divisions and zonal offices in India. It transacts business in India and abroad and has opened its offices in Fiji, Mauritius and United Kingdom. LIC also has joint ventures abroad. It has collaborated with insurance companies like Ken-India Assurance Company Limited, Nairobi, United Oriental Assurance Company Limited, Kuala Lumpur and Life Insurance Corporation (International) E.C. Bahrain. LIC has registered a joint venture company in 26th Dec., 2000 in Kathmandu, in Nepal in collaboration with Vishal Group Limited. An off-shore company LIC (Mauritius) off-shore Limited has also been set up in 2001. Its main objective is to extend its services in the African insurance market.

The LIC's main aim has been to mobilise the savings of the household and to offer protection against death and sickness. In recent years, it has also become a medium for saving tax. The LIC, therefore, collects huge resources of funds from the people.

Types of Life Insurance Policies

The Life Insurance Policies consist of the following policies.

- *Whole life policies* which cover the insured for the whole life. His nominee receives the assured sum with bonus after the date of insured.

- *Endowment policies* in which the insured takes a life cover for a specific period of time. At the expiry of the policy he receives the sum of the insurance policy.

- *Money back policies* are taken by the insured for the advantage of receiving money at regular intervals of the policies. The premium cost is high. If the insured dies, the nominee receives the insurance amount.

- *Children policies* are taken by parents for their education or marriage. This is a fixed term policy and the money is received at a specific age of the child.

- *Pension schemes* are planned by individuals at their young age. The amount is received only at retirement. If however, the insured does not survive, the amount of lump-sum will be given to his nominee.

LIC's Investment Policy

These resources are built into a 'life fund' and invested in various types of classes of investment, to benefit the policy-holders in their time of need. LIC continuously plans its investments in such a way that it has liquid funds for immediate satisfaction of shareholders as well as secured for long-term investments for the purpose of earning a higher rate of interest. For this purpose LIC has an investment policy in which the various investment outlets are specified. Within the framework, the investments are made.

LIC has its investments in government securities, Public Sector, Co-operative Sector, Private Sector and Joint Sector. on the Stock Exchange, it is considered a very powerful security holder. Table 15.1 depicts the investment of LIC from 1979 to 2006. The value of LIC's Stock Exchange Securities as on 31st March, 2006 was Rs. 4,50,557.2 crores. Its sector wise investment shows Rs. 3,78,807.2 crores in the public sector, Rs. 1,05,148.1 crores in the private sector, Rs. 1,915.5 crores in the joint sector and Rs. 1,356.5 crores in Co-operative sector. This has increased manifold since 1979 as shown in the Table 15.1. The total investments were Rs. 4,587.7 crores in 1979 and in 2006 it had increased to Rs. 4,87,227.2 crores.

Table 15.1: Investments by LIC

(Rupees crore)

Year (end-March)	Sector-wise				Instrument-wise *of which*		Total
	Public	Private	Joint	Co-operative	Stock exchange securities	Loans	(2 to 5)
1	2	3	4	5	6	7	8
1979	3411.9	618.1	29.9	527.8	2733.8	1853.1	**4587.7**
1980	3915.5	770.1	0	602.1	3113.4	2173.6	**5287.7**
1981	4707.8	647.2	0	665.5	3591.3	2725.6	**6020.5**
1982	5410.7	698.7	32.0	753.0	4040.6	2612.0	**6894.4**
1983	6189.7	787.4	32.7	825.2	–	–	**7835.0**
1984	7020.8	891.4	40.1	905.3	–	–	**8857.6**
1985	7919.5	1010.6	51.2	972.9	–	–	**9954.2**
1986	9063.8	1121.3	68.0	1036.8	6822.8	4474.1	**11289.9**
1987	10259.3	1408.1	86.9	1058.6	7929.6	4865.0	**12812.9**
1988	11837.3	1624.8	88.4	1161.7	9230.9	5412.0	**14712.2**
1989	14032.4	1973.1	97.1	1240.1	10932.3	5055.5	**17342.7**
1990	16404.3	2640.7	125.5	1333.2	12918.6	7257.5	**20503.7**
1991	19980.2	3310.0	165.2	1444.3	15871.2	7416.6	**24899.7**
1992	24425.4	4239.5	174.9	1562.6	19056.8	10942.3	**30402.4**
1993	28983.2	5397.0	284.3	1657.6	23082.5	11585.4	**36322.1**
1994	36246.5	5894.4	304.6	1716.1	29536.3	12876.3	**44161.6**
1995	44318.9	7017.2	350.3	1793.1	37420.1	14169.4	**53479.5**
1996	54003.4	8814.4	380.3	1858.8	47086.1	18085.6	**65056.9**
1997	65917.4	9588.5	490.3	1941.8	58850.8	16750.7	**77938.0**
1998	79235.7	11834.3	500.0	2030.3	72537.0	18489.9	**93600.3**
1999	96410.5	15048.4	549.3	2094.5	90823.8	26109.7	**114102.7**
2000	117059.0	19268.4	575.5	2129.3	114032.3	28925.5	**139032.2**
2001	141256.2	22779.5	799.7	2168.4	140106.0	32155.4	**167003.8**
2002	180574.1	23707.8	792.8	2128.6	178943.3	34913.2	**207203.3**
2003	219596.7	29406.8	684.5	2082.3	222449.3	27539.8*	**251770.3**
2004	271778.5	51923.6	959.6	2079.5	297566.0	31800.4*	**326741.2**
2005	322021.8	68484.5	1270.2	1408.2	355634.7	37529.5*	**393184.6**
2006 P	378807.2	105148.1	1915.5	1356.5	450557.2	37135.3*	**487227.2**

P : Provisional.
* Excluding policy loans to HPF, Treasury bills, Commercial papers.
Source : Life Insurance Corporation of India.

LIC has been the largest underwriter of capital issues in the Indian Capital Market till the year 1978 after which it has reduced its activities in favour of socially-oriented projects. In the year 1983 itself, LIC underwrote 72 new issues of an aggregate amount of Rs. 156.72 crores. It underwrote firms and preferred large and established companies. As an underwriter, it influenced the capital market considerably and was also able to stabilize the market during the downswings or depression periods. From 1983-85 it began to change its direction in investments.

Since 1970 LIC has been disbursing 'loans' for industrial development. One of the major avenues of investment in 1983 constituted financing through loans. It has given loans for generation and transmission of electricity for agricultural and industrial use, housing schemes, piped water supply schemes and development of road and transport.

The LIC also subscribes to debentures and bonds of various financial institutions and development bank like IDBI and IFCL.

Finally, LIC has resorted to socially oriented schemes in a big way since 1978. This brought down its activities in the capital market. The rationale behind this change has been to go in for developmental work. Own Your House (OYH) schemes have been given priority. Apart from these schemes, loans for sewerage, road and transport and electricity generation have also been given priority in the recent years.

Another direction which he LIC has taken has been to influence the private corporate sector. by virtue of its shareholding it has been recognized amongst the top ten shareholders in one out of every three companies listed in the Stock Exchange in which it has a shareholding. While LIC has invested in large blocks of equities and in later years in debenture holdings, it had kept away and did not interfere in the decisions of the management of the past. In recent years, it has influenced the management to take proper decisions and to tone up the quality of working in the organizations. This is intended to promote confidence in the minds of the public and to exercise control in the corporate sector that often have a very small shareholding but are controlling their organization. In 1984 LIC has dominated the Indian industrial scene. One notable instance which may be cited in which it interfered in the policies of the management has been in the Nanda Group of Companies, *i.e.,* 'Escorts Ltd.' These changes in the direction of the policies of a large institution like the LIC is bound to exert some pressure on the industry and change the complexion of Indian Industrial scenario.

Since 1984 several changes are noticeable in LIC's capital market activity. It continued its policy of withdrawing from investment in corporate securities and enlarging its activities in welfare schemes of the state electricity boards. Consequently their investment in corporate securities declined from 16% in 1956-57 to 5% in 1986-87 and to 3% in 1992-93 and it has lost the rating of *Captive Investor*.

LICs function was to channelize savings. The savings in life insurance from the household sector is Rs. 1,10,964 crores in 2006-07.

The savings in LIC was used for investment through the financial system to lend stability to the financial markets especially during the downswings in the economy. With its shift into socially oriented sector this facility was withdrawn. However with the inception of merchant bankers and brokers the LIC is replaced as an underwriter in the New Issue Market. The UTI has emerged as the single largest purchaser of corporate securities and it can be said that it has relieved the LIC of its responsibility in lending stability to the market.

The LIC's interest towards socially oriented projects and reduced capital market activity had affected the policy holders, *i.e.,* the small savers who had entrusted their life time saving with the objective of insurance cover and prospects of a good return on investment. The premium on life policies was high and return was far lower than the UTI. This did not serve the interest of the policy holders as LIC did not act in the spirit of trusteeship.

In 1993 the Malhotra Committee had suggested reforms for restructuring regulation and liberalization of the insurance sector. The Committee suggested that LIC's policies should be made attractive for the small saver, the insurance services should be improved and LIC should be converted from a monolithic institution to a public limited company. The private sector should be allowed to enter insurance business with a view to encourage competition. According to the committee the insurance sector should also have technology up-gradation and high standards of accounting. It became necessary to institute an Insurance Regulatory Authority (IRA) as a statutory autonomous board in order to improve the standards of insurance business and provide consumer protection.

In 1995 government announced an interim IRA to begin functioning and streamlining procedures and bringing discipline and professionalism in the insurance sector. The interim IRA would have three full time members and a chairman appointed by government. The chairman would take over the powers of the present controller of insurance. This team would be assisted by four other members nominated by government. The IRA was proposed to work under the Ministry of Finance.

Thus the interest of the policyholders has been given great importance and emphasis by Malhotra Committee. The LIC would fail in its purpose if it is not satisfying the policyholders. Private insurance and foreign companies would be allowed to enter into insurance business. Joint venture was considered as a responsibility for the entry of new insurance companies to bring about innovative schemes for attracting policy holders and for linking the ultimate pool of savers and investors in the capital market in India.

Life Insurance has now been extended to the private sector as well. A large number of new companies have been floated for providing life insurance cover. The companies whose life business are notable are Industrial Credit and Investment Corporation of India (ICICI), Tata's Insurance and Housing Development Finance Corporation of India (HDFC). A list of companies in the public sector and private sector are given below:

Table 15.2: Life Insurance Companies in India

> **LIFE INSURERS**
> **Public Sector**
> Life Insurance Corporation of India
> **Private Sector**
> Allianz Bajaj Life Insurance Company Limited
> Birla Sun-Life Insurance Company Limited
> HDFC Standard Life Insurance Co. Limited
> ICICI Prudential Life Insurance Co. Limited
> ING Vysya Life Insurance Company Limited
> Max New York Life Insurance Co. Limited
> MetLife Insurance Company Limited
> Om Kotak Mahindra Life Insurance Co. Ltd.
> SBI Life Insurance Company Limited
> TATA AIG Life Insurance Company Limited
> AMP Sanmar Assurance Company Limited
> Dabur CGU Life Insurance Co. Pvt. Limited

PRIVATE INSURANCE COMPANIES

The private insurance companies in India have made insurance industry competitive. The Life Insurance Corporation of India (LIC) is however still the largest in volume of its life fund.

The ICICI Prudential, HDFC Standard Life and Tata AIG have experienced an increase in their market share. It his stated that the private companies will grow by 20% in the next 3 years. In India insurance requires to be tapped in rural areas because only a small size of the population in India has contributed in insurance policies. The Insurance Regulatory and Development Authority (IRDA) are encouraging the private companies to bring out new and good life insurance product. The Indian customer buys policies for tax benefits and to ensure secure savings for the future. He is sensitive to price of the insurance products. Many private players have initiated education campaigns explaining the benefits and need for insurance.

The private players have been quite successful due to their innovative offers, customer-centric products, increasing awareness levels of consumers through a need-based, structured approach of selling, sound risk-management practices, good service standards, reaching out to the customer through a number of distribution and communications channels, and providing advice to the customer.

The Indian population generally takes one life insurance policy in his life time. Private companies can try to change this habit by giving distinct product.

The endowment plans offered by private companies offer different benefits, but the overall structure is quite similar, but each company has products with unique features. There are new concepts of whole life policy. Private companies have entered into the corporate pension management business, where a corporate house can outsource its pension management system to the insurance company. Companies are also introducing investment-linked company schemes and credit-card insurance, where the bill is insured against death of the cardholder. These product innovations were not available in the past.

When the insurance market grows there will be a distinction in individual products. as compared to similar products in endowment policies, whole life and pension plans. In the current scenario LIC is dominating the endowment market. Private players are major stakeholders in whole life insurance, pensions plans and term insurance.

Private companies provide efficient customer service channels which differentiate from the traditional model of LIC. Many private companies provide good service to the customers. The customer gets quicker turnaround of claims and has access to faster processing then through the LIC.

In the US and Japan, almost 90 per cent policies are sold through personal interactions with individuals. Insurance agents are the key persons in the industry. The profile of the insurance agent has undergone a transformation, with private players in India. Insurance companies have strengthened their internal regulatory training programmes and are trying to emulate the countries life US and Japan to encourage insurance products rather than move in traditional directions like the LIC.

Agents are given 100 hours of training in India and a further 50 hours are spent in securing higher education. This covers the rudiments of insurance, claims, policy protection and an exhaustive background study on the insurance industry. These agents are also trained to interact with the customer. Private players have full-time, ongoing training programmes in India. This is a major competition for the LIC and a challenge to keep its dominating position because the agents do not merely sell policies but also guide the customers on the right choice of the product most suitable for their requirements.

The private insurance companies have invested in multiple and innovative distribution strategies. They reach their customers through Internet and direct mailers. Bancassuarance, or distribution of insurance products through the branches and multiple communication channels of banks, including ATMs, tele-banking and Internet banking, is becoming popular in India.

The majority of India is rural. This market cannot be ignored. The private insurance companies have still to create products for the rural market. The distribution strategy will have to be different. New strategies have to be formulated for cash collection and medical facilities.

The months of February and March are a very busy period for LIC. In comparison the private insurance companies do not offer products during that time to get the same response. New products have to be offered to compete with the LIC which offers tax benefits. However, the opening up of the insurance sector with private companies offers competition and challenges to the LIC which has to move into new product lines to keep pace with the growing private insurance sector.

GENERAL INSURANCE CORPORATION (GIC)

The LIC is regulated by the Insurance Act of 1938 under Section 27A. The GIC is governed by the same Act under Section 27B. GIC was formed as a government company under Section 9 of the General Insurance Business (Nationalisation) Act 1972 and registered as a private company under the Companies Act, 1956 and its four subsidiaries, viz., (a) National Insurance Company Ltd., Kolkata, (b) New India Assurance Co. Ltd., Mumbai, (c) Oriental Fire and General Insurance Co. Ltd., New Delhi, and (d) United India Fire and General Insurance Co. Ltd., Chennai.

General Insurance Corporation (GIC) which was the holding company of the four public sector general insurance companies has since been de-linked from those companies. Since 3rd Nov., 2000 it is recognized as the "Indian Re-insurer". The share capital of GIC and that of the four companies are held by the Government of India.

The general insurance volume of business has increased to a great extent after nationalization. The GIC and its subsidiaries are represented in 16 countries and through associate/ locally incorporated subsidiary companies in 14 other countries. In Singapore Indian International Pvt. Ltd. a wholly-owned subsidiary company of GIC is established. In Kenya Kenindia Assurance Ltd. is in joint venture with GIC. In UK wholly owned subsidiary called New India International Ltd. is registered.

The following companies are doing general insurance business in India in the public and private sector.

Table 15.3: General Insurance Companies in India

GENERAL INSURERS
Public Sector
National Insurance Company Limited
New India Assurance Company Limited
Oriental Insurance Company Limited
United India Insurance Company Limited
Private Sector
Bajaj Allianz General Insurance Co. Limited
ICICI Lombard General Insurance Co. Ltd.
IFFCO-Tokio General Insurance Co. Ltd.
Reliance General Insurance Co. Limited
Royal Sundaram Alliance Insurance Co. Ltd.
TATA AIG General Insurance Co. Limited
Cholamandalam General Insurance Co. Ltd.
Export Credit Guarantee Corporation
HDFC Chubb General Insurance Co. Ltd.
RE-INSURER
General Insurance Corporation of India

GICs Investment Policy

The GIC's had a prudent conservative and rational investment policy with the purpose of fulfilling national priorities. The GIC's in comparison with the LIC were less important in their activities in the NIM. They underwrote capital issues. In small and medium issues and non-group companies and as kept the national priorities in mind. It promoted those companies which did not find support with larger financial institutions.

GIC's pattern of investments is diversified for purposes of liquidity and high return on investments. It had a well balanced portfolio. It has investments in Central and State Government Securities, debentures and equity shares of companies. It also gave loans to banks under participating and bills re-discounting schemes.

GIC's investments are influential in the India Capital Market. Unlike the LIC, the GIC is an active underwriter of capital issues and purchaser of industrial securities. It continues its policy of taking on its portfolio those securities which combine liquidity with maximum return on its portfolio. Reforms were made in 1992 in the insurance sector to make it more efficient and functional. The Malhotra Committee proposed certain changes in its structure and investment pattern. Restructuring the GIC was important in the light of the experience of running the general insurance business. When GIC was nationalized it had been formed with a holding company and four subsidiaries. The subsidiaries had gained experience in functioning and administration. The Malhotra Committee suggested that four subsidiaries should be made. Shares should be held by government and 50% by the public and employees of the General Insurance Companies.

In its investments GIC would be allowed to invest 55% of the annual accretion of funds or additional premium income in the private corporate securities through the financial market. 20% of the share would be in the Central Government Securities, 10% in the State Government Securities and 15% in the housing loans to HUDCO. Thus the share of the private sector was increased from 30% to 55% whereas; other securities were reduced from 70% to 45%.

Premiums from General Insurance

A large volume of funds is collected through various kinds of insurance policies. This is taken in the form of yearly premiums. There are different kinds of policies. General Insurance provides protection against unforeseen events such as accidents, illness, fire, burglary General Insurance does not offer returns but is a protection against contingencies. Products that have a financial value in life and have a probability of getting lost, stolen or damaged can be covered through General Insurance policy. Some of them are fire insurance, marine insurance Property (both movable and immovable), vehicle, cash, household goods, health. Under certain Acts of Parliament, some types of insurance like Motor Insurance and Public Liability Insurance have been made compulsory. Major insurance policies that are covered under General Insurance are: home, health, motor and travel insurance.

The insurance regulatory authority has provided data showing gross direct premium income under written by non life insurance companies for the year 2005-06. This is depicted in Table 15.4. The premiums for the year are given for GIC and its subsidiaries and private companies. The GICs had a total premium of Rs. 15,976.44 crores. Amongst the private companies the ICICI Lombard had the highest collection of premium. Its gross premium for the year was Rs. 15,82.86 crores. Bajaj Allianz was second in premium collection it had Rs. 12,72.29 crores.

Table 15.4: Gross direct premium income underwritten by non-life insurers 2005-06

(Rs crore)

S. No.	Insurer	Fire	Misc	Marine	Total Premium in India	Total Premium including business outside India
1.	National	483.94	2866.30	173.43	3523.67	3536.34
2.	New India	839.63	3652.08	299.78	4791.50	5675.54
3.	Oriental	546.89	2655.11	325.11	3527.11	3609.77
4.	United	645.48	2305.33	203.97	3154.78	3154.78
	Sub-Total	**2515.94**	**11478.83**	**1002.29**	**14997.06**	**15976.44**
5.	Royal Sundaram	91.74	348.61	18.29	458.64	458.64
6.	Reliance	47.76	103.83	10.74	162.33	162.33
7.	IFFCO-Tokio	263.29	583.30	46.13	892.72	892.72
8.	Tata AIG	116.27	408.54	47.88	572.70	572.70
9.	ICICI Lombard	308.47	1188.68	85.71	1582.86	1582.86
10.	Bajaj Allianz	351.40	866.56	54.33	1272.29	1272.29
11.	Cholamandalam	72.83	130.35	17.00	220.18	220.18
12.	HDFC Chubb	5.82	192.28	1.72	199.81	199.81
	Sub-Total	**1257.59**	**3822.14**	**281.80**	**5361.53**	**5361.53**
	Grand Total	**3773.53**	**15300.97**	**1284.09**	**20358.59**	**21337.97**
13.	ECGC					577.33
14.	AIC					555.83

Source: Insurance Regulatory Development Authority.

REFORMS IN INSURANCE SECTOR

The Insurance Sector was working with low efficiency, low productivity, with limited products and poor quality insurance services. The R.N. Malhotra Committee had made several recommendations. As a result the Insurance Regulatory Development Act (IRDA) was passed in 1999. Insurance was opened up to private companies. The IRDA made several reforms on regulation of investment funds, adjudication of disputes between the insurers and intermediaries. With the liberal process the following new aspects were brought about.

Customer Friendly Service: Life Insurance business brought in new products for people. The introduction of flexible and realistic products to suit individuals has improved the insurance market. Products which short term guarantees have been brought about due to volatility in interest rates. Customer's awareness and education programmes have given them and insight into new product.

Marketing of Products: A large number of new products have been started. Every insurance company has to market is products to increase insurance density and insurance penetration levels by marketing new and better products through financial engineering and good services by agents, brokers and Third Party Administrations (TPAs).

Health Insurance: The introduction of health insurance through cashless hospitalization and modification in payment of insurance premium and issue of credit cards has been introduced in the liberalized reform period in India.

Pension Schemes: Life Insurance schemes are now entering into long term retirement savings and pension plans. ICICI prudential was the first to begun retirement planning schemes.

Unit Linked Products: The unit linked products have been flexible. The policy holders have a choice of the amount of premium to pay and the level of the sum assured and the fund in which they would like to invest. There is transparency in charges to the insurers and the net asset values and portfolio allocations of various funds are continuously available. These products are very attractive for the consumer.

Service to Customers: Life Insurance business has become very friendly towards its customers. It provides them with good service and advice. The settlement of claims is done quickly. They reply to customers emails and respond to complaints. Their website can be easily accessed by consumers. Information is readily available for all the insurance products.

Entry of Banks in Insurance Business: The insurance sector has expanded to a great extent. It is now one of the functions of banks. The banks collaborate with life insurance companies to market and distribute insurance products.

The RBI has permitted banks participation in setting up separate joint venture insurance company with risk participation; they have also allowed the banks to participate in fees based insurance services without risk participation and to invest in insurance companies for providing infrastructure and services support.

Entry of Co-operative Credit Institutions in Insurance Business: The co-operative operating in rural areas has also been permitted to distribute insurance product. In 2003 they were permitted to undertake insurance business as corporate agents without risk participation. However, the co-operative which were permitted to enter insurance business have to be financially strong with a minimum net worth of Rs. 100 crores.

Rural Regional Banks in Insurance Business: In 2004, the RBI also permitted the regional rural banks to enter into insurance business if they fulfilled the terms and conditions of positive net worth, NPAs of less than 10%, profits and last 3 years and no accumulated losses. In addition they should fulfil the requirement of complying with prudential norms.

Non-bank Financial Companies in Insurance Business: The RBI opened up insurance business for non bank financial companies in 2000. The registered companies were permitted to setup joint ventures in insurance business with risk participations and were allowed to undertake insurance business as agents on the basis of fees without any risk participation.

Foreign Direct Investment in Insurance Business: In the insurance sector the foreign direct investment was liberalized. They were permitted upto 26% through the automatic route if approved by IRDA. In 2004-05, this was raised to 49%. The companies interested in the foreign equity were to expand their equity base of the existing company or open a new company. The money should be remitted in foreign currency and the proposal should be under the automatic route.

CONTROLS BY IRDA

The Insurance Regulatory Development Authority (IRDA) act was passed in 1999 to regulate, promote and ensure growth of insurance and re-insurance business. It has notified 27 Regulations on insurance companies. These are Registration of Insurers, Regulation on insurance agents, Solvency Margin, Re-insurance, Obligation of Insurers to Rural and Social sector, Investment and Accounting Procedure and protection of policy holders' interest.

Registration of Insurance Company: The IRDA issues licenses and gives registration certificate to insurance companies. Every insurance company has to apply for a licence and if the IRDA is satisfied with the working of the company it may grant a license. However, it will review the financial soundness of the company. It will also take into account the experience and expertise and of the management. On review if the IRDA finds that the insurance company can be given a license it will give it a certificate of registration. Applications were invited by it with effect from 15th August, 2000 for issue of the Certificate of Registration to both life and non-life insurers.

Guidelines for Investment of Funds: The IRDA has framed some important guidelines for insurance companies to follow. These guidelines pertain to the proportion of funds in specified securities. According to the directive, the general insurance companies have to strictly abide by the restrictions on investing funds in stock market securities. They can invest 55% of their fund in approved market securities. They also required investing a minimum of 30% of their funds in government securities and 15% in housing projects which is inclusive of fire fighting equipments of state government.

Monitor Activities of Intermediaries: The IRDA is empowered to give license to the agents and brokers of the insurance companies. It also continuously monitors the activities of the insurance companies and the dealings of the intermediaries. If at any time the agents or the brokers are not entering into transparent deals the IRDA is empowered to take action against them by cancellation of their registration/licensing certificates.

Control of Surveyors: The IRDA issues licenses to surveyors and loss assessors. In the event of losses surveyors interact with insurers to assess their losses. The IRDA is strict about the behaviour of surveyors with clients. It is necessary for them to be fair in their dealings and not to delay in the process of assessing losses. The IRDA will renew licenses only if it is satisfied with the activities of the surveyors.

Price of Products: One of the important reforms in the insurance sector was to price the products reasonably. The IRDA has to be satisfied with the new products marketed by insurance companies. It also has the powers to oversee the pricing of the product. It can control the price and premium rates of the products. This power has been given to it as the chairman of IRDA is the ex-officio chairman of Tariff Advisory Committee (TAC). The price of products and premium is fixed by TAC but the IRDA has the powers to make changes to the prices if it wants to control the price of a product.

Solvency Margin: The IRDA strictly controls insurance companies on their solvency margins. If the companies do not maintain this margin IRDA can take disciplinary action against the defaulting company.

Investigation and Inspection of Companies: The IRDA has powers to appoint an investigator to make an inquiry against any insurance company. The appointed investigator is required to report on the activities of the insurance company as required by IRDA. On the basis of this report disciplinary action can be taken and the company can loose its certificate of registration/license.

Accounts of Insurance Companies: All insurance companies have to prepare balance sheet, annual profit and loss account and a receipt and payments account. They also have to prepare revenue account of each class of business done by them. It has to be audited by a charted accountant and it has to be filed with IRDA.

Appointment of Actuary: The IRDA has issued orders to every insurance company that they must appoint an actuary. It is mandatory to appoint a qualified actuary as specified by IRDA. The qualifications, functions and duties of actuaries have been prescribed by IRDA.

Appointment of Managing Director: An insurance company has to take an approval from IRDA before appointing a managing director, chief executive or whole time director of an insurance company. The IRDA has the powers to appoint any additional directors of the company. It can also remove a director from his position if it is not satisfied with the qualifications or working ability of the management staff.

Monitor Reinsurance Programs: IRDA controls the reinsurance programs of insurance companies. They continuously monitor the programs of the insurers and re-insurers. Insurance companies have been directed by IRDA to give a proportion of their premium to the designated Indian re-insurers. The insurers have to report to IRDA about their outward and inward activities and take approvals from IRDA to continue their reinsurance programme.

Protection of Policy Holder

Protection of Policyholders Interest Regulations 2001 was passed to provide the policy holders relief from unscrupulous life insurance companies. The IRDA issued directives to companies to prepare policy proposal documents in easy and understandable language. The companies were to provide claims procedure in both life and non-life policies. They were to setup grievance redressal machinery for speedy settlement of claims; and policyholders' servicing. The Regulation also provides for payment of interest by insurers for the delay in settlement of claim.

The insurance companies have to disclose clearly the benefits, terms and conditions under the policy and the advertisements issued by the insurers should not mislead the insuring public.

The IRDA would take up complaints received from the policyholders in connection with services provided by them under the insurance contract.

New Insurance Schemes

Many new insurance products have been started in India since 1991. Some of its new schemes to suit the different types of customers are given below. It has taken care to bring schemes for weaker section of the society, the old and aged, schemes for social security and health.

Social Security Group Scheme: Life Insurance Corporation of India has started the social security group scheme to fulfill the requirements of the weaker section of the society. This scheme is an insurance cover of Rs.5000 for natural death and of Rs. 25,000 due to accidental death. It covers people in the age group of 18-60 years.

Shiksha Sahyog Yojana: This scheme provides an educational scholarship of Rs. 300 per quarter per child and it is given for a period of four years. It is working since December 31, 2001.

Jan Arogya Bima Policy: This scheme has a coverage fixed at Rs. 5,000 per annum. It covers a special group of population who are unable to pay for high cost of medical treatments. The premium is low. It is Rs. 70 for adults' up to the age of 45 years and for children it is Rs. 50.

Mediclaim Insurance Policy: This policy is a cashless system of payment in hospitals through Third Party Assures. It is a system of reimbursing the medical expenses. It covers the people of the age group from 5-80 years. There is a deduction from income up to Rs. 10,000. This tax benefit can be availed by the person who takes a medical insurance.

Jana Shree Bima Yojana: On August 10th, 2000 this group scheme was launched. It requires a minimum membership of 25 people in a group. The insurance coverage is of Rs. 2,000 on natural death and Rs. 50,000 for accidental death. The premium amount is fixed at Rs. 200 for single member.

Videsh Yatra Mitra Policy: One of the important requirements of people was to take a medical insurance while traveling abroad. In 1998 four General Insurance Companies started the Videsh Yatra Mitra Policy for providing benefits for medical expenses during the period of overseas travel.

Bhagya Shree Child Welfare Bima Yojana: On October 19, 1998 the policy to cover one girl child in a family was started. It would cover the child upto the age of 18 but the condition is that her parents' age should not exceed 60 years. It has a premium of Rs.15 per annum.

Raj Rajeshwari Mahila Kalyan Yojana: On October 19,1998 this scheme was introduced to provide protection to woman in the age group of 10 to 75 years with an insurance of Rs. 25,000 and premium Rs. 15 per annum.

Ashray Bima Yojana: This Scheme was especially designed for workers. The policy covers workers in case of loss of jobs. The worker is given assistance of a maximum amount of Rs. 3,000 given to the till he/she gets an alternative job. This scheme is operative since October 10, 2001.

Personal Accident Insurance Scheme for Kissan Credit Card: This scheme was introduced in 2001. The Kissan Credit Card holders are covered up to an age of 70 years. Insurance coverage includes 50,000 for accidental death and 25,000 for partial disability.

Universal Health Insurance Scheme: This Insurance policy is specially created for groups of 100 or more families. In this scheme there is a reimbursement of medical expenses upto Rs. 3,0000 towards hospitalization for the members of the family, death cover due to an accident for Rs. 25,000 to the earning head of the family and compensation due to loss of earning head of the family @ Rs. 50 per day upto a maximum of 15 days. This becomes operative after a period of three days, of hospitalization of the head of the family. The premium under the policy is Rs. 1 per day which is Rs. 365 per annum for an individual. For a family of five limited to spouse and children it is Rs. 1.50 per day or Rs. 548 per annum and Rs. 2 per day or Rs. 730 per annum for a family size of seven. It covers dependent parents. A subsidy of Rs. 100 per year towards annual premium for "Below Poverty Life" families is also provided under the Scheme. This scheme is applicable to any hospital which is registered with the local authorities or run NGOs/Trusts/selected private hospitals with fixed schedule of charges. Hospitalization should be for a minimum period of 24 hours. The time limit is not applicable to some specific treatments which do not require 24 hours of hospitalization. The age limit for this scheme is 5 to 65 years.

Varishtha Pension Bima Yojana: This scheme has been designed for Indian citizens of 55 years and above. It is a pension scheme and does not have any upper age ceiling. Pension in this scheme will be paid during the lifetime of the pensioner. If the person dies the purchase price will be paid to the nominee/legal heir of the pensioner. The minimum pension would be Rs. 250 and maximum Rs. 2,000 per month. Only one person from a family can apply. The family for this purpose would comprise of the pensioner, his/her spouse and dependants. Only purchase price is payable in one lump-sum. The exit option would be after 15 years.

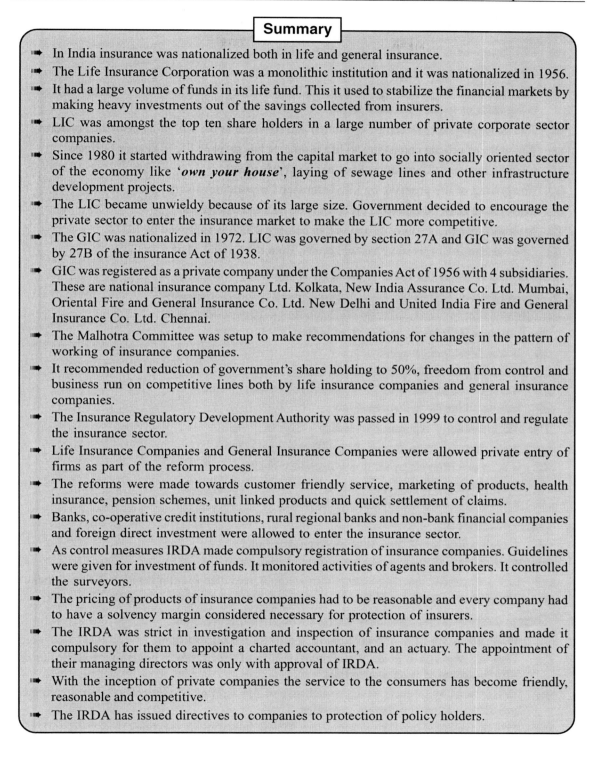

Summary

➡ In India insurance was nationalized both in life and general insurance.

➡ The Life Insurance Corporation was a monolithic institution and it was nationalized in 1956.

➡ It had a large volume of funds in its life fund. This it used to stabilize the financial markets by making heavy investments out of the savings collected from insurers.

➡ LIC was amongst the top ten share holders in a large number of private corporate sector companies.

➡ Since 1980 it started withdrawing from the capital market to go into socially oriented sector of the economy like '*own your house*', laying of sewage lines and other infrastructure development projects.

➡ The LIC became unwieldy because of its large size. Government decided to encourage the private sector to enter the insurance market to make the LIC more competitive.

➡ The GIC was nationalized in 1972. LIC was governed by section 27A and GIC was governed by 27B of the insurance Act of 1938.

➡ GIC was registered as a private company under the Companies Act of 1956 with 4 subsidiaries. These are national insurance company Ltd. Kolkata, New India Assurance Co. Ltd. Mumbai, Oriental Fire and General Insurance Co. Ltd. New Delhi and United India Fire and General Insurance Co. Ltd. Chennai.

➡ The Malhotra Committee was setup to make recommendations for changes in the pattern of working of insurance companies.

➡ It recommended reduction of government's share holding to 50%, freedom from control and business run on competitive lines both by life insurance companies and general insurance companies.

➡ The Insurance Regulatory Development Authority was passed in 1999 to control and regulate the insurance sector.

➡ Life Insurance Companies and General Insurance Companies were allowed private entry of firms as part of the reform process.

➡ The reforms were made towards customer friendly service, marketing of products, health insurance, pension schemes, unit linked products and quick settlement of claims.

➡ Banks, co-operative credit institutions, rural regional banks and non-bank financial companies and foreign direct investment were allowed to enter the insurance sector.

➡ As control measures IRDA made compulsory registration of insurance companies. Guidelines were given for investment of funds. It monitored activities of agents and brokers. It controlled the surveyors.

➡ The pricing of products of insurance companies had to be reasonable and every company had to have a solvency margin considered necessary for protection of insurers.

➡ The IRDA was strict in investigation and inspection of insurance companies and made it compulsory for them to appoint a charted accountant, and an actuary. The appointment of their managing directors was only with approval of IRDA.

➡ With the inception of private companies the service to the consumers has become friendly, reasonable and competitive.

➡ The IRDA has issued directives to companies to protection of policy holders.

Objective Type Questions, Answer True (T) or False (F)

(a) Life insurance is a monolithic institution in India.

(b) General Insurance Companies have many operations in India and abroad.

(c) The Insurance Regulatory Authority of India is an Independent body established to control and bring reforms to the insurance sector.

(d) The managing director can be appointed and removed at the will of an insurance company

(e) The entry of private companies to life insurance has reduced life insurance business.

(f) General Insurance Companies have not been privatized.

(g) The pricing of life products by Life Insurance Corporation is very low.

(h) Banks have been permitted to enter into life insurance business.

(i) Insurance companies have to appoint an actuary which is approved by IRDA.

(j) Life Insurance Corporation has withdrawn from the Capital Market in India.

Answer: (a) F, (b) T, (c) T, (d) F, (e) F, (f) F, (g) F, (h) T, (i) T, (j) T.

Multiple Choice Questions (Tick mark (✓) the right answer)

1. The Insurance Regulatory Authority of India:
   (a) It is a development agency.
   (b) It is a regulatory and development body.
   (c) It is a development body for expanding insurance business
   (d) It is an authority in insurance law

2. The Life Insurance Corporation of India:
   (a) It is a monolithic institution doing life business in India
   (b) It is an autonomous board doing insurance business in India
   (c) It is a nationalized institution doing life business in India
   (d) It is an apex insurance regulatory authority.

3. Health insurance is:
   (a) A core policy for all insurance companies in India.
   (b) Mediclaim is the only health insurance company in India.
   (c) Life and general insurance companies are both permitted to offer health policies in India.
   (d) The exclusive business of health promotional product companies in India.

4. General insurance companies have the following investment pattern:
   (a) They can invest 55% of their fund in approved market securities.
   (b) They are required to invest a minimum of 30% of their funds in government securities and 70% in approved market securities.
   (c) 15% in housing projects which is inclusive of fire fighting equipments of state government and 85% in approved market securities.
   (d) 45% in approved market securities and 55% in government securities.

5. An Endowment Policy is one in which the insured takes a life cover for a specific period of time:

    (a) At the expiry of the policy he receives the sum of the insurance policy.

    (b) The insurer has the advantage of receiving money at regular intervals of the policy with a specific sum of money at the expiry of the policy.

    (c) The premium cost is high. If the insured dies, the nominee receives the insurance amount.

    (d) It covers the insured for the whole life. His nominee receives the assured sum with bonus after the date of insured.

    Answers: 1 (b), 2 (c), 3 (c), 4 (a), 5(a).

Short Answer Questions

1. Discuss the objective of Life Insurance Corporation.

2. Give the recommendations of Malhotra Committee which was appointed in 1993.

3. What are the different kinds of life and non-life policies in India?

4. Discuss the health insurance policy in India.

Long Answer Questions

1. Discuss the insurance sector reforms in India based on the Malhotra Committee recommendations.

2. What is the role of private life insurance companies in India?

3. What is General Insurance? How do they operate and do business in India?

4. What is the pattern of investments of life insurance and non-insurance in India?

Chapter 16

Unit Trust of India and Mutual Funds

Chapter Plan

- Structure of UTI
- Restructure of UTI and Mutual Fund
- Methodology of Operations
- Objectives of Investing in Mutual Fund

- Classification of Mutual Funds
- Net Asset Value
- Schemes of Unit Trust of India
- Significant Mutual Fund Companies in India

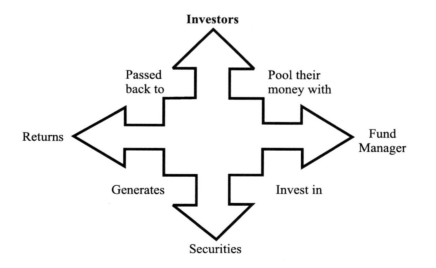

Fig. 16.1: Mechanisms of Mutual Funds

INTRODUCTION

Mutual fund is a mechanism of pooling resources by issuing units to investors and investing their funds in securities to get a good return. Out of the return received the mutual fund keeps a margin for its costs and distributes the profits to the investors. These funds have to be invested according to the objectives provided in offer documents. Investments in securities are spread across a wide cross-section of industries and sectors and thus the risk is reduced. Unit Trust of India was the first mutual fund which was started in India Units as a form of investment is issued by the Unit Trust of India which is a public sector financial institution.

Unit Trust of India began its operations with an initial capital of Rs. 5 crores jointly subscribed by Industrial Development Bank of India, Life Insurance Corporation of India, State Bank of India, Commercial Banks and other financial institutions. In addition, the Unit Trust of India has a unit capital. The unit capital varies from year to year and depends on the subscription of the investors.

The Unit Trust of India (UTI) is a public sector financial institution. It issues *units* as a form of investment.

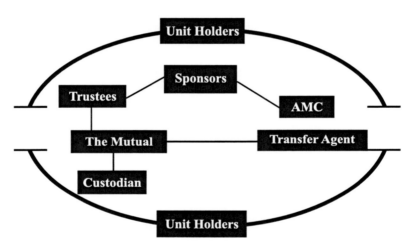

Fig. 16.2: Structure of Mutual Fund

STRUCTURE OF UTI

The role of the Unit Trust of India is to fulfill the objectives of mobilizing savings especially from the household sector and re-investing these funds into different investments outlets. Unit Trust of India was managed by a competent Board of Trustees. Its Chairman is appointed by the Central Government. It also has an Executive Trustee and four other Members who look after the saving of the investors. These members are appointed by the Industrial Development Bank of India, Reserve Bank of India, Life Insurance Corporation of India, and sometimes by commercial banks.

In 1996 SEBI regulations became uniformly applicable to the mutual funds. UTI Mutual Fund is managed by UTI Asset Management Company Private Limited and it was established on Jan 14, 2003.

It has been appointed by the UTI Trustee Company Private Limited for managing the schemes of UTI Mutual Fund and the schemes transferred/migrated from UTI Mutual Fund. UTI Mutual Fund has come into existence with effect from 1st February 2003. UTI Asset Management Company manages a corpus of Rs. 340,500 million and it is the largest in the world.

RESTRUCTURE OF UTI AND MUTUAL FUNDS

The SEBI regulation act of 1996 has defined a mutual fund as one, which is constituted in the form of a Trust under the Indian Trust Act 1882. The structure of a mutual fund consists of an Asset Management Company, sponsor and board of trustees. These are explained below.

Asset Management Company

The asset management company manages the funds of a mutual fund by diversifying its investments in different type of securities. The company has to be registered with SEBI and is setup as a trust. It works under the guidelines of SEBI.

Sponsor

A sponsor has the powers to appoint a person or a body corporate which establishes a mutual fund. It also appoints a Board of Trustees to manage the Trust according to the provisions provided by SEBI.

Board of Trustees

The board of trustees is in a position of trust and confidence mainly for the benefit of the unit holders. The trustees select stock according to the price, quantity of stock and their investment policy. They operate upon the fact that the investors have limited knowledge of the environment as well as of the quality of the investments and its management are superior to the investment in funds by a single naive investor. They are able to draw upon the special dividend as well as capital appreciation factors of a particular security. Their specialized knowledge helps them to diversify in those stocks which give the ideal combination of securities.

The trustees appoint custodian, bankers, and registrar and transfer agents to provide financial services to the mutual funds.

Development of Mutual Fund Industry

The formation of Unit Trust of India in 1963 was the starting point of mutual fund industry in India. The Government of India and Reserve Bank took a major step in initiating the UTI. The history of mutual funds in India is divided into four distinct phases.

First Phase – 1964-87

Unit Trust of India (UTI) was established on 1963 by an Act of Parliament. It was supervised by the Regulatory and administrative control of the Reserve Bank of India. In 1978 UTI was de-linked from the RBI and the Industrial Development Bank of India (IDBI) took over the regulatory and administrative control from the RBI. In 1964 the first scheme was started by UTI.

Second Phase – 1987-93 (Entry of Public Sector Funds)

In 1987 non-UTI, public sector mutual funds were permitted to enter the mutual fund industry by public sector banks and Life Insurance Corporation of India (LIC) and General Insurance Corporation of India (GIC). SBI Mutual Fund was the first non-UTI Mutual Fund established in June 1987 followed by Canbank Mutual Fund in December 1987 Punjab National Bank Mutual Fund in August 1989, Indian Bank Mutual Fund in November 1989, Bank of India in June 1990, Bank of Baroda Mutual Fund in October 1992. LIC established its mutual fund in June 1989 while GIC had set up its mutual fund in December 1990.

Third Phase – 1993-03 (Entry of Private Sector Funds)

In 1993 private sector banks were permitted to enter into mutual fund industry in this year. The first Mutual Fund Regulations came into being, under which all mutual funds, except UTI were to be registered and governed. The Kothari Pioneer which is presently merged with Franklin Templeton was the first private sector mutual fund registered in July 1993. The 1993 a more comprehensive and revised Mutual Fund Regulations came into force. In 1996 the industry was brought under the SEBI (Mutual Fund) Regulations.

The number of mutual funds increased with many foreign mutual funds setting up funds in India and also the industry went through mergers and acquisitions. As at the end of January 2003, there were 33 mutual funds.

Fourth Phase – February 2003-07

In February 2003, the Unit Trust of India Act 1963 was repealed UTI was bifurcated into two separate entities. One is the Specified Undertaking of the Unit Trust of India with assets under management of Rs.29,835 crores as at the end of January 2003, representing broadly, the assets of US 64 scheme, assured return and certain other schemes. The Specified Undertaking of Unit Trust of India, functioning under an administrator and under the rules framed by Government of India and does not come under the purview of the Mutual Fund Regulations.[1]

The second is the UTI Mutual Fund Ltd., sponsored by State Bank of India (SBI), Punjab National Bank (PNB), Bank of Baroda (BOB) and LIC. It is registered with SEBI and functions under the Mutual Fund Regulations. With the bifurcation of the UTI which had in March 2000 more than Rs. 76,000 crores of assets under management and with the setting up of a UTI Mutual Fund, conforming to the SEBI Mutual Fund Regulations, and with recent mergers taking place among different private sector funds, the mutual fund industry is in the phase of consolidation and growth. As at the end of September, 2004, there were 29 funds and in 2007 they were 33 funds.

Growth of Mutual Fund Assets

The growth of assets of the mutual fund industry is phenomenal. At the end of 1988 UTI had Rs. 6,700 crores of assets under management.

In 1993 the mutual fund industry had total assets of Rs. 1,21,805 crores. The Unit Trust of India had the highest fund with Rs. 44,541 crores of assets at the end of 1993, the mutual fund industry had

---

1. Source Association of Mutual Funds in India handbook.

assets of Rs. 47,004 crores. In 2004 the mutual fund industry had 29 funds, 421 schemes and assets of Rs. 1,53,108 crores under their management. In 2007 the funds under the management of mutual funds increased manifold to Rs. 1,218.05 billion and there were 33 mutual funds.

Table 16.1 : Net Resources Mobilised by Mutual Funds

(Rupees crore)

Year	UTI*	Bank-sponsored mutual funds	FI-sponsored mutual funds	Private ector mutual funds	Total (2 to 5)
1	2	3	4	5	6
1970-71	18	—	—	—	18
1971-72	15.1	—	—	—	15.1
1972-73	23.2	—	—	—	23.2
1973-74	30.6	—	—	—	30.6
1974-75	17.2	—	—	—	17.2
1975-76	29	—	—	—	29
1976-77	34.6	—	—	—	34.6
1977-78	73.3	—	—	—	73.3
1978-79	101.5	—	—	—	101.5
1979-80	57.9	—	—	—	57.9
1980-81	52.1	—	—	—	52.1
1981-82	157.4	—	—	—	157.4
1982-83	166.9	—	—	—	166.9
1983-84	330.2	—	—	—	330.2
1984-85	756.2	—	—	—	756.2
1985-86	891.8	—	—	—	891.8
1986-87	1,261.1	—	—	—	1,261.1
1987-88	2,059.4	250.3	—	—	2,309.7
1988-89	3,855	319.7	—	—	4,174.8
1989-90	5,583.6	888.1	315.3	—	6,786.9
1990-91	4553	2,351.9	603.5	—	7,508.4
1991-92	8,685.4	2,140.4	427.1	—	11,253
1992-93	1,1057	1204	760	—	13,021
1993-94	9,297	148.1	238.6	1559.5	11,243
	− 7453				
1994-95	8611	765.5	576.3	1321.8	11,275
	− 6800				
1995-96	− 6314	113.3	234.8	133	− 5832.9
	(− 2877.0)				
1996-97	− 3043.0 @	5.9	136.9	863.6	− 2036.7
	(− 855.0)@				
1997-98	2875	236.9	203.4	748.6	4063.9
	− 2592				

1998-99	170	− 88.3	546.8	2,066.9	**2,695.4**
	− 1,300				
1999-00	4,548	335.9	295.5	16,937.4	**22,117**
	− 5,762				
2000-01	322	247.8	1,272.8	9,292.1	**11,135**
	− 1,201				
2001-02	− 7,284	862.8	406.8	16,134.1	**10,120**
	(− 6,119.0)				
2002-03	− 9,434.1	1,033.4	861.5	12,122.2	**4,583**
2003-04	1,049.9 **	4,526.2	786.8	41,509.8	**47,873**
2004-05	− 2,467.2 #	706.5	− 3,383.5	7,933.1	**2,788.9**
2005-06	3,423.8 #	5,364.9	2,111.9	4,1581	**52,482**
2006-07 P	7,326.1 #	3032	4,226.1	7,6687	**91,271**

P : Provisional.
FI : Financial Institution.
*   For Unit Trust of India (UTI), data are gross values (with premium) of net sales under all domestic schemes.
@   Excludes re-investment sales.
**   Data pertain to UTI Mutual Fund for the period February 01, 2003 to March 31, 2004, being the first year in operation after the bifurcation of the erstwhile UTI into UTI Mutual Fund and Specified Undertaking of the Unit Trust of India.
#   Data pertain to UTI Mutual Fund only.
Note :
1. Data in parentheses pertain to net sales at face value (excluding premium).
2. Data from 1970-71 to 1990-91 for UTI relate to July-June period.
    Also see Notes on Tables.
Source : UTI and Respective Mutual Funds.

METHODOLOGY OF OPERATIONS

Unit Trust of India assures to the investor a safe return of the investment. The trust provides daily price record in its open end scheme and advertises it in the newspapers. The purchase price as well as the sale price of the units is quoted daily. This price fluctuates daily, but the fluctuations are nominal on a monthly basis. The price, however, varies between the month of July and the month of June. The purchase price of units is the lowest in the month of July and an investor seeking investment may purchase his units at this time of the year and receive the lowest offer price for the units. Every year dividend is declared on units on June 30. In June, therefore, price of units is the highest. The face value of the unit is Rs. 10. At any time the re-purchase price of the units will be lower than the price at which it will sell to the investor. The investor, however, is safe in this investment because he may buy his units in July at the lower price and sell back to the Unit Trust of India in June when the price is higher. This will offset any loss to him. The Unit Trust purchases back the units at the operating price at the time of re-purchase of units. The investor can, thus, safely purchase these units and sell them back to the Unit Trust of India, if need be. If he does not sell them he is assured of the safety of the return in the form of dividends.

SEBI and Mutual Fund Regulation

SEBI regulated the mutual funds to protect the interest on the investors. In 1996 new guidelines were issued to regulate the mutual fund investments in India. Some of the important provisions are:

- All mutual funds must be compulsory registered with SEBI.

- The sponsors of mutual funds should have contributed a minimum of 40% of the net worth of the Asset Management Company and should have a record of good reputation in financial services for at least 5 years.

- All new mutual funds schemes have to be approved by the trustees of the mutual fund.

- Mutual funds have to follow investments norms provided by SEBI to protect the investor from high-risk exposure.

- A report has to be published by the mutual fund for each new scheme that it launches.

- A mutual fund has to published sale price and repurchase price of a unit in open-ended scheme at least once a week.

- The repurchase price of a unit should not be less than 93% of NAV and sale price should not be more than 107% NAV. In closed ended scheme the repurchase price should not be less than 95% of the NAV.

- SEBI permits mutual funds to participate in its Security Lending Scheme.

- SEBI permits mutual funds to invest in Indian and Foreign ADRs and GDRs within its guidelines.

- SEBI has provided that 90% of the mutual fund profits should be distributed every year and the earnings have to be shown as current income, short term capital gains and long term capital gain.

- To protect the investors SEBI can impose monetary penalties on mutual funds for violating regulations and guidelines.

OBJECTIVES OF INVESTING IN MUTUAL FUND

Units have many benefits for the investor. It provides security to the small investor as it can be easily converted into liquid cash. It is of nominal value of Rs. 10 each but this varies from day to day depending on its net asset value (NAV) which is widely advertised.

In India, there are a large number of mutual funds. All mutual funds are under the regulatory framework of the Securities Exchange Board of India.

The mutual fund concept is based on sharing of risks and rewards. The profits or losses are shared by the investors in proportion to their investments. The income and capital appreciation arising out of investments are shared among the investors. Their securities are subject to market risk.

The mutual funds have specific objectives for the investor. They have certain representatives called trustees who look after their funds and diversify them into proper portfolio. This diversification is made in the combination of dividend income and capital growth. The diversification pattern involves common stocks, preference shares and bonds. They also diversify according to companies, industries, size of companies and age of companies and have a combination of both risky and non-risky portfolios. Mutual funds are established in a form of a Trust. The Trust consists of Sponsor, Board of Trustees, Asset Management Company (AMC) and a Custodian and a Trust Agreement.

Every investment has advantages and disadvantages. But it's important to remember that features that matter to one investor may not be important to another. Whether any particular feature is an advantage for a person will depend on his unique circumstances. For some investors, mutual funds provide an attractive investment choice because they generally offer the following features:

Management: The professional consultants have the specialized knowledge due to expertise and training in evaluating investments. The have superiority in managing the portfolios.

Small Saver: Mutual funds accommodate investors who don't have a lot of money to invest by setting relatively low rupee value for initial purchases, subsequent monthly purchases, or both.

Liquidity: Mutual fund investors can readily redeem their shares at the current NAV plus any fees and charges assessed on redemption at any time. Investments made in units give the advantage of liquidity to the investor. The investor may purchase the units and sell them at any time in an open ended scheme. The small investor does not even have to find any other investor in the stock exchange or wait for the liquidity of his funds. The terms of payment on re-purchase are low.

Diversification: Diversification reduces the risk because all stocks may not move in the same direction in the same proportion at the same time. Share prices can move up or down. The investor should be aware of these risks while making an investment decision. Even with risks it is expected that the mutual funds are able to perform better than an individual because a careful selection of securities over a diversified portfolio covering large number of companies and industries is made and the portfolio is constantly reviewed. Spreading investments across a wide range of companies and industry sectors can help to lower risk.

Analysis and Selection of Securities: Mutual funds select a large share of equities in the case of growth schemes. Although this has a greater risk and potential for capital appreciation is higher in growth schemes. Besides growth schemes mutual funds also have income schemes. When they have income schemes they invest in securities of a guaranteed return. They generally select a large share of fixed income securities like debentures and bonds. All growth schemes are closed ended and income schemes are either closed ended or open ended.

Professional Management: Professional money managers research, select, and monitor the performance of the securities the fund purchases. This helps the investor in achieving a higher return than he would gain by investing in individual securities without professional help.

All mutual funds in the public sector, private sector and those promoted by foreign entities are governed by the same set of Regulations by SEBI, which is the controlling authority.

- Unit Trust of India was the first mutual fund set up in India in the year 1963.
- In 1987 Government allowed public sector banks and institutions to set up mutual funds.
- In 1992, Securities and exchange Board of India (SEBI) Act was passed to formulate policies and regulate the mutual funds to protect the interest of the investors.
- In 1993 mutual funds sponsored by private sector entities were allowed to enter the capital market.
- In 1996 SEBI revised its regulations to protect the interest of the investors.
- SEBI has also issued guidelines to the mutual funds in order to make the mutual funds as secure as possible for the investors.

CLASSIFICATION OF MUTUAL FUNDS

The Mutual Funds operate under the advantages of diversification, quality of management, and liquidity of funds. These companies are of different kinds. But the most important difference between them is that of closed end and open-end mutual funds. The following classification is given of mutual funds:

> **Types of Mutual Fund Schemes**
> **by Structure**
> - Open – Ended Schemes
> - Close – Ended Schemes
> - Interval Schemes
>   **By Investment Objective**
> - Growth Schemes
> - Income Schemes
> - Balance Schemes
> - Money Market Schemes
>   **Other Schemes**
> - Tax Saving Schemes
> - Special Schemes
>   Index Schemes
>   Sector Specific Schemes

Open-Ended

The Unit Trust of India is an open-end mutual fund company. The open-ended fund is one that is available for subscription and repurchase on a continuous basis. These schemes do not have a fixed maturity period. In such a company the purchase price and sale price change daily because of fluctuations in stock prices. The mutual funds repurchase shares directly from the investing public. The Investors can conveniently buy and sell units at Net Asset Value (NAV) related prices, which are declared on a daily basis. The key feature of open-end schemes is liquidity. The investors should take *load*s into consideration while making investment as these affect their yields/returns. A Load is a charge or a percentage of NAV for entry or exit. That is, each time one buys or sells units in the fund, a charge will be payable. This charge is used by the mutual fund for marketing and distribution expenses. Suppose the NAV per unit is Rs. 10. If the entry as well as exit load charged is 1%, then the investors who buy would be required to pay Rs. 10.10 and those who offer their units for repurchase to the mutual fund will get only Rs. 9.90 per unit. Efficient funds may give higher returns in spite of loads. Mutual funds cannot increase the load beyond the level which is printed in the offer document. If there is any change in the load it will be applicable only to prospective investments and not to the existing investments. In case mutual funds want to increase loads, they are required to amend their offer documents before approaching new investors. Sometimes there are no-load funds this means that there is no charge for entry or exit. It means the investors can enter the scheme at NAV and no additional charges are payable on purchase or sale of units.

Closed Ended

The closed end mutual funds are like any other company operating in an industry. Its main objective is to sell shares to the public, through public subscription. It has its own Memorandum of Association and Articles of Association and Prospectus. It is listed on a stock exchange and its stocks and shares are treated on the stock exchange. Such a company can make additional issues to the public. They can sell their shares at any value above or below the net asset value of their shares. The net asset value (NAV) of the shares is the total market value of funds, performance minus its liabilities divided by total number of shares outstanding. The shares of mutual fund companies often sell at a discount because the closed end companies are considered to be highly risky from the investor's point of view. A close-ended fund or scheme has a stipulated maturity period e.g., 5-7 years. In India, these companies usually belong to part of a group company and use the amount collected by it to put into expansion programs of the other group companies by giving them this amount as loan. The shares of these companies are very often traded at a great discount. When the discount is very high it is worthwhile for an investor to make investments. In these companies, units are listed in order to provide an exit route to the investors. Some close-ended funds give an option of selling back the units to the mutual fund through periodic repurchase at NAV related prices. According to SEBI regulations there should be at least one exit route for investors.

Income Fund

The aim of income funds is to provide regular and steady income to investors. Such schemes generally invest in fixed income securities such as bonds, corporate debentures, Government securities and money market instruments. Such funds are less risky compared to equity schemes because they are not affected with fluctuations that may take place in equity shares. Income Fund has the limitation that it is restricted with certain opportunities. They promise a regular income in the form of dividends but they do not have the advantage of capital appreciation.

Growth Funds

The aim of growth funds is to provide capital appreciation over the medium to long-term. Such schemes normally invest a major part of their corpus in equities. Such funds have comparatively high risks. These schemes provide different options to the investors like dividend option, capital appreciation. and the investors may choose an option depending on their preferences. The investors must indicate the option in the application form. The mutual funds also allow the investors to change the options at a later date. Growth schemes are good for investors having a long-term outlook seeking appreciation over a period of time.

Dual Funds Company: The dual funds company is also closed end. It operates with two different kinds of shares. It has both capital shares as well as income shares. If an investor wishes to buy stocks in such a company he must specify the kind of stock which he wants to purchase. If he purchases stock of capital gains then the return from the company to him will be only in the form of gains and capital. Thus, investors who purchase income shares will receive from the company only dividends and interest, which the company earns. This it will pass on to the investor. Such a company has a dual role and because of these roles it is thus named the dual fund investment company. The investor in such a company thus specifies the kind of interest that he has—capital appreciation or income appreciation. Such companies work well but the quality of management is very important because it is responsible for proper diversification and maintaining the balance of investments. The company has to have a proper combination of diversification into stocks of capital gains as well as stocks of dividend-yield companies.

Index Funds

Index Funds are invested by a mutual fund according to a particular index such as the BSE Sensitive index, S&P NSE 50 index (Nifty). These schemes invest in the securities in the same weight as that of an index. NAVs of such schemes are expected to rise or fall in accordance with the rise or fall in the index, by the same percentage. Information is given through the offer document of the mutual fund scheme. In the Unites States a new type of fund called the index fund is being operated. These funds are based on the fact that the costs are made as low as possible. The costs are taken into consideration by calculating beta. This is based on the Random Walk theory and investments are made according to the index fund by bringing down the unsystematic risk by proper diversification and reducing systematic risk through a study of the market factors with the risk and return factors.

Exchange Traded Funds (ETF)

These securities are listed on stock exchange they are quite similar to index funds and can be traded in the stock exchange. Such funds are different from mutual funds because they do not sell ETF directly to retail investors. An asset management company sponsors the ETF takes the shares of the company and in turn it issues a block of ETF units. The ETF portfolio value changes with the index therefore NAV of an ETF is usually higher than that of index fund of a similar portfolio. The price of ETF is determined by demand and supply conditions and market value of the shares. In India UTI mutual fund has an ETF called SUNDERS listed in Mumbai Stock Exchange. Some of the ETFs traded in American Stock Exchange are called QUBES (this represents NASDAQ 100) SPIDERS (SNP 500) DIAMONDS (Dow Jones Ind. Average).

Money Market Funds

The money market funds are operative, namely, in the United States Government Securities relating to short-term maturities. Large amounts are used for the purchase of these securities. These securities involve complete safety but the yields are not so high. For safety, investment companies make investments in these funds and pass on the benefits to the investors. In India the SEBI regulation 1996 has allowed money market funds to operate in commercial papers treasury bills and commercial bills. They are open-end funds for short-term use and they are completely safe.

Municipal Bond Funds

These funds are also exempt from tax in the Unites States and in the Unites States these are called unit trust. Unlike the Indian Unit Trust the United States Unit Trust does not make a continues offering to the public like tile open end funds. These are sold to the public from time to time whenever there is a new offering and the interest is paid monthly. In India, the incomes from municipal bonds are in the form of Post Office Savings, Pension Funds.

Pension Funds

The pension funds are operative both in India as well as in the United States. These funds are kept aside by an employer so that he can make payments to his employees after their retirement. In this fund also the method is to diversify a large pool of resources into income yielding securities and capital appreciation securities. It requires management of funds through proper consultant as it requires care and combination of securities.

Off Shore Funds

Domestic Funds are usually open within the country but off shore funds are those, which are subscribed in other countries. They bring foreign exchange to a capital market. In India there are off shore funds.

Balanced Fund

The aim of balanced funds is to provide both growth and regular income as such schemes invest both in equities and fixed income securities in the proportion indicated in their offer documents. These are appropriate for investors looking for moderate growth. They generally invest 40-60% in equity and debt instruments. These funds are also affected because of fluctuations in share prices in the stock markets. However, NAVs of such funds are likely to be less volatile compared to pure equity funds.

Gilt Fund

These funds invest exclusively in government securities. Government securities have no default risk. NAVs of these schemes also fluctuate due to change in interest rates and other economic factors as are the case with income or debt oriented schemes.

Sector Specific Fund

These are schemes, which invest in the securities of those sectors or industries, which are specified in the offer documents. For example, pharmaceuticals, software, consumer petroleum stocks. The returns in these funds depend on the performance of the industries. These funds usually give higher returns, but they are considered to be high risk compared to diversify funds.

Tax Saving Schemes

These schemes offer tax rebates to the investors under specific provisions of the Income Tax Act. Government offers tax incentives for investment in specified avenues. For example, equity linked savings schemes and pension schemes launched by the mutual funds offer tax benefits. These schemes are growth oriented and invest pre-dominantly in equities.

Fund of Funds

This scheme invests mainly in other schemes of the same mutual fund or other mutual funds are known as a fund of funds scheme. This scheme enables the investors to achieve greater diversification. It spreads risks and provides diversification.

The mutual funds market values change everyday. This is the region that the net asset value is calculated.

NET ASSET VALUE

The question, however, is whether the performance of open end mutual fund companies of managed funds in terms of performance is better than the performance of investments made by an individual because portfolios are equally important whether they are invested by a managed trust or by an individual. Mutual funds invest the money collected from the investors in securities markets. Market value of securities changes every day. This is the reason that NAV also varies from day to day. The NAV per unit is the market value of securities of a scheme divided by the total number of units of the scheme on any particular date. NAV can be calculated in the following way:

Example:

A mutual fund collected Rs. 8,00,00,000 by issuing Rs. 80,00,000 units of Rs. 10 each. The amount has been invested in different securities. The market value of these securities is Rs. 12,00,00,000 and the mutual fund has a liability of 50,00,000. Calculate Net Asset Value of the fund.

Solution:

$$\text{NAV} = \frac{\text{Market Value of Securities} - \text{Liabilities}}{\text{No. of Outstanding Units}}$$

$$\text{NAV} = \frac{12,00,00,000 - 50,00,000}{80,00,000}$$

$$= \frac{11,50,00,000}{80,00,000} = \text{Rs. } 14.375 \text{ per unit.}$$

Mutual Fund Investment Cost

Mutual funds have different kinds of expenses in order to run the business enterprise. These costs are called Operating Costs. These costs are administrative expenses, consultation fees given to trustees and expenses on Brokerage. These are calculated as shown in the example they are also called Expense Rotio. The operating costs are deducted from the closing NAV assets. This cost is spread out on the unit holders as they receive a reduced NAV to cover the costs of the mutual funds.

$$\text{Expense Ratio} = \frac{\text{Total Annual Operating Expense}}{\text{Average Assets under Management}}$$

A mutual fund has an annual expense of 50 lakhs. Assets in the beginning and end of the year were Rs. 2,50,00,000 and Rs. 7,00,00,000. Find the Expense Ratio.

Solution

$$\text{The expense ratio} = \frac{50,00,000}{2,50,00,000 + 7,00,00,000} \times 100 = 5.26\%.$$

Return from Mutual Fund

A mutual funds investment provides a return in a form of annual dividends and distribution of capital gains. Returns are calculated by taking into consideration dividends, capital gains, NAV in the beginning of the period and NAV in the end of the period. This is shown in the example 16.3.

$$\text{Return} = \frac{\text{Div} + \text{CG} + (\text{NAV}_1 - \text{NAV}_0)}{\text{NAV}_0}$$

Div   = Dividends.

CG   = Capital gain.

NAV_0 = NAV in the beginning.

NAV_1 = NAV at the end of the year.

$NAV_1 - NAV_0$ shows change over the period.

Example:

A mutual fund has a Nav of Rs. 10.60 in the beginning and Rs. 10.90 at the end of the period. Calculate the return of the mutual fund.

   (i)   When dividend of Rs. 2 is distributed.

  (ii)   If there is a capital gain also distribute of 0.50 Paisa.

Solution:

   (i)   Return $= \dfrac{2 + (10.90 - 10.60)}{10.60} \times 100 = 21.7\%$

  (ii)   When capital gain is distributed

$$= \dfrac{2 + 0.50\,(10.90 - 10.60)}{10.60} \times 100 = 20.75\%$$

SCHEMES OF UNIT TRUST OF INDIA

UTI has provided a large number of schemes of investors. These are very popular in India, due to the possibilities of providing suitable and risk-less return. Although some schemes may have a greater return than other, units by and large suit the needs of different kind of investors, and can cover a single small investor to a large investor.

While evaluating the investments under the Unit Trust investments and life policies the risk and return framework must be carefully studied. While these investments provide attractive benefits in the form of security, annual returns, liquidity, the greater disadvantage of this scheme is the purchasing power risk that it provides to an investor. Over the years inflationary trends have been increasing and especially so this has been noted in Indian conditions. One of the greatest disadvantages in fixed time securities is that the increase in return in investment is not high as the rise in prices. As a form of investment this is essential for every investor because of family protection and stability of income and tax benefits but for the prospects of growth, other investments may also be taken on a person's portfolio. An investor should also include investments on growth securities like equities which are highly risky as form of investment to provide capital appreciation.

The Unit Trust of India operated ten different schemes and plans. These are Unit Scheme 1964 Re-investment Plan 1966, Children's Gift Plan 1970, Unit Linked Insurance Plan 1971, Unit Scheme for Charitable and Religious Trusts and Registered Societies 1981, Capital Gains Unit Scheme 1983, Income Unit Scheme 1982, Monthly Income Unit Scheme 1983, Growth and Income Scheme 1983, and Unit Scheme 1985. Many of these have closed down. There are many new schemes since 1990 but the 1964 scheme is open ended and still popular.

Unit Scheme 1964

The Unit Scheme 1964 was the first to be issued by the Unit Trust of India. It is the called the flagship scheme of Unit Trust of India. It has the face value of Rs. 10 and the sale price and re-purchase price moderately changes every day. It is normally about Rs. 14.50 at the higher end and Rs. 11.90 at the lower end. These figures were identified in 1984. Each year the price keeps on changing. These units can be bought in multiples of tens with a minimum of ten units.

Some New Schemes of UTI (Since 1990)

UTI had many schemes but most of them were closed because they became non-remunerative and could not be continued. Since 1990 new schemes was started by UTI.

Seven Year Monthly Income Scheme (MSIG)

This scheme was started in 1990 and modified in 1991. According to this scheme monthly income option (A) provides dividend of 12% per annum payable every month plus 1% early bonus dividend at the end of each year. In cumulative option (B), the dividend is re-invested automatically in a way that original investment grows 2.5 times in 7 years. In this scheme the minimum investment is 100 units, if the scheme is of non-cumulative option. The investor must make a minimum investment of 500 units.

Monthly Income Unit Scheme (MIVS)

The first scheme of this nature was started in 1983. The new scheme is called GMIS 91 of growing monthly unit scheme. This has a face value of Rs. 10/- and the minimum investment required is 500 units in multiples of 10. The units must be held by the investor for at least 5 years. There are 2 options under this scheme. Under option (A), dividend is payable every month and there is 2% capital appreciation on maturity. Under option (B), the amount is re-invested every month and the original investment grows 21 times in 5 years. GMIS 92 was introduced with the same features of profits and bonus at the end of 3 year.

Deferred Income Unit Scheme (DIUS 1991): This scheme offered investment of 5 years with 2 options. In the first option (A), it offered 18% dividend in the third year of investment, 24% in the fourth year, and 30% in the fifth year. But no dividend is payable in the first 2 years. Bonus dividend was to be declared at the end of 3rd and 4th year. Under option (B), Rs. 1,000/- would grow to Rs. 2,000/- in 5 years and there was no provision in bonus dividend.

Master Equity Plan 1991 (MEP 1991): The face value of the units in this plan is Rs. 10/- and there is no maximum limit. This option is available to all citizens of India above 19 years of age, Hindu Undivided Family (HUF) as well as parents of minor children. This scheme has capital appreciation and also provide dividend to investors depending on income realisation. Master Equity Plan was also further introduced in 1992 with modifications of MEP 91. MEP was also introduced in 1993 with the same characteristics, with listing provided on major Stock Exchanges after initial locking period of 3 years. MEP was also introduced in 1995 for providing the benefits of tax rebate and growth. Re-purchase of unit is allowed after a lock in period of years. The investor must purchase a minimum of 50 units in multiples of 50 units. The face value of the unit is Rs. 10/-.

Capital Growth Unit Scheme 1991 (GVS Master Gain 1991): The investment in this scheme is multiples of 10 and an investor has to take 50 units having a face value of Rs. 100/-. This scheme is also for long capital appreciation and its holding period of 7 years and 15 years.

Rajlakshmi Unit Scheme 1992

Investment in this scheme can be made for a girl child upto the age of 5 years. This scheme has a face value of each unit of Rs. 10/-. The investor can invest in multiples of 10 in the minimum investment is 100 units. In 20 years this scheme grows 21 times.

Bhopal Gas Victims Mainly Income Plan 1992

This scheme has been formulated by the UTI with the approval of Government of India and under the orders of Supreme Court. The victims certified by the commissioner can benefit by this scheme. This plan is for 8 years and distributes the dividend of 15% per annum. All maturity schemes offers capital appreciation.

Capital Growth Unit Scheme 1992 (Master Gain)

This was introduced in similar to CGVS scheme 1991. This scheme has a holding period 7 years. It has a face value of Rs. 10/- and minimum investment of 200 units in multiples of 100 units. Grand master 1993 was introduced on the same line as Master Gain 1992.

Unit Scheme 1992

This scheme introduced by UTI was also for the benefit of the investors for long-term capital appreciation. This scheme is listed on major recognized stock exchanges in the country and it declares a reasonable dividend after an initial lock in period of 3 years. The face value is of Rs. 10/- and minimum unit has to be 500 in multiples of 100 units.

Children College and Carrier Fund Unit Plan (CCF) 1993

This plan supports a child on completion of School Education. This scheme can be taken for a child upto 15 years of age. The minimum amount of investment is Rs. 2,000/-. The investment grows by 11 times in 18 years and 21 times in 23 years. The face value is Rs. 10/-. This helps a child in Higher Education or in setting up a business.

Senior Citizen Plan 1993

This plan is prepared with the collaboration of New India Assurance Company. One of the main objects of this scheme is to provide Hospitalization benefits to Senior Citizens. After the age of 58 years the Senior Citizen can approach in all the hospitals in which UTI has made the arrangements for Free Treatment. This scheme is applicable to both the applicant and spouse. An investor between the age of 21 years and 51 years can join this plan. The investor is also entitled to yearly return declared by UTI. The face value is Rs. 10/-.

Institutional Investors Special Fund Unit Scheme (IISFUS 1993)

This scheme is designed for large institutional investors. It provides a return of 16% per annum with scope of capital appreciation. At the time of encashments it is open for re-investment. The units have a face value of Rs. 10 and investment should be for a minimum of 2.5 lakhs units. This scheme involves an investment multiples of 50,000 units. The units cannot be transferred or pledged.

Grihalakshmi Unit Plan 1994

This plan is like a Gift to a daughter/grand daughter/niece/close female relative. It has a limit of 1 lakh per year. The donee gets a regular income. The face value of the unit is Rs. 10 and minimum investment is 200 units. This plan is for 30 years. No dividend is declared for the first year. After that annual dividends are paid.

Scheme for Charitable and Religious Trusts and Registered Societies (CRTS 81)

This scheme is specially for Religious and Charitable Trust and Societies. The objective is to provide a good rate of return with a minimum Guarantee of 12%. The face value of the unit in this scheme is Rs. 100 and there should be a minimum of 100 units. But there is no maximum limit. The investment must be for atleast 3 years. Repurchase of unit can be made by the investor in multiples of 10.

Income Unit Scheme (IUS)

This scheme was introduced for lower and middle income group of people, especially those of the salaried class. The main objectives of this scheme are to provide a share income to the investors. The minimum investment in this scheme is Rs. 2,000/- with a holding period of 5 years. Under IVS scheme 1985 the ceiling of investment was raised to 1 lakh.

Unit Growth Scheme 2000 (UGS 2000): In this scheme the investors of unit scheme 1964 and CGP 1990 could make the investment. The maximum investment could be 200 units and the minimum investments would be 50 units. The face value of the units is Rs. 10/- and can be purchased any multiples of 50 units. There is no dividend for the first 2 years and the holding period of the scheme is 10 years. UGS 5000 was introduced as a modification of UGS 2000.

SIGNIFICANT MUTUAL FUNDS COMPANIES IN INDIA

In India, a large number of mutual funds have been floated. Some of these are:

Some of the major mutual funds in India are given below. Unit Trust of India ranks first in the resources into its fund. After that some of the following mutual funds have become large companies.

ABN AMRO Mutual Fund: This mutual fund was setup on April 15, 2004 with ABN AMRO Trustee (India) Pvt. Ltd. as the Trustee Company. The AMC, ABN AMRO Asset Management (India) Ltd. was incorporated on November 4, 2003. Deutsche Bank A G is the custodian of ABN AMRO Mutual Fund.

Birla Sun Life Mutual Fund: Aditya Birla Group and Sun Life Financial have formed a joint venture mutual fund. It is called Birla Sun Life mutual fund. Sun Life Financial is a global organisation. It started in 1871. It is represented in Canada, the US, the Philippines, Japan, Indonesia Bermuda and India. Birla Sun Life Mutual Fund is a conservative long-term investor.

Bank of Baroda Mutual Fund: Bank of Baroda setup its mutual fund on October 30, 1992. It was sponsored by Bank of Baroda. The Asset Management Company is Bank of Baroda Limited. The mutual fund and was incorporated on November 5, 1992. Deutsche Bank AG is the custodian.

HDFC Mutual Fund: The Housing Development Finance Corporation Limited and Standard Life Investments Limited are the two sponsors which setup HDFC mutual fund on June 30, 2000.

HSBC Mutual Fund: This mutual fund was setup on May 27, 2002 with HSBC Securities and Capital Markets (India) Private Limited as the sponsor. HSBC Mutual Fund is the Trustee Company of HSBC Mutual Fund.

ING Vysya Mutual Fund: This mutual fund was incorporated on April 6, 1998 and was setup on February 11, 1999. It is a joint venture of Vysya and ING.

Prudential ICICI Mutual Fund: The mutual fund of ICICI is a joint venture with Prudential Plc. of America, one of the largest life insurance companies in the US of A. Prudential ICICI Mutual Fund was setup with two sponsorers, Prudential Plc. and ICICI Ltd. on 13th of October, 1993. The Trustee Company formed is Prudential ICICI Trust Ltd. and the AMC is Prudential ICICI Asset Management Company Limited and it was incorporated on 22nd of June, 1993.

Sahara Mutual Fund: It was sponsored by Sahara India Financial Corporation Ltd. set up on July 18, 1996. Sahara Asset Management Company Private Limited incorporated on August 31, 1995 works as the AMC of Sahara Mutual Fund. The paid-up capital of the AMC is Rs. 25.8 crores.

State Bank of India Mutual Fund: This is the first mutual fund to offer offshore fund, the India Its Magnum Fund had a large volume in corpus. It is the largest Bank sponsored Mutual Fund in India. It has 35 Schemes. It has an investor base of over 8 Lakhs in 18 schemes.

Tata Mutual Fund: The sponsorers for Tata Mutual Fund are Tata Sons Ltd., and Tata Investment Corporation Ltd. The investment manager is Tata Asset Management Limited and its Tata Trustee Company Pvt. Limited. Tata Asset Management Limited is a Trust under the Indian Trust Act, 1882.

Kotak Mahindra: This is a subsidiary of Kotak Mahindra. It has more than 2 lakhs investors in its various schemes. Kotak Mahindra Mutual Fund offers schemes investors with varying risk and return profiles. It was the first company to begin gilt scheme which invested in government securities only.

Unit Trust of India Mutual Fund: UTI Asset Management Company Private Ltd. manages the UTI Mutual Fund with the support of UTI Trustee Company Private Limited. It was setup in Jan 14, 2003; UTI Asset Management Company manages a corpus of over Rs. 20,000 crores. The sponsors of UTI Mutual Fund are Bank of Baroda (BOB), Punjab National Bank (PNB), State Bank of India (SBI), and Life Insurance Corporation of India (LIC). The schemes of UTI Mutual Fund are Liquid Funds, Income Funds, Asset Management Funds, Index Funds, Equity Funds and Balance Funds.

Reliance Mutual Fund: Reliance Mutual Fund is sponsored by Reliance Capital Ltd. and Reliance Capital Trustee Co. of was established as trust under Indian Trusts Act, 1882. The Reliance Capital Trustee Co. Limited is the Trustee. It was registered on June 30, 1995 as Reliance Capital Mutual Fund was changed on March 11, 2004. Reliance Mutual Fund was formed to contribute to the capital market by diversifying investments and providing the investors with opportunities for a balanced risk free growth.

Standard Chartered Mutual Fund: It was set up on March 13, 2000 sponsored by Standard Chartered Bank. The Trustee is Standard Chartered Trustee Company Pvt. Ltd. Standard Chartered Asset Management Company Pvt. Ltd. is the AMC which was incorporated with SEBI on December 20, 1999.

Franklin Templeton India Mutual Fund: It is one of the largest financial services groups in the world. Investors can buy or sell the Mutual Fund through their financial advisor or through mail or through their website. They offer many kinds of schemes such as Open end Diversified Equity schemes, Open end Sector Equity schemes, Open end Hybrid schemes, Open end Tax Saving schemes, Open end Income and Liquid schemes, Close end Income schemes and Open end Fund of Funds schemes.

Morgan Stanley Mutual Fund India: Morgan Stanley is a worldwide financial services company and is a market leader in investment management, credit services and securities. In 1975 Morgan Stanley Investment Management was established. It provides customized asset management services and products to governments, corporations, pension funds and non-profit organisations. It also gives service to high net worth individuals and retail investors. In India it is known as Morgan Stanley Investment Management Private Limited India and its Asset Management Company is Morgan Stanley Mutual Fund. It focuses on long term capital appreciation and has started the first closed end diversified equity scheme for the Indian retail investors.

Escorts Mutual Fund: It was setup on April 15, 1996 with Escorts Finance Limited as its sponsor. The Trustee Company is Escorts Investment Trust Limited. Its Asset Management Company was incorporated on December 1, 1995 with the name Escorts Asset Management Limited.

Alliance Capital Mutual Fund: This mutual fund with its corporate office in Mumbai was setup on December 30, 1994. This mutual fund was sponsored by Alliance Capital Management Corp. of Delaware (USA). The Trustee is Alliance Asset Management Trust Company Pvt. Ltd. and Asset Management Company is Alliance Capital Asset Management India (Pvt.) Ltd.

Benchmark Mutual Fund: This mutual fund was sponsored by Niche Financial Services Pvt. Ltd. as the sponsor and Benchmark Trustee Company Pvt. Ltd. as the Trustee Company. It was incorporated on October 16, 2000 and setup on June 12, 2001. Its headquarters are in Mumbai. Its asset management company is Benchmark Asset Management Company Pvt. Ltd.

Canbank Mutual Fund: Canara bank sponsored the canbank mutual fund. It was setup on December 19, 1987. The asset management company is Canbank Investment Management Services Ltd. The Corporate Office of the Asset Management Company is in Mumbai.

Chola Mutual Fund: Cholamandalam Investment and Finance Company Ltd. sponsored Chola Mutual Fund. It was setup on January 3, 1997. The asset management company is Cholamandalam Ltd. Cholamandalam Trustee Co. Ltd. is the Trustee Company.

LIC Mutual Fund: Life Insurance Corporation of India set up LIC Mutual Fund on 19th June 1989. The Company started its business on 29th April, 1994. It was constituted as a Trust with the provisions of the Indian Trust Act, 1882. The Trustees of LIC Mutual Fund have appointed Jeevan Bima Sahayog Asset Management Company Ltd as the Investment Managers for LIC Mutual Fund. It contributed Rs. 2 Crores towards the corpus of the Fund.

GIC Mutual Fund: This mutual fund is a government of India undertaken. It is sponsored by General Insurance Corporation of India (GIC), and the four Public Sector General Insurance Companies National Insurance Co. Ltd., New India Assurance Co. Ltd., Oriental Insurance Co. Ltd. and United India Insurance Co. Ltd. It is constituted as a Trust according to the provisions of the Indian Trusts Act, 1882.

Summary

➡ A mutual fund pools its resources through the issue of units to investors. Its main objective being to give a good return to its investors.

➡ The Unit Trust of India was the first mutual fund in India. Its started with Units – 64 plan which became its flagship schemes. It was the first open ended unit scheme in India.

➡ In 2003, the UTI mutual fund was established. Its assets management company is the largest in the world and it has a corpus of 340,500 million.

➡ Since 1996 all mutual funds have to be registered with SEBI.

➡ The structure of mutual fund consists of an Asset Management Company, sponsor and board of trustee since 1996.

➡ The development of mutual fund has been in four phases. The first phase was the establishment of UTI. In the second phase, there was the entry of public sector funds in the mutual fund business. In the third phase the private sector and foreign funds entered the mutual fund business. In the fourth phase from 2003-07 the Unit Trust of India was divided into two parts. One in which the UTI had its assets under the rules of government of India and it is not under the purview of mutual fund regulations. The second one is the UTI mutual fund which is sponsored by SBI, PNB, BOB and LIC. This is under the SEBI mutual fund regulation.

➡ The mutual fund assets in 2007 were Rs. 1218.05 billion and there were 33 mutual funds.

➡ Every mutual fund has to publish a report for each new scheme launched by it.

➡ Mutual funds are permitted to invest in India. They can also invest in foreign countries through ADRs and GDRs within the guidelines of SEBI.

➡ The benefits of mutual funds are derived through the specialized knowledge and expertise of management. It is useful for small investors. It has the advantage of liquidity as in an open ended scheme the investor can by and sell units through out the year. The investments of mutual funds are diversified through carefully selection of securities by professional manager.

➡ Mutual funds can be classified into open ended, closed ended, income fund, growth funds, dual funds, index funds, exchange credit funds, money market funds, municipal bond funds, pension funds, offshore funds, balanced funds, gilt fund, sector specific fund, tax saving schemes and fund of funds.

➡ The net asset value is the market value of securities minus liabilities divided by number of outstanding units.

➡ Mutual funds have administrative expenses, operating cost and consultation fees. Thus it had many expenses.

➡ UTI has many schemes. Some of the closed ended schemes are closed. There are many new schemes since 1990. Some of them being monthly income scheme, deferred income unit scheme, master equity plan, capital growth scheme, rajlakshmi unit scheme and senior citizen plan. It also has a unit growth scheme.

➡ There are many significant mutual funds in India. Some of them being ABN AMRO Mutual Fund, Birla Sun Life, Bank of Baroda, HDFC and HSBC mutual fund.

Objective Type Questions, Answer True (T) or False (F)

(a) The market price of units is measured by NAV.

(b) Mutual funds are broker agencies buying and selling securities for investors.

(c) An open ended fund is popular because of its feature of liquidity.

(d) The scheme of mutual funds is based on entry and exit load.

(e) Mutual funds have a regulatory body in India.

(f) Mutual fund has a sponsor, a trustee and a manager.

(g) Index funds are invested through a particular market index.

(h) Unit Trust of India was started in 1960.

(i) Government permitted public sector bank and institution to setup mutual funds in India.

(j) The mutual fund is based on sharing of risks and rewards.

Answer: (a) F, (b) F, (c) T, (d) T, (e) T, (f) F, (g) T, (h) F, (i) T, (j) T.

Multiple Choice Questions (Tick mark (✓) the right answer)

1. The Unit Trust of India:
   (a) It is a government organization
   (b) It is a private trust
   (c) It is a mutual fund
   (d) It is a Public sector bank

2. The sponsor of a mutual fund:
   (a) It selects the stocks of the mutual fund
   (b) It is the registrar of the mutual fund
   (c) It establishes a mutual fund
   (d) It manages the funds of a mutual fund

3. The open ended scheme of a mutual fund:
   (a) It is the purchase and sale of units on a daily basis
   (b) It is the purchase and sale of units for a fixed number of years
   (c) It has purchase and sale through the market index
   (d) It has dual funds in the company

4. The closed ended scheme of a mutual fund:
   (a) It is investment for a number of years
   (b) It is based on net asset value
   (c) It is based on capital appreciation
   (d) It is a money market fund

5.   A load is:

   (a)   A return on units received by the investor

   (b)   A cost which is in built in the cost of the asset

   (c)   It is the purchase value of the units

   (d)   It is the net asset value of the units

   Answer: 1 (c), 2 (c), 3 (a), 4 (a), 5 (b).

Short Answer Questions

1.   What is a mutual fund? Discuss the benefit of a mutual fund to an investor.

2.   What are the advantages of investing savings in Unit Trust of India?

3.   What is a load? How does it affect investors?

4.   Write notes on: (i) open ended and closed ended funds, (ii) Index fund and exchange traded funds.

Long Answer Questions

1.   What is a mutual fund? Discuss the structure of mutual fund in India.

2.   Why are mutual funds considered to be indirect investments? Are mutual funds good investments? Is NAV important for mutual funds?

3.   Discuss the regulations of SEBI towards mutual funds in India.

4.   What are the different schemes of mutual funds in India?

Chapter 17

Development Banks

Chapter Plan

- Introduction
- Industrial Development Bank of India (IDBI)
- Industrial Finance Corporation (IFC)
- Industrial Credit and Investment Corporation of India (ICICI)
- Industrial Investment Bank of India Ltd.
- State Financial Corporations (SFCS)
- Export-Import Bank of India (Exim)

INTRODUCTION

Development banks were instituted in India as gap fillers in providing credit for promotion and development of industry. Their role was to be quantitative but they were to support the financial mechanism qualitatively as well. Their objective was to develop backward regions, small, medium and large enterprises. They were to provide finance to new entrepreneurs who had the technical qualifications but not the financing ability. They differed from financial institutions in their functions. While the financial institutions linked the sources and uses of funds, the development banks were considered to be the backbone of the financial system. The development banks were to act as facilitators of trade as well as act in an advisory capacity.

The development-banking era began in India with the setting up of the Industrial Financial Corporation of India (IFCI) in 1948. While IFCI was set up at the all-India level, State Financial Corporations (SFCs) were regional institutions. The first SFC was formed in 1951. The IFCI and SFCs were organized to assist small and medium enterprises and to work in the form of industrial mortgage banks. IFCI's working was an orthodox line. A more dynamic and modern approach was brought about with the introduction of Industrial Credit and Investment Corporation of India (ICICI) in 1955. It was considered to be a pioneer in its participation in the private corporate sector. It brought into India foreign currency loans from the World Bank and also entered the Industrial Securities Market as an underwriter of capital issues. Subsequently, the Government of India set up the Refinance Corporation of India (RCI) in 1958 to provide refinance to banks against term loans granted by them to medium and small enterprises. Subsequently, the RCI merged with the Industrial Development Bank of India (IDBI) in 1964. In the same year, IDBI was established as a subsidiary of the RBI. Later the IDBI was elevated to the position of an apex institution to provide finance and to co-ordinate the activities of all the financial institutions. At the state level, the State Industrial Development Corporation (SIDC)/State Industrial Investment Corporation were created to meet the financial requirements of the States and to promote balanced regional development. In 1971 the IDBI and LIC and jointly set up the Industrial Reconstruction Corporation (IRCI) to rehabilitate sick mills.

The expansion in size and the number of institutions has led to a considerable degree of diversification and increase in the types of financial instruments. The impetus given by planning led to rapid industrialization, relative decline in the private proprietorship type of business organization, growth of corporate sector and the growth of the government sector. The financial instruments grew in addition to those already in existence, new instruments were introduced in the form of innovative deposit scheme of banks, time deposits, recurring deposits and cumulative time deposits with post offices, public provident fund accounts, participation certificates, new schemes of LIC, UTI, National Development Bonds and Rural Debentures.

The Indian financial system is both developed and integrated today when compared to the initial period in 1950. Integration has been through a participatory approach to the granting of loans as well as in savings schemes. Banks and term lending institutions are linked between themselves. One of the well-known examples is the Unit linked insurance scheme of the Unit Trust of India in which the UTI is linked with the LIC. Also, the IDBI's refinance and rediscounting schemes promote integration.

The financial sector was wholly owned by the government. As a result, the government was also the controlling body of these institutions. One of the problems faced by such a system was the need to coordinate the working of different financial institutions. Financial institutions of the large size of LIC and UTI led to monopolistic/oligopolistic market structures in the Indian financial system. In India, there was only one organization conducting insurance business or unit business. The insurance bill was passed to bring about private entrepreneurs for promoting business. The working of a large structure had led to inefficiency and mismanagement, or lack of effort in mobilizing savings and in the development of the national financial system.

In 1991 with the new phase of liberalization and new economic reforms all the financial institutions and development banks began to change and bring in policies which were relevant for the country in its present situation. Many development banks had to shift from completely financing agencies to commercial and viable institutions. They had to move on to new directions. The purely financial institutions became open to private sector contributing to it to become competitive. It was also an era for mergers and amalgamations. Development banks had become non-competitive with raising non-performing assets. They started to change by beginning their operations as commercial banks. Some of the development banks went in for reverse mergers and got themselves attached to commercial banks which started their business late in terms of years of formation but became very prosperous. The commercial banks became financial conglomerates. The country moved towards universal banking. The ICICI Bank proved to be the first universal bank by offering numerous services to customers. Thus there is a change in the operations of development banks.

The Development Banks

Development Banks are special financial institutions, which discussed in the earlier part of the chapter are different from investment type financial institutions. These have been essentially viewed as gap fillers. They are like artificial limbs specially instituted to compensate for the slow growth of the normal sources of finance. The accent of these banks is on providing development finance. As development agencies they are concerned with the development of total financing and its impact on the economy. These banks are IDBI, IFCI, ICICI and State Financial Corporations. Since 1991 there have been many changes in their working. Their role and activities is discussed in the following part of the chapter.

INDUSTRIAL DEVELOPMENT BANK OF INDIA (IDBI)

The IDBI was set up in 1964 as a subsidiary of the RBI. Subsequently, it was de-linked and made an independent institution in 1975 under the Public Financial Institutions Act. It became the apex special financial institution in the economy. IDBI made a public issue in July 1995, where government reduced its shareholding to 58.47% Its objective was to strengthen the resources of financial institutions including banks. To meet emerging challenges and to keep up with reforms in financial sector, IDBI reshaped its role from a development finance institution to a commercial institution. With Industrial Development Bank (Transfer of Undertaking and Repeal) Act, 2003, IDBI attained the status of a limited company. It was named Industrial Development Bank of India Limited (IDBIL). The Central Government notified October 1, 2004 as the 'Appointed Date' and RBI made a notification on September 30, 2004 incorporating IDBI Ltd., as a 'scheduled bank' under the RBI Act, 1934. IDBI, the Development Financial Institution of the country, entered into banking business.

As of July, 2006 the employees association of the Industrial Finance Corporation of India have demanded its merger with the Bank.

Role of IDBI

The IDBI follows a flexible approach in its financing pattern. Being a development agency it is not interested in receiving high profits on amounts it loans to industrial units. Also, it prefers to assist industrial organization indirectly through other institutions. It has set up a special 'Development Assistance Fund' for assisting deserving projects which other financial institutions are not likely to finance. It also acts as a 'lead' institution by coordinating the work of other financial institutions through regular appraisals, supervision of projects and follow-up meetings. IDBI has been engaged in re-financing industrial loans granted by eligible financial institutions like banks, IFC, SFCs, LIC, etc. It also re-discounts machinery bills and subscribe to the shares and bonds of IFC, ICICI and SFCs.

Promotional Role: The IDBI plays a promotional role in backward and underdeveloped countries. It has set up Technical Consultancy Organizations (TCOs) in backward areas to fortify institutional structure for growth in these areas. It offers concessions in financing in backward areas. It provides facilities for joint industrial surveys to identify growth potential in backward areas. IDBI co-ordinates the working of institutions engaged in financing, promoting and developing industries. Its promotional activities include entrepreneurship development programs for new entrepreneurs, provision of consultancy services for small and medium enterprises, up-gradation of technology and programs for economic improvement of the underprivileged.

Underwriting: IDBI's role in industry takes various forms. It helps industry directly through underwriting operations and provisions of loans. It also undertakes guarantees for repayment of loan. Indirectly it re-finances the loans given to industry. It also subscribes to bonds and debentures of other financial institutions.

IDBI's Role as a Catalyst: IDBI's role as a catalyst to industrial development encompasses a wide spectrum of activities. It can finance all types of industrial concerns covered under the provisions of the IDBI Act.

Innovative Role: IDBI also renders technical and advisory help to industry. Another innovative role in has played has been to revive sick industrial units. IDBI has been of great help to the industrial small-scale sector. It has provided them with financial concessions, refinancing and re-discounting bills and acting as a channel of foreign currency loans under the IDA credit from the World Bank.

Export Finance: IDBI also provides export finance through the scheme of direct participation; re-finance and medium-term export credit and overseas buyers' credit. It functions as the *Export Import Bank of India.*

Technological Advancement: Since 1986 many changes have taken place in India's Economic Policies. IDBI's role in the capital market has remained undiminished due to the dynamism it has shown in keeping pace with the reforms in the economic policies in India. Its major effort has been in the direction of technical up gradation scheme. It has given liberal assistance to those established industries, which have desired to import machinery. It also established a venture capital fund scheme for promoting new and risky ventures. Since environmental conditions have been the primary concern of India, IDBI has been identifying and implementing cost effective programs for controlling pollution. It has assisted industries in effluent treatment and promoting new techniques for reducing pollution. It conducts a training program on environmental issues.

Refinancing Activity: Since 1985 it has been refinancing SFCs and State Industrial Development Corporation's on their equipment financing schemes. It provides refinancing assistance to a single project up to Rs. 5 crores.

Development Role: IDBI's role in energy conservation is especially noteworthy. It finances plant and machinery instruments acquired for energy audit including erection, installation changes, technical know-how and fees paid for designs and drawing to the technical consultant. Its development role includes entrepreneurship development, self-employment and wage employment in the industrial sector for the weaker sections of society through voluntary agencies, support to Science and Technology Entrepreneurs' Parks, Energy Conservation, Common Quality Testing Centres for small industries.

Borrowing Pattern of IDBI

IDBI has also made changes in its borrowing pattern. Initially IDBI's borrowings were from government and Reserve Bank of India but since 1971 it has strengthened its resources through market borrowings. IDBI has issued bonds and debentures in India as well as abroad. The borrowing is approximately Rs. 20,000 crores as on June 30th 1996.

Institutions Sponsored by IDBI

Industrial Development Bank of India (IDBI) is the tenth largest bank in the world in terms of development. The National Stock Exchange (NSE), The National Securities Depository Services Ltd. (NSDL), Stock Holding Corporation of India (SHCIL) are some of the institutions which has been sponsored by IDBI. IDBI is a strategic investor in a plethora of institutions which have revolutionized the Indian Financial Markets.

IDBI Bank, promoted by IDBI Group started in November 1995 with a branch at Indore with an equity capital base of Rs. 1000 million.

IDBI also setup Technical Consultancy Organizations for consultancy and advisory services to entrepreneurs.

Technical Consultancy Organizations: IDBI collaborated with other All-India Financial Institutions and has set up a network of Technical Consultancy Organizations (TCOs) in India. TCOs offer diversified services to small and medium enterprises in the selection, formulation and appraisal of projects, their implementation and review.

Entrepreneurship Development Institute: IDBI played a dominant role in setting up the Entrepreneurship Development Institute of India for encouraging entrepreneurship in India. It established similar institutes in Bihar, Orissa, Madhya Pradesh and Uttar Pradesh. It extends financial support to various organizations in conducting studies or surveys of relevance to industrial development.

IDBI has played a pioneering role in development banking from 1964 to 1991 in industrial development of the country. IDBI's activities comprised long-term lending to industry and balanced industrial growth through development of backward areas, modernization of specific industries, employment generation, entrepreneurship development and support services for creating a deep and vibrant domestic capital market, including development institutional framework.

Role in Retail Finance Sector: In September 2003, IDBI diversified its business by acquiring the entire shareholding of Tata Finance Limited in Tata Home finance Limited. It entered into the retail finance sector. The fully-owned housing finance subsidiary has been renamed 'IDBI Home finance Limited'.

IDBI Commercial Bank

In the post reforms period after 1991 Government of India decided to transform IDBI into a commercial bank without changing its secular development finance obligations. The entry to the new business model of commercial banking, with its objective of low-cost current, savings bank deposits, would help overcome most of the limitations of the current business model of development finance while simultaneously enabling it to diversify its client/asset base. The IDB (Transfer of Undertaking and Repeal) Act 2003 was passed by Parliament in December 2003. The Act provides for repeal of IDBI Act, for making the IDBI into a corporate organization with majority Government holding of 58.47% and transformation into a commercial bank.

Merger of IDBI and IDBI Bank

On July 29, 2004, the Board of Directors of IDBI and IDBI Bank approved to the merger of IDBI Bank with the Industrial Development Bank of India Ltd. to be formed incorporated under the Companies Act, 1956 pursuant to the IDB (Transfer of Undertaking and Repeal) Act, 2003 (53 of 2003), subject to the approval of shareholders and other regulatory and statutory approvals. The merger was expected to be completed by March 31st, 2005.

Corporate Governance

IDBI proposes to maintain high standards of governance in running its business. To maintain good corporate governance practices this role has been designated to the Board of Directors. Two Committees of the Board comprising of the Executive Committee and the Audit Committee are empowered to monitor implementation of good corporate governance practices and making necessary disclosures within the framework of legal provisions of the bank.

New Directions of IDBI

IDBI's objective of transformation into a commercial bank was to continue to provide its products and services as part of its development finance role even after its conversion into a banking company. In addition, the new entity would also provide an array of wholesale and retail banking products, designed to suit the specific needs cash flow requirements of corporates and individuals. It planned to provide low-cost deposits like Current and Savings Bank Deposits to have a positive impact on the Bank's overall cost of funds. It proposed to lend funds at competitive rates to its clients. The commercial bank planned to offer various retail products, under its existing Suvidha Flexi-bond schemes.

In its new role the IDBI has the objective of becoming a one stop super-shop and most preferred brand for providing total financial and banking solutions to corporate organizations and individuals.

INDUSTRIAL FINANCE CORPORATION (IFC)

IFC was set up in 1948. It is a pioneer development bank in India. Its main objective is to provide long and medium-term requirements of capital to industry. It does not give assistance for short-term purposes, *i.e.,* for working capital or for repayment of existing liabilities but the IFC encourages loans for setting up new industrial projects and also loans for expansions of existing units' diversification, modernization and renovation. It is the only known agency for providing import of capital goods such as machinery, but it does not import capital goods for the purpose of trading. The various activities of the IFC are centered around public limited companies, or the corporate sector. Private companies, partnership and proprietary concerns are beyond their purview. The constitution of IFCI was changed in 1993 from a statutory corporation to a company under the Indian Companies Act, 1956. Subsequently, the name of the company was also changed to "IFCI Limited" with effect from October 1999.

IFC assists industrial enterprises in all States in the country. Maharashtra, Tamil Nadu, Uttar Pradesh, West Bengal and Andhra Pradesh have from its inception in 1949 till the year 1982 received substantial financial help which accounts for three-fourths of IFC's net approval. The IFC has generally provided industries in these States concessional finance up to Rs. 1 crore. The maximum loan to one concern at a time has been up to Rs. 2 crores. The concessional rate of interest is 9.5% on the rupee and 10% on the foreign currency loan, while the normal rate of interest is 11%. IFC has always encouraged new enterprises. It has also assisted the new technician entrepreneurs. Apart from financial assistance it has extended necessary guidance to them in formulating their projects so that they become technically feasible and economically viable so that they qualify for assistance from development banks. IFC has been assisting these organizations since 1975 through its own sponsored institution called the 'Risk Capital Foundation' for assistance to new entrepreneurs.

IFCIs Support to Industry: The IFC assists schemes in industrial areas in more than one-way: (a) It grants loans both in rupees and in foreign currencies. (b) It underwrites issues both 'initial' and 'further' in the NIM. (c) It makes direct subscriptions to shares and debentures of public limited companies. (d) It guarantees deferred payments for imported machinery. (e) It raises foreign currency loans from institutions.

IFC's assistance has been especially noteworthy to sugar and jute industries. It has been a 'Lead Institution' for providing funds on a priority basis for revial of their sick units. Assistance under this scheme was based on the need of each individual organization and there was no ceiling for individual loans.

Its contribution to the modernization of Indian industry, export promotion, import substitution, entrepreneurship development, pollution control, energy conservation and generation of both direct and indirect employment is noteworthy. Some sectors that have directly benefited from IFCI's disbursals include Consumer goods industry like textiles, paper and sugar. Service industries such as hotels and hospitals have been benefited by IFCs. Basic industries such as iron and steel, fertilizers, basic chemicals, cement, capital and intermediate goods industries like electronics, synthetic fibers, synthetic plastics, miscellaneous chemicals; and Infrastructure power generation, telecom service have also been financed by IFCI.

Merchant Banking Activities of IFCIs: The IFC has broadened the scope of its activities. Well-established in merchant banking activities in India, it has extended these outside India as well. It also provides credit syndication assistance by providing documentation and registration services. Since 1989, IFC has actively promoted tourism related projects, sponsoring Tourism Finance Corporation of India (TFCI) and Tourism Advisory and Financial Corporation of India Ltd. (TAFSIL) for promotion of financial and advisory services to tourism.

In 1994-95 the IFC set up subsidiaries for merchant banking and stock exchange services. Industrial Finance Corporation Investor Services Ltd. was set up for transfer agents and registrars services. The Industrial Finance Corporation Custodial Services Ltd. was primarily set up to be a custodian of shares and securities and Industrial Finance Corporation Financial Services Ltd. was directed towards merchant banking activities.

Promotion of New Institutions: IFC played an influential role in co-promoting agencies such as the OTCEI, National Stock Exchange of India and Investment Information and Credit Rating Agency of India Ltd. (ICRA). This role it performed in association with other financial institutions to bring about better trading and assessment facilities to investors and creditors in the capital market. IFC has always encouraged professionalism in management. It sponsored the Management Development Institute (MDI) in 1973 and a development-banking centre in 1977. Their main activities are research and training programs. It has made a significant contribution towards co-promoting and developing Stock Holding Corporation of India Ltd. (SHCIL), Discount and Finance House of India Ltd. (DFHI), National Stock Exchange (NSE), Securities Trading Corporation of India (STCI), LIC Housing Finance Ltd., GIC Grih Vitta Ltd., and Bio-tech Consortium Ltd. (BCL). It promoted the Tourism Finance Corporation of India (TFCI) for promotion of the hotel and tourism industry. It also sponsored Rashtriya Gramin Vikas Nidhi (RGVN) for developing voluntary agencies in uplifting rural and urban poor in east and northeast India. It developed the Institute of Labor Development (ILD) for rehabilitation and training of displaced and retrenched labor force.

Economic Role of IFCI: The role of IFCI in financial assistance of industries has provided direct employment of almost 1 million persons. It has played a pivotal role in the regional dispersal of industry IFCI's assistance have been granted to units located in backward areas, helping to mobilize investments of more than 1 billion. It has played a key role in the development of cooperatives in the sugar and textile sectors and acted as a nodal agency in both sectors. Many cooperative societies in these sectors have been assisted by IFCI. It has promoted Technical Consultancy Organizations (TCOs), in less developed states to provide necessary services to the promoters of small- and medium-sized industries in collaboration with other banks and institutions. It has been instrument in providing assistance to self-employed youth and women entrepreneurs under its Benevolent Reserve Fund (BRF) and the Interest Different Fund (IDF).

Entrepreneurship Development Programme: The IFCI was keen to upgrade the knowledge of the entrepreneurs. It supported the Entrepreneurship Development Programs (EDPs) conducted by National Science and Technology Entrepreneurship Development Board (NSTEDB) and Entrepreneurship Development Institute of India (EDI).

Leasing and Higher Purchase Financing: IFC has extended financial services in new areas of industrial activity. It provides loans to leasing and hire purchase companies, which lease equipment and machinery to industries. It also has an equipment credit scheme through which it finances the full cost of equipment purchased by an industrial concern. Since 1988 it has an equipment procurement scheme for new areas such as computer pollution control and those equipments under national priority. It pays the cost of the equipment directly to the supplier and later recovers it from the user. In November 1991 it introduced the installment credit scheme whereby IFCI would pay the supplier the total cost of the equipment purchased. It would then recover the amount in 36/48 monthly installments from the beneficiary. It has also provided assistance to users of equipment through leasing facilities.

IFCI however went into losses in 1999. It reported high NPAs and its cost of borrowing exceeded its income from operations. This made IFCI terminally sick. Government of India based on the recommendations of Basu Committee made a plan for restructuring IFCI. Government suggested a Rs. 100 crores package for reviving IFCI. This was to be in two parts. Rs. 400 crores were to be given by government in the form of subscription to long term convertible debentures and Rs. 600 crores by government control institutional shareholders. This plan was prepared in 2001. The government appointed Mc Kinsey consulting company to revive IFCI. This company suggested that IFCI should be divided into two companies. One company was to have good assets, the other one with bad assets. The good assets company was to provide finance to mid sized companies and to take fee based services. It also suggested a merger with a potential universal bank and change in the top management positions of the company.

INDUSTRIAL CREDIT AND INVESTMENT CORPORATION OF INDIA (ICICI)

ICICI was formed in 1955 at the initiative of the World Bank, the Government of India and representatives of Indian industry. It was instituted as a 'private sector development bank' for providing 'foreign currency loans' and for developing 'underwriting facilities in the NIM'. The special feature of the ICICI was that it was to be privately owned and its assistance was to be given to private sector industries only. It was to provide project financing for medium and long term to industries in India. Since the reforms in India in 1991 ICICI Bank has taken many progressive steps. It is India's largest private sector bank in market capitalization and second largest overall in terms of assets. In 1994 there was a change in the structure of the ICICI. It established the ICICI banking corporation as a banking subsidiary. The ICICI Banking Corporation was renamed ICICI Bank Limited. In 1999 ICICI became the first Indian company to list itself on New York Stock Exchange. In 2000 it acquired the Bank of Madura. In 2002 the Board of Directors of ICICI and ICICI decided jointly to merge both the institutions with ICICI Bank integrating their financing and banking operations into a single entity. ICICI extended its services beyond the national boundaries. In 2002 it established its representative offices in New York and London. In 2003 it opened subsidiaries in Canada and the United Kingdom (UK). It also started an Offshore Banking Unit (OBU) in Singapore and representative offices in Dubai and Shanghai. In 2004 it extended its services to Bangladesh by opening and establishing its representative office in that area. In 2005 it acquired a Russian Bank Investitsionno-Kreditny Bank (IKB) with its head office in Balabanovo in the Kaluga region and with a branch in Moscow. ICICI renamed the bank ICICI Bank Eurasia. In the same year it established a branch in Hong Kong and in Dubai International Financial Centre. In 2006 ICICI Bank UK opened a branch in Antwerp in Belgium. It also started its representative offices in Bangkok, Jakarta, and Kuala Lumpur. In 2007 ICICI amalgamated Sangli Bank, in Maharashtra State. ICICI was also permitted by the government of Qatar to open a branch in Doha and from the US Federal Reserve to open a branch in New York. ICICI Bank Eurasia opened its second branch in St. Petersburg. In 2008 ICICI Bank introduced iMobile which is a comprehensive Mobile banking solution. iMobile is a breakthrough innovation in Indian Banking. It allows its customers to make their banking transactions through a GPRS-enabled mobile phone.

Objectives of ICICI

The objectives of the ICICI were: (i) to create, expand and modernize enterprises, (ii) to encourage private capital both external and internal to grow, (iii) to provide finance for long and medium-term needs, (iv) to underwrite new issues, (v) to guarantee loans, (vi) to provide guidance in managerial, technical and administrative matters.

Resources of ICICI

The ICICI's resources came from several sources. Its rupee resources are: (i) share capital, (ii) reserves, (iii) loans from government, (iv) advance from IDBI, (v) debentures issued to public. Its foreign resources consist of: (i) credit from World Bank, (ii) loans from KFW, (iii) sterling loans from U.K. Government, (iv) funds from USAID and public issues of bonds in Swiss Francs.

Listing of ICICI Shares

ICICI Bank's equity shares are listed in India on stock exchanges at Mumbai, National Stock Exchange of India, Kolkata and Vadodra. Its American Depository Receipts are listed on the New York Stock Exchange (NYSE).

Role of ICICI in Industrial Development

The ICICI has provided a major share of assistance in foreign currency. The industries to which it has given credit have generally been those, which require foreign credit. Non-traditional and growth-oriented industries like chemicals, metal products, machinery manufacturers have received a major share of finance. Its assistance to these industries has been concentrated in Maharashtra, Gujarat, Tamil Nadu and West Bengal. The ICICI has also given assistance to backward and less developed regions in the country. It has provided concessional finance for their promotion.

Modernization of Industries: The ICICI has also participated in the consortium of IDBI, IFC and other financial institutions to provide assistance on 'soft' terms for modernization of industries like cotton textiles, jute, sugar, cement and engineering industry.

Merchant Banking Division: The ICICI is the first financial institution to have a Merchant Banking Division in 1974. It assists new entrepreneurs through this division by giving them sound advice on the nature of the project. It also promotes their venture through the NIM. It also supervises and follows up the progress of these concerns. Another new and promotional role has been to appoint its nominee directors on firms, which have received its assistance for constant evaluation of these projects.

ICICI's Merchant Banking activities have undergone major changes based according to the needs of the economy. In 1993, ICICI floated a new company called ICICI Securities and Finance Co. Ltd. (I-SFC), which is a joint venture with the subsidiary of J.P. Morgan. 60% of the shares are owned by ICICI. This company is engaged in New Issue Management, security trading, underwriting and company advisory services. It is registered as a member of the OTCEI and the NSE and is registered as a merchant banker with the SEBI.

Research and Development Financing: It has also participated actively in financing industrial firms for initiating research and development through its sponsored scheme called SPREAD or Sponsored Research and Development Program. It has focused its attention to agriculture through ACE or Agricultural Commercialization and Enterprise Project. This project aims at increasing agricultural business sector through private investment. It provides funds for new technology and equipment. ICICI is entrusted with the responsibility for providing funds for commercial energy research. The scheme is called Programme for Acceleration of Commercial Energy Research (PACER). The ICICI has another Programme for Advancement of Commercial Technology (PACT), which is based on market-oriented research and development.

Promotion of Institutions: The ICICI also sponsored a mutual fund in 1993. It was called ICICI Trust Ltd. This mutual fund launched its first 100 crore issue on November 30, 1993. To provide even more services to the investor, it promoted another wholly owned subsidiary called ISERV with the objective of offering services as registrars and transfer agents. In 1994, ICICI also set up a bank called the ICICI Banking Corporation Ltd. This bank has a 75% ownership of ICICI.

The ICICI also formed a joint venture in 1993 for the Exports of Auto Components. This is formed to act as a single window-trading house. It has also set up the Credit Rating Information Services of India Ltd. (CRISIL) with the UTI – with the objective of rating the different financial instruments offered to the investors.

It promoted the Technology Development and Information Company of India Ltd. (TDICI) to undertake venture capital and technology up gradation financing. It has also associated itself with UTI and IFCI for promoting OTCEI and Stock Holding Corporation of India for streamlining trading of shares.

IFCI has promoted academic learning in Financial Management by setting up three institutes. These are—Institute for Financial Management and Research, the ICICI Foundation for Research and Development and Indian Institute for Foreman Training. Using the Indian academic it set up a Foundation for Globalization of Indian Industry in 1993. This foundation aims at restructuring value engineering and competition analysis.

The ICICI's resources pattern and functioning has undergone a change since it was set up. Its foreign currency resources have declined. It now relies on domestic Rupee Resources. Thus ICICI has continues to change its financing activities in accordance with the economic scenario in India.

There have been further developments in the ICICI. Its commercial banking operations have done well. It has offered a reverse merger whereby the ICICI will now merge with the commercial bank.

Insurance Business: ICICI has also entered into insurance through ICICI prudential. Its single premium scheme is rated very high and is extremely popular with individuals who have taken retirement under the Voluntary Retirement Scheme. It has launched 8 schemes. One of the new schemes called Pru Lifetime combines protection with market linked returns.

Consumer Financing: ICICI also facilitate other lending services. Commercial banks have been lending to private individuals for purchasing cars. ICICI has also stepped into financing of cars. This has brought about good returns to the bank.

ICICI and Universal Banking

ICICI Ltd. established in 1955, facilitated industrial development in line with the economic objectives of the time. The principal objective was to create a development financial institution for providing medium-term and long-term project financing to Indian businesses. In the 1990s, ICICI transformed its business from a development financial institution offering only project finance to a diversified financial conglomerate offering a wide variety of products and services, both directly and through a number of subsidiaries and affiliates like ICICI Bank. It evolved several new products to meet the changing needs of the corporate sector. It has provided a range of wholesale banking products and services, including project finance, corporate finance, hybrid financial structures, syndication services, treasury-based financial solutions, cash flow based financial products, lease financing, equity financing, risk management tools as well as advisory services. It also played a facilitating role in consolidation in various sectors of the Indian industry, by funding mergers and acquisitions. In the context of the emerging competitive scenario in the financial sector, In October 2001, the merger of ICICI Ltd. and two of its wholly owned retail finance subsidiaries with ICICI Bank Ltd., the ICICI Group's financing and banking operations, both wholesale and retail, have been integrated into a single full-service banking company in May 2002.

ICICI Bank has become a universal bank in India. It offers a wide range of banking products and financial services to corporate and retail customers through a variety of delivery channels and through its specialized subsidiaries and affiliates in the areas of investment banking, life and non-life insurance, venture capital and asset management. ICICI Bank set up its international banking group in fiscal 2002 to cater to the cross border needs of clients and leverage on its domestic banking strengths to offer products internationally ICICI Bank was originally promoted in 1994 by ICICI Ltd., an Indian financial institution, and was its wholly owned subsidiary. ICICI's shareholding in ICICI Bank was reduced to 46% through a public offering of shares in India in fiscal 1998. In 1999 after consideration of various corporate structuring alternatives in the context of the emerging competitive scenario in the Indian banking industry, and the move towards universal banking, the managements of ICICI and ICICI Bank formed the view that the merger of ICICI with ICICI Bank would be the optimal strategic alternative for both entities, and would create the optimal legal structure for the ICICI group's universal banking strategy. The merger would enhance value for ICICI Bank shareholders through a large capital base and scale of operations, seamless access to ICICI's strong corporate relationships built up over five decades, entry into new business segments, higher market share in various business segments, particularly fee-based services, and access to the vast talent pool of ICICI and its subsidiaries. In 2002 consequent to the merger, the ICICI group's financing and banking operations, both wholesale and retail, have been integrated in a single entity.

After the merger of ICICI with ICICI bank, all the subsidiaries companies are now the subsidiaries companies of the bank. There are 11 such subsidiaries. The principal subsidiaries are ICICI Securities and Finance Company Ltd., ICICI Venture Funds Management Company Ltd., ICICI Prudential Life Insurance Company Ltd., ICICI Lombard General Insurance Companies Ltd. and ICICI Home Finance Company Ltd. Its other subsidiaries are ICICI brokerage services Ltd., ICICI Securities Holding Incorporated, ICICI Securities Incorporated, ICICI International Ltd., ICICI Investment Management Company Ltd. and ICICI Trusteeship Services Limited. Its affiliate companies are ICICI Infotech Service Ltd., ICICI Web Trade Ltd. and ICICI One Source Limited.

ICICI as a Universal Bank has the following services.

- ICICI Securities and Finance Company Ltd. was setup in 1993-94. It provides advice to companies on corporate strategy, capital structure and capital raising. It has taken up the entire investment banking services. It advises companies on mergers and amalgamations. In the government securities market it is a primary dealer. Its subsidiaries are ICICI securities holdings Inc and ICICI securities Inc.

- ICICI Venture funds management companies provide skills and services for making equity investments. Its objective is to provide a high return to its investors.

- ICICI Prudential Life Insurance Company Ltd. began its business in 2001. It is a leading private insurance company in India. 74% of its holdings are of ICICI Ltd. and 26% of Prudential Corporation Holdings Limited. It has the life insurance business which comprises of non linked participating, non-linked non-participating, annuities and linked policies.

- ICICI Lombard General Insurance Companies Ltd. began its business in August 2001. Its principal shareholders are ICICI Ltd. which has a share of 74% and the other partner is Lombard Canada Ltd. which has a share of 26%.

- ICICI Investment Management Company Ltd. is a mutual fund. It is registered with SEBI. It is an asset management company of ICICI securities fund.

- ICICI Trusteeship Services Ltd. this company provides services for enterprises which are of strategic importance to ICICI bank and its group.

- ICICI Home Finance Company Ltd. provides loans for purchasing a house on floating rate loans. It has expanded its services for retail and corporate fee based clients.

- ICICI International Ltd. is an investment and fund management company. It was incorporated in the Republic of Mauritius in January 1996.

- ICICI bank has designed many services for its retail customers. Its retail products are personal loans, credit cards, consumer durable loans, commercial vehicle and construction equipment financing, automobile and two wheeler loans.

- ICICI bank has wholesale services for its clients. It deals with corporate banking, credit portfolio management, financing and structured financing for its clients. It provides advisory services to the public sector during its investment process. It offers letters of credit and bank guarantees. It provides cash management services and internet banking services to its clients.

ICICI Bank which was earlier known as Industrial Credit and Investment Corporation of India is India's largest private sector bank in market capitalization and second largest overall in terms of assets. ICICI Bank has total assets of about USD 79 Billion by March 31st 2007 a network of over 950 branches and offices. It has approximately 3600 ATMs and the customer's base was 24 million by the end of July 2007.

INDUSTRIAL INVESTMENT BANK OF INDIA LTD.

The industrial investment bank of India is one of oldest banks in India. The Industrial Reconstruction Corporation of India Ltd., set up in 1971 for rehabilitation of sick industrial companies, was reconstituted as Industrial Reconstruction Bank of India in 1985 under the IRBI Act, 1984. With a view to converting the institution into a full-fledged development financial institution, IRBI was incorporated under the Companies Act, 1956, as Industrial Investment Bank of India Ltd. (IIBI) in March 1997. IIBI offers a wide range of products and services, including term loan assistance for project finance, short duration non-project asset-backed financing, working capital/other short-term loans to companies, equity subscription, asset credit, equipment finance as also investments in capital market and money market instruments.

In view of certain structural and financial problems adversely impacting its long-term viability, IIBI submitted a financial restructuring proposal to the Government of India on July 25, 2003. IIBI has since received certain directives from the Government of India, which include restricting fresh lending to existing clients approved cases rated corporates, restrictions on fresh borrowings, an action plan to reduce the overhead expenditure, disposal of fixed assets and a time-bound plan for asset recovery/ reconstruction. The Government of India gave its approval for the merger of IIBI with IDBI.

STATE FINANCIAL CORPORATIONS (SFCS)

Many State level institutions have been set up to provide assistance to State level industrial units but the SFCs were established as far back as 1951 under the State Financial Corporation Act with the specific purpose of being development banks for promotion and balanced development of each state. The first SFC was formed in 1953 in Punjab. SFCs are confined to one State and also cover those neighboring states or territories which do not have their own SFC. The scope of this discussion is limited and, therefore, we will take its activity as a total group.

The objectives of the SFCs are to confine themselves to small and medium enterprises. It is prohibited from granting loans to any industry whose paid up capital and free reserves together exceed Rs. 1.0 crore. Further, the maximum loan it sanctions is Rs. 90 lakhs to companies and co-operative societies and Rs. 15 lakhs to other borrowers. Moreover, SFCs holding of a company and 10% of its own paid up capital and reserves, whichever is less. SFCs are also prohibited from entering into a business in which any of its directors is a proprietor, partner, director, manager, agent, employee, or guarantor.

The SFCs provide assistance through loans or advances not exceeding 20 years. They also subscribe to debentures repayable within 20 years. They guarantee loans for industrial purposes. They provide assistance by underwriting issues of shares; bonds or debentures and they subscribe to shares and bonds of special financial institutions.

SFCs have emerged as primary lending institutions. They have liberal terms of lending. Their areas of operation are wider than All India Development banks. They have been significant developers of backward regions. They have assisted industrial units of divergent fields ranging from artisan enterprises to units engaged in sophisticated lines of manufacture. It has been of great help to technician entrepreneurs. The assistance to them has been on liberal terms regarding interest, margin requirements and repayments. The assistance ranges between Rs. 2 and 3 lakhs. Its efforts have been noteworthy in providing 'seed capital' to small entrepreneurs. It has also provided assistance for meeting the foreign exchange requirements of medium and small projects through the International Development Association (IDA).

The SFCs have since the New Economic Policy of 1992 made several changes in their assistance pattern. They have provided loans for modernization and technology up gradation especially in the areas of energy saving, conservation of raw materials, anti-pollution measures and export oriented and import substitution products. They have also enlarged their areas of operation into industries like hotels, transport, research and development. They extend loans up to Rs. 5 lakhs to medical graduates for setting up clinics. They also provide loans to women entrepreneurs to the extent of Rs. 10 lakhs, under the Mahila Udyam Nidhi Scheme.

SFCs are extending their functions of term lending. They are also entering into new areas like merchant banking and equipment leasing keeping in view the financial reforms in the economy.

The SFCs also have a change in their methodology of resource mobilization. The SFCs drew strength in receiving inexpensive funds directly and through refinancing from the IDBI. SFCs have started investing in stocks, shares, bonds and debentures of industrial concerns. To meet the growing demand of financing SFCs has started the process of finding new areas such as financial services sector to improve profitability.

EXPORT-IMPORT BANK OF INDIA (EXIM)

The Export-Import Bank of India is wholly owned by government. It began its operations in 1982. Its main objective is to promote foreign trade in India by financing and facilitating the exporters and importers.

The bank provides the following financial services to exporters and importers.

- It provides loans to exporters and importers.
- It refinances loans of banks and financial institutions that encourage export and import trade.
- It disburses overseas investment finance to Indian companies for making equity participations in joint ventures abroad.
- It gives merchant banking services to export oriented industries.
- It provides pre shipment and post shipment term finance.
- It finances individuals and companies engaged in export marketing,
- It rediscounts export bills.
- It provides services advisory services to export and import units.

Activities of Exim

Exim bank has been involved in many promotional and developmental activities. It has worked towards developing rural projects and small scale industries for export and import trade.

Development of Small Industries: Exim has provided marketing support to rural products and small enterprises. It has launched an export marketing services program to benefit these units. It assists the SHGs / NGOs in different states to establish the small enterprises in the export market through its overseas offices. It organizes seminars and workshops for small enterprises.

Consultancy Services of EXIM: Exim has provided consultancy services in Malaysia by setting up an Exim Bank in Malaysia. It has also established an Export Credit Guarantee Company in Zimbabwe and plans to establish an Exim Bank in Zimbabwe. It has made feasibility studies for setting up the A frexim Bank. It has designed many export financing and developing programs in Turkey, South Africa: Ukraine, Vietnam, Armenia and Mauritius.

Research Studies: Exim bank has conducted research studies on products in different sectors and countries, in subjects relevant to international trade and investment. It has also published many news letters and magazines for informing the exporters and importers of trade benefits in different countries.

Development Activity: The Exim bank was the first institution in India in 1986 to finance and promote computer software exports. It supported Infosys to develop into a large export company. It setup Global Trade Finance Ltd. as a joint venture with IFC and West LB for providing export factoring facility as an alternate trade financing instrument for Small Industry sector. In 1996 it initiated Global

Procurement Consultants Ltd. as a joint venture with 10 Indian private and public sector enterprises to take up overseas assignments in procurement advisory services. It started the Asian Exim Banks Forum in 1996 to bring together Exim Banks operating in Asia to promote intra-regional trade and reduce transaction cost. Bank signed Multilateral L/C confirmation facility with other Exim Banks.

Summary

➠ Development banks were conceived in India as gap fillers for providing credit to industry.

➠ The focus of development banks was to developed backward region as well as small, medium and large enterprises particularly in the private corporate sector.

➠ The first development bank to be setup was IFCI in 1948. It was instituted as an all India level development bank to assist large enterprises in the private corporate sector.

➠ The State Financial Corporation's were instituted in each state and their work was to assist the enterprises developed in a particular state.

➠ The IDBI was setup in 1964 as a subsidiary of the RBI but in 1975 it attained an independent status.

➠ IDBI became the apex development bank in India.

➠ In 1995 government reduced its shareholding in IDBI to 58.47% and in 2003 IDBI became a limited company.

➠ In 2004 IDBI started functioning as a commercial bank.

➠ IDBI has played a promotional role in developing backward regions. It has underwritten many companies at the time of their new issues. It has been a catalyst to industrial development by providing finance for development purposes to many companies. It has revived sick companies. It has provided export finance. It has participated in technological advancements by providing loans to industries for controlling pollution and energy conservation. It has refinanced SFC's and SIDC's. It has sponsored many institutions including Technology Consultancy Organizations and Entrepreneurship Development Institute. It has contributed to the stock market by sponsoring the National Securities Depository Services Ltd. and Stock Holding Corporation of India.

➠ IDBI has diversified by becoming a commercial bank and has started a new model with the objective of low cost current and savings bank accounts. It has also provided finance to the retail customers.

➠ The IFCI assists large industries it underwrite issues in the new issue market. Its subscribes to shares and debentures of public limited companies and provides foreign currency loans. It has contributed to the modernization of Indian industry, entrepreneurship development programs. It has sponsored many financial institutions. It has setup subsidiaries for merchant banking and stock exchange services. Its sponsored ICRA, National Stock Exchange and Management Development Institute. It has gone into new areas of financing predominant among them being leasing and hire-purchase of equipments.   *Contd.....*

➠ The ICICI was developed as a private sector development bank for providing foreign currencies loans and developing the new issue market in India. ICICI has taken many progressive steps since 1991. It started a commercial bank and later on merged with it in 2001. It has extended its operations in foreign countries. It was the first Indian company to be listed on the New York Stock Exchange. ICICI had the first merchant banking division in India to help the new issue market. It has sponsored research and development program. It had promoted many institution such as a mutual fund, CRISIL rating and promoted OTCEI with other financial institutions. Being progressive it entered into insurance business and consumer financing. It became the first universal bank in India. It transformed itself from a development institution which offered only project finance to diversify into many new products in the wholesale and retail sector. It also provide service in corporate finance, syndication services, lease financing, equity financing and in advisory services. It has many subsidiary companies through which it enters into insurance, mutual fund, brokerage, investment ant trusteeship services.

➠ The SFC's were started in 1951. They were instituted in every state in India to develop the small and medium companies. Their focus was to develop the resources of the state in which they were initiated. They participated in providing feasibility studies and promotion of industries in the state.

➠ The Export Import Bank of India gives its service to exporters and importers of the country. It has played a promotional and developmental role in promoting exports from the country. It has given pre and post shipment loans. It has also helped the entrepreneurs to develop their products in rural areas with the help of NGO's. It has provided consultancy services and made research studies to benefit the export and import trade in different countries.

Objective Type Questions, Answer True (T) or False (F)

(a) The IFCI is the first universal bank in India.

(b) The development banks were started to support the financial institutions in India.

(c) ICICI was the first Indian company to be listed on New York Stock Exchange.

(d) The Export Import Bank of India has developed industries in rural areas for export trade.

(e) Lombard Insurance Company has been sponsored by IDBI.

(f) The IDBI and the ICICI bank have entered into reverse merger with each other.

(g) The State Financial Corporation's are subsidiaries of International Financial Corporation.

(h) The Export Import Bank of India is a subsidiary of IDBI.

(i) The ICICI has sponsored ICRA.

(j) IDBI has sponsored CRISIL.

Answer: (a) F, (b) F (c) T, (d) T, (e) F, (f) F, (g) F, (h) F, (i) F (j) F.

Multiple Choice Questions (Tick mark (✓) the right answer)

1. The ICICI was started in the year:
   - (a) 1957
   - (b) 1959
   - (c) 1951
   - (d) 1955

2. The ICICI carries out the following business:
   - (a) Buying and selling of shares
   - (b) Brokerage from foreign companies for giving it business
   - (c) Life and General Insurance business
   - (d) Setting up medical clinics in India

3. The IDBI promoted:
   - (a) CRISIL
   - (b) ICRA
   - (c) IFCI
   - (d) RBI

4. The IDBI promoted large and medium companies:
   - (a) At all India level
   - (b) At the State level
   - (c) In Maharashtra State
   - (d) In Gujarat State

5. The development banks are called:
   - (a) Universal Banks
   - (b) Financial Institutions
   - (c) Development Financial Institutions
   - (d) Non-bank Institutions

   Answer: 1 (d), 2 (c), 3 (b), 4 (a), 5 (c).

Short Answer Questions

1. State the objective of development financial institutions. How are they different from other financial institutions?

2. Discuss the new directions of ICICI since 1991.

3. Briefly discuss the role of State Financial Corporation's in India.

Long Answer Questions

1. What is universal banking? What services does ICICI provide since its transformation into a universal bank?

2. Discuss the role of Export-Import Bank of India. What are its development and promotional activities?

3. What is the role of IDBI as a development bank of India which institutions has it promoted?

Part – Seven
Financial Services

18. Financial Services
    - Merchant Banking
    - Underwriting
    - Leasing
    - Hire-purchase
    - Consumer Finance
    - Housing Finance
    - Venture Capital Finance
    - Factoring & Forfaiting Services
    - Securitization
    - Credit Rating

Financial Services

Chapter Plan

- Phases of Financial Services in India
- Types of Financial Services
- Financial Services – Players
- Merchant Banking
- Underwriting
- Leasing
- Hire Purchase
- Consumer Finance
- Housing Finance
- Venture Capital Finance
- Factoring & Forfaiting
- Securitization
- Credit Rating

INTRODUCTION

The last chapter of this book is concerned with an overview of the financial services offered in India to mobilize and allocate savings through the transformation of savings into investments. Financial services are rendered through specialized institutions which organize the work of the client to raise funds, manage funds and transform savings into investments. The financial services market consists of market players, financial instruments, specialized institutions and regulatory bodies. The specialized financial services are merchant banking, underwriting, leasing, hire-purchase, consumer and housing finance, venture capital finance, factoring services, securitization and credit rating.

The financial services offer different types of financial instruments like equity, debt, hybrid and financial engineering instruments and specialized institutions in this market are the discount houses, depositories, venture capital institutions, acceptance houses, credit rating agencies and many others. The main regulatory bodies are the Reserve Bank of India, Securities Exchange Board of India, Insurance Regulatory Development Authority, Department of Banking and Insurance of the Central Government.

Phases of Financial Services in India

The financial services in India have grown since 1960 but its development took place since the new economic reforms in 1991. The slow growth of the financial sector was due to lack of experts, professional bodies and number of institutions providing financial services. This sector suffered due to the absence of computer and telecommunication technology. The process of information was slow as it used to be done manually. The quality of the work was not according to world standards. There was no proper regulation of the market to provide investor protection. The growth of financial services can be discussed in four different phases.

Phase I : The first phase of financial services was from 1960. This is often called '*the merchant banking'* phase. The merchant bankers assisted companies to develop new projects by preparing project reports and feasibility studies. They also undertook advisory positions on legal and technical matters. They arranged working capital loans for companies and made underwriting arrangements.

Phase II : In the second phase the development of banks, life insurance and general insurance companies and investment companies were developed. LIC was incorporated in 1956 but it began to make an impact only in the 70's. Banks were nationalized for the first time in 1969 to take up priority sector lending and other financial services for developing the savings and investments position in the economy. By 1978 leasing companies started providing service in India. This phase is popularly called the period of development of *investment companies*.

Phase III : The third phase was in the 80's when many new services were developed in India. The new services consisted of credit rating, venture capital funding, factoring, mutual funds and share transfers. Factoring was useful for short term financing in internal as well as international trade. Credit rating brought about branding of industries and creating confidence for the investor for freely investing in capital market securities. In this phase *new services* were initiated.

Phase IV : In this phase many new development were brought about in India to internationalize and globalize the Indian markets. Many reforms were made in the new issue market and the stock market. Book building was introduced in the new issue market. The depository system for dematerializing shares to move towards a paperless trading system was brought about. The Bombay Stock Exchange, Delhi Stock Exchange and National Stock Exchange were computerized and online trading was started in India. The foreign institutional investors entered the Indian capital market. SEBI brought out guidelines to bring about discipline in the capital market. Several legislations were passed by regulatory authorities to develop the capital market. Finally the Indian market with its liberalized structure was accepted globally. With the opening up of the Indian capital market many new financial services were initiated for creating a sound institutional mechanism.

TYPES OF FINANCIAL SERVICES

There are different types of financial services in India. These are fund based services, fee based services, commercial financial services and securities related financial services.

- *The fund based financial services* comprise of equipment leasing and hire-purchase, venture capital, housing finance, factoring, bills discounting and loans and investments.

- *The fee based financial services* are corporate counselling, issue management, portfolio management, loan syndication, foreign collaboration, mergers and acquisitions and capital restructuring.

- *The commercial financial services* are largely bank based services. These are advisory and custodian services, letter of credit for financing trade, financial management and transaction services and credit card services.

- *The securities related financial services* are mutual fund services, private placement, underwriting services, securities trading, clearance, and lending and settlement services.

FINANCIAL SERVICES – PLAYERS

The financial services have a large number of players. Households, firms, government and foreign financial institutions play an important role in the demand and supply of funds. Banks, financial institutions, insurance companies, mutual funds and financial services companies assist in development of the financial market.

Households: In an economy the household sector is a supplier of funds. It is an important player because the people save from their current income for current consumption, as a precautionary measure and first speculative purposes. They have current needs and they also save for retirement. They are looking for current gain above their normal income as well as capital gain out of their investments. However, savings of the household sector largely depends on certain factors like age, income level, personal taxes and the willingness of the people to save and invest.

Firms: All institutions which are engaged in commercial activity would be classified as firms. This is the sector which has a demand for funds for carrying on business activity with the end result of making a profit. The demand for funds will be high when the economy is flourishing. In the downward trend when there is recession, it is expected that the demand for funds will diminish.

Government: The government sector plays an important role in the financial services market. It regulates the market. It is also a player in the form of lender and borrower in the financial market. It requires large amount of funds for development work carried out in a country. When it has excess funds, it lends in the market.

Financial Institutions: These companies and institutions provide many services to get the savers and the investors together. Their main function is to act as an intermediary between those who supply funds and those who demand them.

Insurance Companies, Mutual Funds: These companies function as service oriented companies or intermediaries between the savers and the investors. They have a large resource base collected from the household sector. This surplus is invested in securities thus brining about development in the financial markets.

Financial Services: A large number of institutions have been developed to provide financial services for moping up the savings of the people and investing them. While promoting savings and investments they provide innovative customer oriented financial products. They provide attractive financial instruments. They give advisory services to their customers for which they charge their fees. The financial services market has developed since the new economy reforms in 1991. They provide financial instruments which give liquidity, marketability and quick transferability of financial instruments. Some of the important financial services are discussed in this chapter because a book on financial institutions and markets do not seem complete without some reference to this challenging sector.

MERCHANT BANKING

Merchant banking is a financial service which has the function of providing advice in corporate matters. *It is an intermediary between issuers and purchasers of securities*. Their focus is on *issue management*. Merchant bankers in India take up a number of services. They are engaged in the following services:

- *Issue Management:* The Merchant bankers manage the *new issue* of companies. They give services in designing the capital structure of a company, the timing of the public issue. Selection of brokers and underwriters. They also hire issue houses and advertising agencies for pre and post publicity of the issue. They prepare the prospectus and application forms of the issue and they arrange for listing of shares with the stock exchanges. The merchant bankers have pre and post issue obligations. Pre issue they have to file the prospectus and relevant documents with SEBI. Post issue they have to allot the shares and despatch shares or refunds within 30 days to the applicants. They have to arrange the bankers, registrars and underwriters of the issue and file their names with SEBI. As per SEBI guidelines there has to be a 100% net offer to the public through book building or 75% through book building and 25% at the price determent through book building. All the functions of issue management are required to be done to the best of a merchant bankers' ability and with full disclosures required by SEBI.

- *Portfolio Management:* Merchant bankers help their customers to make the correct choice of their investments. They take decisions regarding the type and quantity of the securities to be invested. The time of purchase and the mix between the different assets to maximize the return and minimize the risk of the client.

- *Project Feasibility Advice:* This service relates to project counselling and guiding the company in identifying a potential project. Merchant bankers assist in getting approvals, grants, licenses and permission from government agencies for making collaborations. They also assist in preparing the technical, economic and financial feasibilities studies for a company.

- *Financial Counselling:* Merchant bankers provide advisory services in investment decisions, capital management, and marketing strategy, choice of product, mergers and acquisition. They assist in taking over sick companies and in revitalizing them. They evaluate industrial products through financial appraisals. They also give advice in capital restructuring services.

- *Credit Syndication:* Merchant bankers undertake the service of credit procurement and raising loans in India and abroad. They prepare the loan application forms and follow up the loan procedure with financial institutions and banks.

- *Venture Financing:* Merchant bankers advise companies on obtaining venture capital. They also interact between the venture capitalists and the company requiring funds and give every possible help in obtaining capital.

- *Lease Financing:* Merchant bankers give advice on leasing of equipment. They assist in identifying the right product useful for the requirements of the purpose of the project. They prepare proposals and acquire capital equipment through leasing for companies. They do not however do any leasing business themselves.

- *Foreign Currency Financing:* Merchant bankers provide services for foreign currency loans and export import trade financing. They arrange for different kinds of loans through negotiations with other parties. They arrange for pre shipment and post shipment credit, bridge loans and other foreign currency loans through euro currencies, bank guarantees, and syndication of euro loans. They also provide assistance in currency and interest rate swaps.

Regulatory Framework of Merchant Bankers

The merchant bankers have to follow certain operational guidelines as directed by Securities Exchange Board of India.

Code of Conduct: The merchant bankers are governed by a code of conduct. According to this code they have to follow a high standard of integrity and provide good quality service to their clients. They have to be honest and fair in their dealings while advising their customers. While providing advice they should be professional and give the adequate information to their clients. They should comply with the Act, rules and regulations relevant to their functioning. They should not discriminate amongst their clients. They should also not make any oral or written statements which misrepresents their clients in any way.

The merchant bankers have to obtain certain clearances for carrying out their business as per operational guidelines of SEBI.

Registration: Merchant bankers have to register themselves with SEBI for conducting their services to clients. They require compulsory registration for acting as sponsors of a capital issue. Although merchant bankers are of four types, since 1997 there is a uniformity and only category I merchant bankers are allowed to do issue management. In the function of issue management they have to prepare prospectus of the company, its capital structure, allot shares and also refund subscriptions. They have to advise the company as its consultant and manager. They take the role of a *lead manager* to an issue. If they act as *underwriters or portfolio manager* of the company they must obtain from SEBI a separate registration certificate.

Capital Adequacy Requirement: The registration fees have been raised to Rs. 5 lakhs since 1999. The four categories had to apply for different types of renewal fees but from 1999 the renewal fees is Rs. 2.5 lakhs per annum for 3 years.

Restriction of Business: A merchant banker is allowed to carry on the business of securities market. They cannot enter into fund based activities like leasing. When a merchant banker is registered with RBI as a primary/satellite dealer he will be permitted to carry on only that business which is permitted by RBI.

Lead Manager

The main merchant banker will be the lead manager. These lead managers can have associate merchant bankers to the issue.

Number of Lead Managers: The number of *Lead* managers to be appointed would depend on the size of an issue.

- If the size is lees than Rs. 50 crores two lead managers have to be appointed by a company.
- When the size is between 50 crores and 100 crores, 3 lead managers would be appointed.
- Companies in the size group of 100 to 200 crores can appoint *four* lead managers.
- When the issue size is between 200 and 400 crores *five* lead managers would be appointed.

Role of Lead Managers: The role of lead managers is to furnish a statement to the SEBI one month before the ***new issue about the date of the issue***. They have to prepare an agreement with the issuing company about their rights, liabilities and obligations towards the issue. In particular they have to provide information on allotment and refund relating to ***the issue.*** If there are more than one lead managers/ merchant bankers both the lead managers have to furnish a statement with SEBI giving details of their responsibilities. A lead manager cannot associate with a company in managing its issue if the issuing company is its associates. It can also not work with a non registered merchant banker. The lead manager and other merchant bankers have to be compulsorily registered with SEBI to conduct the business of issue management with a company. The lead manager has to take a minimum underwriting commitment of 5% or Rs. 25 lakhs (whichever is less) of the total underwriting commitment. In case he has a problem, the associate merchant banker can pay the amount and notify SEBI.

Documents filed with SEBI: The lead manager has to submit the documents of the issue to SEBI two weeks before it is to be filed with the register of companies and regional stock exchanges. The documents consist of letter of offer/draft prospectus and complete information related with the issue and to be circulated to investors/shareholders. The offer document has to accompany the prescribed fees.

- If the size of the offer is upto Rs. 5 crores the prescribed fees is Rs. 10,000.
- If the size is between 5 crores and 10 crores the fees is Rs. 15,000.
- Companies making and issue of the size of 10 crores to 50 crores would have to pay fees of Rs. 25,000.
- Rs. 50 to 100 crores issue would be a fee of Rs. 50,000.
- Rs. 100 to 500 crores issue would have to pay Rs. 2,50,000 to SEBI, and
- Issues worth more than Rs. 500 crores would pay a fees of Rs. 5 lakhs.

Certificate of Due Diligence: The lead manager has to furnish the ***due diligence certificate*** to SEBI. This certificate has to be sent two weeks in advance of the issue. The lead manager has to make a written statement that the prospectus/letter of offer prepared by him confirm with the regulations of SEBI and the disclosure made by the company is true and fair for the investors to make that decision relating to the investment.

Disclosures to SEBI: A lead manager and associate merchant bankers have to furnish documents regarding matters of the issue. If any information is changed after receiving the certificate of registration the information should be immediately submitted. The information may pertain to any issue which is necessary for complying with the rules and regulations of SEBI in respect of new issues.

Inspection of Records: The merchant banker has to comply with the rules and regulations of SEBI. He has to submit all information regarding the records and books relating to its business. At any time

SEBI can inspect the books and records of the merchant banker in order to protect the interest of the investors. SEBI can also ask for explanations from the merchant banker if it finds that the rules and regulations are not complied with. SEBI has the right of appointing an auditor and inspection committee which is qualified to inspect the books of account of a merchant banker.

Penalty of Merchant Bankers: A merchant banker can be penalized by ***suspension of his registration*** if he violates the ***Acts, rules or regulations*** of SEBI. He can be suspended from his activity of merchant banking if he submits incorrect documents giving false information or is not co-operative at the time of an enquiry. If he does not submit periodical returns he faces penalty. In the following cases his certificate of registration can be suspended.

- When he does the activity of price rigging, manipulation or cornering of share prices.
- When he is guilty of unprofessional and unethical conduct in his work.
- When he does not pay his fees in time.
- When he does not comply with the registration of SEBI.

In Serious cases merchant banker's registration can be ***cancelled.*** In the following cases registration can be cancelled.

- When his improper activities affect the interest of the investor in the securities market.
- When he misrepresents his financial statement and SEBI on inspection finds out that merchant banker is guilty of fraud.
- When a merchant banker is convicted in the case of a criminal offence.
- When the merchant banker does not improve in his activities after his suspension his registration can be cancelled.

In the above cases if SEBI decides to cancel the registration of the merchant banker, he will have to refrain from any activity of merchant banking. SEBI will publish the suspension or cancellation of the merchant banker's registration in to leading daily news papers.

Penalty Points of Merchant Bankers: Merchant Bankers will get penalty points in case of defaults. The defaults may be of different kinds. They can be general, minor, major or serious defaults.

- *General defaults* are when the lead manager does not submit the draft prospectus/letter of offer from lead manager, certificate of due diligence, certificate of subscription of minimum of 90% of the issue. Another general default is when the shareholders refund orders or share certificates are not sent in time.
- *Minor defaults* are when a circular or an advertisement relating to the issue is not in accordance with SEBI guidelines or prospectus is drafted incorrectly or adequate disclosure is not provided to shareholders. Such defaults also occur when there are delays in mailing refund or allotment letters. If investor grievances are not handled within a time framework and there are delays it will be taken as a minor default.
- *Major Defaults* are when the merchant banker does not conduct underwriting according to the mandatory regulations and the number of lead managers is more than required for the issue. If unauthorized merchant bankers are hired it is a major defaults.

- ***Serious Defaults*** are when a merchant banker violates his code of conduct and his activities are unethical. If a merchant banker does not co-operate in providing information or documents required by SEBI it is a serious defaults.

When the merchant banker gets eight penalty points his registration can be suspended or cancelled by SEBI. In a single issue the merchant banker can get a maximum of four penalty points. If there are a number of lead managers associated with an issue and they have joint responsibility, each one of them will get four penalty points.

Negative Points: The merchant bankers can also get ***general negative points*** if they have not highlighted the risk factors or listing details.

Grading Points: Deficiencies in preparing a prospectus will get negative points. The prospectus is graded according to the points. The prospectus get full 10 points if it is correct in all respects and graded A+, A, B or C according to the number of points.

Thus, the merchant bankers have certain responsibilities and obligations towards their clients. They have a code of conduct to be followed they have to prepare an agreement or memorandum of understanding with the company with whom they are dealing. They have to prepare a due diligence certificate. In an issue there are lead managers and co-managers. They have to submit the draft prospectus or offer with SEBI. Their books can be inspected by SEBI. Their certificate can be suspended or cancelled according to the negative points. They must be responsible and manage an issue in a way that it complies with the rules and regulations of SEBI.

UNDERWRITING

The main function of underwriting is to subscribe to the new issues that are not fully subscribed. The underwriters commit before the new issue, the number of shares they would like to subscribe to. They have the option to subscribe the shares themselves or by other underwriters but they have to give the names of the underwriters in advance of the issue. The underwriters are appointed by the merchant bankers or lead managers to the issue by signing a contract between the company and the underwriter. The contract is called a Memorandum of Understanding (MOU). Since 1995 underwriting is not mandatory for the issuing company. However, it is an important service and underwriting continues to exist in the new issue market. The following aspects are important for conducting the business of underwriting.

Certificate of Registration: In order to become an underwriter a certificate of registration has to be applied for to the SEBI. To grant this certificate SEBI inspects the following details of the applicant:

- The infrastructure of the applicant relating to office space, manpower and equipment required for carrying out the business of underwriting.
- The experience of the applicant in the function of underwriting. If he does not have any past experience he should have at least two employees who have experience in underwriting.
- The applicant past record. The person should not have any record of negligence of duty or any disciplinary action taken against him.

- The applicants past record should not show any criminal offence against him or any of his partners for which he or any of them was convicted.
- The applicant should have a capital adequacy requirement of a minimum amount of Rs. 20 lakhs of net worth which includes capital and free reserves.

If after inspection the records of the underwriter are clear SEBI will grant them a certificate of registration for commencement of business after they have paid a fees and have understood the code of conduct that they have to follow to do business.

Fees: SEBI charges a fees from the date of granting a certificate. Since 1999 the fees is Rs. 5 lakhs for the first year and there is a renewal fees of Rs. 2 lakhs for every 3 years. In order to continue with the business renewal of registration has to be applied for.

Code of Conduct: The following code of conduct has to be maintained by underwriters to continue the business.

- An underwriter has to be professional in his dealings with his clients and carry out the business efficiently and promptly.
- He must protect the interest of his clients honestly and be fair in his dealings with them.
- He has to maintain a high standard of integrity and not misrepresent his clients in any oral or written statement made by him.
- He has to disclosed all information in the interest of his clients and avoid any conflict of interest and has to be objective and unbiased in his dealings with them.
- He cannot discriminate amongst his clients except for carrying out moral responsibility and obligations.
- He cannot participate in price rigging or manipulation of information to any person about securities listed with stock exchange.
- He has to follow the guidelines acts and rules of SEBI and comply with the OMBUDSMAN regulations 2003 as advised by SEBI.
- He must follow good corporate governance and corporate policies by acting within the sphere of law.

Memorandum of Agreement: An underwriter has to enter into a contract with the issuing company. The contract should state clearly the responsibilities and obligations of the underwriter. It should also have clear written agreement on the number of shares to be subscribed, period of underwriting contract and commission and brokerage to be received for the service undertaken. The underwriter can take a maximum subscription of shares up to 20 times his own net worth. He has to subscribe to shares within 45 days of   receiving a notification from the issuing company.

Inspection: SEBI has the right to inspect the books of account and records of the underwriter. If the underwriter fails to comply with the conditions of SEBI, he will be faced with cancellation or suspension of his certificate of registration.

LEASING

A lease is a financial arrangement or agreement between the lessor and lessee for use of an asset in return for a rent for a certain period of time. Lessor is the owner of the asset. He gives the right to the other person to use his asset for a periodic payment of rent. The lessee is the person who wants to pay a rent to use the assets without owning it.

The following are the important aspects of a lease agreement.

- *Assets:* A lease agreement is made for using a *high value asset*. Examples of these assets are building, plant and machinery and automobile.

- *Agreement:* It is an agreement between two parties. They are known as the lessor and lessee.

- *Time period:* The agreed period for use of the asset is the term of the lease. In India there can be a perpetual lease. However, lease term must be stated in the agreement because after the expiry of that period the asset goes back in favour of the leaser.

- *Owner:* The ownership of the asset is different from the use of the asset. When an agreement is signed and the lease period is continuing, the ownership of the asset is with the lessor but the asset is used by the lessee. When the term is over the asset goes back to the original owner or lessor. Lease period can have a continuous specified term period. It can also have two periods like *primary term period and secondary term period*.

- *Rent:* The rent of the lease is written in the contract it covers cost of interest repairs, maintenance and service charges paid by the lessor. It also covers depreciation on the asset.

Types of Lease

Lease can be of different types. There can be financial lease, operating lease, conveyance type lease, leverage lease, consumer lease, import lease and international lease.

- *Finance lease:* It is also called 'capital lease'. This has been defined by Institute of Chartered accountants and by International Accounting Standard. According to their definitions a financial lease is one in which the lessee has the major role in taking over all the risks and expenses of maintenance for using the assets. He also receives all the rewards. The lessor receives the rent. He does not give any service while leasing out his asset. He receives the full value of his leased asset through rent and residual value. He also receives the tax benefits and depreciation of the assets.

- *Operating lease:* It is a short-term lease for the economic service provided by the lessor. All the risks and the rewards are received by the lessor. The period of lease is usually less than the life is the asset. The lease period can be cancelled or renewed by the lessor. The cost of maintenance is paid by the lessor and it is a non payout lease as the lessor may give this asset on lease to many different people.

- *Conveyance type lease:* Lease provided on immovable properties for a long term period of time covering 99 years to 999 years is called a conveyance type lease.

- *Leverage lease:* The assets having a high value are leased through leveraged lease. It is leased through a financer.

- *Consumer lease:* Retail consumers who buy items like refrigerator, television, computer, air conditioner take a lease contract. Such contracts are for purchase of personal household goods. Most of these contracts are with the option of purchasing the asset when the lease expires.

- *Import lease:* When capital goods are imported through a leasing agreement, it is called an import lease. It is of advantage to the lessee because they are not able to get finance for paying import duty. The simplest method is to arrange the goods through leasing. However, import leasing is possible only by receiving permission from the licensing authorities. The Memorandum of Association should allow the leasing. The lessor and the lessee become jointly responsible for terms and conditions of the authorities. Thus both the parties have to give a letter of consent with submission of the leasing agreement.

- *International lease:* International leasing is done by a company by operating in more than one country. It can also be done through cross border leasing when more than one country is involved in the lease. International leasing has to be done within the framework of the countries rules and regulations. It has two kinds of risk namely '*country risk and currency risks*'.

Leasing has many benefits for the lessor and the lessee. It also has some limitations. The advantages and its limitations are listed below:

Advantages of Leasing

- *Advantages to lessor:* The lessor has the advantage of owning an asset without making any capital payment for it. The lessee pays him a rent out of which he acquires his asset. He is able to get tax benefits on lease rentals as tax on leasing is lower than tax on sale of asset. He also gets the advantage of tax relief on depreciation. He is the owner of the asset even after receiving rent for a number of years. It is a very profitable business with the potential of high growth.

- *Advantages to lessee:* The lessee procures capital goods without making a down payment for the product. He can give a rent and begin his business. The greatest advantage to the lessee is that he can avoid taking loans from institutions which is a cumbersome procedure. He takes a lease for the period that suits him. He selects the lease in which he has the capacity to repay the amount through rentals. He can get a tax advantage on the rental that he pays because his taxable income is reduced by paying the rentals. His risk of obsolescence on a capital product is avoided as such a risk is borne by the lessor.

Limitations of Leasing

One of the limitations of leasing is when it suffered from double taxation due to these state laws. Lease rental can be taxed at the time of sale and again when it is leased out. Another limitation is that the lessee does not get any ownership rights against the use of the assets. The risk of default is high. In other words it is a firmed of debt financing and it is expensive because of high rents. The lessee does not receive the residual value because he has to return the asset after using it. Hence, it is a lost to him.

The lessor has an equal problem as the lessee because though he owns an asset he cannot use it because he his given at rent. While using it the lessee can damage the product and thus when he receives it, the product may not be in a workable position. Thus it is of high risk to the lessor.

Lease financing has become popular in India since the amendment of the Banking Regulation Act. The commercial banks in India offer leasing benefits to clients. The ICICI and the Asian Development Bank jointly provide leasing arrangements for consumer durable, manufacturing and electronic industries. The IFCI provides lease financing to both corporate and non-corporate sectors. In the private sector there are many leasing companies engaged in consumer credit and leasing services. The Infrastructure Leasing and Financing Services (ILFS) were formed for providing leasing services especially for infrastructure development in co-operation with central government and state government agencies.

HIRE PURCHASE

Hire purchase is an agreement between two parties in which the goods are taken on hire with the option of purchasing them by making the payment of the goods through instalment. In India hire purchase is very popular for consumer durables machinery and automobiles. Hire purchase is in two parts. In the first part of the contract the goods are given in the form of a bailment of goods. In the second part of the contract when the hirer buys the product, it is the contract of sale. The owner of the goods continues to have the right of ownership until the purchasing party exercises the option of acquiring it. Hire purchase can be distinguished from instalment payment and lease financing.

- *Instalment:* An instalment sale is a contract in which the seller transfers the ownership rights to the buyer. The time period of payment is specified and the buyer makes his payments through instalments.

- *Leasing:* In lease financing the lessor has the ownership of the equipment which he gives on rent. The ownership does not get transferred.

- *Hire purchase:* The hire purchase is a system which resembles both instalment sale and lease financing but it is also different from them. In hire purchase there is a ***call option*** according which the purchaser has the right to make the full payment and buy the asset. He can terminate the contract as soon as he pays the full value of the asset. In lease financing the lessee can use the asset but has to return it because the lessor is the owner. In hire purchase the moment the contract is made a small down payment is made with the promise of ***equated monthly instalments*** till the full payment.

Hire Purchase Contract

The hire purchase contract is between 3 parties. These are the seller, the hirer and the financer. The seller prepares a hire purchase agreement between the hirer and a finance company. An agreement is signed by the seller and the financer with the terms and condition of the hire purchase. The financer prepares a hire purchase agreement with the hirer of the product with his terms and conditions. The hirer makes a down payment to the seller. The seller requests the finance company to make the payment and purchase the goods. The finance company makes the payment to the seller. The hirer pays monthly instalments to the financer and when last payment is made he receives a clearance from the finance company. Thus the hirer becomes the owner of the asset.

Calculation of Interest

In hire purchase the method of calculating interest is through the effective rate of interest, sum of digits method and straight line method.

- *Effective rate of interest or annual percentage rate method:* The internal rate of return technique is used to find out the effective rate of interest. The hire purchase which is paid is greater than the cost of the asset. It equates the present value of all future annual instalment payments with the hire purchase principal paid in the beginning of the contract.

- *The sum of digit method:* It is the total amount payable multiplied by a continuous flat rate of interest.

- *Straight line method:* This is annual amount of interest which is found out the basis of the total interest payable during the hire purchase period divided by the number of hire purchase period.

Tax Treatment

The tax treatment in hire purchase is in favour of the hirer. The depreciation of the asset can be claimed by the hirer. He can also get a deduction on the interest paid by him in his instalment.

CONSUMER FINANCE

Consumer credit is given to customers for purchasing consumer durables. The credit is available for personal consumption items like refrigerator, air-conditioned, computer, television, geyser etc. There are different kinds of consumer finance available in India.

- *Revolving credit:* The credit facility given to a consumer can be a *revolving credit* in which the consumer has a maximum credit limit sanctioned to him. In the modern concept the credit cards are like a revolving facility for a customer.

- *Cash loan:* Banks and financial institutions give cash in the form of loans to customers for purchasing products for their personal use.

- *Fixed credit:* A fixed credit is a term loan for a fixed period of time. At the expiry of the period the customer has to return the principal.

- *Hire purchase:* It is a system of giving credit to consumers to buy certain asset of their choice. In hire purchase the seller is different to the lender. The lender does not own the asset that he is financing.

- *Instalment purchase:* A payment made through a number of instalments for the cost of the assets is the instalment credit system. The buyer becomes the owner of the asset after the first instalment. Then he continues to pay till the cost of the asset is cover.

- *Secured credit:* A secured loan is given by a bank or a financial institution to a consumer against collateral supplied by the borrower. The collateral may be in the form of property or value based assets.

- *Unsecured loans:* When a bank or a financial institution provides a loan to a persona without any collateral. It is an unsecured loan.

Consumer Credit Contract

The consumer credit contract is between two parties. These are the *seller* and the *buyer*. There can be three parties involved when the financer provides the finance. Usually in hire purchase there are three parties involved in the contract.

- *Period of credit:* Consumer credit is given for short periods of time. The term of loan is decided by the type and value of asset purchased. Usually the maximum time period of providing loan is 5 years.

- *Rate of Interest:* The rate of interest is high because the seller does not take any collateral from the buyer for purchasing consumer durables. It is based on the personal rapport between the buyer and the seller. The seller judges the personal integrity of the consumer and accordingly gives consumer credit.

- *Instalments:* If the buyer purchases assets through instalments the seller works out the equated monthly instalments (EMI) for the period of payment.

- *Payment method:* The seller takes post dated cheques in advance from the buyer. Every month he deposits the cheque in the bank and it is cleared until the final instalment is paid.

- *Other charges:* In case third parties are involved in the firm of financers they charge processing fees, documentation charges, service charges and collection cost above the interest charged by them.

- *Customer Verification:* The seller makes an enquiry about the integrity of the buyer from his banker or previous record of loans taken by him. He has he right to verify the details relating to the borrowing capacity of the buyer.

Benefits of Consumer Finance

Consumer finance is beneficial both for the buyer and the seller. The benefits of such a sale are discussed below.

- **Benefits for buyer:** A buyer can increase his standard of living by being able to acquire goods for his family and his home. He does not have to pay the whole of the amount immediately. He can purchase goods which he is unable to do without any credit. Thus consumer finance makes it convenient for buyers to purchase goods of their choice.

- **Benefits for seller:** The seller is able to get the advantage of immediate sale of his product. Many goods like unsold for a long time because consumers cannot pay for them in one down payment. The seller is thus losing money by stocking goods. The costs of storage, electricity and depreciation all increase in the form of interest charges on the products. Consumer credit lures a buyer to take advantages of convenience of payment in instalments. This enhances the sales of the seller.

Disadvantages of Consumer Finance

The buyer and the seller must take caution in selling products through credit. It has some disadvantages for both the buyer and the seller.

- ***Disadvantages for buyer:*** Consumers purchase more than their capacity because of the ease and advantages of instalment payment. However, the instalment becomes a burden on the family resources. Credit cards of buyers carry heavy debt to be paid for purchasing consumer durables. Sometimes people buy but find it very difficulty to pay and take further credit to return the amount. This creates a bad personal financial position and they can end up by being insolvent. Another disadvantage is that the consumers have to pay an amount higher than the cost of the asset because interest charges are added to the cost for providing credit to consumers.

- ***Disadvantages for seller:*** The seller is faced with a heavy risk. If the buyer defaults in his payments the seller will lose finance. He will ultimately be faced by bad debts which will accumulate thus reducing his profits. Further the seller creates an artificial boom in an economy through credit sales. Thus the true position in the economy is not reflected through credit sales.

Thus consumer credit should be taken very carefully. The buyer should be sure of his financial position before he decides to purchase goods which he actually cannot afford. The seller should also be careful in taking the risk of giving consumer credit. He should judge the customer through his capital and integrity and be very sure that he will receive the full value of his goods once he has given a credit.

HOUSING FINANCE

Housing finance has become very popular in India for purchasing an apartment. There are many housing finance institutions like National Housing Bank (NHB), Housing Development Finance Corporation Ltd., (HDFC) Housing and Urban Development Corporation Of India (HUDCO).

- ***National Housing Bank (NHB):*** NHB was established in 1987 with the objective of promoting housing finance institutions at local and regional areas. They provide finance for housing, directly and indirectly. They promote and support housing financing institutions. They participate in housing mortgage insurance. They provide advisory services to government by assisting in preparing policies for growth of housing in India. The NHB had three functions. They had a promotional role, a regulatory role and a financing role in assisting in housing credit.

Role of NHB

- The role of NHB is to provide a regulatory mechanism for creating confidence of the investor in taking housing loans.
- NHB was setup to create and develop institutional infrastructure by promoting housing companies.
- It has to provide financial assistance to institutions through refinancing of their financial requirements.
- It has the role of financing housing projects of local authorities as well as public agencies.
- It has to participate in equity of the housing finance corporation and draw out a proper procedure for home loan account schemes.
- It has to coordinate with the central and state government in creating a good support system through legal reforms regarding rent control, registration and stamp duties.

Activities of NHB

- NHB has supported housing finance institutions by providing loans to then.
- It has promoted and established Housing Finance Institutions.
- It has guaranteed the financial obligations of Housing Finance Institutions. In respect of their purchases of equity shares, bonds and debentures.
- It has discounted and rediscounted bills of exchanges promissory notes, debentures and bonds of housing finance institutions.
- It has promoted mutual funds engaged in housing finance activities.
- It has coordinated with LIC, UTI and GIC in housing finance activities.
- It has given advisory services to government at the centre and at state level for formulating policies relating to housing finance.
- Since 1999 it has promoted self help groups and NGOs for housing loans through its refinance schemes.
- It has started refinancing rural housing through its scheme called Swarana Jayanti rural housing scheme.
- It has raised funds through tax free and priority sector bonds by from the Asian Development Bank and LIC.

It has given loans for purchasing, constructing or upgrading houses in rural areas by extending refinancing to Rural Development Banks, Regional Rural Banks and Co-operative housing societies. In this way NHB has an important role in purchasing, selling and giving loans for immovable properties to banks and housing finance institutions.

- *Housing Development Finance Corporation Ltd. (HDFC):* HDFC was incorporated in 1977 with the objective of providing housing finance for increasing the number of residential houses. They wanted to have houses which were economical but modern. Another objective was to enter into mutual fund services, leasing, commercial banking and insurance and o provide their share holder with a good return. They provide loans to an individual which was based on their repaying capacity. The loans were to have a maximum period of 20 years. They provide loans for purchase of land for constructing a house, repairing and modernizing, existing housing.

Subsidiaries of HDFC

HDFC has 118 offices. It has 9 subsidiaries. It also has outreach programs in about hundred locations and extension counters and in many companies. It appoints direct selling agents to provide service to customers for home service. The 9 subsidiaries are listed below.

- HDFC Investment Ltd. is engaged in investment of stocks shares and debentures.
- HDFC Developers Ltd. conducts real estate development business.
- HDFC Trustee Company is the trustee of HDFC mutual fund is the trustee company.
- HDFC Standard Life Insurance Company was formed for conducting life insurance business.

- HDFC Holdings Ltd. are coordinating investment business of stocks share and debentures.
- HDFC Chubb General insurance Company was formed for transacting general insurance business.
- HDFC Asset Management Company was formed for managing the assets of HDFC mutual fund.
- GRUH Finance Ltd. was formed for giving of a financing long term housing projects.
- HDFC Realty Ltd. is carrying on the business of real estate brokerage and services relating to real estate development.

Role of HDFC

- HDFC has provided housing loans for purchase of land, house, repairs, renovations and extensions to individuals.
- It has provided housing facility to weaker section of the society by the concept of low cost housing.
- It has borrowed foreign currency from Internal Bank for reconstruction and development and the International Finance Corporation Washington for its housing development projects.
- It has managed its mortgage business through export risk management.
- *Housing and Urban Development Corporation of India (HUDCO):* HUDCO was incorporated in 1970 with the aim of providing long term finance for constructing houses in urban and rural areas. They also had the objective of financing or jointly setting up new or satellite towns. They were to promote and assist housing and urban development projects in India. They also have the objective of subscribing debentures and bonds of state housing and Urban Development Boards and development authorities.

Role of HUDCO

- HUDCO has been engaged in providing finance for constructing houses in urban areas.
- It has provided loans for constructing night shelters for pavement dwellers in cities.
- It has financed repairs, extensions and renovations of houses.
- It has financed scheme of NGOs and self help group for providing houses.
- It has also given funds for ownership of houses for working women.
- HUDCO has provided consultancy services for housing development in India and in foreign countries.
- *Commercial Banks:* RBI has permitted commercial banks to give loans for housing directly to individuals or through housing finance companies and private housing institutions. They have to follow the guidelines as setup by RBI. Banks provide loans to professionals for purchasing or renovating clinics and also modernizing their clinics. They give loans not only for housing but also for other reason like personal loans, housing loans, loans for purchasing consumer durables and for purchasing automobiles.

- *Financial Institutions:* The Life Insurance Corporation of India is a leading institutions for giving loans to the housing sector. It does not give loans directly to individuals. It provides funds to central government, state government, housing boards, HUDCO and Co-operative housing societies. It has a subsidiary by the name of LIC housing finance limited. Other financial institutions engaged in housing finance are GIC, ICICI, IFCI and SBI.

Housing Finance Contract

The housing finance contract consists of the borrower and the lender as well as a financer. The important aspects of the contract are the term period of the contract, the amount of loan required for the purchase of a house and the interest charged on the loan. Housing loans are to be evaluated for long term periods of time. Besides these factors there are other aspects to be considered while making a contract for taking a loan for purchasing a house. These are the processing charges involved in taking a loan, the foreclosure charges and the EMI calculations. The housing finance contract is binding on the borrower and the lender. Once it has been signed both the parties have the obligation to make their commitments. Both the borrower and the lender should understand that purchase of property involves long term commitment. The contract should be clear and there should be no ambiguity in the contract. It is a legal paper and if any party defaults, the court will have to decide the legality of the issue.

VENTURE CAPITAL FINANCE

Venture capital is a private equity investment provided to investors in return for monetary gains as well as shareholding in the business financed and the right to acquire it. The objective of this service is to be part of the ownership of an enterprise in the process of its growth for capital gains.

Venture capital finance has its origin in USA after the Second World War when investors wanted to begin new ventures but they did not have the requisite capital to do so. In 1946 the first venture capital company was started. It was called the American research and Development Corporation. Venture capital business in UK and Europe became known since 1980 for promoting new corporate organizations. In India venture capital was recognized in 1972 with the appointment of Bhatt Committee for development of small and medium enterprises. The first venture capita fund was started in 1975 it was called the Risk Capital Foundation (RCF) and was established by Industrial Finance Corporation of India (IFCI).

Features of Venture Capital

Venture capital is required in developing countries for supporting entrepreneurs for establishing their organizations. Entrepreneurs have technical qualifications and skill but require financial support and consultancy for promotion, development and growth of their business. Venture capital is required in different stages of business. It is required in the initial stage for research and development. It is also called *seed capital.* After the project begins then venture capital is required for developing the product and marketing it. In the next stage of business large amount of funds are required for business development. Once the business has developed and goods have been marketed then the risky stage has passed then venture capital is required for growth and extension of business. The following features of venture capital are described below.

- *Finance:* Venture capital is based on equity contributions made in ***new small and medium sized companies***. It is usually in the form of equity investment but it can also be in the form of convertible debt and loan finance.

- *Period:* Venture capital covers long term period of investment in small or medium firms which are growth oriented.

- *Capital appreciation:* Venture capitalists invest in companies to get a capital appreciation on their contribution.

- *Involvement:* Venture capitalists provide funds and business skills to companies in which they invest their funds. They participate in developing the firm and they can active interest in its working.

- *Controlling interest:* Venture capitalists do not interfere with the management of the firm. They do not have a controlling interest in the company in which they invest. Their prime interest is to earn a capital gain at the time of exit from the company.

- *High risk:* Venture capital is provided for new companies. The risk in these companies is very high because it is a new idea or concept in business. It may develop and give profits or losses may occur. It is only after its development that its capital appreciation can be received. Hence venture capital is highly risky.

- *High return:* Venture capital is given with the objective of receiving a high return on the investment made by them. The return is expected only after the firm is well developed. The return is assumed to be in the form of capital appreciation.

- *Idea based:* Venture capital is based on certain ***new ideas***. Its concept is growth oriented. It is not based on high technology or for established companies. Its focus is on new companies.

Types of Venture Capital Funds

Venture capital funds in India are of four different types. These are the sponsored venture capital funds by development financial institutions, the state level sponsored development financial institutions, promoted by public sector banks and private venture capital funds.

- *Development financial institutions:* Venture capital funds have been promoted India by the national level venture capital funds. These are the Risk Capital and Technology Finance Corporation Ltd. sponsored by IFCI and Risk Capital fund, and Technology Development and Information Company of India Ltd. sponsored by ICICI.

- *State financial institutions:* Venture capital funds have been sponsored by state level financial institutions these are Andhra Pradesh venture capital limited has been sponsored by Andhra Pradesh State Financial Corporation and Gujarat Venture Capital Ltd. by Gujarat Industrial Investment Limited.

- *Banks:* Commercial banks have sponsored venture capital funds. The Canara Bank venture capital fund is promoted by Canara Bank and its subsidiary the Can Bank Financial Services Ltd. The State Bank of India has also promoted a venture capital fund for financing new companies.

- *Private Venture Capital Fund:* Venture capital funds have been promoted by private sector companies, financial institutions and foreign banks. Some notable examples are Grindlays Bank which floated two funds. The capital of these funds was contributed by non-resident Indians and internal institutions. It gives equity finance and also gives venture capital. Indus venture capital fund provides venture capital. IDBI, IFCI, Internal Finance Corporation are major contributors to this fund.

Stages of Venture Capital Finance

Venture Capital is required by a firm at different stages of business. These stages are explained below:

Stage – I Seed Capital: Venture capital is required for developing a product in the initial stages. Funds are required for research and development. This fund is called seed capital. At this stage of the business enterprises there is high risk involved. The business venture has to be initiated and developed. This can be called the pre start up stage of a business venture.

Stage – II Start up Capital: Venture capital is required when a firm begins its activity it requires funds for research and development, transfer of technology whether within the country or from oversees. Funds may also be required for appraising the proposal of the entrepreneur. The venture capitalist reviews the passed record of the entrepreneur the cost structure of the project, its market potential and the time that will be required for completing in the project before it actually takes this decision of providing finance. The venture capitalist also evaluates the project through a financial analysis and portfolio analysis because it is interested in capital appreciation.

Stage – III Early Stage Financing: This stage in the firm is when a firm has not yet started making a profit. Funds have to be pumped into the system for costs to be covered for completing the project. If the start up stage has been successful then the project actually begins to take shape. During this stage if funds are not provided the firm will not be able to stand competition from other companies. Hence the role of venture capitalists is very important at this stage to make the firm successful.

Stage – IV Follow on Financing: When the project has started its working and it appears that it will become a successful venture the venture capitalist feel that funds should be invested to make the organization attractive. In UK and USA this is the time for venture capitalist to enter into providing funds for companies. This is also called mezzanine finance. At this stage the firm is getting ready to make a public issue.

Stage – V Expansion Financing: Venture capital provided for expansion of production capacity or for take over or acquisition of a company is called expansion financing. At this stage of firm has got a good market share and is interested in making a profit by increasing its production capacity. This is the also called bridge finance. It is the last round of finance before a firm becomes successful and it is the time of decision to be taken by venture capitalist to make an exit.

Stage – VI Replacement Financing: This is also stage of financing when venture capitalist provide for the financing of shares. The venture capitalist by shares and convert them into preference share with a fixed dividend. After a certain waiting period when the company is listed on some stock market the venture capitalist converts the preference shares back into ordinary shares and then the share can be sold.

Stage – VII Turn Around Financing: Venture capitalist provide finance when firms became unprofitable. They provide relief to sick units to recover. This type of finance is provided in the US to non listed and unprofitable companies which require equity funds for a turn around become successful.

Stage – VIII Buy Outs: When the transfer of management control is to be considered it is called a ***management buy out or a management buy in***. A management buy out is when the management surrenders a portion of its equity and gets finance from the venture capitalists. It is usually the acquisition of a company or it shares in that company from the existing owners by the internal operating management. A management buy in is when an external group of managers by a running company. Management buy outs are more popular than management buy ins.

The Venture Capital Process

The venture capitalists provide finance by following certain steps. The process requires the exploration and decision of investment opportunities, analysis of the investment proposal, valuation of the proposal, price, monitoring and exit.

Investment Opportunities: The venture capitalist look for good opportunities and new ideas. The objective of the venture capitalist is to support a venture in order to get capital appreciation in the future. To get an advantage the venture capitalist makes fundamental analysis of an economy, industry and tries to find out possibilities where new ventures will be able to take the pressure of competition from other established firms. It makes a constant evaluation of investment opportunities to select good projects.

Analysis of the Investment Proposal: Venture capitalist analysis specific proposals by making an appraisal of the entrepreneurs requiring the funds, the nature of the projects, the stage of financing required and the method of financing. They also look into the economic and financial position of the firm and its management. The capitalist also tries to find out the future exit mechanism and the profitability at that time from the firm.

Valuation of the Proposal: Proposals are valued through the conventional valuation method, first Chicago method and the revenue multiplier method.

- ***Conventional Valuation Method:*** This method takes into account the starting time of the venture and the exit time. The venture capitalist calculate the revenue at the beginning period and at the liquidating period and compound it by the expected annual growth rate for the period that they decide to hold the investment in the firm. They calculate the expected earning levels which is equal to future earnings level multiplied by after tax margin percentage on liquidation. After this they compute the future market valuation by multiplying the expected P/E ratio with the earnings level. Then they value the investment of the company by using a discount factor. If the present value of the venture capital undertaking is 50 lakhs and the entrepreneur is interested in 25 lakhs. The venture capitalist ownership will be 50%. This method ignores the losses and concentrates on exit. To explain this method calculates ***annual revenue, expected earning levels, future market valuation, present value of venture capital and minimum percentage of ownership.***

- *First Chicago Method:* This method takes the complete earning stream and the starting point and the exit. To calculate this method three alternative routes are calculated. These are success, sideways survival and failure rate. They are then given a probability rating. The venture capital undertaking is then discounted to its present value with a discount rate higher than the risk. The discounted present value is multiplied by the probabilities assigned. The expected present value of the venture capitalist is equal to the three alternate situations. If the present value of the undertaking is Rs. 10 crores and the fund requirement is Rs. 5 crores the minimum ownership requirement is 50%.

- *Revenue Multiplier Method:* This method is used in the early stage of venture capital investments when the earnings based on after tax profit is low or negative. The venture capital investment is calculated by multiplying annual revenue of the company with estimated revenue multiplier.

Price: Venture capitalist then negotiates with the firm by structuring or preparing a financial deal. There are many instruments which are used for structuring a deal. The venture capitalist invests through the following instruments.

- *Preference Shares:* Venture capitalist may take redeemable or convertible preference shares.

- *Debt:* Venture Capitalist invests in *convertible debt* through debentures and convertible loans. They also invest in *non-convertible debt* through loans and non convertible debentures.

- *Quasi Equity Instruments:* They invest in bridge loans, share warrants, optionally convertible debentures and partially convertible debentures.

- *Equity investments:* This form of investment is through quoted investments, unquoted venture investments and unquoted development investments.

Monitor: The venture capitalists take a continued interest in the working of the company that they finance. They monitor the activities of the company because they are interested in its growth and survival as they are looking for profit. If the company fails they will lose their investments because they are the advisors of the company as well as their financial partners. Thus they continuously monitor the investments of the company.

Exit: The venture capitalist exit by buying the shares of the company and then selling it again at an initial public offering. They can also make an exit by sale of shares to employees, by sale to another company, by liquidation and by selling to new investors.

SEBI Regulations in India

SEBI has made many regulations in India for protecting the investors. In 1996 the Venture Capital Funds Regulation was passed and in 2000 SEBI Foreign Venture Capital Investors Regulation was enacted. In January 2000 Chandrasekhar Committee was appointed to identify the problems of venture capital industry in India and to suggest methods for their growth. The committee recommended that the regulation should be simplified and the venture capital fund structure should be amended. They also recommended resource raising, investments and exit regulations. Some of the important regulations are the following:

- *Registration*: Venture capital funds must be registered with SEBI for doing business in India. They have to apply for registration after taking approval from RBI. The applicant has to be in the prescribed form showing the eligibility of the fund by providing the track record of experience, financial soundness and competence. They also have to submit registration fees of US $10,000.

- *Custodian:* A domestic custodian has the appointed to make arrangements with the banker. The custodian has to be registered with SEBI.

- *Investment Norms:* SEBI has prescribed norms for investing the funds of the venture capitalist. They cannot invest more than 25% in one venture capital unit. A minimum of 75% of their funds invested should be in unlisted equity shares, equity linked instruments, preference shares, share warrants and convertible securities compulsorily convertible in to equity. 25% of the funds to be invested as subscription to initial public offer.

- *Responsibilities:* The foreign venture capitalists have to maintain for a term period of 8 years their books of account, documents and records. SEBI may ask for the documents at any time. Further they have to be monitored by their custodian in India for their domestic investments. They also have the responsibility of furnishing periodical reports to SEBI.

- *Investigation:* SEBI has the right to investigate and inspect books of account maintained by the venture capitalist. They have the power to examine any person or record of the activity of the venture capitalist. SEBI may order them to dispose of any security or investment. It may even prohibit the fund from entering into the capital market for a specified period of time.

- *Suspension:* SEBI may suspend the venture capital if it does not furnish information required as per law. It may also suspend it if it gives any misleading statements or does not cooperate with it at the time of enquiry.

- *Cancellation:* Venture capital fund may be cancelled if they are guilty of fraud or have been convicted in a moral turpitude or guilty of repeated defaults or suspension of registration.

Structure of a Venture Capital Fund

The venture capital companies are structured into an investment company, a unit trust, as a scheme of the Unit Trust of India and as a division of a financial institution or bank. It is explained in the following way.

Investment Company Structure: This form of venture capital is like a company. In this form the liability of the shareholder is limited. They have tax benefits on long term capital gains. The income of their shareholders is taxable as per the guidelines the 1988 but in 1995 the new guidelines extended the exemption to dividend income from equity investment. However the shareholders would continue to be taxable. Example of such a fund is the Lazard Credit Capital Venture Finance Corporation Ltd.

Unit Trust Structure: Venture capitalist fund which has been setup under the Indian Trust Act takes the form of unit trust structure. It is managed by an asset management company. It has a management fees and carries interest. It has a capital contribution by individuals and corporate bodies.

UTI Scheme: The venture capital funds are part of UTI schemes in collaboration with other organizations. They are called venture capital unit schemes. The Risk Capital and Technology Finance Corporation and The Technology Development and Information Company of India which have been sponsored by UTI offer venture capital unit schemes. It is called VECAUS or Venture Capital unit schemes. VECAUS I and II have been offered by the Technology Development and Information Company of India and VECAUS III by the Risk Capital and Technology Finance Corporation. The VECAUS schemes get tax exemptions which are available to UTI.

Division of Financial Institution / Bank: The venture capital fund is division in a bank. It does not have a separate legal entity. IDBI Venture Capital Fund Scheme, Canara Bank Venture Capital Fund, Grindlays Bank - India Investment Fund.

Venture Capital Funds in India

There are many venture capital funds in India. Some of these are given below:

- ***IDBI Venture Capital Fund:*** The IDBI encourages development and innovative projects. It also emphasizes on seed capital and technology oriented projects. It has supported many projects in the Information Technology Sector. It invests in projects at the start up stage or at the seed level. It aims at a return 30% on a security investment and it adopts an exit root of 3 to 5 years. It finances 80% of the project costs and expect the promoters to contribute at least 20% of the cost. It finances through equity shares, preference shares, and convertible debt and term loans. It gives a large proportion of its funds through unsecured loans. It finances ventures directly and indirectly. It contributes to the corpus of venture capitalists. It has contributed to South Asia Regional Apex Fund, Andhra Pradesh Industrial Development Corporation and Gujarat Industrial Investment Corporation.

- ***ICICI Venture Funds Management Company Limited:*** The ICICI venture was started for venture financing in India. It provides loans for high-tech industries like pharmaceuticals, computer and energy. In 1998 it was renamed ICICI Venture Funds Management Company Limited. ICICI has 10 funds and it has also sponsored private equity funds. The venture capital funds of ICICI are given below.

Venture Capital Schemes

- ***VECAUS I and II:*** In 1989 the venture capital was launched and VECAUS – I was established as a 10 year closed ended fund in 1994. The major contribution to this fund was from UTI. It invested in high technology ventures and new products in the early stage of the investments. In 1999 VECAUS – II a 12 year closed ended fund was established. Funds of VECAUS - II were invested in innovative instruments like bridge loans, partially convertible debentures and convertible preference shares.

- ***Software Funds:*** In 1997 software funds were established by ICICI and World Bank together. They invested in unlisted companies at the early stage with innovative investment instruments.

- ***Structured Product Funds:*** This fund was established as a managed account in 1999. Its fund is invested in retail sector which is not high tech. It was originally purposed for knowledge based sectors but it changed its course.

- ***Information Technology Funds:*** This fund was specially made for high tech investments in the IT sector. It was collaborated with Japan Investment Corporation with the objective of setting up a parallel offshore fund.

- *JAIC Fund:* This fund was setup in Mauritius in collaboration between the ICICI and Japanese Investment Corporation (JAIC).

- *Global Opportunity Fund:* This fund has its base in Mauritius. Its objective is to give funds for healthcare and service sector. It is focused on knowledge based sector and Information Technology.

- *Incubator Fund:* The objective of this fund is to develop commercially viable proposals with a minimum start up time. The fund finances the early stage also called the incubator stage. This fund is innovative and invests in high risk and small sized ventures.

- *Brand Equity Fund:* This fund has been setup jointly between the Ministry of Information Technology and ICICI. It is focused on the growth of IT industry and on IT exports.

- *Life Science Fund:* This fund finances healthcare and biotechnology at the early stage of the project.

- *Retail Services Fund:* This fund is for the development of the retail sector at the expansion level.

- *Small Industries Bank of India Venture Capital Finance:* This fund was established in 1993 for assisting entrepreneurs who had ideas for innovative products. It provides equity capital and conditional loans. It takes the exit route by of loading its shareholding at the right time through the OTCEI. It provides loans at the start up stage for working capital and other technical financial assistance. It promotes state level in collaboration with state governments and their corporations. The national venture fund for software and IT industries was started by it with government.

- *IFCI Venture Capital Funds Limited:* This fund was renamed Risk Capital and Technology Finance Limited in 2000. It provides financial assistance to new enterprises through soft term loans to fill the gap in promoters' equity contribution. It has provided funds for research and development and on new technology and development of new markets. It also has the *Risk Capital Scheme* which is for medium scale projects promoted by technocrats. It promoted VECAUS – III with the UTI and assisted by World Bank as a 15 year closed ended fund.

- *Can Bank Venture Capital Fund:* This fund was the first venture capital fund started by a nationalized by bank in India. In 1989 the Can Bank Financial Services Ltd. managed the fund as a trustee. It is now managed by Can Bank Venture Capital Fund Ltd. It provides fund for technically qualified entrepreneurs starting a project with the potential to grow. Venture capital is financed only in companies which are not listed in recognised stock exchanges in India. The focus areas of financing are information technology, bio technology, pharmaceuticals and software technology in south and western regions of India.

- *Gujarat Venture Capital Finance Limited:* This fund was established in 1990. It was professionally managed in association with the World Bank. This was the pioneer venture capital form in India. It invests in different types of small and medium industries. It has many funds. Its other funds are *Gujarat Venture Capital Fund* 1990 which was a 15 year closed ended fund for innovative products and imported technology. Its focus was on up-gradation of projects requiring imported technology. *Gujarat Venture Capital Fund* was launched in 1995.

Its focused was on start up and early stage ventures. It preferred to give loans to first generation entrepreneurs. The funds requirement is a return on 30% over a period of 12 years. It takes a maximum share of 40% of the paid of capital of the venture. In 1997 the Gujarat software venture capital fund was launched specifically for entrepreneurs of small software unlisted companies. Another fund was setup by it by the name of *Gujarat Information Technology Fund.* This was setup for promoting technology sector in Gujarat.

There is many other important ventures fund in India. Some of them are South Asian Regional Apex Fund, Auto Ancillary fund, Indus Venture Management Ltd., Marigold Capital Management Ltd. and HSBC Private Equity Management Ltd. and Walden Nikko India Management Company Ltd.

Thus the venture capital concept is new to India but there are a large number of funds operating in India. The major interest of these funds is to provide finance and to make an exit at the right time to earn profits. Such funds are of advantage to the entrepreneurs for getting finance at the right time. They are also useful for the venture capitalists as they are able to earn profits.

FACTORING & FORFAITING

Factoring refers to credit sales in which the receivables are sold by a firm to a specialized agency called *factor.* The factor is a financial intermediary who becomes responsible for the management of the credit sales. The factor provides the services of *finance, maintenance of accounts, collection of debts and protection to a company from its credit risks.* Factoring is a fund based service. A factor takes a commission for undertaking the responsibility of realizing the receivables from the customers. There are 3 parties in factoring. *These are the seller, the buyer and the factor.*

Forfaiting is financing of receivables that arise out of international trade. Banks of financial institutions purchase trade bills or promissory notes through discounting and cover the risk of non-payment at the time of collection of dues. The *forfaiter/purchaser* becomes responsible for the risks. He pays cash to the seller on discounting of the bills.

Mechanism of Factoring

The mechanism of operation of *factoring service* is explained below.

The Seller: The seller prepares a memorandum of understanding with the buyer and sells goods on credit to him. He gives him the delivery invoice and instructs the buyer to pay the amount due on credit sales to his *agent or factor.* The factor deducts his service charges and pays 80% of the amount on receivables.

The Buyer: The buyer makes an agreement with the seller after negotiating his terms and signing a memorandum of understanding. Then he receives the delivery of the goods and the instructions from the seller regarding mode and date of payment to his agent/factor. The buyer then makes a payment to the factor on the due date. If he cannot keep his commitment on the due date he can ask for an extension of time from the factor. The factor may agree to extend the time through the same conditions or ask for a higher charge. He also has the right to go for legal settlement.

The Factor: The factor is a financial intermediary between the buyer and the seller. He is an agent of the seller as he makes an agreement with him for looking after all his credit sales. The seller sends the sale documents to the factor. The factor pays 80% of the price in advance and receives the payment from the buyer on the due date. He then remits the balance to the seller after deducting his commission.

The sale deed should clearly state the name of the factor and the agreement made with him to enable him to recover the money on credit sales from the buyer on the due date.

Functions of the Factor

The factor has a very important role to play. He maintains the sales ledger, he collects the account receivable, he provides financing facility and takers of the credit risks.

Sales Ledger: The factor administers the sales ledger. When he receives the sales invoice his work on opening the ledger begins. He writes the entries of receipts from the customer and sends periodic reports to the seller. He keeps the seller informed of his account with the buyer of goods. On the due date when he receives the full payment, he sends the final account to the seller on whose behalf he is the factor.

Collection of Receivables: The factor keeps a record of the collection that he has to make on behalf of his client. He sends notices to the debtor reminding him of the due date. For collection of the receivables the factor maintains a trained staff. The staff should be courteous while making demands on customers but they also have to be firm so that the debt is collected on the desired date.

Financing: A factor purchases the book debts from the seller in his own favour. He makes advance payments to the seller for assigning the debts to him. On factoring ***without recourse to debt*** the factor becomes responsible if the buyer does not make a payment because the seller will not refund the payment to the factor. On factoring ***with recourse*** the factor is refunded by the seller in case of defaults by the buyer. This is the unique financing function of the factor.

Credit Risks: Factoring service is usually ***without recourse to debt***. The factor takes up the entire risk of collection of debt and protects the seller in the event of default by the buyer. This service helps the seller to spend his time in fruitful business ventures and leave the collection work to the factor. The factor does the service of assessing the customers. It makes a report on the buyers' background and earlier business dealings and gives it to the seller before entering into a sale deed. Further he keeps in constant touch with the buyer and updates him on due dates. Thus the seller can concentrate on other important work in business transactions and the factor takes care of all the credit risks.

The factor thus becomes a close associate of the seller/client. He gives information to his clients about emerging trends in the market. He also gives advice on banking, leasing, merchant banking and other services if required to do so.

Types of Factoring

Factoring is the function of collection of receivables and all formalities attach to it. There are many types of factoring these are given below.

With Recourse Factoring: When an agreement between a seller and the factor is with recourse the factor can take from its client any amount which is due by the purchaser and he defaults to pay on the due date. In with recourse factoring, the factor does not take any credit risk which is associated with receivables. The factor still has the right to receive his commissions and his expenses for maintaining a sales ledger and for any expenses that occur for collection of dues.

Without Recourse Factoring: The factor has to bear all losses that arise out of irrecoverable receivables. For this service he charges a higher commission which is a premium for the higher risk and it is called *del credere* commission. In this type of factoring the factor takes a great interest in the business matters of the client. He makes a summary of the purchasers credibility and background and makes a rating before giving him goods on credit. This precaution is taken by the factor because in case the purchaser does not pay the dues the factor has the bear the loss as he does not have the right of recourse.

Advance Factoring: When advance factoring is being agreed upon, the factor makes an advance payment which covers 70-80% of the receivables which are factored. The factor then collects interest on the advance payment made. The interest is charged according to the short term rates prevailing in the market. On the date of maturity the dues are collected and deposited with his client.

Maturity Factoring: This type of factoring is called collection factoring. This means that the factor does not give any advance payment to his client. He guarantees a payment date or promises to pay on the due date after collecting the receivers.

Full Factoring: In this type of agreement the factor does not have any recourse to the seller. It is a comprehensive type of factoring where by the factor promises to pay an advance of 70-80% and also keep the books of account and spend on collection of debts.

Bank Participation Factoring: In this type of agreement the factor arranges advance from a bank. For this service it pays interest to the bank and with the banks participation it makes the advance to the client.

Disclosed Factoring Agreement: This type of factoring is without recourse agreement. The name of the factor is disclosed in the invoice which is sent to the purchaser. The factor is the agent between the seller and the purchaser and he is responsible for collection and assumption of risks of non-payment.

Undisclosed Factoring Agreement: In this factoring agreement the name of the factor is not disclosed in the invoice sent to the purchaser. However, the factor maintains the control of books and collection of dues. The factor does his work in the name of the clients company.

Domestic Factoring: When an agreement is made between a factor and his client within the boundaries of his own country it is called domestic factoring. There are 3 parties involved in the deal. The 3 parties are the seller, the buyer and the factor.

International Factoring: Factoring beyond the country's boundaries is done through cross border or international factoring. In this system there are four parties involved in the transaction. These parties are the exporter client, the importer customer, the export factor and the import factor. This is called two factor system of factoring. The import factor is a link between the export factor and the importer. There are to separate types of agreements. One agreement is between the exporter client and the export factor. The second agreement is between the export factor and the import factor. The goods are sold on open credit. To make an agreement the following steps have to take place.

Step I: The exporter makes an agreement with the export factor and informs in about the goods to be exported to a particular country and a specified importer.

Step II: The export factor will right to the import factor in the importers country to finds out details of the importer.

Step III: The exporter delivers goods to the importer with relevant documents. The export receivables are on a non recourse factoring system.

Step IV: The export factor maintains sales ledger and all documents required for collection of dues from the import factor.

Step V: The import factor on the due date collects the payment from the importer and gives the payment to the export factor as per regulations of the country and currency requirements.

Step VI: The export factor gives the payment to exporters.

There are certain legal aspects of a factoring contract. These must be considered before entering into a contract.

Legal Aspects of Factoring

In India there is no regulation of code of conduct for regulating it. It is of recent region and is based on the recommendations of the Kalyansundaram Committee which was appointed by RBI in 1989. The first factoring company in India was SBI Factors and Commercial Limited (SBI FACS). The first service in the private sector was started in 1992 with the inception of Fair Growth Factor Ltd. This service was started in April 1991 by them. The following legal implications should be considered.

- *Approval:* The business of factoring can be started in India by RBIs approval. Banks can undertake indirect participations of factoring services with the approval of RBI by investing in shares of other factoring companies. Banks can open subsidiaries for carrying out factoring business individually or jointly with other banks if the get approval from RBI for this business..

- *Genuine transactions:* The factoring contract can arise only out of genuine business transactions between the buyer and the seller.

- *Compensation:* The factor receives a commission as compensation for his services. He also has the right to receive all expenses in connection with the factoring work that he undertakes.

- *Agreement:* It is a sale purchase agreement governed by the law of contracts. The time framework and mode of termination are provided in the agreement.

- *Payment:* The buyer has obligation of making the payment to the factor. The factor has the legal status of an assignee. He has to receive the payment and then remit the same to his client. The factoring agreement has to give in detail the mode and date of payment.

FORFAITING

Forfaiting is a form of financing of receivables which arise out of international trade. In forfaiting, a financial institution or a bank agree to purchase the trade bills or promissory notes without recourse to the seller. Purchasing internationally is done through discounting of documents which cover the risk of non-payment on the due date of collection of funds. The risks are responsibility of the forfaiter/purchaser. When the bills or promissory notes have been discounted then the forfaiter pays cash the seller.

Advantages of Forfaiting

Forfaiting has the following advantages.

- It protects the exporter from any type of default risks for non-settlement of claims.
- There is no international risk to the exporter due to foreign exchange fluctuations during the period between the date of insurance and the maturity date of the paper.
- Exporters are free from collection problems and maintenance of sales ledger and other documents.
- Exporters are able to over come any problems due to financial requirements.

Forfaiting Contract

The following terms and condition are required for making a forfaiting contract.

- *Agreement:* A forfaiting agreement is between the exporter and importer. They have to draw up the terms and conditions in the form of a commercial contract. The agreement is without recourse.
- *Finance:* A forfaiter provides 100% financing arrangement of the receivables amount.
- *Time Period:* A forfaiter finances through promissory notes and bills for a deferred credit period of 3-5 years.
- *Risk:* The forfaiter covers risks of exchange rate fluctuations.
- *Premium:* The forfaiter charges of premium for covering the entire risk of international contract.
- *Contract:* The forfaiter and the exporter enter into a contract. Usually the forfaiter is a bank.
- *Payment:* The forfaiter receives the payment from the exporter on the face value of the promissory note of bill of exchange after deducting the discount. The forfaiter can hold the bills or promissory notes till the maturity of the amount and receive the payment from the importer banks. He can also securitize the bills and sell them in the secondary market as short term unsecured loan with a high yield.

In India, exporters have been allowed to enter into forfaiting contracts since 1992. The contract is without recourse. It is used as post shipment finance for export deals.

SECURITIZATION

Securitization is a process through which certain receivables are converted into marketable securities by restructuring cash flows which are generated by them. These receivables are not liquid but they have to be processed through conversion by repackaging of asset in the form of collateral securities or loans. The purpose of securitization is to create marketability to financial claims. The entity that intermediates between the originator of receivables and the end investors is called the *Special Purpose Vehicle*. The originator transfers the assets to the special purpose vehicle that holds the asset for the investors and issues to the investors its own securities. The special purpose vehicle is in other words the issuer of the security.

The securitization mode can be explained through the following process.

- *Originator:* The Company that sells its securities is called be originator. The original ownership of the securities are in the name of the company.

- *Special Purpose Vehicle:* The originator transfers the asset to the special purpose vehicle which issues securities in its own name. The special purpose vehicle (SPV) can be a trust or a company. The securitized assets now become separate from the originator. The SPV acts as a trustee and owns the assets when they are securitized. The Special purpose vehicle becomes responsible to the investor for repayment of principal and recovery of interest. The securities are called *asset backed securities.* These securities are rated by a separate credit rating agency.

- *Regulator:* The role of the regulator is to find out the capital adequacy liquidity and credit quality of the asset back securities and the methodology of transfer of the assets.

- *Credit Rating Agency:* It provides the estimate of credit risk in the securitization process.

- *The Trustee:* He is the investor representative and acts in the interest of the investors.

- *Types:* Asset backed securities are of four types. These are *Pass through, Asset backed bond, Pay through and Real estate mortgage investment conduit.* In *pass through* securities a prorate share of assets is in a pool of securities in which the principal and interest payments pass through to the investors own a schedule. The issuer does not have these assets on its balance sheet. In India pass through securities are popular. *Asset backed bonds* are debt obligation where the schedule of interest and principal are different from the asset. The issuer keeps these assets on its balance sheet. *Pay through* assets and asset backed bonds do not have any difference between them accept in the balance sheet entry. Pass through assets do not remain on the issuers balance sheet. *The real estate mortgage investment conduit* the principal and interest pass through one of the regular types of securities and one residual class.

- *Listing:* The securitized paper is listed on the National Stock Exchange. These securities can be traded on the stock market. The securities are assets for the seller but it becomes a debt when it is listed on the stock market. This is the reason that it is called debt securitization.

- *Cost of Funds:* Securitization is a method of raising funds at low cost through new sources. It is called off the balance sheet method. It adds value to the issuer portfolio and the investors get a high term.

Benefits of Securitization

Securitization provides the advantages of converting non liquid assets into liquidity. It creates tradable securities out of financial claims. It diversifies the assets amongst a wide number of savers in marketable lots. The following benefits are derived from securitization. It recycles funds and effectively utilizes capital of a country.

- *Benefit to Originator:* Securitization provides off balance sheet funding by converting non-liquid assets into liquidity. It is a means to quick recovery of funds leading to profitability. It provides credit rating to the instrument infusing confidence amongst the investors. It creates new instruments at low cost through credit enhancement and diversification of risks.

- *Benefits to Investors:* Securitization creates multiple new investment instruments for matching preferences of investors and minimizing risk. It provides a high yield. It is negotiable instrument and it can be traded in the stock market.

Securitization in India

Securitization in India was first initiated in 1991. The first securitization deal was made by Citi Bank, HDFC and ICICI. Securitization up to 2000 was not popular in India. Electricity boards securitized their assets. In 2001 ICICI merged with ICICI bank. It off loaded its assets of Rs. 7,000 crores through securitization. To meet its statutory liquidity requirement it securitized corporate loans of Rs. 2,250 crores and 50 crores of housing loans. In 2000 HUDCO securitized Rs. 1,500 crores of its infrastructure portfolios.

In India securitization became popular after the securitization ordinance was passed in 2000. It was called the ordinance on *Securitization and Reconstruction of Financial Assets and Enforcement of Security Interest.*

After the Ordinance was passed securitization became very popular especially with banks and financial institutions that wanted to make their assets liquid. Government planned to setup the Asset Reconstruction Company Limited with 51% holding and 24.5% to be held by ICICI. 25.5 were to be held by other financial institutions.

Many securitized issues have been rated by credit rating agencies like CRISIL. Banks like Citi bank and ICICI issued *pass through certificates* for securitization

In India securitization is more popular in the case of auto financing and personal loan portfolios. Securitized notes and other new flexible securitized instruments are being introduced in India.

Securitization requires being transparent in its dealings. In order to make a popular there should be a regulatory framework for Special Purpose Vehicle. It also requires awareness and participation from banks. At present it has a narrow investor base. There is participation from mutual funds, private banks and foreign banks. It requires to be extended to public sector banks, provident funds, trust and foreign institutional investors in this market. Public awareness is also required. Finally to developed this market there should be standard procedures and accounting standards to improve the quality of assets.

CREDIT RATING

The credit rating agencies are companies, which are in the business of rating of securities which are offered to public. Rating is essentially an opinion which is expressed through standard symbols by the credit rating agencies. In India credit rating first started in 1987 with the inception of CRISIL (Credit Rating Information Services of India Ltd.) was incorporated. CRISIL is the only rating agency to operate on the basis of a sectoral specialization, which analyses and disseminates information to a large number of investors.

Credit rating is the method of assigning standard scores to a particular debt instrument. It facilitates trading in debt securities as it helps participants to arrive at a quick estimate and opinion about various instruments. In 2007 credit rating agencies have started evaluating equity issues also. There are 4 rating agencies in India. These are CRISIL (Credit Rating Information Services of India), ICRA (Investment

Information and Credit Rating Agency of India), CARE (Credit Analysis and Research Ltd.) and Duff and Phleps. These rating agencies are registered and regulated by SEBI. CRISIL has about 42% market share and Care 36%.

Objectives of Credit Rating

The objectives of credit rating are to analyze and give an opinion on the type of instrument. The following are some of its objectives:

- To provide credence to financial commitments made by a company.
- To provide information to the investor in selecting debt securities.
- To help the company by providing it with the service of marketability through grading of debt securities with technical expertise of rating securities.

Grading System

Every rating agency has a different code for expressing rating of debt securities. CRISIL has four main grades and many sub grades for long-term debentures/bonds/fixed deposits. The grades are in decreasing order of quality. Their grades are AAA, AA+, A, BBB, BB, B, C, D.

The following tables are given by CRISIL and ICRA for rating the securities.

Table 18.1: Rating Symbols of CRISIL

Debenture rating symbols	Fixed Deposit rating symbols	Commercial papers rating symbols
AAA Highest safety	FAAA Highest safety	P1 Highest safety
AA High safety	FAA High safety	P2 high safety
A Adequate safety	FA adequate safety	P3 adequate safety
BBB moderate safety	FB Inadequate safety	P4 Inadequate safety
BB inadequate safety	FC High risk	P5 default
B high risk	FD default	
C substantial risk		
D Default risk		

Table 18.2: Rating Symbols of ICRA

Rating	Debentures/bonds/preference shares	Fixed Deposits	Commercial papers
Highest safety	LAAA	MAAA	A1
High safety	LAA	MAA	A2
Adequate safety	LA	MA	
Moderate safety	LBBB	–	
Inadequate safety	LBB	MB	A3
Risky	LB	MC	A4
Substantial risk	LC		
Default	LD	MD	A5

Credit Rating Factors

Credit rating depends on many factors which are dependant on the judgment of the rating agency. The important factors influencing the safety of the bond are given below:

- The Earning capacity of the company and the volatility of its business.
- It is dependent on the liquidity position of the company.
- The overall macro position of business and industrial environment has to be ascertained.
- The financial capability of the firm to be able to raise funds form outside sources when in need of temporary requirement.
- The leverage existing with the firm and its financial risk position are important factors for analysis of credit worthiness.
- The funds position of the firm to meet its irrevocable commitments must be analyzed.
- Support from financially strong companies and banks existing in the market are important for a good rating in the market.
- The credit rating agencies evaluate in detail, Fundamental and Technical data of the firm before coming to any conclusions.

Importance of Credit Rating

The importance of credit rating is three-fold. It is useful for investors, companies issuing securities and intermediaries which are providing funds to corporate organization.

- *Investors* It is useful for the investors as data is presented to them to take decisions on investment
- *Companies* It helps the companies as they are ranked according to the security and safety of their instruments. It provides them with credibility. They are the issuers of security and they offer the instrument to public. To get a good rating from the credit agency will enhance their credibility.
- *Intermediaries* Merchant Bankers, Market traders, brokers and financial institutions and other market players use the information for pricing placement and marketing of issues.

Limitations

Credit rating also has certain limitations. These are:

- Credit rating is an opinion often these opinions have gone wrong so buyer beware. These are not offered as guarantees or protection against defaults and frauds.
- Rating is made specifically for an instrument and not a business house.

Bonds also require to be evaluated. The evaluation is by finding out basic values of the bonds. These are based on the basic principles of time value of money. Credit rating agencies offer a service to the public. Although they express an opinion to an issue, they do not claim responsibilities for incorrect judgments on the basis of which people apply for issues of bonds which has now become extendable to equity issues also. In India the investors are of the opinion that there should be a law to enforce the responsibilities of a credit rating agency.

Summary

➡ This chapter provides an overview of the financial services that are offered in India.

➡ The financial services market consists of market players, financial instruments, specialized institutions and regulatory bodies.

➡ Financial services offer different types of financial instruments. There are new types of innovative financial instruments specially prepared through financial engineering.

➡ The regulatory bodies like Reserve Bank of India, SEBI, Insurance Regulatory Development Authority and Department of Banking and Insurance of the Central Government are committed to the protection of investors and law and order in the capital market in India.

➡ Financial services developed slowly in India. Their development has been through various stages since the year 1960. The new economic reform in India accelerated the pace of development in the financial services. The first service that was developed was merchant banking. This was followed by changes in banking, underwriting, and insurance and investment companies. Many new services were developed in India. These were venture capital funding/factoring and credit rating. Finally services were developed to internationalize the capital market and its institutions.

➡ Financial services are different types. They are fund based, fee based, commercial financial services and securities related services.

➡ Households, firms, government, banks, insurance companies, mutual funds, financial institutions and foreign financial institutions are important players in providing and receiving financial services in India.

➡ Merchant bankers are an important service for *new issues* of companies. They provide the complete pre issue and post issue management service. They also provide other advisory services like portfolio management, project feasibility advice, corporate financial counselling, credit syndication, venture financing, lease financing and foreign currency financing.

➡ Merchant bankers have a regulatory framework. They are governed by a code of conduct. They should have capital adequacy and they have restrictions in carrying out fund based business like leasing.

➡ Merchant bankers act as lead managers. The number of lead managers depends on the size of the issue. The role of the lead manager is to take charge of the new issue, to furnish a due diligence certificate and other disclosures to SEBI.

➡ SEBI can inspect their records of merchant bankers and if they violate acts, rules or regulations they can be suspended or their certificate can be cancelled. They get grading points.

➡ Underwriting is the service for subscribing to new issues which are not fully subscribed. The underwriters sign an MOU with the company. Underwriting is not mandatory in India.

➡ Underwriters have to be registered with SEBI. They have to pay fees and submit documents for registration. They have to maintain a code of conduct. SEBI can cancel their registration if they do not follow the acts governing them.

Contd.....

➠ Leasing is a service for the use of an asset in return for a rent paid for a specified period of time. The agreement is between the lessor and the lessee.

➠ The important aspects of leasing are that it is an agreement for using a high value asset. The ownership of the asset is different from the use of the asset. Lease can be of different types like finance lease, operating lease, conveyance type lease, leverage lease, consumer lease, import lease and international lease.

➠ Hire purchase is another service through which goods are taken on hire with the option of purchasing them by making the payment of the goods through instalment. Hire purchase is a contract in two parts. The first is a contract is through bailment of goods and the second part is a contract of sale. It is very popular in India.

➠ The contract is between three parties. These are the seller, the hirer and the financer. The interest is calculated through effective rate of interest, sum of digits method and straight method.

➠ Consumer finance is another service given to retail individual customers for purchasing consumer durables. The credit facility can be given through revolving credit, cash loans, fixed credit, hire purchase, instalment purchase and through secured and unsecured loans. A consumer credit contract is signed between the parties specifying the period of credit, rate of interest, instalment, other charges and payment method.

➠ Housing finance has become popular in India for purchasing an apartment. There are many housing finance institutions in India to support this service. These are National Housing Bank, Housing Development Finance Corporation Ltd. and Housing, Urban Development Corporation of India and Commercial Bank and Financial Institutions.

➠ Venture capital finance is a private equity investment service provided to investors. The objective of the venture capitalist is to finance to new, small and medium enterprises at the infancy stage of a venture. In order to make profit it makes an exit at the right time. This service is based on new innovative ideas of business.

➠ Venture capital fund can be promoted by banks, private venture capital fund, state financial institutions and development institutions. Venture capital can be as seed capital, start up capital, early stage financing, follow on financing, expansion financing, replacement financing, turn around financing and buy outs and buy ins.

➠ Venture capitalist finds out investment opportunities, analyzes investment proposals, calculates price, makes a bid, monitors the organization and makes an exit.

➠ SEBI regulates venture capitalists in India. They have to get themselves registered, follow investment norms and responsibilities of keeping books of account. SEBI can investigate the books and cancel or suspend registrations if the regulations are violated.

➠ Venture capital companies can be in the structure of an investment company, unit trust structure, UTI scheme or as a division of a financial institution/bank. In India ICICI has floated many funds. IDBI, IFCI, Can Bank and Gujarat Venture Capitals also have many funds.

Contd.....

➡ Factoring refers to credit sales sold by a firm to a specialised agency called a factor. The factor is responsible for financing, maintenance of accounts and collection of receivables within a country. When financing of receivables arises out of international trade. It is called factoring.

➡ In factoring there are three parties. These are the seller, the buyer and the intermediary call the factor. In forfaiting there are four parties, these are the exporter, the exporters factor, the importer and the importer factor.

➡ The factoring can be with recourse or without recourse but forfaiting is a service without recourse. The factor has to bear all the losses of the seller.

➡ Securitization is an asset backed service. In this service the securities are sold by the originator to a special purpose vehicle who packages the securities and makes them liquid. The securities can be listed on the National Stock Exchange and is tradable. This service has become popular in India since 2000. ICICI repackaged its securities and sold them when it merged with the ICICI bank. This service suffers from lack of standardization. It is more popular in securitization of vehicles rather than houses.

➡ Credit rating is a service which helps to identify rated companies. Credit rating agencies offer their own opinion through fundamental and technical analysis. In recent years the credit worthiness of the credit rating agencies is being questioned in India.

➡ Thus there are many financial services in India. Most of these services have developed after the opening up of the financial sector. These services require a lot of improvement to be organized and highly developed for the requirements of the investors. SEBI has be responsibility of creating investor awareness and providing investor protection.

Objective Type Questions, Answer True (T) or False (F)

(a) Forfaiting is without recourse but factoring is with or without recourse finance.

(b) Securitization is packaging of illiquid assets and reselling them for liquidity.

(c) Venture capitalists start new companies and sell them for making profit.

(d) Credit rating services are certified and regulated by SEBI in India.

(e) Leasing is a rental contract between the lessor and the lessee for using an asset.

(f) Hire purchase is a rental contract between the vendor and the hirer.

(g) Housing Finance is provided by forfaiters.

(h) Merchant banking is the service between a merchant borrower and a lending banker.

(i) Underwriting is statutorily necessary for companies issuing an IPO.

(j) Leasing creates value addition to products.

Answer: (a) T, (b) T (c) F, (d) F, (e T, (f) F, (g) F, (h) F, (i) F (j) F.

Multiple Choice Questions (Tick mark (✓) the right answer)

1. Venture capital provides the service of:
   - (a) Seed financing
   - (b) Purchasing a company
   - (c) Selling a company
   - (d) Borrowing and lending from the company.

2. Lease financing is:
   - (a) A sale of goods to the lessee
   - (b) It is a hire of goods on rent
   - (c) It is a transfer of ownership of goods
   - (d) It is a financing partnership between lessor and lessee

3. A hire purchase agreement is:
   - (a) A contract for sale of the goods
   - (b) It is a hire for the goods provided
   - (c) It is an instalment scheme for purchasing goods
   - (d) It is an instalment paid for goods with the option of purchasing the goods

4. Securitization is a service provided for:
   - (a) Sick units
   - (b) Small companies
   - (c) IPOs
   - (d) Creation of asset pool and sale through stock exchange

5. A lead merchant banker has the task of:
   - (a) Pre issue and post issue documentation
   - (b) Pre issue organization of IPO
   - (c) Documentation, organization and obligations towards pre and post IPOs
   - (d) Post issue documentation and organization of issue

6. A merchant banker has a:
   - (a) Job of a specialist in issue management
   - (b) Project syndication job with the company
   - (c) Job for redressal of investor grievances
   - (d) Job to provide documentation for banks

   Answer: 1 (a), 2 (b), 3 (d), 4 (d), 5 (c), 6 (a).

Short Answer Questions

1. Discuss the activities of a merchant banker in connection with financial counselling.
2. Describe the code of conduct to be followed by merchant bankers.
3. What is due diligence certificate? Why is it issued?

4. Describe the different kinds of factoring.

5. What is consumer finance? What are the different sources from which such finance can be received?

6. What is the need of underwriting of new issues? Which agencies underwrite securities in India?

7. Discuss the process of venture capital in India.

8. Discuss the different stages in which venture capital can be financed.

9. What is the need for securitization of assets? What does the Special Purpose Vehicle do in the process of securitization?

Long Answer Questions

1. Discuss the pre and post issue functions of a merchant banker.

2. What is merchant banking? Discuss the various functions of a merchant banker?

3. Who is a lead merchant banker? What are his functions?

4. Who is a factor? What are the different kinds of factoring? How is it different from forfaiting?

5. What is hire purchase? Discuss its features and its merit and limitations.

6. What is leasing? How is it useful for a lessor and lessee? What are its limitations?

7. What is venture capital financing? In which stage do venture capitalists invest their funds? When do the exit?

8. State some of the important venture capital funds in India.

9. What are the different institutions dealing with housing finance in India? Has it been successful in India?

10. Securitization process started in India in 2000. Explain the process and methodology of this service in India.

Glossary

Acceptance House: It is an institution which specializes in accepting commercial bills of exchange which are discounted by discount houses.

Accommodation Bill: An accommodation bill is an instrument which is created by borrowers and lenders to help each other. There is no backing of any trading transactions.

Allocation Function: This is a capital market function which allows the saving of the investors to be chanellized in different productive avenues of investments.

Allocative Efficiency: This is stock market efficiency to ensure a continuous flow of marketing information to all the investors to decide the issue in which he is interested in investing.

American Depository Receipts (ADRs): This is a negotiable certificate which is dominated by dollars. It represents non-U.S. company's public clay traded equity, to help American's in stock trading in overseas securities.

Arbitrage: It is a process in which a dealer of a security indulges in buying and selling activity to take advantage of price difference of different markets. The speculator purchases a security from a market where the prices is low and sells it in a market where the price is high.

Arbitrageurs: A risk averse player in a derivate market. He inters into contracts which will earn a profit that is risk less through arbitrage. He buys in one market and simultaneously be sales in

another market to earn a risk less profit through an imperfect market.

Ask (offer) Quotation: This is the quotation in one currency at which dealer will sell another currency. The quote is usually more than the big price.

Asset Management Company (AMC): An investment manager that manages the assets and is also responsible for operating the schemes of a mutual fund is called an asset management company.

Asset Securitization: This is the process in which some assets are separated from the balance sheet and they are used as collateral for issuing securities, for example loan receivables.

Bad Paper: It is a forged, lost, fake, stolen and duplicate certificate. It is in physical form with the clearing house.

Badla System: It is stock exchange trading method. It is the carry forward of a transaction for clearing from one settlement period to another. The buyer is not allowed to make a payment in full at the time of the purchase. It is a purchase against blank transfer deed.

Balloon Lease: This is an arrangement in a lease agreement in which the rent is low initially, high in the middle years and again low at the terminal period of the lease.

Banker's Certificate: It is a certificate which is issued to a banker to get rediscounting facility on account of genuine trade transactions. The bank certifies that the drawers of the bill are credit worthy and financial sound. It also certifies that the signatures are genuine.

Bear: Another name for speculator. In India he is called the '*mandiwala*' on a stock exchange. He expects of a fall in prices of security ant take advantage of the fall by selling securities which may not be in his possession.

Bearish Trend: When the stock market is falling, the security prices also fall. It is an atmosphere of gloom and pessimism.

Bid-ask Spread: This is the difference between buying and selling rates.

Bill Brokers: Agents and firms that buy and sell credit instruments on behalf of their clients.

Bill Discounting System: In this system the seller draws a bill on the buyer's bank. The buyer's bank discounts the bill and sends the amount to the seller.

Book-building: A system through which the demand of the public is assessed for a security, through a bidding process.

Bull: He is a speculator on the stock market. In India he is called the '*tejiwala*'. He excepts arise in the price of security and buys the security without taking delivery of the security. He then sells the security to make a profit at higher prices.

Bull Campaign: It is an atmosphere of optimism in the stock market by spreading rumors of an excepted rise in prices of securities.

Bullish Trend: This is a spirit of optimism in stock exchange because of rising prices.

Call Money Market: This is a market for borrowing and lending money of very short term maturity.

Call Option: This is a contract which gives the owner a right but not an obligation to buy an underlying asset. The owner makes a profit on the sale at high current prices and purchase at lower future prices of a security.

Capital Market: This is a market for long term securities with the definite purpose of directing the flow of savings into long term investments.

Carry Forward: This system of trading is unique in India. It is not genuine trading. The buyer does not have the money to pay for shares at the time of settlement. The seller does not have shares to deliver. Sometimes one party is genuine but the other is fraud. This is called '*badla*' trade.

Chicago Method: This is an evaluation method which is used by a venture capitalist. He considers the complete stream of earnings through the propose venture.

Chip Card: This is a plastic card which has an embedded circuit or a microchip. This is the modern operated card. This is different to the conventional card which has magnetic strips.

CHIPS: This is a computer network or a clearing house for transferring inter-bank payments. This is used for international dollar payments. It is linked to depository institutions and its affiliates in New-York city.

Close-ended Scheme: A scheme issued by a mutual fund which is liquidated after the completion of the specified period.

Cornering: It is a speculative activity. An individual or a group of people have the entire supply of a security. In this situation the bears must posses the securities they want to sell.

CRISIL: A premier credit rating agency in India. It grades debt securities.

Demand Bills: This is a bill of exchange which is paid 'at sight' or on presentation of the bill to the drawee.

Dematerialization: Process of conversion of securities from physical to electronic form. It helps in trading and settlement of securities quickly.

Depository: The agency which transfers the securities from physical to electronic form.

Depository Market: The market which except deposits and uses the funds to participates in debt market to make loans or purchase debt securities and treasury bills.

Derivatives: It is a contract or agreement, bilateral in nature. The value is derived from an underlying asset.

Directorate of Stock Exchange: The institution for enforcing the regulatory provisions of the Act.

Discount House: An organization in the money market. It specializes in commercial bill discounting.

Dunham Green-berg Formula: A consumer's loan proposal in which different parameters regarding income, finance, employment and past loan records are evaluated. The scoring points of 100 are allotted and if the consumer scores 70 points it means he has a good credit rating.

E-Commerce: Is the use of electronic transactions for contracting and other business. Through it digital signatures can be used.

Economic Barometer: It is a thermometer which shows the health of a company or a trend in a stock market or events in an economy.

Economic Growth: It is an economies total output. It refers to the addition made to the assets of the country.

Effective Rate of Interest (ERI): It is the calculation of interest which a person actually receives.

Electronic Cards: Cards which eliminate paperwork because they have an electronic mode for clearing and settlement of accounts.

Equity shares: These are ownership shares. They are also called ordinary shares.

Factor: An intermediary between a buyer and seller for taking the responsibility of collection of credit sales.

Gilt-edged Market: Government securities market. The securities are as pure as gold. There is full surety of the genuineness of these securities.

Global Depository Receipts (GDRs): These are securities issued by companies. There are traded in at least two countries outside the issuing company's country.

Global Financial Systems: Financial markets in which global capital transactions are transacted.

Hedging: Trying to minimize risk by buying different types of securities and selling them to set off losses with gains. This is applied when some share prices are falling and others on the portfolio are rising.

Holding Company: When one company is controlling another company it is called a holding company. The other company is called the subsidiary company.

Hurdle Rate: It is the minimum cut of rate acceptable for a project. It is useful to estimate it while selecting and investing in a project.

Hot money: These are funds which move from one country to another, wherever the interest rate is high. These are usually for short term uses.

Insider Trading: Use of price sensitive information for trading purposes.

Interest Rate Risk: The change in the market interest rates of a security brings about risk in a security. This is called interest rate risk.

Intrinsic Value: This is the investment value of an asset. It is calculated through the present value of the stream of expected benefits from an asset.

Jobber: A jobber is a market participant who buys and sells particular scripts for profits. He is also called a market maker.

Junk Bonds: Such bonds have low ratings with high yields. Its market is called high yield debt market.

Kerb Deals: These are illegal deals while trading in securities. These deals are made before and after trading hours outside the official stock market.

Lame Duck: He/she is a speculator who cannot meet his commitments at the appointed time. He is in temporary difficulties to make payments.

Leasing: A lease contract is between the leaser and the lessee for using an asset without owning it. It is a rental agreement by paying a rental charge.

Life Insurance: This is a contract in which the insurer pays a sum of money to the assured on the death or date of maturity of the policy which ever event is first.

Listed Securities: Those securities accepted for trading on a recognized stock market, after permission has been granted by SEBI.

London Inter Bank Offered Rate (LIBOR): This is a deposit rate in the Euro currency market in inter bank transactions.

Merchant Bank: It is an organization which advises firms on making new issues, underwriting, and corporate mergers. It is engaged in providing financial alternatives and suggestions.

Minimum Public Offer: This is the minimum amount of securities to be offered to public for becoming eligible in listing of securities with a stock market.

Net Asset Value (NAV): Market value of mutual fund-net assets divided by number of shares outstanding. This gives the net asset value per share.

OTC: It is a recognized stock market in India and it works through security dealers who trade in financial assets.

Pegged Rate: It is the currency rate which is controlled by government. It can be pushed up or down according to government rated value of currency.

Pegs and Baskets: This is the exchange rate which is pegged to a large number of currencies instead of pegging it against one currency.

Portfolio Management: This is the activity of making the right choice of the assets that a person has by combining them in such a way to maximize profit and minimize risk.

Portfolio Revision: Review of assets and changes in combination of assets in order to make continuous profits. Without review the portfolio may not give a good profit. After reviewing the portfolio can be revised according to the current scenario in the economy.

Price Band: It is a range of price offered by a company to investors for making bids by the book building system.

Put Option: A contract which gives the owner the right but not the obligation to sell an underlying asset, at a specified price on a specified date. This option is used for purchasing and asset at a lower price at the current date and selling it at a higher price in the future to make a profit.

Red-herring Prospectus: A prospectus which is issued after a company offers its securities through book building method. It does not furnish complete details of the price and quantity of securities offered.

Reverse Repos: It is a repurchase agreement. A short term loan is made to the primary seller of securities. The securities return to the lender when the reverse repurchases transaction matures.

Rigging the Market: It is artificial rise in price due to a bull movement in the market. Speculators create a demand for securities and when the price increases then they off loads the shares to make a profit.

Ringless Trading: Trading online through computers which does not require any market place or ring to conduct a sale. OTC exchanges are an example.

Rolling Settlement: It is a settlement system through which the trade is executed after a certain number of days according to the rules of the stock exchange.

Safety Net Scheme: This is a pricing method of public issues in which merchant bankers give the option to investors to buy back their shares if the price falls after its listing on the stock market.

Screen Based Trading: Electronic trading system which is completely transparent. Information of shares regarding price and volume of securities is publicly available for every transaction.

Scripless Trading: This is called paperless trading. Transaction takes place through an electronic mode by dematerialization.

SEBI: Securities Exchange Board of India is an apex body setup in India by government in 1988 for promoting the capital market and protecting the investor.

Secondary Market: When the IPOs are made it is called a new issue market transaction. When the shares are listed on the stock market and transactions of purchase and sale take place it is called a secondary market transaction. The secondary market is another name for stock market.

Securities Market: This is a stock market in which the sale and purchase of shares and debentures takes place.

Securitization: This is a method of creating a pool of assets and issuing them to investors through the special purpose vehicle. After they are repackaged, they are sold in the stock market.

Sensex: This is a share index on the Bombay stock exchange. 30 shares which are sound blue chip companies and are actively traded represent the index.

Smart Card: This card is embedded with a computer microchip which has intelligence as well as greater memory capacity.

Speculation: It is the activity of purchase and sale of securities with the aim of making profit in a short time.

Speculator: A speculator is a person who makes profit by finding out and guessing the price of a security. He buys and sells securities. His objective is to make a profit but he can in the course of the contract make a loss also.

Spot Delivery Contract: When securities are purchased or sold and the delivery takes place on the same day or the next day. It is called a spot delivery contract. A spot market conducts transactions where delivery has to take place immediately or on the following day.

Stag: A stag applies for shares in an IPO but he does not have any intention of keeping the shares on his portfolio. His main aim is to appear like a genuine investor but to off load shares for profit.

Stagflation: In a stagnant economy where inflation and unemployment coexist, it is called stagflation.

Strike Price: This is the price of the security at which the contract between the buyer and the seller has been executed.

Swaps: A swap is a transaction in which two counter parties exchange payments. This is a derivative instrument. Currency and interest rate swaps are popular.

SWIFT: The international electronic communication network of banks is called the SWIFT. This is the mode of trading in a foreign exchange market. It links all traders and brokers in foreign exchange.

Tax Havens: A country which has liberal tax incentives and very low level of tax. It is used by corporate organizations to trade through such a country to get the benefits of low taxation.

Trading Cycle: This is the minimum time taken for settlement and payment in a transaction.

Underwriting: It is a financial service in which an undertaking is made that if the shares are unsubscribed, the underwriter will purchase all or a part of the unsubscribed lot of shares.

Unit Trust: This is like a mutual fund. It sells its units to subscribers and pools in a large volume of funds through many subscribers. The fund is used to make investments. The profits are given as a dividend to the unit subscribers. It can also be called an investment company.

Venture Capital: This is a form of equity financing to new small and medium companies. After the companies are developed the venture capitalist exit and earn a profit.

Wash Sales: This is a fictitious transaction. A speculator sells a security and buys it at a higher price to mislead other people. There is no delivery of documents.

With Recourse Factoring: When a factor has the backing from his client that if the credit sales are not recovered from the purchaser he will have his money returned to him it is called with recourse factoring.

Without Recourse Factoring: When a factor is not able to receive his money from his clients and he is burdened with unpaid claims it is called without recourse factoring.

Z Group: These are listed companies which have defaulted on listing agreements.

Zero Coupon Bonds: These bonds are issued at a discount but they are redeemed at maturity on par.

Index

A

American Depository Receipts (ADRs) 189, 192
Anti money laundering (AML) 224, 243
Asian Development Bank 189, 194, 199, 352, 356
Asset Management Company 70, 72, 145, 300, 301,
    305, 309, 316, 317, 318, 333, 357, 363

B

Bank for International Settlements (BIS) 195
Banking Ombudsman 33, 227, 245, 248
Banking Sector Reforms 27, 30, 32, 205, 214, 216
Banking Supervision 19, 205, 218, 220
Bolt 31, 69, 111, 140, 146
Bombay Stock Exchange 23, 31, 70, 72, 75, 103, 107,
    108, 111, 115, 143, 144, 145, 146, 160, 342
Book-building 23, 31, 67, 87, 95, 139, 344
Broker 71, 87, 89, 99, 170

C

Call money market 20, 55, 149
CAMELS 220, 249
Capital adequacy norms 20, 30, 71, 97, 99, 130, 216,
    218, 229
Capital Market 7, 55, 140, 248, 288, 316
Capital risk weighted ratios 216
Certificate of due diligence 346, 347
CHIPS 192, 193
Chore committee report 157, 213

Circuit Breakers 81, 107, 146
Classification of mutual funds 299, 307
Closed Ended Schemes 22
Close-ended mutual fund schemes 308
Commercial banks 16, 18, 53, 205, 300, 357
Commercial bills market 20, 21, 154
Consumer finance 238, 341, 353, 354
Conventional Valuation method 361
Convertible bonds 55, 186, 190
Convertible debentures 22
Co-operative Banks 237
Credit rating 17, 151, 264, 341, 372
Currency option bonds 190

D

Debentures 21
Debt oriented schemes 310
Deep discount bond 22, 211
Dematerialization 23, 31, 69, 81, 140
Dematerialization (demat) 69, 81, 117, 140
Depositories Act 74
Derivatives trading 110
Direct Finance 5, 6
Discount and finance house of India Ltd. 328
Discount market 149, 157
Diversification of services 205, 215
Domestic Market 7, 8, 46
Due diligence certificate 346, 347, 348

E

Electronic Money 224
Equity shares 21
Euro Bonds 189, 190
Euro notes 191
Exchange Traded Funds 111, 309
Export – Import Bank of India 53, 321, 325

F

Factoring 10, 215, 336, 341
Fair practices code 227, 257, 260
Financial Assets 9, 37, 38, 372
Financial engineering 5, 21, 23, 290
Financial Institutions 5, 21, 290, 341
Financial Market 6, 7, 19, 149
Financial sector reforms 27, 45
Financial Services 10, 23, 215, 317, 327, 342
First Chicago Method 361, 362
Fixed and Flexible Exchange rates 167, 170
Floating rate bonds 22, 190
Floating rate certificate of deposits 191
Floating rate notes 190, 191
Foreign Banks 35, 56, 169, 208
Foreign capital 185, 187
Foreign capital flows 185, 188
Foreign exchange risks 167, 177
Foreign institutional investors (FIIs) 34, 55, 64, 72, 146, 153, 189
Forfaiting 366, 369
Forward rate agreements 52, 191
Function of RBI 45, 47
Functions of a Financial System 4

G

GDRs/ADRs (see Euro issues) 189
General insurance companies 16, 29, 89, 280, 288, 317, 322, 333
Global banking 185, 192
Global bonds 191
Global Depository Receipts (GDRs) 189, 192

Globalization 4
Government gilt edged securities market 7, 161
Government securities market reforms 27, 32
Growth Fund 308

H

HDFC 215, 225, 285, 316, 355, 356, 357
Hire purchase 341, 352
Housing finance 10, 19, 242, 328, 355
HUDCO 289, 355, 357, 358, 372

I

Impact of financial reforms 27, 35
Importance of foreign capita 187
Important stock market in India 107, 108
Income Fund 308, 316
Income recognition and asset classification 219
Index Fund 309
Indirect financing 213
Industrial Credit and Investment Corporation of India (ICICI) 9, 16, 89, 285, 321, 329
Industrial Development Bank of India (IDBI) 9, 16, 52, 225, 301, 321, 322, 323, 325
Innovative investment instruments 364
Innovative Schemes 4, 258
Insider Trading 107, 143
Insurance regulatory and development authority (IRDA) 18, 286
Inter Connected Stock Exchange 107, 108, 114
International Development Agency (IDA) 193, 194
International Finance Corporation (IFC) 194
International Market 8, 172, 186, 275
International Monetary Fund 171, 172, 189, 194
Investment 3
Investment norms 218, 259, 363
Investor Education 61, 112
Investor grievances 61, 66
Investor Protection 61, 65
Investor protection fund 78, 111
Issue mechanism 90

J

Joint ventures 189, 207

L

Lead bank scheme (LBS)   212

Leasing   328, 341, 350

Lessee   350

Lessor   350

Liability Transformation   8

Life Insurance Corporation (LIC)   16, 89, 279, 280, 302

Lok Adalat   54, 223

M

Malhotra Committee Recommendations   279

MAPIN   61, 78, 80

Market Discipline   218

Market for commercial papers & certificate of deposits   156

Market for financial guarantees   7, 20, 149, 158

Maturity Transformation   8, 9

Mechanics of security trading in stock exchanges   107, 114

Membership rules in a stock exchange   107, 128

Merchant bankers/lead managers   20

Mergers and acquisitions   63, 143, 189, 342

Mergers and Amalgamations   225, 230, 241

Model Code of Conduct   61, 65

Money market   7, 149

Money market funds   309

Multilateral financing agencies   193

Multilateral investment guarantee agency (MIGA)   193, 194

Multiple tranche bonds   190

Mutual funds   18, 55, 72, 107, 145, 156, 299, 301, 307

N

National securities depositories Limited, (NSDL)   20, 69, 325

National stock exchange (NSE)   20, 31, 72, 107, 108, 109, 144, 325, 328

Nature of foreign exchange market   167

Net asset value   145, 262, 290, 299, 307, 310

New issue and stock market reforms   28, 31

New schemes of UTI   313

Non bank finance companies   31

Non-banking financial companies   29, 54, 56, 258

Non-performing assets (NPAs)   219, 221

Note issuance facility   191

O

Offer for sale   35, 90, 91, 113, 135, 153

Offer to public procedure   87, 91

Offshore Banking   192, 193, 329

Ombudsman   61, 78, 227, 248, 280, 349

Open ended schemes   305, 306

Options   71, 72, 107, 119, 144

Origination   88

OTCEI   17, 20, 31, 67, 68, 92, 97, 107, 112, 113, 140, 327, 330, 331, 365

P

Participatory notes   191

Pension funds   73, 146, 269, 309

Phase of banking consolidation   302

Phase of prudential banking   211

Portfolio managers   20, 62, 70, 74, 168, 193

Post office schemes   22, 169

Preference shares   21, 61, 93, 138, 264, 305, 361, 362, 373

Private insurance companies   18, 279, 286, 287

Promotional role of RBI   45, 52

Prospectus   90, 93, 131, 308

Provident funds   22, 32, 160, 215, 269, 272

Prudential norms   33, 54, 206, 216, 240, 257, 262

Public issue through prospectus   90

Public sector and private sector banks   206

R

Reforms   5, 19, 27, 28, 281

Regional rural banks   205, 229, 238, 356

Relationship between new issue market and stock exchange   87, 102

Reserve bank of India   10, 16, 45, 46, 66, 149, 157, 161, 168, 172, 205, 206, 212, 238, 239, 300, 324, 341

Revenue multiplier method   361, 362
Right issues   91
Risk management   205, 219, 220, 242
Risk Transformation   8, 9
Rural co-operative banks   237, 248

S

SARFAESI   221, 262
Saving   269
Scheduled and Non-scheduled banks   206
Secondary Market   62, 63, 107
Securities and exchange board of India (SEBI)   61, 88, 100, 112, 306
Size Transformation   8, 9
Small Savings   269
Stages of Financial Development   3, 5
Structure of venture capital fund   363
SWIFT   168, 192, 193
Syndicated Euro currency loans   189

T

Tax havens   193
Technology   187, 205, 223, 239
Tender/book building method   31, 342, 344

The relationship of the new issue market and stock exchange   87, 102
Transparency and disclosures   219
Types of Banks   205
Types of foreign capital   185, 188
Types of lease   350

U

Underwriters   62, 99, 131
Underwriting   10, 138, 324
Unit Trust of India   16, 17, 18, 52, 89, 274, 299, 300, 322, 363
Universal banks   209
Urban Co-operative banks   56, 150, 237, 239

V

Venture capital funds   217, 359, 364
Venture capital investments   362
Vision documents   34

W

With recourse factoring   367, 368
Without recourse factoring   368
World Bank   189, 193, 321, 364